D0049494

STILL DREAMING

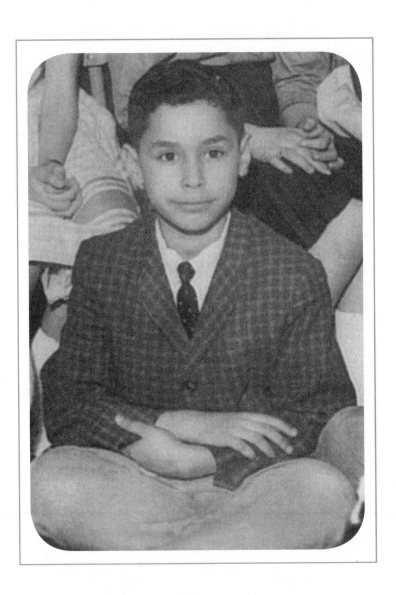

STILL DREAMING

MY JOURNEY FROM THE BARRIO TO CAPITOL HILL

LUIS GUTIÉRREZ

with DOUG SCOFIELD

W. W. Norton & Company | NEW YORK • LONDON

To write this book, I've relied on my memory and many interviews
with family and friends. I've also consulted media coverage
and books that reference some of the more noteworthy events. In order to
be respectful of the privacy of others, I've changed the names of
some people outside of my family who are not public figures. Overall, the
work reflects my personal experience and recollection, and I have
worked to make it as accurate as possible.

For information about permission to reproduce selections from this book,
write to Permissions, W. W. Norton & Company, Inc., 500 Fifth Avenue,
New York, NY 10110

For information about special discounts for bulk purchases, please contact
W. W. Norton Special Sales at specialsales@wwnorton.com or 800-233-4830

Manufacturing by Courier Westford
Book design by Brooke Koven
Production manager: Anna Oler

Library of Congress Cataloging-in-Publication Data

ISBN: 978-0-393-08897-7 (hardcover)

W. W. Norton & Company, Inc., 500 Fifth Avenue, New York, N.Y. 10110
www.wwnorton.com
W. W. Norton & Company Ltd., Castle House,
75/76 Wells Streets, London W1T 3QT

1 2 3 4 5 6 7 8 9 0

For Soraida, who despite my long periods away,
has never once complained. She always had one simple
message for me—"Go and fight for what you believe
in." And for Omaira and Jessica, proud Puerto Rican
daughters of a proud Puerto Rican woman,
children who have grown to be kind, compassionate, and
intolerant of injustice. I love you all.

CONTENTS

STILL DREAMING

Ring of Fire

I T WASN'T the heat or the smoke that woke me, it was the crashing sound, like a car accident right in my living room. I opened my eyes and saw flames shooting all the way from my floor to the ceiling.

Even though I was disoriented from coming out of a dead sleep at three fifteen in the morning, I noticed the fire didn't look normal. It looked as if it were created by the special-effects guy in a science-fiction movie. It swirled like a Hula-Hoop of flames, blasting up fast from the floor, like the song "Ring of Fire"—except real.

Waking up to a crash and a burning living room gets you moving quickly. It was hot, and the ceiling was turning black. I jumped off the couch, where I had fallen asleep, and ran up the stairs, shouting to my family to get out of the house. I went to my daughter Omaira's bedroom in the back of the house and grabbed her, still sleeping soundly. Then I sprinted to our bedroom, directly above the burning living room, to get my wife, Soraida. She was already heading down the hallway, still groggy. She had heard the crash too. I yelled, "The house is on fire, we have to get out!" Carrying my little girl in my arms, we ran down the stairs, straight for the front door. We could see that the entire living room was burning. The couch was on fire and the flames were attacking the ceiling.

I had dry-walled that ceiling myself, and gone to the emergency room when I stepped on a nasty, rusty old nail from one of the boards I'd ripped from the ceiling. Our house was an old, single-family, brick home. It was our little part of the American Dream. It had big double windows in the front and a postage-stamp-size Chicago front yard, where we had planted azaleas. We had three small bedrooms on the second floor. The house was a wreck when we bought it, and we had done most of the work ourselves. I wanted it to be the nicest house on the block, determined not to let even one of my mostly white neighbors think the new Puerto Rican family was ruining their nice community. Now our home was going up in flames.

It didn't take us more than a minute to grab Omaira. By the time we headed down the stairs, the living room was practically destroyed. It was 1984, long before cell phones, so we were nearly out the front door when it occurred to me that we hadn't called the fire department. I handed Omaira to Soraida and doubled back inside to call 911 from the phone in the front hallway. It was hot and I was sweating. The walls looked like they were melting. I shouted "Fire, 2246 Homer!" into the receiver and then ran down the front steps, away from the flames.

Just then the front windows exploded from the heat, spraying glass into the front yard. Some of the shards landed inches away from me, close enough to make me wonder why I hadn't called 911 from a neighbor's house. Lights went on up and down the block and the street started to fill with curious and concerned neighbors. We lived three blocks from the fire station and you could hear the sirens almost immediately. Now the flames were jumping out of the first floor windows and the smoke was rising toward the second story, where my wife had been sleeping five minutes before. Soraida, Omaira, and I stood quietly and watched our house burn.

I loved our house. I couldn't believe we were losing it. I thought about my daughter's room filled with her huge stuffed Big Bird that she loved so much, our wedding album by the TV in the living room, my record collection. Then I thought about how much worse it could have been, about how rare it was for me to fall asleep downstairs.

Soraida and I had gone out to dinner with friends that night. On the way home, I stopped to get the early Sunday edition of the *Chicago Tribune,* to catch up on the Mondale-Reagan coverage, hoping that Mondale might still have a comeback in him. It was October, a mild Indian summer night; Soraida had put Omaira to bed and I fell asleep watching the news and reading the paper. Our house was quiet—so quiet that Soraida and I had slept soundly while burglars stole everything from unpacked boxes we'd left downstairs the very night we moved in. If I had been sleeping upstairs, and the crash hadn't woken me right away, we might have been jumping out a back window to escape the fire. Or maybe we wouldn't have gotten out at all.

Omaira did what any five-year-old would do; she cried and asked about her toys, her room. We told her we would save everything we could, but as I looked at the house I didn't think we were going to save much besides ourselves. Soraida took Omaira to our neighbor's house and they called my wife's sister, Lucy, to tell her we would need a place to stay for a while.

Before long, the firefighters were there, breaking more windows to let out the heat. The water from their hoses gushed into the living room. It didn't take long to get it under control, but as I looked at the giant streams of water pouring in through the windows I knew that whatever the fire didn't get, the water would.

As the firefighters moved their hoses around for better angles, a Chicago Police Department cruiser pulled up. I hadn't yet completely embraced the idea that the police could be your friends. I was a Puerto Rican who grew up in a neighborhood where cops stopped you whenever they felt like it. They asked you and your teenage friends where you lived and what you were doing and where you were going. They assumed you existed to cause trouble. Seeing the police as allies didn't come naturally to me.

So I wasn't expecting a warm blanket, hot coffee, and a lot of sympathy from the police, but I thought the officer might at least have gotten out of his cruiser. Instead, he turned on his spotlight and motioned me over to his car. He stayed in the front seat with his report book open. He hardly looked at me while he took notes, as if it were nothing more than a routine fender bender. He didn't seem thrilled to be called out to a burning building on a Saturday night. His physique suggested he wasn't crazy about much of anything that required movement.

"This your house?"

I told him it was, and what happened. I described the crash that I had heard and the way the ring of flames had shot up from the middle of the room to the ceiling.

"Probably an electrical fire," he said.

I told him I had rewired the whole house and put in 220-amp circuits. I wanted him to understand my hard work, that I was a responsible homeowner. Besides, the fire looked like it had started right in the middle of the room. And what about the crash?

"Probably something with the boiler."

"But there is nothing wrong with the boiler," I said. "It's a warm night, it's not even on. The boiler's in the back of the house."

"The TV probably overheated." The officer had still barely looked at me.

I try to get along with people. Really, I do. That's a statement some people would laugh at, including Republican members of Congress who've fought with me about immigration, or Democratic members of Congress who've fought with me about stopping their pay raises. I can hear laughter from Chicago aldermen who screamed at me when I read—out loud, on the city council floor—the surprisingly low amount they paid in property taxes. The president of the United States, who saw me get arrested on Pennsylvania Avenue in front of his house, might even be amused at that assertion. But I do try to be agreeable.

I have my limits. I had just raced up and down my stairs to get my family out of my burning home. Many of my belongings were smoldering twenty feet away. My burning couch was lying in my front yard, where it had been tossed by the firemen, and it was crushing my azaleas. My daughter was crying. My heart was still pounding. I didn't expect much sympathy, but in exchange for my tax dollars and my burning house, I was hoping for at least a little courtesy. But it was obvious that the policeman assigned to the fire that night was about as interested in figuring out what caused it as he was in running the Chicago marathon.

I resisted the urge to call him the names that were on the tip of my tongue; instead I explained to him why I didn't think it was the TV. Or the boiler. Or the wiring. I was still talking when he looked up at me for the first time and said, "Board it up and call your insurance company." And he drove off.

By 1984, I had come a little ways from being just another kid in a poor Chicago neighborhood who stood politely with my hands on a car hood whenever a policeman stopped me on my own block. So instead of just calling my insurance company, I also called my new boss, Ben Reyes, the deputy mayor of the city of Chicago. He reported directly to the mayor, a mayor I would soon meet with pretty regularly. I explained my situation. My house had burned and the police weren't exactly being helpful. He called the deputy mayor in charge of the police and fire departments. Just as the last flames from my house were crackling out and the smoke was starting to drift away, two younger and more interested investigators from the bomb and arson squad showed up. They had gotten a call.

I told them what happened. The crash, the weird cone of flame. They didn't look at me like I was crazy. They were less interested in their report book and more interested in what I had to say. We talked while the water dripped off the front of my now-exposed living room and the house started to cool down.

The younger investigator said we should go in and look around. It looked dangerous to me, but I was eager to see what I could salvage. The glow of his flashlight illuminated what was left. The fire department had put the fire out quickly, and the back of the house was still in decent shape. The front—upstairs and down—was burned down to the floors, framework, and bricks. I hoped I could save a few toys from my daughter's bedroom, maybe a few things from the kitchen. There wasn't going to be much. As the investigator and I carefully walked through what used to be my living room, he stopped. It was hot. He sniffed and looked at me.

"Electrical fire, huh?"

I wasn't sure if he was making fun of me or the other cop. His flashlight scanned the floor, then stopped.

"You collect bricks, Mr. Gutiérrez?"

He shined his light on a brick smoldering in the debris, just a few feet away from where I had been sleeping on the couch.

"No sir, I don't collect bricks."

"You ever seen that brick before?"

He moved his light over the area around the brick, and then looked back at me.

"Have you been drinking, Mr. Gutiérrez?"

I wasn't quite sure whether to be mad or amused.

"No, I haven't been drinking." And I hadn't. My only liquid vice is drinking Coca-Cola for breakfast.

"Well, that sure looks like the bottom of a big jug of wine to me," he said.

He was right. Near the brick was the still-intact bottom of a Gallo or Paul Masson wine jug. It looked like a green Frisbee made out of glass.

Then he leaned down and found the handle and the top of the jug, with part of a rag still sticking out of the hole. He held it up. He was smiling. He pushed the rag up toward me.

"Take a look at this, and smell the house. What do you smell?"

I hadn't thought too much about the smell—it just smelled like fire and smoke. It smelled like it was going to cost me a lot of time and money. But once I really sniffed, the smell was unmistakable, the same thing you smelled every time you pulled into the Mobile station. It smelled like gasoline.

I was still confused.

"Why the brick?"

"They threw the brick through the window. That was probably your crash. Then they threw the jug filled with gasoline through the hole where your window used to be. The jug filled with gasoline won't break the window. It would just break and catch on fire when it hits the window. That just gives you an exterior fire, and they wanted to make sure they got the gasoline inside the house."

"But why?" I asked, still not quite convinced.

He looked at me like I was a little slow.

"Because they wanted to hurt you."

IN MARCH OF 1980, just four years earlier, my wife and I had moved into our new home, on a very nice street. Even the name of the street was cozy—"Homer." We were surrounded mostly by white people—a significant change for two Puerto Ricans from poor neighborhoods. We religiously watched *This Old House*, letting Bob Vila teach us how to fix almost anything without having to hire expensive contractors. Bob showed me that making our old, broken-down house on Homer Street that we had bought for $28,000 into a place where we could raise our family took only a little ingenuity and sweat equity. Bob taught me how anything old and beaten up could be turned into something vintage and hip. And Soraida and I were pulling it off together. New drywall, newly sanded hardwood floors, exposed woodwork. We found old furniture people had thrown away in the alley and refinished it. We were young and married, new parents and homeowners. We were moving on up.

For us, even though the move had been only a mile away, we were generations away from our previous house. Before, we had a little place on Rockwell Street, where our living-room window looked out over five abandoned lots. At night, the gang members would drive stolen cars into the middle of the lots, get out their tools, and go to work. Feeling like secret agents, Soraida and I would crouch down beneath our front windows, call 911, and tell the operator, "If you hurry, you can make it, they are just taking the tires off the car."

In a few minutes we would call back and say, "Now they are taking parts out of the engine. You need to get here right away."

Then we would call back again and tell them, "There's not much left. It looks like they are cleaning out the interior. They have a gas can. You need to get here now."

The gang members would douse the car with gasoline, light a match, and be on their way. We watched this no fewer than six or seven times. The lots were like the gang's assembly line. We called 911 every time because we thought it was our responsibility as good citizens. The police never once showed up in time to arrest anyone. A patrol car would accompany the fire truck once the car was torched. The cops would make their report and head home. When enough cars piled up, sometimes three or four, a tow truck would come to haul away what was left of the cars to make sure there was plenty of room for the next chop job.

The last straw was the day we were in the living room and we heard a giant crash. I ran out to find that our brand-new Toyota Tercel—the cheapest Toyota you could find—was missing the entire front right part of the car. The car had been knocked to the curb; most of the quarter panel was in the street. People were out all over the block— drinking on one porch, playing dice on another—listening to music and hanging out. I turned a hopeful circle in the middle of the street, saying to the twenty people within earshot, "What happened?" The crash had taken place sixty seconds before, but we didn't get one lead from our neighbors. Nobody saw anything. Soraida and I knew it was no place to raise our daughter. It was time to move.

In our new Bucktown neighborhood, we thought we had gone upscale. The house wasn't big or fancy, or in very good condition, but we were in love with it. We loved the big windows in front, we loved that it had three bedrooms—all upstairs. We knew we could make it a home. We were both social workers. I was at the Department of Children and Family Services, checking on families and investigating allegations of abuse. Soraida was at Casa Central, a major social service agency in the neighborhood, doing exactly the same thing. We cared about our work and we cared about our community, but there had never yet been any other time in our lives that we had the luxury of being so focused just on us.

When I talk to young people today, I call it our *Mork & Mindy* period. We cared for Omaira, we worked hard at our jobs, and we fixed up the house. We attended our friends' parties and weddings. A really big weekend might be to play a few rounds of dominoes to five hundred points with my brother-in-law Juano. And we laughed at that crazy Robin Williams on Thursday nights. It was nice—a calm and peaceful time.

Until four of Dan Rostenkowski's precinct captains showed up at our door.

In 1983, the Chicago Democratic machine was humming along efficiently, fueled by city workers who relied mostly on aldermen and party committeemen for their jobs. They got a government paycheck, and in return for their paycheck they made sure their political sponsors were elected and re-elected. The machine recovered from Jane "beat the machine dame" Byrne's defeat of its candidate for mayor by simply making Byrne its candidate. The machine was practical: if you can't beat 'em, co-opt 'em. So they made peace with Jane until Rich Daley decided to run against her. While Daley's and Byrne's political armies fought to the death, Congressman Harold Washington's supporters diligently went from church to church on the West Side, and from block club to block club on the South Side and registered black voters. Daley and Byrne ignored him. To them, he might as well have been running for mayor of Mars.

On Election Day, Harold's supporters waited in long lines to cast their ballots while the Irish candidates split the white vote. And when the results came in, 63 percent of Chicago voted for Byrne or Daley— 33 percent for Jane, 30 percent for Rich. With 37 percent, Harold found just enough voters to win the primary and put Chicago on the verge of having its first black mayor.

I loved it. To me, it felt like the two biggest bullies on the playground had kept swinging at each other until they finally knocked each other out, and now the nice kid who never bothered anybody got to be in charge. The nice kid also happened to be an articulate, smart, and progressive leader who wanted to make real changes in the way Chicago worked. But this was Chicago in 1983, and the nice kid was also black, so the bullies figured out they had one last shot to stay on top. After Harold Washington became the Democratic nominee for mayor, the machine went to work. And Rostenkowski's precinct captains started making the rounds in my neighborhood.

Dan Rostenkowski had been our neighborhood's member of Congress for twenty-five years and had recently become the chairman of the Ways and Means Committee of the US House of Representatives. He was the man who wrote the nation's tax laws, and was at Mayor Daley Sr.'s right hand for two decades.

But in the neighborhood, what mattered even more was that he was the Democratic committeeman of my home ward, the 32nd Ward. In Chicago, the committeeman was an elected Democratic Party position. Chicago has fifty wards, with fifty aldermen who comprise the city council. Each ward also has an elected Republican and Democratic committeeman. The Republican is a powerless and irrelevant nod at bipartisanship. The Democrat runs things.

He's responsible for the workers who run the polling places on Election Day. He also decides where to put them. Maybe in the basement of a friendly senior center. Maybe in a friend's living room. In 1980s Chicago, you might go vote in a corner bar—if that's what the committeeman decided. He called the shots.

He also controlled the jobs. Committeeman was the integral position in the Chicago machine—the party official who turned out votes, and then turned those votes into city jobs, county jobs, state jobs—jobs you might not even know existed until Dan Rostenkowski got you one and made you one of his precinct captains. They were the soldiers, the guys who went house to house, knocked on doors, and kept the machine running.

The machine really was brilliant. It thrived for decades by turning basic city services that you deserved and should receive simply because you paid your taxes into favors that were delivered personally by your precinct captains and committeemen. If the Chicago Democratic machine had been in charge of America's Social Security system, you would feel a surge of gratitude every time some guy from the Sewer Department showed up at your house to drop off your check.

Soraida and I knew Rostenkowski's precinct captains, and when they knocked, we were happy to let them in. They had helped us to get the city to trim a tree in our yard, and to get a sewer in front of our house unclogged. Even more impressive, they brought us brand-new garbage cans, and not just any garbage cans—the ones with lids attached by a metal chain so they wouldn't disappear right away. We're talking top-of-the-line garbage cans for the Gutiérrez family. They were helpful guys.

Soraida and I had never made any waves in our neighborhood. I didn't like Dan Rostenkowski's politics—he played footsie with Ronald Reagan too much for my taste. Still, I didn't think too much about our neighborhood's committeeman and powerful chairman of the Ways and Means Committee. Like most everybody else, I was just happy that his captains unclogged the sewer. And they were still Democrats, after all.

So when his garbage-can-delivering precinct captains showed up in the spring of 1983, I said, "Come on in guys, what can I do for you?"

We all stood in my living room. They were holding clipboards, and it looked like they had some campaign signs with them. It felt a little crowded. The machine found a lot of really big guys for city jobs. But I'm only five-foot-six, so maybe it's a matter of perspective.

"Well, we have a problem," the older guy said. He had lived in the neighborhood a long time—a Polish guy who worked for the Water Department.

"We've got a bad nominee for mayor. Could you do us a favor? Would you put an Epton sign in your window? We can't have Harold Washington as mayor of the city of Chicago."

Three months earlier these same guys had campaigned for Rich Daley. In the November general election the year before, they came to our house and told me I didn't even have to waste my time voting for individual candidates, I could just punch number 10 and vote straight Democratic. Now they wanted me to put up a sign for a Republican. In three months had they undergone a philosophical epiphany? Had they been enchanted by the Republican promises of low taxes and small government and family values?

No, I knew—and they knew—that their reversal was much more basic. Bernard Epton, the Republican nominee for mayor of Chicago, was white. Harold Washington was black.

But to come to my house and ask me to put a Bernard Epton for Mayor sign in my front window? The idea seemed absurd. The guy was an unknown. A *Republican* unknown. Before Harold Washington was nominated, you couldn't have found a person outside of the Epton family who could have told you anything about him. Being the Republican nominee for mayor of Chicago was like being the Communist Party nominee for president of the United States. Epton was destined to be what every Republican nominee for mayor was—the answer to a Chicago trivia question.

I'm sure Soraida could tell I was trying to remain calm, and she probably knew I would fail. I felt like I had done something wrong just by letting them in my house. One of the precinct captains was a Puerto Rican guy. I glared at him. I thought he should have known better.

I have to admit that I thought about my sewer, and my trees, and my garbage cans. About how much I loved my house and my block, and how easy it is to just go along. But I also thought about the Che Guevara and Malcolm X posters on my college dorm walls. About all of the grief my family had taken because of my activism for Puerto Rican independence. But most of all how happy I was for Harold Washington that he had taken on the machine and won. The guys in my living room seemed like a direct challenge to my sense of right and wrong. In the lengthening silence, I think the captains began to figure out that while I had never given them trouble before, they had chosen the wrong house that day.

I tried not to yell. I don't think I succeeded. "How could you come in my house and ask me to support a Republican? You're only for him because Harold is black. Get out of my house; don't ever come back in my house. Epton for mayor? Are you guys nuts?"

They looked stunned. I should have left it at that, but then I added, even though I had absolutely no idea what I was talking about, "And I'm going to make sure Harold Washington wins this precinct."

That was the wrong thing to say to these guys. They looked dumbfounded when I told them they were just supporting Epton because Harold was black. They didn't want to be lectured about race. But they could debate who was going to win the precinct on Election Day.

That they were all a good fifty pounds heavier than me probably didn't help make my campaign boast very intimidating. I'm a little guy—always the smallest in my class. In the early 1980s, the only thing big about me was my hair and my Zapata mustache. I didn't look like the kind of guy who could convince my white neighbors to vote for the black candidate for mayor. My boast loosened them up. They laughed.

"You're going to beat us? We've been doing this for thirty years. We've lived here for thirty years. We've taken care of everyone in the precinct. We'll crush you. Harold Washington will never win this precinct."

They were happy they could speak their own language again—winning elections. They weren't really fluent in the language I was speaking—that it's bad to support a white guy you've never heard of because his opponent is black. They kept their signs; they turned and headed out.

Suddenly, I felt like I hadn't done enough to get their attention.

I ran out the front door. I'm sure Soraida was wondering what trouble I was going to get her into now. I followed them as my neighbor opened her door. "Sally, don't talk to them. You don't have anything to say to them. They're racists. Don't let them in your house. They're for Epton!" The guys and my neighbor looked at me like I was crazy, a ranting, long-haired Puerto Rican shouting at them. But they didn't get a sign in her window that day.

They tried to ignore me. I followed them down the street. I told the Puerto Rican guy he should be ashamed of himself. He should know what racism is. I told him his three white friends probably called him names behind his back. They all glared at me. They were hot and getting hotter while I created a spectacle in the middle of our nice, calm block. People didn't know what was going on, but they didn't want to be around any of us. I kept after them. People got busy with anything but paying attention to the short guy yelling at those nice fellas who brought their garbage cans. Anyone they tried to approach, I approached.

"Don't talk to these guys. They're for Epton. They don't want a black mayor."

It didn't take long before they retreated and called it a day. They probably went back to report to the alderman that there was a crazy

Puerto Rican in the 2nd precinct of the ward and we better keep an eye on him. But I'm sure they didn't think that I would be so angry and motivated and upset that I would decide to run against Dan Rostenkowski for Democratic committeeman. And I know that it definitely never occurred to them, not even for a second, that they would lose their precinct for mayor.

But they did lose their precinct. To me and Soraida, and Juano and Lucy, and the few friends we could talk into helping us spread the gospel of Harold Washington. We beat them by 60 votes—a total of 280 for Harold Washington to 220 for Bernard Epton.

AFTER WE BEAT Epton in our precinct, I did run for Democratic committeeman against Dan Rostenkowski. He wasn't too happy about it. Neither were his captains.

Just one year after that campaign, someone had tried to burn down my house. A brick and a busted-up jug of gasoline gets your attention. But it takes a while to sink in. I knew that ring of fire didn't come from the TV, or the wiring, or the boiler. But a Molotov cocktail in my living room—that wouldn't have been my first guess. The fire investigators collected the brick and the wine jug and made their report, and the police file from my 1984 fire is plain and simple: arson.

The next day the police detectives arrived at Lucy's house, where we were staying. They took out their notebooks and said, "We're investigating your fire."

Their first question was simple: "Have you had any run-ins with anyone?"

My answer was just as simple: "Where do you want me to start?"

The list was long. I ran through it for them. Maybe the tough-guy political operatives posing as community organizers on Milwaukee Avenue, who worked against me when I ran for committeeman. Maybe some of the guys who worked for me now at the city of Chicago. I was supervising electricians—the linemen, big guys who climbed the poles. I wrote them up for drinking in the corner bar while they were supposed to be doing their work down the block.

I'd spoken in public at community groups about dictatorships in

Central America. Archbishop Romero's assassination in El Salvador had turned my attention toward Ronald Reagan's meddling in the Americas. Maybe that made somebody mad.

"But," I told the detectives, "if you really want to know who would try to blow up my house, I have some simple advice on where to start: Dan Rostenkowski might know who did it. Why don't you ask him?"

Three days after the police detectives questioned me about people I had run-ins with, and I told them to check with Rostenkowski, they came back to my sister-in-law's house, our temporary home.

"We don't have any leads. Anyone else you've had trouble with?"

I knew they hadn't talked to Rostenkowski or the people around him in the campaign. I would have heard about it. But they did talk to the "political operatives" on Milwaukee Avenue I had mentioned. And the police had told these guys—a group that included plenty of gang members and ex-cons—that I told the detectives that they were the ones who had burned down my house. That was something I heard about very clearly. Some very scary guys found a friend of mine at a bar one night and strongly suggested that I should stop saying they did it.

So on the second visit, when the detectives came back, I sat quietly.

"No, sir, I don't have any more leads for you."

They never came back, and the case was closed without anyone ever being arrested. I never learned who filled the jug and lit the rag and threw the brick.

I did learn something far more important, however. I found out that when you stand up to the machine, you get people's attention. It's a risk, and sometimes there is a price to pay. But you also feel the thrill of doing the right thing. The excitement of being in the ring, fighting the fight. I knew then that my *Mork & Mindy* period was over.

In the nearly thirty years since that day, I've often thought of how things might have been different if Dan Rostenkowski's precinct captains hadn't come to my house with Bernard Epton for Mayor signs. I probably wouldn't have won that precinct for Harold Washington, and almost certainly wouldn't have made the run against Dan Rostenkowski for committeeman.

If I hadn't run for committeeman—and been crushed by Rosty and his troops, getting less than 25 percent of the vote—I wouldn't have run for alderman in the election that finally turned an obstructionist Chicago City Council—one that fought every initiative of our first black mayor—into a supportive city council that helped Harold Washington change the city. From the city council, I eventually made my way to the US Congress, where I represent much of Dan Rostenkowski's old district. If those precinct captains are still around today, they just might be my constituents.

As I think about my story, I keep coming back to that afternoon in Chicago. I was young, and mostly naïve about politics. When I told the city workers who came to my house that I would beat them in their own precinct, I didn't have a clue how to do it. All I knew was that someone needed to do something.

Now I feel lucky that seventeen political campaigns—a total of sixteen wins, and one very lopsided loss to Dan Rostenkowski for Democratic committeeman—have brought me exactly where I need to be, fighting not just for the 32nd Ward, or Chicago, but fighting for immigrants all across America.

You never know which knock on your door might change your life. Sometimes it turns out to be a couple of guys from the Water Department who want you to support the white Republican guy for mayor.

Looking back now, I'm glad they showed up. They pushed me onto a path that I never imagined for myself as a poor kid growing up in a Puerto Rican neighborhood in Chicago—a path that led from Chicago to the hills of Puerto Rico and back, and from a two-bedroom apartment where I slept on a cot in the hallway to the halls of the Congress of the United States of America.

Very belatedly, I offer my thanks to Rosty's precinct workers. I never gave you a place to put your Epton signs, but you started me on the journey of my life.

CHAPTER TWO

When Lincoln Park
Was Puerto Rican

EEP DOWN, I knew what was coming when my parents started buying things: a stereo, a television, finally a car. I could feel the truth, but I was fifteen and having fun in Chicago, and didn't want to admit it to myself.

My parents' idea of extravagance was springing for Vienna hot dogs and French fries from the stand down the block. That happened once every couple of months and was about the closest we came to a restaurant. But one day, French provincial furniture arrived at our apartment. We didn't even have to carry it in. It came on the back of a regular delivery truck and workers put it right in our living room. Deliverymen in our living room was a spectacle; my parents worked for other people, and I wasn't used to having anyone work for us.

Heavy, dark, and ornate, the furniture looked to me like something rich white people might own. We were ordered not to sit on it until the store could install plastic covers on the pristine cushions. It didn't look to me like the kind of furniture my mom and dad would buy for our apartment on Willow Street in Lincoln Park. My parents had dispatched me to a makeshift bedroom in the hallway when they decided my sister, Ada, and I were too old to share a bedroom. My dad hung up a curtain to give my hallway some privacy and there was just enough room for a cot. I kept my few clothes on some hallway shelves.

Not too long afterward, a new TV was sitting in front of the sofa, and then a nice stereo. I wondered if they had hit the *bolita*—the neighborhood Puerto Rican numbers game—and not told me. One thing I knew—as a fifteen-year-old who found new things every day in shop windows he longed to own—was that my parents saved, they didn't spend. When they did spend, they saw it as an investment. In our Lincoln Park neighborhood, we were comparably well off, but that's not saying much. This was Lincoln Park when it was Puerto Ricans living in two- and three-unit apartment buildings, with a few bigger ones here and there, before the traders and investment bankers tore them down or rehabbed them into million-dollar single-family mansions. We were doing OK because my mom and dad both worked hard. And we felt lucky because they were supporting only my sister and me, putting us at one-third the size of many of the families in our neighborhood.

In our first apartment down the block at 849 West Willow, I remember about a dozen Puerto Ricans who had just arrived from the island and were living in the basement of the building. Their apartment was smaller than ours, and I thought ours felt cramped, though there was plenty of room for the roaches and the mice. When we moved to the nicer apartment down the street, I felt even luckier. We had a few things that other people didn't. We always had newspapers around the house. My dad would bring them home when he finished driving his cab. He bought the newspapers for his passengers. "That newspaper cost me a nickel, but it made me fifty cents in tips," he would say. He didn't spend if he didn't see how some profit would come back to him. So for the Gutiérrez family, the stereo and television—a nice Zenith color TV, made in Chicago—and the big, heavy, fancy furniture should have made things clear to me. But as a teenager listening to Motown, more worried about girls and whether I could talk my dad into buying me bell-bottoms, I wasn't following the family clues as clearly as I should have.

Until my dad brought home the Chevy Impala station wagon.

"We will need this for deliveries in Puerto Rico," he said, as casually as if he had asked how my day went at school.

Deliveries in Puerto Rico? Now I was paying attention.

And the rest of the purchases? My mom and dad had come to Chicago to get ahead. They weren't going to return to Puerto Rico poor; they wanted to show everyone they had made the right decision. Now they had fancy furniture and a color TV to show for their time in the United States. And a 1966, sky-blue, mint condition Chevy Impala station wagon.

MY DAD LEFT Puerto Rico seventeen years before with nothing. He was a teenager working as an assistant projectionist in a movie theater in Aguadilla, a town on the coast that survived mostly because of a US Air Force base. He didn't imagine a big future for himself in the movie business.

If it's possible to have less than nothing, that's what my mother had in Puerto Rico. She lived in Aguadilla too, but in the *cerros*, the cliffs that were home to some of the poorest people in town. She grew up in a wooden shack built into the side of the hill. They were surrounded by families that couldn't afford to live anywhere else. The family shack had one open area, divided by a half wall and a curtain. My mom shared the bigger "room" with her two sisters and a brother. My mom's mother slept in the other one. My grandfather had died young. My grandmother and the kids were left to make it on their own, in not much more than a hut built into the cliff.

Their shack never had running water. They thought they were lucky to have a community water spigot at the bottom of the cliffs. They would take buckets down and fill them for cooking and cleaning and drinking. Their first house on the *cerros* was at the bottom of the hill, near the spigot. Eventually, they traded that for a house closer to the top. They needed the money. It wasn't more expensive to live up top—there was no premium for their beautiful view of the Atlantic

Ocean. It was cheaper because they had to walk farther to get to the water spigot. Even today, ask my mom where they lived in Aguadilla, and she will smile and say, "In the penthouse."

They made ends meet—which essentially meant finding enough money to eat every day and buy material for their clothes—by working and pooling their money. My mother's sister Cucha got a job in the photo shop of a pharmacy and brought the money home to share with her family. Her sister Rose had been hurt in a fall when she was just a little girl, and had trouble walking. One of my mom's responsibilities was to help take care of her. My grandmother, like thousands of other Puerto Rican women, took in sewing. Piecework at home, the *aguja* industry, was a big part of the economy. My grandmother worked on high-end gloves and handkerchiefs that a man would drop off at the house. She was good at what she did. The fancy gloves would eventually find their way from the *cerros* of Aguadilla to high-end department stores to be purchased by wealthy women in America.

My mom's family remembers when electricity arrived in the cliffs of Aguadilla. In the 1950s, the government of Luis Muñoz-Marín aggressively started bringing electricity to Puerto Rico. My mom was thrilled when her little hut joined the modern world. I asked her what it was like after they put the electricity in their shack.

"It was much better. We had a lightbulb hanging from the ceiling in the middle of the room. It was much easier to see," she said. It seemed like great progress to her.

My mom's reaction taught me of the political power of a public works program. That lone lightbulb bought Muñoz-Marín's Popular Democratic Party, called La Pava because their symbol was the hat of the Puerto Rican worker, a lifetime of loyalty from my mom. "La Pava brought us electricity," she always said. After we returned to Puerto Rico, when La Pava's candidate for governor won, my mom drove through the streets, honking her horn with the rest of the partiers. When the competing Statehooders won, she took a sleeping pill and went to bed early.

It was a land of sporadic electricity, few jobs, and water carried in buckets that my parents fled. They didn't leave because Puerto Rico didn't feel like home but because they felt their home held no future for them. They weren't alone. Planeload after planeload of Puerto Ricans left their home island in the 1940s and 1950s. Nearly a half million Puerto Ricans—from an island of just over two million—left Puerto Rico at that time. Nearly a quarter of the population. And the government was more than happy to help. Muñoz-Marín's "Operation Bootstrap" was designed to kick the island's dependence on sugar plantations and sugar production. Diversifying the economy was not a bad idea, but the promised new manufacturing jobs couldn't keep pace with the collapsing world of agriculture. Work disappeared. Farmers had little to do and nowhere to go. Young people were restless. The government worked to assist Puerto Ricans who wanted to leave. Hundreds of thousands of Puerto Ricans felt they had no choice. Unemployment was near 20 percent for most of the decade. No Puerto Ricans were returning to the island from Chicago in the 1950s; they were looking for a way to leave.

Fortunately for them, as American citizens, a more promising future was just a plane ticket away. And my parents were ready to go. Just like thousands of their friends and family and fellow Boricuas— which is how we Puerto Ricans often refer to ourselves because the island was once called Boriken by the native people. They took the same step that people who are in a place without jobs and without hope have taken for thousands of years. They packed up and left. They went looking for work. This very human instinct, shared by generations of Poles, Germans, and Irish—to go where the jobs are—seems bewildering to many of my colleagues in Congress today. It wasn't bewildering to my parents. It was a necessity. They loved Puerto Rico. They didn't want to leave. They felt they had no choice. They definitely didn't come to Chicago for our great weather. They came for the work.

NOW THEY WERE headed back, with stereos, furniture, and a son and daughter along for the return trip. From my teenage perspective, we went to Puerto Rico without any preparation at all. My dad was not the kind of parent to hold family meetings, or lead group discussions. He didn't seek my input on what clothes I wanted to wear or what we had for dinner, so he certainly wasn't looking for guidance on whether we should move away from the only home we had ever known. He was not a parent who stayed up nights worrying that my feelings would be hurt or that the transition would be painful for my sister and me. I can't picture my dad sitting down with us and sympathetically saying, "I know this will be tough, but Mom and I will do everything we can to make this work out for you." He'd be more likely to put on a tie-dyed shirt and protest the war with the hippies in Lincoln Park. What my dad said was, "Start packing," which was easy because I didn't own much. So I did what I was told. My dad's view of parenting was pretty similar to that of most working-class parents in the 1960s: work hard, provide for your family, make rules, and watch your children follow them.

Looking back, there was always talk in the air of moving to Puerto Rico. But the talk was of a possibility, a goal, a dream. After a while it became like talk of a Cubs World Series to me. My dad might want it, he might enjoy it, but I didn't think it would actually happen. All of the Puerto Ricans in our neighborhood talked about going back. Their chatter was constant, about the warm weather and the open spaces. "You can breathe in Puerto Rico," my mom would say. They missed their hometown's patron-saint festivals. They missed knowing everyone you saw on the street. They missed the sense of home, of their birthplace, their *patria*. But all of the longing didn't mean they were actually going to load up their family, book the ticket on Pan Am, and get on the airplane. "We are going to Puerto Rico," was background noise, part of the soundtrack of being Puertorriqueño in Chicago in the 1960s.

But if I had been paying more attention, I would have known it was more than just a dream to the extended Gutiérrez clan. By 1968 my family was on the move. My uncle Keko—the brother closest to my dad—took my two cousins and went back to San Sebastián, my father's hometown.

My uncle Richie—who was only a year older than me as the youngest of my father's fourteen brothers and sisters—went back with my grandma. They had lived in Gary, Indiana, working in the steel mills.

I loved our trips to Gary. The town was overflowing with Puerto Ricans in the 1960s, and our family contributed more than our share of the population. We visited the Indiana family at least once per month. Right behind by grandmother's house was another house full of Puerto Ricans, home to several teenage girls, all cute and all coveted by my teenage uncles. When I was nine or ten, my desperate uncles would send me over to the girls' house with notes to deliver and songs to sing. I would take a little 45-record player and say, "This song is for Lolita from my uncle Ismael. He wants me to perform it for you." The girls would sit in their living room, listen politely, maybe giggle, and then go on their way. I don't remember my ten-year-old serenading as being very effective, but I liked the attention the girls paid to me. I wasn't shy. I would have sung all day. Trips to Gary were a weekend outing. We would drive through Hammond and other little Indiana towns to avoid paying tolls on the Skyway. When my dad was feeling generous, he would buy us fried shrimp with the toll money he saved.

But the steel mills were already declining, and most of my Indiana relatives had gone back to the island. I missed Uncle Richie. I liked to play basketball with Richie and his friends. They were good players and even though I wasn't, they let me tag along to their games at the park. I remember what they said to me the most—"Don't shoot, don't shoot." But now Richie was gone.

My relatives in New York were moving around too, some to Puerto Rico, some out of Spanish Harlem to nicer places like the Bronx. Suddenly, it was like my whole family couldn't sit still. By the late '60s, going to Puerto Rico was more than background noise for the Gutiérrez family, it was a game plan.

I grew up in Chicago listening to my mother say *"Esta no es mi tierra*—This is not my land." She said it a lot in the winters, after snowstorms. In Puerto Rico you never woke up in the morning, looked out your window, saw a sheet of ice, and wondered how you would get to work. My mom said *esta no es mi tierra* when people broke into our apartment and stole things. Once, the thieves came in and literally emptied every drawer and cupboard and cabinet in the apartment. They even dumped out the containers of sugar and flour, apparently convinced that my parents must have a few hidden dollars mixed in with the staples. Most everyone I knew had their apartment broken into at least once. She said it when my aunt Wilda had her purse snatched off her shoulder in the middle of the day; she said it when she saw the Latin Kings gang members hanging out on our corner. *Esta no es mi tierra* was true for my mother. It wasn't true for me. Chicago was my land.

The winters seemed foreign to my mom, but they seemed fun to me. They meant snowball fights and the occasional snow day off from school. The Latin Kings were part of the neighborhood. We always thought the really dangerous Kings were in Humboldt Park, anyway, far across the Kennedy Expressway from where the comparatively lucky Lincoln Park Puerto Ricans like us lived. Back then the Latin Kings still wore sweaters—black and gold to distinguish them from the Harrison Gents, who wore purple and black. It would be nice if the gang members still wore fancy sweaters today so the police could pick them up more easily. Then, we mostly coexisted with them.

To get to our bodega, you had to walk by the Harrison Gents. They controlled the corner of Burling and Willow, around the corner from our apartment. They had dropped out of high school, rented an apartment, and hung out. They yelled at people who walked by, smoked, laughed, and harassed most everyone. The Gents were in charge, and intimidating.

One of them, Israel, decided he liked me. He was from the neighborhood and I think he looked out for his immediate neighbors, and always kept the rest of the Gents from bothering me. One day after I had returned from a weekend in Gary, Israel wasn't around. I asked what happened. He had been killed, shot dead on the playground at Newberry school in a gang fight. I was stunned, devastated. I couldn't sleep. I felt awful for him, but his Harrison Gent buddies weren't interested in carrying on any of his traditions. The next time I went by the corner, another Gent slapped me on the back of my head as I walked by. "Your friend isn't here anymore to protect you," he said. He hit me hard enough that I was still showing the effects when I returned home and saw my dad.

My dad was not sentimental, but he was the protector of our family. And loyal. I never doubted for a minute that my dad would stand up for us.

"What happened, Quiro—did someone hit you?" he asked. My mom and dad always called me Quiro, a Puerto Rican nickname he gave me so I wouldn't become a 70-year-old who was still called "junior." My dad was ready to take the fight to someone. And I remember thinking he could take care of any of those kids on the corner. My dad was in shape, solid and tough. He could handle himself. I knew, because I'd felt his belt on my behind more than once. The Gents were mostly kids, not that much older than me. But I also remember thinking that they would get my dad back eventually. That's how gangs think. Wait for the right time to surprise someone, outnumber them. I didn't want him to get hurt, so I never told him who hit me, and we coexisted with the Gents until we headed to Puerto Rico.

I didn't really worry about the Kings or the Gents or much of anything else. I was a fifteen-year-old Chicago kid surrounded by friends. I never once longed for a Caribbean island. Puerto Rico *no es mi tierra*.

Still, I packed. I hoped it was a false alarm, but I knew it wasn't. The closest I came to rebellion was raising the courage to ask my dad, "Why do we have to move, why now?"

"Because it's time, Quiro." That was that.

IT DIDN'T SEEM FAIR. I was being forced to move even though any trouble I found in Chicago was mostly harmless. At school, my teachers told me I talked too much. One day my teacher, a very polite and proper white lady, told me she would have to talk to my parents because I wouldn't listen in class. I begged her not to do it. "You don't understand what that letter will mean. My house isn't like *Leave It to Beaver* or *Father Knows Best*," I told her. I wanted her to understand that her letter home wouldn't lead to a quiet discussion in my dad's study. It would mean serious attention from my dad's belt. She gave me one reprieve, but she called home the next time I disrupted her class, and the red welts from my dad's belt kept me quiet for a while. As a parent now, the use of the belt is hard to understand, but it seemed like standard punishment then.

Still, no amount of corporal punishment changed my basic nature. I liked to have fun. One year our class was collecting funds for the Red Cross, and my fifth-grade teacher, Mrs. Morrison, turned it into a competition to see whether the boys or the girls in class could bring in the most money. The nickels and dimes added up, and Mrs. Morrison tracked the totals on the chalkboard. The competition was close.

At home, my dad kept his tips from the cab in a cigar box in his bedroom. Some of the tip money went to the bodega right away, some eventually made it to our account at the savings and loan, but a lot of it sat in that cigar box. Was it tempting? It was, but I basically viewed my dad as all-knowing and unforgiving, so his tips always stayed in the cigar box. Until the Red Cross donation drive. In a lesson in moral relativism, I figured it couldn't really be that bad if I took a little bit of money and gave it to the Red Cross at school. And so I did, and not just a nickel. I thought if you're going to break the rules for a good cause, why go halfway? So I took fifty cents—a fortune for a mid-'60s school fund-raiser in a poor neighborhood.

When I donated the money, I made one of my first smart campaign moves. I gave the teacher my—or my dad's—fifty cents. This generosity impressed everyone in class, particularly the boys, who were about to move ahead in the collection competition because of my largesse. Except that I told Mrs. Morrison to count my half buck to the girls' side, which caused the girls in the class to cheer me and increased my popularity by a value exponentially greater than my contribution. That I don't really remember the boys' reaction tells you about how much I was worried about it at the time. I was mostly relieved that my dad never missed the fifty cents.

If we were leaving Lincoln Park, I wondered, why did I put in all of those years as an altar boy? Since I was little, I had been getting up early to light the candles for the priests at St. Michael's, the parish that was our home church in Lincoln Park.

St. Michael's wasn't very advanced in how they treated Latinos. The Spanish Mass wasn't held in the main sanctuary, but in a common room next to it. On Sunday mornings the place often smelled of the beer that was served at wedding receptions the night before. So being an altar boy put you up front in the main sanctuary. It was like a club. It set you apart from the rest of the kids and families in the parish. It helped you in St. Michael's Catholic School. When I got in trouble for talking too much, or not showing enough respect for authority in class—which happened fairly regularly—the brothers would look out for me and help me out because I was an altar boy.

Devoting the time to the church also kept me out of trouble because it was a lot of work. My mom and dad made sure I was on time, so they regularly scheduled me for the earliest Mass, at six a.m nearly every day. But not everyone was as diligent. So if the altar boy for the six thirty and seven o'clock masses didn't show, I just stuck around. I lit a lot of candles at St. Michael's between six and eight in the morning. On Sundays I carried a lot of crosses into the sanctuary. There was competition for which lucky altar boy would walk in the front and carry the cross, but there were tradeoffs too; if you carried the cross, you didn't help with the communion. I liked being the one with the cross. You led the way and had less work during the service.

On Sundays after church my mom and I would head down to Maxwell Street, Chicago's buy-anything, open-air market. At Maxwell Street, people always said, "If you had something stolen on Thursday, you could buy it back on Sunday morning." Maxwell Street Market was not, to explain it kindly, highly regulated or policed. It seemed as if the vendors had a Chicago exception from the normal rules of commerce. The market felt like a Turkish bazaar, with bonfires burning in oil drums in the winter, and a rotating roster of vendors selling everything from car parts to doughnuts. The prices were always moving. If the vendors posted honest signs, they would have read, OUR PRICE IS THE MAXIMUM WE CAN POSSIBLY TALK YOU INTO PAYING. Maxwell Street was a good place for a kid to acquire negotiating skills. Every future member of Congress should have spent some time there.

My mom regularly bought—and haggled—at Maxwell Street. One

week we needed a comforter for my new "bedroom." It was probably a guilt purchase because this was when I was being moved onto a cot in the hallway. The vendor wanted fifteen dollars. My mom didn't want to pay more than ten. She held firm and they made a deal. I remember he folded up the comforter and told my mom, "That will be $10.50 with tax." My mom quickly put her money back into her purse and turned and walked away. "You told me ten dollars. I won't pay more than that," she said over her shoulder. Any member of Congress can tell you that walking away is sometimes the best negotiating tactic. My mom knew it worked even then. The vendor called her back and she got her comforter for ten dollars even, and then she taught me one more lesson. "Only pay tax to someone who is actually going to give it to the government," she said as we carried my new comforter home.

TO ME, it seemed unnecessary to move to the Caribbean to experience Puerto Rico. Amost all of the people at Spanish Mass were Puerto Rican. Most of my friends were Puerto Rican. We bought almost everything we needed from the bodega on the corner, which was a kind of town hall for Puerto Ricans. The whites had their little shop a block away, but we went to Mr. Rivera, the Puerto Rican man who kept an account book under the counter. My mom always thought of it as a little piece of Puerto Rico, the place where you felt most at home. You could play the *bolita* at the bodega and hope your numbers hit that week. You could come back from the bodega with *morcilla*— Puerto Rican blood sausage—and with newspapers and magazines from San Juan. If you were from the neighborhood and the owner trusted you, you could also come back with a bottle of Pitorro—Puerto Rican moonshine, a handmade rum that came straight from a still in somebody's basement or kitchen. That was mostly for the holidays, but I knew families that treated every day as a holiday and always had some Pitorro around.

Owning the bodega was considered a status symbol in our modest world. Mr. Rivera was our neighborhood's Puerto Rican entrepreneur. Taking credit from people in the neighborhood made him important;

his ledger book helped more than a few families get through to payday with enough food. I don't ever remember him charging interest. He just wanted people's business. I would take a couple of dollars down to the corner, with my mom's instructions for a three- or four-pound chicken, whether she wanted it cut up or not. I'd come home with chicken, a can of beans, a bag of rice. We never went hungry.

Even Chicago baseball had a Puerto Rican flavor. My dad usually didn't drive his cab on the weekends, and he loved baseball and took me to the games. We would go to Comiskey and cheer for the White Sox and Juan Pizarro. And we would go to Wrigley to cheer for the Cubs—except when the Pirates were in town. Then, we would go to Wrigley with all of the other Puerto Ricans and cheer for Roberto Clemente.

"Watch when they hit the ball to Clemente," my dad would say. "Just watch and see if anyone tries to take an extra base, if they try to tag up. On anyone else, that guy would have scored. Not on Clemente. Nobody ever runs on Clemente."

Growing up in a world where every person of authority was white, the fact that one of America's greatest baseball players was from the tiny island where your parents grew up altered your sense of what it meant to be Puerto Rican. In a world where you never saw a neighbor wear a suit to work or drive a fancy car, Roberto Clemente's fame allowed you to dream big. And Clemente couldn't have been more Puerto Rican. He was poor, he came from nothing. He was dark—almost black. And he was proud. When you watched Roberto Clemente patrol right field, or swing the bat, you felt like you could aspire to much more than just putting food on the table.

And we needed somebody to dream on. In 1960s Chicago, the mailmen, the bankers and the bus drivers were white. The doctors, the teachers, and the lawyers all were white. Movie stars? A bunch of white people and Sidney Poitier. Television was the same. Bill Cosby was breaking through for African Americans, but what Latinos did you see on TV? There was Lucy's husband, the Cuban musician with the accent that made everyone laugh. At least he was smarter than Lucy, I thought to myself. If there was a Puerto Rican policeman in

Chicago in the 1960s, I never met him. I met lots of white cops, most of whom weren't crazy about me and my friends. And even most of the baseball players were white—with a few blacks here and there.

But we had Roberto Clemente, a Puerto Rican guy with a rifle arm who hit .300 every year and moved like he was running in a dream. My first Puerto Rican hero, a man who still stands for honor and courage.

MY DAD didn't care that I was fifteen and discovering girls. To impress the girls, some friends and I had even started a band. We were terrible. As far as I can remember, none of us really played any instruments very well, we just loved the music. We practiced in my friend Frankie's garage. I borrowed a bass guitar and spent weeks trying to learn the bass line from "Louie Louie." Now every DJ at every campaign victory party wants to play that song for me. They don't know it just reminds me of our awful band.

We argued about the best radio stations, and Frankie and I would get his portable, box-shaped 45 record player and prank call people. We would pick the most obvious songs, the Beatles singing "She Loves You" and "I Want to Hold Your Hand," call someone, put on our best disc jockey voice, and say to the unlucky person who picked up the phone, "Name this tune and you have won a trip to Hawaii!" Eventually we would find some gullible person who would shout— very excited, picturing the hula girls and luaus—"I Want to Hold Your Hand!" and we would laugh and hang up. Trust me, it seemed funny to two teenagers with lots of time and no money to spend.

I was too young to be troubled by the momentous world events happening right in my city. My friends and I would sneak away from home and go down to Wells Street to watch the hippies hang out and smoke pot and play their music. Old Town was a fifteen-minute walk from our neighborhood, and my friends and I knew every inch of Piper's Alley long before Wells Street was mostly yuppies and tourists going to Second City. I ate my first deep-dish pizza on Wells Street. The cool stores on Wells now seem like time capsules of '60s hipness; tie-dye and sunglasses, head shops that we hadn't quite figured out were head shops. And a lot of the women obviously weren't wearing bras. We were more gawkers than participants in the Wells Street scene, but what fifteen-year-old—even a fifteen-year-old with no money—would want to move away from that excitement?

When we weren't watching the hippies on Wells, Frankie and I were always coming up with elaborate explanations that might allow us to stay out ten minutes later. My dad was a tyrant about coming home precisely on time. When we went to the freshman dance at St. Michael's School, my dad dutifully showed up at nine thirty p.m. to pick me up. I was the first of my friends forced to go home. They laughed at me as I moped to my dad's car. The dance lasted until eleven. It was being supervised by a battalion of nuns. My dad apparently thought the nuns would go crazy and let the dance turn into a frenzy of sex and drugs in the last hour and a half.

In Lincoln Park, we had our own Puerto Rican world mapped out. We knew every inch of our neighborhood. We knew where to look for cute girls. We knew which guys were just wannabe gang members trying to act tough, and which guys were really dangerous. We knew what streets not to cross so you didn't end up in the black neighborhood or the white neighborhood. It was simple—everything south of North Avenue was black, everything east of Larrabee was white. Mostly, the black kids thought Puerto Ricans were too white and the white kids definitely thought we were too dark, so we kept to our own neighborhood. North Avenue, the gateway to the black neighborhoods that led eventually to the Cabrini–Green housing project, had an impassable median running down the middle, making it harder to cross. In the 1960s, segregation could be accomplished just by establishing the right traffic patterns.

IT WAS HOME to me; all of it. All of those trips carrying the cross up and down the aisle, all of the work to keep the Harrison Street Gents from bothering me, all of the time practicing my bass for our terrible band.

But for my dad, Chicago had turned into something very different from what my sister and I saw. In 1969, the riots after Martin Luther King Jr.'s death were still fresh in everyone's mind. People had lost their businesses and their houses. In our neighborhood, I remember watching people bust out the windows of CET, the big appliance and television store on North Avenue. They shattered the windows and carried out the televisions in the window displays. It was a bad day for the stores. The Woolworths was looted that day too. I was on my way home from school and moved fast to get off North Avenue. I ran home. For days, the National Guard patrolled the neighborhood, driving up and down the streets in jeeps. My father had no sympathy for the rioters.

Where I thought Wells Street was a wonderland of the counterculture, filled with cool people not much older than me, my dad saw drugs and chaos. Where I saw the Harrison Gents and maybe even the Latin Kings as part of the neighborhood, he saw an imminent and dangerous threat to his family. And where I saw *The Ed Sullivan Show* and *I Spy* and Motown as my day-to-day entertainment, he saw something entirely alien and foreign.

My dad saw gang members as teenage bullies with knives, who would never be tolerated in Puerto Rico. He saw the riots in Lincoln Park at the 1968 Democratic Convention and saw nothing but danger. My dad cheered for Mayor Daley in his showdown with the troublemakers protesting the war. He was disturbed and worried by the assassinations of 1968. Like many Puerto Rican families, we had two pictures other than family members hanging in our apartment—John F. Kennedy and Jesus Christ. If the president of the United States, and then his brother—good Catholic men—couldn't be protected, how could anyone be safe? Everywhere he looked, my dad saw good people trying, and failing, to control the turmoil of the 1960s.

He also saw small signs of unrest right in his own home. He would have to send me back to the neighborhood "barber," a Puerto Rican guy who cut hair for a buck in his basement two blocks down from the apartment, to tell him to cut my hair even shorter. I had already asked for bell-bottoms, which my dad laughed at. "They're for sissies," he said. I scraped together enough money to buy John Lennon glasses—

small, round sunglasses that I thought shouted out that young Luis Gutiérrez was hip. My dad thought they looked ridiculous. They were confiscated. He didn't want me to go out at night, so I would have to tell him I was sleeping over at Frankie's house.

Disorder in the streets was bad enough. My dad wasn't going to tolerate even the smallest disorder under his roof.

IT DIDN'T MATTER to my dad that I was making some money myself. I had gotten a paper route. When I signed up, the only route available was downtown. I took the train to the Loop, picked up my papers, and dropped off the evening edition of the *Chicago Tribune*—mostly to office buildings. After paying my bus fare, I would still have five dollars a week left over, a fortune to me then.

My boss sold me Christmas cards to give to my customers. I hoped he was right when he told me it would be worth it, because he charged me ten bucks for the cards. I gave them away and made my rounds before Christmas. Some of the people I saw every day—maybe a building manager, or a lawyer in an office or a doorman or two— would throw a quarter or even a dollar my way. City Hall was on my route too. I liked heading into the fancy building where all of the decisions were made. Every day I dropped off the afternoon paper to the mayor's office.

Before Christmas, the mayor's security guy took my paper and then told me to wait. Another tip, I thought. Great. I waited expectantly for my quarter. Heck, it was the mayor's office, maybe it would be a buck or two if I were lucky. I waited a minute, worried that I was getting late on my route. Then I looked up, and it wasn't the security guard who came back. It was the man. It was Mayor Richard J. Daley, heading toward me. Just like on television, big and round and powerful. He walked right up to me. He didn't have a quarter; he gave me a five-dollar bill. "Merry Christmas, son," he said. He handed me the bill and gave me a handshake with a quick pump of his very strong right hand. And then he was gone.

The mayor of Chicago. I was stunned. Not just by the five bucks but by seeing a celebrity right up close. The man who ran everything. He took on the protesters, told everyone what to do, made all of the decisions. It never would have occurred to me for a second that one day I would be sitting down and meeting with his son in the same office that Mayor Richard J. Daley had walked right back into after he gave me that huge tip.

MY DAD DROVE a cab for a long time, but not long before we left he changed jobs and became a building manager for the man who owned our apartment building and many others in Lincoln Park. A businessman, John Krenger believed Lincoln Park was going to improve, that the building stock was good, and that the location near the lake and downtown made it invaluable. Others looked and wondered who would want to live near a bunch of Puerto Ricans and other poor people. But Krenger believed in the future of Lincoln Park and saw my dad as reliable and trustworthy, just the kind of man he wanted for a building superintendent.

And he was right. My dad cared for all of the properties like they were his own, kept them clean, kept an eye on the residents, negotiated away problems. I helped him sweep and mop most weekends. We didn't get our first phone until my dad took the job; Mr. Krenger might call, and we needed to be available. No more going down to the bodega with a stack of quarters to use the pay phone to call my mom's relatives in New York. Now we would call from our own phone, a little status symbol for the Gutiérrez family.

One evening, not too long before we left, Mr. Krenger and his wife came over to our small apartment for dinner. We prepared for it like it was a state visit and the secret service might be coming to check out our place to be sure it was clean and that nobody would be the target of snipers. We didn't have a dining room; we had a small kitchen with a Formica-topped table. Today you find them in antique stores being sold as vintage, 1960s retro. Back then they were the kind of cheap furniture owned by working people living in apartment buildings. We put out our best plates and silverware and treated it like Christmas.

Ada and I were warned upon the threat of corporal punishment to be on our best behavior, even though we were banished to a table in the living room. "Do not embarrass us," we were told. This was important. It is the only time I remember white people being in our apartment.

The dinner was a success. Mr. and Mrs. Krenger were nice and funny and easy to get along with. I thought they would be scary and intimidating—like having the pope over for dinner—but they were kind people. Mr. Krenger liked having my dad as part of his business. He and my dad seemed like friends. Ada and I quietly ate our food. Isn't that how white people acted at dinnertime? Dignified and quiet?

I learned much later that John Krenger wanted my dad to go into business with him. He would give him a small part of his business in exchange for looking for good properties and managing them, helping him find trustworthy tenants. This was Lincoln Park, Chicago, in the 1960s, when property values were a fraction of what they are today. Fraction doesn't even really describe it. A fraction of a fraction. John Krenger was inviting my dad in on the ground floor of a real-estate Microsoft, asking him to become a millionaire.

My dad never even thought about it. He just wanted to go home. It was as if the American Dream had knocked on my dad's door and he said, "I'll pass. I like the weather in Puerto Rico. It's safer. It's better. It's home." That's how much going back to the island meant to my parents.

I think now that moving wasn't a choice for my dad, it was an obligation. Were my parents tired of snow and English-language radio stations? Yes, but in the end it was the chaos—the drugs and hippies and gangs and riots and assassinations. It was no place to raise their children, even if a wealthy developer wanted to cut my dad in on a bright American future. His son's love of Motown and the neighborhood girls were not reasons to stay in Chicago. He had a family to think about, and an island calling him home.

It was time to go to Puerto Rico.

CHAPTER THREE

Leaving Home, Going Home

W E WERE crammed in the back of our Impala station wagon, crowded by our luggage, watching Chicago disappear out of the big back window, driving toward New York. Ada and my mom would stay in Harlem with our relatives while my dad and I went ahead to San Sebastián, a little town up in the mountains. I felt like we were waving good-bye to the civilized world. My sister and I sang "Yesterday" over and over loudly, in protest. My parents hated the Beatles. My sister cried, and I cried with her. It was true. We were moving to Puerto Rico. My mom and dad were going home. My sister and I were leaving home.

We couldn't cry all the way to New York. Our singing voices eventually gave out. I'm sure my parents preferred our sullen silence to our forlorn Beatles sing-along. My sister mostly slept. I looked out the window and watched the Midwest roll by. My parents were happy. For me, the drive was a journey away from everything I had ever known.

We had driven to New York many times, so the cross-country trek wasn't new. Going to my grandmother's apartment in Spanish Harlem was our summer vacation—our only vacation—every year. My grandmother's apartment in Spanish Harlem was our Hilton Head, our little Puerto Rican Nantucket.

I had always liked the Gutiérrez family road trips. Gas stations and road maps and the highway stretching out before us. The idea of spending money on a motel was ridiculous. I don't ever remember even talking about it. We drove straight through and slept in the car. But we had to stop to eat, so our summer vacations accounted for most of my restaurant visits as a kid. We would stop in cheap roadside places. Almost every stop, my dad ordered apple pie and ice cream, which seemed exotic to us. Sometimes my mom would make flan, but we never once had apple pie in the house. It reminded me that my dad had a whole life away from us, driving his cab and stopping at diners. We couldn't order anything expensive, but the places seemed fancy to me—sometimes the food was brought by an actual waitress.

The first half of the drive went quickly as I looked forward to my upcoming cheeseburger. That usually happened about halfway through Ohio. Then we were in for the long drive through Pennsylvania. We never asked if we were there yet, we asked if we were out of Pennsylvania yet. Once you made it across Pennsylvania, New Jersey was a piece of cake. Forty years later, I still think of members of Congress from Pennsylvania as the guys who represent the long state.

Before, there had never been anything to be sad about as we saw Chicago fade away, because we always had a return option. We used to look forward to going away. Our time in New York would be filled with stickball and lots of visits with cousins and aunts and uncles. We would go to Orchard Beach and swim. The beach wasn't new to us; we walked to North Avenue Beach all the time in Chicago. It was the saltwater that was a novelty. It was easy to float. We would go to Yankee Stadium, and I would boo the Yankees because they were the guys who always came to town and beat the White Sox. My family treated us like tourists, and over the years I'd made it to the World's Fair and the Empire State Building and saw the Rockettes at Radio City. We would always take the subway downtown in New York. In Chicago, we would go months without going downtown. Lincoln Park was my world. Until my paper route, the Loop was foreign territory. My grade-school class took a bus downtown once to see *Mary Poppins*, and it felt like I was on a spectacular outing.

But in New York, my relatives wanted to get out of their neighborhood and do things. New York was crowded. The time we spent in New York every summer was just enough to make me appreciate living in Chicago. At home, even if I didn't have a room, at least I had a hallway to myself. We had a Boys Club right around the corner, where I could hang out with my friends. In Lincoln Park, there was at least a little distance in between the buildings. In fact, the walkways between buildings were just wide enough that you could stand in between, put your left foot on one building and your right foot on the one next to it, twist yourself in, and climb up as high as you dared, one foot on each building, back and forth, just like Spider-Man. I knew kids who went all the way to the roof. I went about halfway up and then came back down. The room between buildings helped you feel like you could breathe in Chicago.

New York was different. My grandmother's front door opened right into her kitchen. You had to walk through two bedrooms to get to the living room. The toilet had a pull chain. At night, people hung out on *el balcon*—the balcony—which looked a lot like the fire escape to me. There really wasn't enough room for everyone inside. Her grown daughter was living with her, and she was raising another grandson, and she was visited by a revolving door of other relatives. You never knew who was going to show up. It was a rotating cast of Puerto Ricans—even without the extra Gutiérrezes from Chicago. And the building—like most of the buildings—felt like it could collapse at any minute. The smell of your neighbors' cooking floated through the hall and under your doorway. You felt like you lived with your neighbor's fried chicken and pork chops, their rice and beans. You couldn't mop the smells away. The buildings were taller, too; four long stories to walk up and down. My dad and Mr. Krenger didn't take care of any buildings like the one my grandmother lived in. Mr. Krenger wouldn't have wanted any part of it.

Back in Lincoln Park, we had alleys to hide the garbage. In New York it piled up right in front of the building and never quite disappeared. Chicago had parks everywhere. New York's park plan? Central Park, and good luck to the rest of you—go play in the street. New York had neighborhood pools, but they were packed with people. You were lucky if you found a place to stand in the water. I told my cousins we had neighborhood pools too; they were called fire hydrants and all you needed was a wrench and the ability to run away and hide when the cops came. Put a tire over the fire hydrant and jam a board down into it to make the fire hydrant spray. We had invented our own little water park that was way better than the New York pools. When I became alderman, I used to have to have to tell people to stop opening up the fire hydrants because it made the neighborhood water pressure dangerously low. "Your house will burn down," I would tell them, and the Puerto Ricans in the neighborhood would look at me like I was some crazy enforcer sent from City Hall to ruin their fun. Even my daughter would be mad at me. She always told me to close the hydrant next to our house last. The truth is, I always wanted to get in the spray with them. I remembered those hot summer days.

Every time we had driven to New York before, I had a great vacation with my family and then was thrilled to go back home. Compared to New York, I thought Chicago was bright and grass-filled. Chicago shined. Trips to my grandma's made me feel like we were the affluent part of the Gutiérrez clan.

This trip was different. I would have gladly stayed in New York forever. At least the smells and the fire escape and the crowds seemed familiar and safe. From my previous summer vacations, I knew my way around the city. But New York wasn't a vacation this time. To me, it was a farewell tour of my familiar past.

My dad and I rushed around New York for nearly a week making final preparations for San Sebastián. We double-checked the things we were shipping. We dropped off the car at the port to be shipped over by boat. My dad was serious and steady, checking things off of his to-do list before he finally returned home. He also took some pity on me. Almost every day, before we returned home from our schedule of errands, we would go down to Forty-Second Street and catch a movie. That week, we probably saw three or four WWII movies. Maybe a western. I remember a lot of John Wayne. We sat in the dark in the New York movie theater, two men ready to embark on a new life. The time had finally come, and what choice did I have?

My uncle drove us to the airport, and we left the women behind.

It was my first time flying. I had never even been on a train except for the CTA. The whole process was dramatic. Checking in at the airport, having our tickets taken, putting away our luggage in our own overhead compartments. Flying on a plane in 1969 was much different from how it is today. The stewardesses—and everyone called them stewardesses—were happy and friendly. They seemed glamorous to me. The pilot welcomed you aboard. The bankrupt airlines hadn't cut everyone's salaries and taken away their pensions yet. Passengers weren't complaining about security lines and baggage fees and struggling to fit everything under their seats. People were dressed up. It was a special occasion. I felt like I was in some exclusive club.

But we weren't just flying. We were on a plane with a little lounge area with actual tables. The best part? I could drink all of the Coke I wanted. For free. The best part for my dad? He could smoke all the airline cigarettes he wanted. Also free. My dad and I sucked down the airline's free cigarettes and Coke for the duration of the flight. If Pan Am was looking for two people who knew how to take advantage of giveaways, they found it in Luis Gutiérrez senior and junior. For at least a few hours, my dad and I talked and laughed. We were moving ahead to the new world, modern-day conquistadores.

Almost twenty years after he'd left the island, my dad was almost back home. His new Chevy Impala station wagon was safely stored on a boat chugging across the sea. His new furniture, his TV, his stereo— all about to arrive. My mom had departed from a wooden shack with one lightbulb swinging from the ceiling, two rooms carved perilously into the side of a hill. She was returning with a family and enough possessions to decorate a comfortable home. In Chicago, they were poor. In San Sebastián, they returned rich.

I think this sense of pride was very much in my dad's mind as we flew toward San Juan. We enjoyed our trip and took our Pan Am freebies without shame. For a while, as we relaxed on the plane, with the pretty stewardesses asking us regularly if we needed anything, I thought that just maybe Puerto Rico wouldn't be so bad after all.

* * *

OUR PLANE LANDED and we gathered our suitcases and walked down the airplane's portable steps and across the concrete tarmac to the terminal. My first impression of my new home was simple.

Puerto Rico is hot.

Not hot like a summer day in Chicago. It was the hottest day I had ever felt. My shirt, a nice knit one I had worn to look respectable on the plane, suddenly seemed too heavy, a made-for-Chicago short-sleeved shirt that might as well have been a parka. It was definitely not designed for the tropics. I looked at my dad. He seemed nice and cool.

My first question was simple too.

"Dad, can I have a Coke? I'm thirsty."

My dad turned to me and said, "Speak Spanish now. You're in Puerto Rico. If you speak English, people will think you're arrogant. That you think you're better than them." Then he turned and kept walking toward the terminal.

He said it as if he were saying "Wasn't that a nice plane ride?"

Speak Spanish? I had just spoken to him on the plane for four hours. In English. I always—*always*—spoke to my dad in English. We had been preparing to come to Puerto Rico for months. Buying and sorting and packing and throwing away and making plans. Never once did he put his arm around me and say, "Hey, son, by the way—one thing you might want to do for this Caribbean island we're moving to is brush up on your Spanish. I know you've been speaking English for fifteen years, but remember, we were conquered by the Spaniards long before Teddy Roosevelt and the gang came along, so practice a bit, amigo."

At home, my parents spoke Spanish to each other all the time. I understood most everything they said, but I spoke English back to them. My dad, because of his years in the cab dealing with passengers, spoke English well. My mom was a different story. If the Gutiérrez family had starred in a sitcom, my mom would have been the lovable Puerto Rican matriarch with the broken English mispronouncing words to the delight of a studio audience full of amused white people. But her Spanish was excellent. I heard it all the time on the Puerto Rican radio stations my mom loved. I spoke it, poorly, to my grandmother and other relatives whose English was worse than my mom's. I could get by in Chicago.

My dad just kept on walking toward the terminal. He hadn't given his Spanish directive a second thought. I hustled to catch up. Speak Spanish? To my dad? Great, I thought, and in the evenings I'll design a rocket ship.

Looking back, it should have been obvious to me.

I knew that I would be speaking more Spanish, but I never fully thought through what school would be like, or trying to make new friends. Or buying a Coke at the store. Had I been smart, I would have spent more time thinking about my new life in Puerto Rico. Instead, I thought about Frankie and our band and all the cute girls in the neighborhood and the radio stations I would never hear again. I didn't ask myself what Puerto Rico would really be like. All I knew was Chicago and New York. I assumed it would be something like that, only with even more Puerto Ricans. I was so busy looking back, I had no idea what was coming right at me. I'd spent most of my time preparing to miss Chicago instead of preparing to get by in Puerto Rico.

I watched my dad enter the terminal, a man coming home. He looked as happy and carefree as I had ever seen him. The only thing I wanted to say in Spanish was "I want to go home."

WE WAITED FOR a public car to fill up with travelers heading somewhere near San Sebastián. It was a big old Ford that carried my dad, me, and three or four other people. As instructed, I spoke Spanish to him. If his goal was to make me fit in with other Puerto Ricans, making me speak his native language wasn't helping. The other passengers gawked at me—a Puerto Rican teenager who for some reason couldn't speak Spanish. Their looks said "How can you let your son butcher such a beautiful language?"

We stopped and started out of San Juan. We waited at traffic lights. The car had no air-conditioning. That was new to me. We'd had air-conditioning in our car at home. We'd had air-conditioning in our apartment, too, but my dad was cheap about it. He didn't like to turn it on. When I was home alone I would crank it way up. As soon as I heard my dad coming, I would jump up and quickly switch it off. On a hot summer day, he would walk into an apartment as cool and comfortable as the lobby of the Hilton. He would say, "This costs me money. You've been running the air conditioner again." I would shake my head and look bewildered, like maybe a random cold front had moved exclusively through our little apartment.

But there was no cold front in our public car in Puerto Rico the day we arrived. There were no expressways in 1969, so we took Route 2 out of San Juan and down the coast. We saw a little bit of San Juan, and it looked kind of familiar—busy streets, lots of people, big buildings . . . Then, we were on the open road, heading toward Camuy, where we would turn inland toward the hills to San Sebastián. We passed through towns I had never heard of. Dorado. Arecibo. Suddenly, the trees were exotic. Palm trees and banana trees and mango trees. And the air was filled with a smell that was new to me. What was it? It took a while to know. It was pineapple. The air was fragrant with pineapple.

Then, we hit Camuy and turned inland. And suddenly it was nothing remotely like New York, or Chicago, or even Ohio or Pennsylvania. The two-lane highway felt like a country road, traffic backing up, people waiting to pass. We saw chickens all along the way. We saw lots of small houses, leaning, looking like they might fall over. We saw kids without shoes. Everyone I knew in Chicago had shoes. I remember lots of small towns and lonely intersections and stop signs.

I was a city kid. I had never seen anything like this. Or smelled anything like it. I had never seen pineapple anywhere but at the bodega or cut up on my plate. Never growing on the ground. In sixth grade, my class had taken a field trip to a farm somewhere outside of Chicago. A very nice, very patient farmer in overalls gave us a tour, talking about eggs and milking and plowing. I was bored. I remember seeing pigs and chickens up close for the first time, and thinking, This is food. I don't have any reason to get too friendly with it.

Now there were chickens everywhere I looked. I saw one huge, empty green field after another. Even the fields didn't look like the ones I had seen in Pennsylvania. I asked my dad what they were. "Sugarcane," he said.

"But there's nothing there. It's empty," I said in my fractured Spanish.

"It's out of season. It's summer. They've already chopped it down," he told me.

After an hour or so, we were in the hills leading to San Sebastián. The road narrowed and became steep. I worried every time a car passed us on the other side. It didn't look like there was room. And we were up much higher than I had ever been in a car. I thought my dad had brought me to a place where a stranger was going to send me over a cliff down to my death in some remote Puerto Rican valley. Eventually, after what seemed like hundreds of turns, my dad pointed out the window and said, "San Sebastián."

I looked, and I looked again. I remember my word-for-word thoughts clearly: You have got to be fucking kidding me.

It was San Sebastián. Not just a part of it, like Wrigley Field or North Avenue Beach or Wells Street or even Lincoln Park. It looked like everything. You couldn't climb a tall hill and see Chicago. But there was San Sebastián, a little town down in the valley, right below us, surrounded by a vast cushion of sugarcane and farms. It looked like a very small bull's-eye of civilization in the middle of a very large dartboard of nothing.

I asked my dad, hoping I had misunderstood, "That's it?"

"That's it." We were looking at our new home.

We drove out of the hills and safely made it down into the town, and I gazed at the quiet streets and modest shops. I hoped we were related to the Méndez family, because they seemed to own everything. The Méndez pharmacy, Méndez grocery, Dr. Méndez . . . I wondered if they had any teenage daughters. We passed through the Méndez empire and headed to Pueblo Nuevo—New Town—a neighborhood just off the town center. In Puerto Rico, small or large, I learned over time that there is a very Spanish sameness to the small towns. These towns weren't designed by New England Puritans or Midwestern farmers; these were towns designed by Spanish conquistadores and their descendants. The Spaniards built towns that placed the necessary main functions of daily life firmly in the plaza; the church and the city hall. Everything grows from the places of God and government.

When my dad told me we were going to stay in Pueblo Nuevo in San Sebastián, I pictured our own neighborhood, something like Lincoln Park. It turned out to be one long street. But just like the name said, it was new, and in San Sebastián it passed for the rough part of town. A nighttime spot where you might go to get a drink, or play some pool.

My uncle Keko was one of the newcomers looking to make his way in Pueblo Nuevo. My uncle had returned to Puerto Rico more than a year before, a Gutiérrez family trailblazer. At the top of the one uphill street of Pueblo Nuevo, he bought a house and implemented his plan to make money. His family, including my younger cousins, lived on the first floor. In the basement, nestled into the hillside, uncle Keko started Cuchilandia, home of the best *cuchifritos* on the island.

At least, he said they were the best. And the customers who came and went all night seemed to agree. It seemed everyone showed up at Keko's door for *cuchifritos* eventually, from the mayor to street hustlers. I don't know if they were the best, because in Chicago I never had *cuchifritos* before. I had never heard my parents mention *cuchifritos*. I'd never smelled *cuchifritos*. But I smelled them now, because a huge cauldron of *cuchifritos* was bubbling just outside the window of my new bedroom.

Saying *cuchifritos* are cooking beneath your bedroom window isn't exactly like saying your mom is making chocolate-chip cookies in the kitchen. When I say cauldron, I'm not kidding around. Think *Macbeth*. Think hungry cannibals cooking dinner in the center of their village. Something from a Tarzan movie. The smell that overflowed the pot was of boiling pig parts. People use lots of pig parts for different kinds of *cuchifritos*, from the ears to the tongue, but my uncle specialized in pig stomach, a delicacy some people called *buche*. *Cuchi* means "little pig." *Fritos* means "fried." That tells you all you need to know about *cuchifritos*.

My uncle's cauldron was three or four feet across, the right size for a smallish lost Amazon explorer or pounds and pounds of pig stomach. It stood over a wood fire built into a pit. The cauldron was in back of our house, on a cement slab, a kind of unfinished deck. In the morning, once a week, a truck would drop off huge boxes of pig stomachs. My uncle would take them out back and hack them into big pieces on a table and put them in his huge vat to boil down. To cook them down you had to keep stirring them in the pot, work that I would soon share. You stirred and stirred, with a huge wooden paddle that was big enough to row a boat. He would boil them until they were soft and then take them out and put them in the refrigerator. Eventually, he would take those out, chop them into bite-size pieces, and throw them in a deep-fryer. You fried them quickly—you didn't want them to be crunchy. The smell filled the neighborhood, and Uncle Keko sold the finished product out of his basement in paper cups.

Puerto Rico wasn't big on zoning laws in the 1960s. If your neighbor wanted to boil pig stomachs in a giant vat in the backyard and sell it from his basement, I'm pretty sure San Sebastián didn't have a city department to handle your complaints. Your best bet was to ask your neighbor for a *cuchifritos* discount.

Or, better yet, negotiate a deal on my uncle's *alcapurria*, a Puerto Rican delicacy that he also made in our backyard. He had a special, very specific recipe where he took both green bananas and plantains and grated them into a pulp that you could spread around like a doughy paste. You would then divide it up like pieces of bread, and fill it with meat and spices, olives, and capers. We usually made pork. When your *alcapurria* was assembled, you dropped it into the fryer as well—a bit like an empanada, except with more crunch and flavor.

All my life I had been eating Puerto Rican food. Rice and beans and chicken and pork accounted for about 90 percent of my Chicago diet. I had consumed vastly more pork chops and beans than slices of pizza and hot dogs. The Mexican kids in Chicago would call Puerto Ricans "pork chops." It wasn't a term of admiration. Of course, as a kid I heard more than a few Puerto Ricans call Mexicans "tortilla face," so we all looked to native menus for insults.

But this food being prepared in my backyard, *cuchifritos* and *alcapurria*, was new to me. And incredibly delicious. I understood why the neighborhood men wandered in at night to buy their paper cup full of *cuchifritos*. There was barely room to stand in Cuchilandia, so nobody came for the décor. I was frustrated that I had spent so much of my life eating potato chips. *Cuchifritos* tasted exotic, different. That I liked them immediately said something to me about genetics. I'm not sure a fifteen-year-old Norwegian kid dropped into Puerto Rico would have taken an immediate liking to boiled pig stomach, but I did. It was something I tasted for the first time and thought, Why haven't I been eating this all my life?

I HAD ALWAYS gotten along with my uncle and my cousins in Chicago. But getting along in Chicago was different from living with them. My cousins, Carlos and Edwin, were six or seven years younger than me but had been in Puerto Rico just long enough to be comfortable. They were happy to have a newcomer to taunt and torment. They liked having an advantage in language over their older cousin. But they weren't too thrilled to make room in their bedroom for my cot and my meager belongings.

Edwin was expert at capturing the lizards that filled the streets and yards of Puerto Rico the way squirrels populate Chicago. He showed me how to take a piece of long grass and tie a knot, kind of like a noose, at the end to corral a lizard like you were roping a calf. Unfortunately, they had both become even more expert at releasing the lizards into my cot, or throwing them at me when I was least expecting it. Eventually, I came to expect it all the time. They thought it was hilarious that they could scare their older cousin at will.

As soon as we were settled, my dad was off to scout possible locations for the restaurant that was going to become our livelihood in Puerto Rico. Sometimes he took me along, but more often he didn't. That left me lying on a cot in an apartment in a hill town of Puerto Rico, being laughed at by lizard-tossing cousins and smelling plantains and pig parts. I was speaking a mix of bad Spanish and more familiar English to my cousins and uncle. It was more than a month until school started. I needed something to do.

My choices were limited. I didn't have Wells Street to explore, and nobody to explore with me. Wrigley Field was a memory. We had moved to Puerto Rico, but Roberto Clemente seemed farther away. There was no television for my dad and me to watch together. My dad liked Johnny Carson. Gone. I liked *The Monkees*. Gone. Instead, we had one TV station. It seemed to broadcast nothing but local news and variety shows. I remember puppets and pet tricks and lonely-looking guys with guitars. It looked like they had taped our church's talent show and forced all the acts to perform in Spanish. I was thrilled to find out that there was an English-language radio station in San Juan, but we couldn't get it up in the hills. There were no more WWII movies. For me, there were no movies at all, because everything came to Puerto Rico many months after it opened in Chicago. In San Sebastián, I had already seen everything that was playing.

The lizards and the loneliness and the distance from everything I knew turned me into an angry, sullen teenager. The free Coke in the airplane had started to seem more like a last supper than an omen of future happiness. My bitterness made me feel like I had been banished to a supermax prison, the kind of place with twenty-three-hour-a-day lockdown in solitary confinement. My cousins were too young and too annoying. My dad was busy. My sister was lucky. She was still hanging out in Harlem, being doted on by her aunts and speaking English.

Back in Chicago, I knew the rules. The places to go and stay away from, what pranks I could get away with pulling with my friends. In Chicago, I was starting to talk to girls and they even occasionally talked back. In San Sebastián, I wrote letters to a girl I had made friends with not long before I left. The letters we exchanged kept my hopes alive that this new friendship might become a romance. When I told her I hoped to make it back to Chicago soon, she wrote me back and asked me how tall I had grown since I saw her last. I answered honestly—I had made it all the way to five feet, four inches tall. I never heard back.

In Chicago, my dad worried about us all the time. He was furious when I stayed out with Frankie a few minutes later than I was allowed.

Now we had moved thousands of miles away, and my dad's parenting routine had become little more than fixing me some breakfast in the morning and telling me he would see me that night. I was on my own. His new discipline philosophy seemed simple: nothing bad could happen to me in San Sebastián, Puerto Rico. After my dad left, I would help my uncle around Cuchilandia, but I didn't really want to stir pig parts all day. I started to explore. It didn't take long to cover all of San Sebastián.

As I studied my new home, I began to think my mom and dad had lost their minds. They brought me to this little town for *safety?* There were bars and guys wandering around at night with paper cups of rum. I had noticed women dressed to attract the attention of men who came to Pueblo Nuevo late at night to drink and have some unsupervised fun. In Chicago, my uncle was just another ordinary guy working a boring nine-to-five job. Now he was a do-it-yourself butcher, wandering around my backyard with a huge cleaver. The truth was, at night things got a little rough in my new neighborhood; yelling and arguing, singing and celebrating. My dad wasn't even supervising me. It didn't seem that long ago that my sister and I were sitting politely as we hosted a rich white real estate tycoon for dinner at our apartment. Now, in Pueblo Nuevo, I could wander around all day and then have a cup of fried pig stomach for dinner.

Finally I thought I might as well try the Pueblo Nuevo pool hall. I had never been in a pool hall before. I walked in one afternoon and quickly understood why Pueblo Nuevo was a magnet for Puerto Rican men who didn't do much during the day. It looked like fun; the chatter, the back-and-forth taunting, a roomful of guys laughing. Pool tables had money sitting on the side rails. The pool hall was crowded at night, and guys overflowed out onto the street. Some of the guys looked familiar—they had probably been by Cuchilandia. Inside, there were four or five tables with a bar in the back. Nobody seemed too concerned about a fifteen-year-old kid wandering in unsupervised.

Soon enough, the guys in the pool hall put me to work. They didn't mind if I was there, but I had to do something useful. They would give me a nickel to rack the balls or chalk the cues, a dime to go get them a soda or a beer. The owner would let me play for free. I watched and learned. I listened carefully to their stories. Even if I wasn't talking much, I hoped my Spanish was improving by immersion. They could tell I wasn't from San Sebastián. I didn't sound like it, and I didn't look like it. I was still wearing knit shirts made for Chicago summers.

The pool hall became my summer hangout. I really didn't have anything else to do. I did enough stirring of *cuchifritos* to help out at Cuchilandia, and then I took a lot of long walks, covering Pueblo Nuevo and the rest of the town. It wasn't as interesting as Wells Street. No head shops. No tie-dye. No hippies. No gangs. Instead, I had the guys at the pool hall. My dad had moved me across the sea for safety and to learn some traditional Puerto Rican values. I wondered how well my dad's plans were working out. A couple of months in San Sebastián, and mostly I had learned how to shoot pool, take long walks, and make *cuchifritos*.

But finally I met another exiled American teenager. His name was Carlos, and the minute he walked into the pool hall I knew he wasn't from San Sebastián either.

I immediately thought to myself, He's American. He had the same not-quite-Caribbean summer clothes. And he had greased back his hair, a look I associated with the Harrison Gents. If that look existed in Puerto Rico, I hadn't seen it. Like most kids my age, he was much bigger than me. He got people's attention in the pool hall. He knew his way around a pool cue and hustled the older guys, usually taking their money. He watched my game and shook his head, like it was embarrassing that a fellow Puerto Rican played like I did. He took the time to show me how to play. He taught me to back up the ball, to put sidespin on it, to scatter the balls like an explosion on the break.

I wasn't surprised to learn that Carlos was from Brooklyn. He would have been right at home in my grandmother's neighborhood. His family had also torn him from everything he had ever known and dropped him into San Sebastián, like a toddler thrown into a pool and told to swim. We started hanging out away from the pool hall too, because we had exactly zero other choices for friends. I don't know what the rest of the Puerto Rican teenagers were doing that summer before school started, but they weren't playing pool. So as summer started to wind down, Carlos and I played pool and talked about what we missed about home. We compared favorite music and TV shows. We talked about what we expected at school. We hung out together, racking the pool balls and collecting dimes. We spoke English. In Chicago, I doubt that Carlos and I would have been spending much time together. For all I know, he might have been hanging around with the Harrison Street Gents and hitting me on the back of the head as I walked by him.

But in the hills of Puerto Rico, in the remote and lonely town of San Sebastián, we were like soldiers shipped out together to a distant land. We were the only ones who spoke our language and remembered what it was like back home. But unfortunately for us, we had an open-ended deployment. And the relative calm and security of a summer in Pueblo Nuevo was about to come to an end. My mom and sister had finally arrived from New York. My dad had found a location for the restaurant and an apartment that went with it. School was about to start, and we were a family again, making our new life seem real and permanent. There was no turning back.

CHAPTER FOUR

The Gringo Is Bothering Me

EVEN THE SCHOOL looked different in Puerto Rico.

I had a very American idea of what a school should look like—a large rectangular building, two or three stories tall, brick or concrete, institutional. In Chicago, my Catholic high school had long hallways, square rooms, and stern nuns. The windows looked out over the streets of the city.

Manuel Méndez Liciaga High School in San Sebastián was open and airy, with balconies facing a courtyard. It was designed to keep down electricity costs and to let the Caribbean sunshine in. The courtyard was filled with trees. Most of the building was on one story, with a new wing and an old wing. If you parked cars in the back it would have looked like a meandering, tropical Motel 6.

If I cared about aesthetics, I would have been impressed by the lush setting of my new school. But I just thought it looked odd, unlike any school I had ever seen. It reminded me that I was an outsider. On that first day, as I heard other students chattering in Spanish, I knew I should have practiced more. I was happy to speak English with my American friend from Brooklyn. I spoke English to Ada when she showed up to keep me company at the end of summer. My pool-hall days had taught me to say "The balls are racked," and "Do you want another beer?" in Spanish pretty well. I didn't think that was going to help me at school. I knew I wasn't ready.

I looked around and wondered where all these teenagers had come from. Nobody was running up to me, eager to make a new American friend. Seeing a few hundred Puerto Rican kids my own age should have set me at ease. It didn't. I felt the isolation of being alone in a crowd of my peers. In Chicago, I was in the mix; I was talkative, always up for a joke. Here, I was invisible. Carlos, my buddy from Brooklyn, didn't seem to care about hanging around with me at school. He didn't care about fitting in. His outlook was simple: I don't want to be here, I won't be here for long, and I don't care what anyone thinks of me. He glared. I worried.

My homeroom was in the old wing of the Motel 6. The room was surrounded by huge trees that must have filtered out more of the daylight than the school's architects imagined. I found my seat and kept waiting for the teacher to flip on a light switch. He didn't. I think of Puerto Rico as a place where you attend school in the shade.

My homeroom teacher was Señor Hernández, a young, physically fit guy. He wore a shirt and tie. He started going over the basic rules of the class. I was hoping he would ignore me. He didn't. He asked me a question, and I answered using the informal *tu* instead of the formal *usted* in addressing him. Kids laughed. There was no formal and informal in English. I had never thought about it and didn't understand the difference. I never worried about formal and informal when I spoke Spanish to my relatives in Spanish Harlem.

When I spoke to him, I pronounced the *h* in "Hernández." I pronounced the *h* in all my words. For fifteen years, if a word had an *h*, I made the *h* sound. I learned quickly that was not acceptable in Señor Hernández's class.

I said "Hernández"—hard *h*—and in response, slightly offended, he said, "I am professor Hernández," the *h* sound rolling and diving and disappearing into an "eh" off of his tongue.

He enjoyed giving me more examples of his perfect Spanish pronunciation.

"The girls in *Hermosa* are beautiful." Air-mosa.

"This is *history* class." Istoria.

No *h* to be found. Or heard.

When it came to pronunciation, my new teacher was very digni-fied, very proper, and very formal. And very pleased with himself. I just wondered where all the *h*'s had gone. Probably packed away in a box somewhere with my Motown records.

Kids kept chuckling. I knew exactly how I must have sounded to my new classmates. I heard it in the English my relatives from Puerto Rico spoke when they arrived in Chicago. They brought a child's vocabulary accompanied by clunky pronunciations. I never had much sympathy for them before. I did now.

This was my first day, my first class, my first hour, and I was already the center of attention. Finally, the teacher moved on to other kids. I thought I was safe, but at the end of class, Señor Hernández began looking carefully through the information cards we had filled out. He came to one and paused.

He looked directly at me, and asked me what my name was.

I answered a very Anglicized "Lou-is Goo-terrez." I always pro-nounced "Luis" with the emphasis on "lou," like Lou Gehrig. Certainly not "Lu-*ees*," with the emphasis on "ees." I crunched "Gutiérrez" into three syllables and had never rolled my *r*'s. Until then, I pronounced my name the way my Republican colleagues from South Carolina pronounce it today. It was the way most people said it in Chicago.

The teacher stared at me.

"Don't you have a mother?"

The classroom filled with muffled giggling. The kids thought I was the school's most entertaining sideshow. I looked Puerto Rican. But I didn't sound Puerto Rican. I'm a kid who doesn't know *tu* from *usted*. Apparently, I didn't even know my name. I'm a curiosity from America.

But he made me angry. Why did the teacher bring up my mother? You don't make fun of someone's mother. That's playground taunting. I had no idea what he was talking about.

He continued with his dignified glare.

"I don't know what it's like in the US, but in Puerto Rico, to enroll in high school, knowing your complete name is a minimum requirement."

My complete name was Luis Gutiérrez. I was bewildered. Trying to get through my introduction to a new school was hard enough without facing a teacher who was taking a personal interest in making it worse.

That was all he said. He thought he had made his point. Class was over. I was mad. And confused. I don't remember much of the rest of the day. I was in a fog. My complete name? That wasn't the riddle I expected in homeroom. I expected to get lost in the language, but I was pretty sure I knew my name.

I went home and told my mom what happened. I told her I thought the teacher was mocking her. What did he mean when he said I should know my complete name? Why would he ask if I had a mother? Isn't it obvious that everyone has a mother?

My mom smiled.

"In Puerto Rico, your complete name includes my maiden name."

My mom felt sorry for me. She looked at me, and for the first time in my life, pronounced my full Puerto Rican name.

Luis Vicente Gutiérrez-Olmedo.

I had never heard my mother's maiden name before. Olmedo? That was a news flash to me. That my name includes part of my mom's name was another little Puerto Rican custom my parents might have clued me in on while we were getting ready to move to the island.

Luis Vicente Gutiérrez-Olmedo. I felt challenged. This was a test I could pass. Now, at least I knew my name. I would just have to figure out how to pronounce it. I went to my room and practiced it over and over again. I looked in the mirror. I trained myself to roll the *r*. Lou-is became Lu-ees with an accent on the second syllable. Luis Vicente Gutiérrez-Olmedo. I put the lost Spanish syllable back in "Gu-ti-er-ez." I did it over and over again. Eventually, I practiced for my mom.

I thought my new name sounded pretty good. Very Puerto Rican. I had to admit, it was much more lyrical than my Chicago pronunciation. There was some rhythm to it. Luis Vicente Gutiérrez-Olmedo. The more I thought about it, the more I liked it. Sounded like a movie star. It might have been nice to have known my name on the first day of school, but I was determined to nail it on day two. I probably dreamed of my full name that night, and I woke up the next morning to practice at breakfast.

I didn't approach my second day of school with confidence. I knew I was still an outsider. But at least I knew my full name, and I would show my arrogant bastard of a homeroom teacher that I could learn it and repeat it as easily as the kids who had been in San Sebastián their whole lives.

I took a new information card to fill out for Señor Hernández. I wrote Luis Vicente Gutiérrez-Olmedo. I'd put the accent over the *e*. It was the first time in my life I had written an accent. I was proud of myself. I was eager to show off my new knowledge of my real Puerto Rican identity. I was so eager I couldn't wait for the teacher. I couldn't even be sure he would call on me. I walked toward the corner of the classroom, where some girls were talking. I chose one of the girls to receive the good fortune of hearing the symphony of me articulating my complete name. I looked right at her.

"*Mi nombre es Luis Vicente Gutiérrez-Olmedo.*" I smiled.

She looked shocked, almost scared. She immediately raised her hand to get the teacher's attention. She shouted "Mister, mister"—the Puerto Rican formal address for "teacher"—as if she needed his urgent assistance. He quickly asked her what was wrong.

"*El gringo me está molestando,*" she said.

The gringo is bothering me.

This time, everyone laughed, including my teacher. He thought it was hilarious.

The words echoed around my head. *The gringo is bothering me.*

It felt like I had been punched in the stomach. I wanted to disappear.

I thought I had figured it out. I knew my name. I had practiced. I said it late into the night in front of the mirror. I was ready. But now there was just laughter. I was out of place and sinking into the quicksand of teenage humiliation. I had never felt so completely isolated and useless, like a boat stranded in the desert.

I didn't know the language. I couldn't figure out the customs. I was far away from everything I had ever known. But it was the one, specific word she used that paralyzed me.

Gringo.

Was she really talking about me?

I took my seat. I put my head down.

Today, looking back with forty years' reflection, I wished I had yelled or complained or told the teacher to stop laughing. That would have been more my style than trying to hide. But I didn't do any of those things. Instead I just hurt. I sat through my classes and wondered how a Puerto Rican kid from Chicago had somehow turned into a gringo. I had been called a lot of things before, but never gringo.

When I arrived in San Sebastián, I thought I was as Puerto Rican as a person could be. Before my family left Chicago, the neighborhood group that my friends and I most admired was the Young Lords. They had taken over an old church three blocks from our house on Willow Street and were using it as a headquarters. They would give out food and hold community meetings. When a young Puerto Rican was shot and killed by the police, they led a march down Halsted that attracted over a thousand people. They were a slightly more peaceful Puerto Rican version of the Black Panthers.

They gave out buttons that said "TENGO PUERTO RICO EN MI CORAZÓN"—I have Puerto Rico in my heart. I had one. Above the Spanish saying was an outline of the island—my island—in green. I wore that button everywhere I went. I wanted people to know who I was, where I came from. My dad thought it was kind of radical, and he didn't trust the Young Lords, but it was hard for him to argue with a button that said I HAVE PUERTO RICO IN MY HEART.

I wore the button and I believed it, never doubted it for a minute. In Chicago, I didn't have an identity beyond being Puerto Rican. It existed in everything I did. The white cops who stopped to ask me and my friends what we were doing when we were just standing on the corner clearly thought of me as Puerto Rican. The Mexican kids who called me pork chop thought I was Puerto Rican. So did the bodega owner, and the *bolitero* who played the numbers in the neighborhood, and my distant relatives who spoke only Spanish.

Being Puerto Rican was all I had ever known. Why else would I go to Wrigley Field and cheer for the Pittsburgh Pirate right fielder who was trying to beat my team, the Cubs?

At home, I had been called a spic. I didn't like it, but I didn't really worry about it either. It was part of growing up Puerto Rican in Chicago. You tried to turn the other cheek. Maybe some days you yelled back, or threatened to fight. Now I was in Puerto Rico, in a Puerto Rican school with a Puerto Rican teacher. And the cutest Puerto Rican girl in class called me a gringo.

I felt set adrift with no compass to find my way back to shore. I was a short, brown-skinned kid with curly hair who couldn't have passed for white in Chicago if someone had offered me a costume and a makeup kit to pull it off. Now I was a gringo.

In Chicago, I might have had Puerto Rico in my heart, but in Puerto Rico, I didn't have Spanish on my lips.

That girl taught me that I would need to learn much more than Spanish in Puerto Rico. She didn't tell Señor Hernández that the gringo was bothering her because I had messed up the pronunciation of my name. My obsessive practice the night before led to a perfectly rolled r and accents in all the right places. The gringo was bothering her because I was being impertinent by addressing her directly. It was inappropriate to be so forward. I was a stranger, and in this case a stranger who talked funny and who should not have been so audacious in addressing a young lady.

In Chicago, walking with my friends, I might have gone ahead and yelled, "Hey, what's up?" to a pretty Puerto Rican girl who I saw for the first time across Fullerton Avenue. She might have ignored me—in fact, I can relate from personal experience that it was likely she would ignore me—but she wouldn't have thought I was offending her. After all, we were just a couple of Puerto Ricans from the neighborhood. Our race was our class—whatever our parents did for a living, we were just a couple of Puerto Rican kids trying to get by in Chicago.

But in San Sebastián, we were all Puerto Ricans. And the Puerto Ricans went to work finding other ways to divide ourselves and rank our families, finding reasons to be better than one another. Clearly, for

Señor Hernández, my fractured Spanish and not knowing my complete name put me in a class beneath the other kids. That pretty girl called me gringo because I wasn't in the club. Nobody would call my skin white. Nobody would call my hair straight. But I was an outsider.

Having Puerto Rico in my heart wasn't going to be enough to cut it in San Sebastián.

I went home and cried that night. I was too embarrassed to tell my parents what had happened. I wanted to go home. Still, I knew Señor Hernández was wrong to belittle me. I didn't want to give up. I didn't want to let him win.

WHILE I WAS misconjugating verbs and being called names, my dad was busy preparing for our future. He had found the restaurant that was going to make him a Puerto Rican entrepreneur.

It was a good location, right on the way out of San Sebastián. There was lots of traffic, a grocery next door, and a couple of small factories just up the road. We moved to the basement apartment below the restaurant. I was happy to leave my lizard-filled cot and Cuchilandia's boiling pig stomachs behind. Having our furniture and our belongings delivered to and arranged in our home by my mother made things a little better. I was glad to have my sister there. I was happy we could re-create a little bit of our formerly happy life in Chicago.

But still, I wondered if my parents were really living their dream. I know my parents felt they had returned rich, but they were comparing our apartment in San Sebastián to a wooden shack on the cliffs of Aguadilla. I compared it to our place on Willow. I didn't think it was any better. And while my parents were proud of their success, it wasn't like we were the richest people in town—far from it. San Sebastián had genuinely wealthy landowners and merchants—Puerto Rican landowners and merchants who weren't that impressed by our Chevy Impala station wagon.

I thought we had left behind as much family as we gained by moving. At home in Chicago, we had uncles and aunts and cousins everywhere, from Gary to New York. It wasn't like my parents had left

Puerto Rico to search for their fortune in Alaska and had spent the last seventeen years panning for gold and surrounded by Eskimos. In Chicago, we were surrounded by people who'd left Puerto Rico. Lincoln Park always seemed plenty Puerto Rican to me; I don't know why we had to live under a restaurant in the hills of San Sebastián to get the real Puerto Rican experience.

But there we were, reunited as a family. After I'd been called a gringo, my sister was the one who comforted me. She was my only friend. She missed home and her friends, but the transition was easier for her. I learned quickly that pretty, outgoing, English-speaking American girls in Puerto Rico were much more interesting and sympathetic than short, gangly American guys. Maybe if I had looked like Antonio Banderas it would have gone easier. My sister received a lot of attention, and it wasn't name-calling attention. Plenty of guys who were San Sebastián natives were eager to help Ada with her Spanish. Ada's friendship helped me a lot at home, but having an exotic sister wasn't helping me feel any better at school.

My dad's plan to help me was simple: keep me too busy to feel sorry for myself.

If you want to spend plenty of quality hours each week working and sweating side by side with your family, I highly recommend running a restaurant. I can't tell you one thing my parents knew about the restaurant business before they decided to move to San Sebastián. We virtually never went to restaurants. Then, suddenly, opening a restaurant was the completely obvious plan to my dad. He might as well have told me we were opening a dentist's office or becoming a family of traveling circus performers. I knew just as much about flying on a trapeze as I did about working in a restaurant.

In front of our very own family café were two picnic tables covered by canopies. When you walked through the door, the small place had seven or eight tables and a long counter with stools that ran the length of the restaurant to your right. The counter was for lunch during the day and was a bar at night. My dad had bought the café mostly ready to run, with equipment and furniture included, and even bottles of liquor still sitting on the shelves behind the counter. He shopped for a few more things he needed. He bought a rotisserie—four rows across, usually filled with chickens that dripped grease and smelled delicious. There were deep-fryers and a huge stove that completely filled the small kitchen.

The Gutiérrez restaurant consortium didn't need to conduct any employee search. We all worked together to clean the place, filling buckets with water and bleach and mopping, making sure the fryers and grill were spotless and in working order. One day, my dad received his first food delivery and we were in business. My dad was head chef, which consisted mainly of cooking chicken. Ada and I took orders, cleaned, and swept floors. My mom was stationed wherever she was most needed—sometimes at the cash register, sometimes making rice.

That the previous owner was so eager to turn over the keys probably should have been more of a concern to my dad, but he wasn't worried. He saw a business opportunity, and a chance to have something of his own. Until we owned our own restaurant, I had never seen my dad cook. Maybe he made an occasional sandwich. My mom had done all of the cooking at home. Now my dad tied on a white apron and stood in front of his stove, cooking chicken and pork chops, stirring huge pots of rice and beans. I wondered if the parents I had known for fifteen years in Chicago were some sort of impostors, now replaced by their true Puerto Rican identities—cook and waitress, owners of a tropical café.

My dad was still just as stern. "Don't touch the sodas or the custards. They are expensive. They are for the customers. Leave them alone," the restaurant tycoon told us.

What was the point of owning a restaurant, and working at a restaurant, if you couldn't drink the soda? We had crates of it sitting around. But my dad was serious about his ban on pilfering his valuable soda. And he was always around the restaurant. Always. I didn't have much time to sneak in and guzzle one down while he had his back turned. I learned right away that trying to down a Coke in one gulp is just too much. Coke spilled all over the front of your school shirt doesn't help you get away with your crime.

But I was a persistent soda thief. The orange Fanta and the orange and grape Old Colony were better targets. They had less carbonation, and some came in ten-ounce bottles. I became adept at a swift, well-orchestrated maneuver: lift the Fanta out of the wooden crate, drink it in one smooth gulp, just as quickly put it back in the crate. As fast as an old-west gunslinger, it could be accomplished while my dad was talking to a customer or putting beans on a plate. Those sodas cost my dad quite a few dimes.

I didn't feel too bad about enhancing my wages with the occasional soda, because whatever I could drink and eat was all I was paid. In the Gutiérrez family restaurant, the minimum wage was no wage. It never occurred to Ada or me to even ask about being paid. It was just the way things worked. The customers weren't too crazy about leaving the Gutiérrez family any tips, either. They considered our restaurant a fast-food place. They weren't leaving the owners' teenage kids any of their hard-earned money.

Our hours weren't short, either. We ran the front of the restaurant for our parents. I specialized in sweeping and cleaning and keeping our restaurant spotless. I waited on customers too. We served breakfast every weekday, and I went in early before school. Our breakfast specialty was ham, cheese, and egg sandwiches. We had the McMuffin before McDonald's. If we had been savvy marketers, I'd be retired on my Puerto Rican McMuffin income.

I would eat a big breakfast in the café and then head out to school. In the middle of the day, I would hurry back to the restaurant, a twenty-minute jog in the tropical sun. It was a sweaty, fast trek every day. We had to be ready for the lunch rush at noon. That's when we made our money. The restaurant was down the road from several factories. The workers, mostly women, would come in for a quick, cheap lunch. My dad came up with a lunch special every day. Something simple and affordable, and 90 percent of the customers ordered it. If you eliminated pork chops and chicken from our menu, we would have closed immediately. Ada and I would spend the hour before noon helping my dad get ready for hungry, impatient factory workers. Every night, I peeled potatoes for french fries—thirty, forty, fifty potatoes. We could never have enough potatoes. I always tried to go too fast. I'm lucky I didn't leave all my fingertips in San Sebastián.

I was quickly learning that the restaurant business was tough, even if you were just running a simple café that specialized in Puerto Rican staples. We were far from fancy. We wrote the menu for the day on a chalkboard. We never even gave the restaurant a name. I would ask my dad about it. "What's the name of the restaurant? Kids ask me." He would just shrug. He was too busy making rice to worry about it. Why bother? The same factory workers who had been coming to lunch at the previous restaurant just kept coming once we took it over—so why expend the energy to name it? I don't remember any advertising or marketing of any kind. My parents' menu strategy was to make what they thought working-class Puerto Ricans would eat. And it had to be something my dad could cook.

As I waited on tables, I learned customer satisfaction was sometimes an impossible goal. We only charged a dollar or two for the lunch special, but we still had regulars who were exceedingly adept at finishing most of their meal, and then locating the leg of a bug in their food. Or the wing of a bug. They would call Ada or me over to the table. They would stare down at their food, appalled. They would look up at us.

"There is part of a bug in my food."

I would look and never see anything, but I would retrieve my dad from the kitchen. He would negotiate. He knew that he would always lose. My dad did not have the stomach for forcing people to pay or throwing them out of the restaurant. Most of our customers were honest. He saw the few who wanted to scam a free plate of chicken for lunch as a cost of doing business. But eventually we knew who to look for.

I would tell my dad, "One of the bug ladies is at the front table." We would serve her a pristine plate, wiped clean, looking beautiful. I would stand by and watch her closely as she ate. The special service and attention was usually enough to stop an outraged bug spotting. For a while.

In the evenings, our restaurant turned into a bar and a neighborhood hangout. In San Sebastián, few people ate out in the evenings. The lunch rush, working people fitting a quick meal into their noon break at the plant, was our moneymaker. At night, my dad made money by pouring rum and serving Lowenbrau beer. I always thought our restaurant seemed more like a social club than a bar. Usually the same guys would come by, sit at the same table, and replay the same games of dominoes. My dad was a champion domino player. Dominoes is all about memory and strategy and patience. He excelled at all three. I rarely beat my dad at dominoes. At the restaurant at night, he sat in on game after game. I would watch him play, and help out by grabbing beers for the customers out of the refrigerator. San Sebastián wasn't concerned about child labor or kids working in bars. Night after night, my dad would sit at the table, counting and remembering the tiles, serving his rum in paper cups, enjoying the warm island breeze, counting up the money bound for his cigar box.

I looked at my dad—a restaurant owner and nighttime domino player—and wondered what happened to the building manager and cabdriver in Chicago. It was obvious that my mom was happier in San Sebastián. No more taking two buses to work, no more marching through the snow. She just walked upstairs to the restaurant from our basement apartment. She didn't struggle to understand the language. My mom was in her land. She had set up a very comfortable apartment. She wasn't worried about anyone breaking in or snatching her purse. She didn't have to search for her favorite radio stations. She hummed along all day to the popular and traditional Puerto Rican music. She was happy to be back home.

But my dad was working harder than ever. He never used to drive his cab on weekends in Chicago. He was home with us. Now we were cleaning the restaurant on Saturday mornings, serving a few weekend lunch stragglers, and preparing the food for the following week. Peeling and chopping and cooking in the small, hot kitchen, even on the weekends. My dad was there more than anyone. I think he would rather have been downstairs with us than pouring beers and playing dominoes every night. It was just part of the job to him. He looked tired when he came home. He worried about money. The price of chicken. People who didn't want to pay. Slow days when fewer customers came in. I was around him all the time, but we were working. He never relaxed. The restaurant was stealing my dad away.

*   *   *

BUT I WAS FIFTEEN, and most of my worries were about school. My time waiting on tables was helping me with my Spanish a little. I certainly learned "I'll have the special." But at school, I was still struggling. Eventually, Señor Hernández grew bored with my mispronunciations and he stopped targeting me. Kids, however, are always looking for laughs at school, something new, something different to break up the monotony. They thought my Spanish was always good for some comic relief.

I would say "I have a hunger" instead of "I'm hungry"—the kind of mistakes that your middle school Spanish teacher would usually correct. The difference between formal and informal was still beyond me. Kids weren't exactly trying to be helpful. I would answer a question with a nice, solid Spanish sentence and feel proud of myself. But I would use the informal, and someone in the classroom would raise their hand and say to the teacher, "Luis disrespected you." Mixing up *tu* and *usted* was more than bad Spanish. People treated me like I was trying to threaten the whole Puerto Rican social order. I would try to make friends with someone and they would say I wasn't treating them with respect. *Tu* and *usted* and respect. I heard it all the time. In Chicago respect was about whether the police were going to harass you, whether the Harrison Street Gents would leave you alone. Now I was battling for respect with a platoon of Caribbean teenage grammarians.

As I worked on my Spanish, I found a few other refugees from America at Manuel Méndez Liciaga High School, but the few who had come back to San Sebastián were all from New York. They tended to stick together. Even with kids who had returned, I was an outsider among the outsiders. A lot of the kids in San Sebastián had no idea where Chicago was. When they thought of Puerto Ricans in America, all they thought about was New York. They all knew *West Side Story*. They would ask me, completely seriously, "What part of New York is Chicago in?"

So I was thrilled that fall when a couple of kids approached me and invited me to do something with them.

They told me about a club they thought I should join, something that was a good fit for me. Their organization was called Young Americans for Freedom. Their goal was simple: they wanted Puerto Rico to be part of the United States, and not just a commonwealth like we already were, but a full-fledged state. They thought it seemed natural that I would agree. I spoke English, and they thought everyone in Puerto Rico should learn to speak English. Puerto Rico is a part of America, after all.

I didn't think about it a whole lot. I was just glad someone was paying attention to me. The club leader was a nice guy, and it was the first time anyone had praised me for my English skills. The truth was most people I met weren't exactly enthralled by the idea that all Puerto Ricans should speak English, but at least this guy was talking to me. I took the flyers, American flags prominently displayed on them, and headed out in front of the school one morning to help spread the word about freedom to our fellow students. I just wanted to be part of something, and who could argue with a name like Young Americans for Freedom?

I found out who could argue. A lot of Puerto Ricans could argue. I might have made a friend or two in my new club, but most of the kids I offered my flyer to ignored us, or shouted at us, or laughed at us. They looked at us like we didn't have any idea what we were talking about. They shouted, *"Viva, Puerto Rico!"* Well, I thought, I'm not really sure why they are so upset, but that's the price you pay for friendship.

Eventually, Luis, a guy from my grade, stopped to watch. I had noticed him before. I thought he was one of the smartest guys in the school. He hung around with another really smart kid, Tino, who had asked me some questions about Chicago. Tino had spent a summer in Chicago and liked the city. I remembered having a conversation—or the best conversation I could have in my Spanish—with him about Division Street. At least he knew Chicago wasn't in New York.

Luis looked at me, the skinny kid who spoke terrible Spanish, hanging out with the Young Americans for Freedom, passing out flyers for statehood. He seemed amused, but also kind of concerned. He kept watching. Eventually, he came over and grabbed my arm. He made a motion for me to come and talk to him.

"What are you doing?" Luis asked. "These guys are crazy. They're for statehood. They're Republicans. They want Puerto Rico to be just like America. You're from Chicago. Does Puerto Rico seem just like America to you?"

Well . . . Luis was making a pretty good point. From the minute I stepped off the plane, Puerto Rico had seemed pretty different to me. It was a place where I could be called a gringo.

"Look, nothing they say makes sense," he told me. "I'll help you out."

It seemed like a kind gesture to me. Most people were ignoring me. The Young Americans for Freedom seemed most interested in recruiting someone to pass out their flyers. Luis seemed more interested in me.

Pretty soon I was talking with Luis and his friend Tino. About Chicago and about Puerto Rican politics. About school and about girls. About how bad my Spanish was, and how to improve it.

And with that, I had some friends. Real friends. Luis Águila and Tino Núñez, two kids who started out trying to save me from the Statehooders, but instead took the first step toward being my friends for life.

CHAPTER FIVE

Paying Sugarcane Cutters Under the Flamboyán Tree

E VERY SATURDAY, early, I would make my way to Central Plata, the sugar refinery outside of San Sebastián. Some days I would walk, some days I would hitchhike. Everyone hitchhiked then. In our small town, most of the time when you saw someone hitching a ride, you knew who it was. It wasn't hard to find someone who would pick you up, and everyone knew the way to Central Plata. The refinery was built on a hill about a mile and a half out of town. It was the largest building in the area, overlooking the fields and farmers who fed it the cane that kept the mill running.

I would meet Luis and Tino and we would hang around in the front office of Central Plata, waiting for the jeeps to come and take us far out into the sugarcane fields. This was long before jeeps became cool. These jeeps looked like General Patton should be riding in the back. Most of them were wide open. The nicer ones were covered in canvas. Old Army jeeps were everywhere in San Sebastián, a daily reminder driving down the road that I was a long way from Lincoln Park. Luis and Tino and I would wait inside the front doors, goofing around, in a good mood because we knew we were lucky to have this Saturday-morning job. Eventually, the jeeps would pull into the lot out front with Luis's dad's workers at the wheel, ready to take us to our assigned spot.

Luis's dad was a foreman at Central Plata. Paying the sugarcane workers—being a paymaster—was a prime part-time job for a Puerto Rican high school kid. There were usually ten or fifteen of us, and most of the other paymasters were older. Luis was taking care of his pals, and we appreciated it. Groups of workers were paid in the fields where they worked, usually several miles away from San Sebastián. The sugarcane cutters who worked closest to town came in to Central Plata to get their money. Each Saturday, Luis and Tino and I would hope that we were assigned out into the fields. It was always better to get away from Central Plata to pay the workers. If you were stuck at the refinery, you had to wait there most of the day for the cutters to trickle in one by one. The waiting cost you most of your Saturday.

But we were rarely stuck there. We would briefly celebrate our assignments out of town, and then split up. Every paymaster was driven away in his own jeep. We would nod hello to the much older and usually silent driver, and then charge out of San Sebastián to where the sugarcane cutters would gather every Saturday to collect their envelopes of cash. We would drive right into a clearing in the fields. At several of the spots, the jeep would pull up and park under a Puerto Rican Flamboyán tree, a tropical tree with long branches a bit like a willow tree. They were huge and filled with spectacular red blossoms that covered our heads like fireworks and provided shade for us while we did our work.

The drive out to the fields wasn't really that far in miles, but it felt like an excursion into Puerto Rico's past. For me, San Sebastián was already small and remote, a distant outpost from civilized Chicago and New York. The world of the cutters made San Sebastián and Pueblo Nuevo seem like Times Square by comparison. The fields were quiet, especially on Saturday mornings, a time of calm between all the hours of hard work. Outside of San Sebastián, there wasn't much else but sugar cane, and once you were deep into the country you saw very little other than rolling hills blanketed with tall, green stalks. The payment sites under the Flamboyán trees were isolated. It felt hidden. We took side roads off of side roads and then drove through the field and into a clearing. Directions wouldn't have gotten you there; you had to know where you were going. The drive out and back usually took longer than it did to pay the men.

Most of the workers would already be waiting for us when we arrived. They stood quietly and patiently, lingering in the morning heat, waiting to line up. They were used to standing in the sun, so waiting for a high school kid to give them their money was the easiest part of their week.

You paid the men right out of the back of the jeep. No tables, no chairs. The Flamboyán tree was your office, the jeep was your desk. The driver just sat and waited. Usually, he didn't even turn around to watch. Why they didn't just have the driver pay the men I'll never know, and I didn't ask. I didn't want to give them any ideas and lose my nice Saturday gig. I would turn around, facing out of the back of the jeep, and take out my box stacked with envelopes. It wasn't much more than a large shoebox. I would put it down next to my ledger. The ledger was old, like a secret, ancient manuscript, with the name of every man I would be paying that day. The men watched me gather everything together, waiting to sign for their envelope and get their payment. I would nod and the workers would approach the jeep one by one.

My first Saturday, I noticed the workers' hands. I had never seen such callused hands, solid like carved wooden blocks that had been sculpted at the ends of their arms to use like tools. Even the thick calluses weren't enough to protect them from the danger of hour after hour of swinging machetes, and most of them had scars and many had fresh cuts. To say the cutters' skin was burned by the sun would be wrong; their skin was transformed—color stained permanently onto their bodies by a glowing sun. I'm Puerto Rican. We're not particularly light-skinned people. But the brown skin the cutters were born with was long gone, replaced with coffee-colored leather that protected them every day.

They were made darker by the sun even though they all wore

pavas—large straw hats that helped to keep the sun out of their faces. Most of them had scarves tied around their necks. They always wore their field dress, simple khaki pants and shirts. Most of the clothes were stained and looked like they hadn't been replaced in a very long time. There were a lot of older men, and some of them looked like they should have retired long ago. Some were stooped over a bit. The machetes were a couple feet long, and many of the men wore them through a big loop on their belts, even on Saturday. The machetes were a way of life for them, part of their uniform. I wouldn't have wanted to be in a bar with most of these guys after a hard week of work. You would read in the papers about the machetes being used as weapons, the words *pelea de machetes* screaming loudly in the headlines. Machete fights didn't usually end with a scrape or bruise. People died, or maybe, if they were lucky, just lost a finger or two.

The men would approach the jeep and tell me their name, and I would hand them their pay envelope. Then I watched to make sure they signed on the correct line in the ledger. As long as I didn't give anyone the wrong envelope, I was a successful paymaster for Central Plata. I paid close attention to those lines in the old book. Regularly, the men signed with just an *x*. The first time I saw a man make the quick *x* and walk away, I thought he had made some sort of mistake. I had never seen anyone use an *x* for their name before. But nobody else gave the one-letter signature a second thought. Back at Central Plata, I was told that I had to write their names on the line for them if they signed with an *x*. I learned from those men that there were harder things than not knowing how to pronounce your name for your homeroom teacher.

The men were patient and polite. In my two years working as a paymaster, I don't remember a disagreement. They collected their money, and many of them went back out into the fields to work some more. I remember most of the envelopes containing between thirty and forty dollars for a week's work under the burning sun swinging a machete and gathering sugarcane. For our Saturday-morning work—driving out in the jeep, sitting in the back under the shade of the Flamboyán tree, keeping track of the envelopes and ledger—we were paid $4.99.

I remember when I first got the job, Luis told me to be sure to bring a penny, so they could just give me a five-dollar bill. I always made the trip out with a penny in my pocket.

I looked at the men and thought that Luis and Tino and I were getting so much for so little. In 1970 in Puerto Rico, you could choose your San Sebastián movie theater, La Gloria or Mislán, and see a movie and get a bucket of popcorn and a giant soda for less than a dollar. My five-dollar Saturday made me feel rich. But I also remember thinking that the cutters were getting so little for so much. To harvest sugarcane you have to bend down low and cut the cane close to the ground. You want to chop right above the dirt and take away as much of the stalk as you can. The ground is often wet and swampy. You then take your machete and get rid of all the leaves on the top of the stalk. The leaves are useless, so you discard those into a pile. The leaves are sharp enough to cut your hands. Then you do it again. Bend, cut, stand, cut, throw, and do it over and over a thousand times in a day. If you miss by an inch you could lose a finger. And the men lined up quietly for their envelope, happy enough to have some money to take back home.

The Puerto Rican men waiting in line made me think of the taunts thrown at me and my friends back in Chicago. The white kids pointed at us and laughed, saying "All you Puerto Ricans are on welfare," or "You guys are a bunch of lazy welfare cheats." It was common to hear it. Lazy Puerto Ricans—it was something that bullies threw at you all the time. It was the go-to line when a Puerto Rican made somebody mad. "What do you know? You're all on welfare."

The welfare cheats danced through my mind like ghostly, mystery Puerto Ricans. I didn't know any Puerto Ricans who were on welfare. Where were they? I'm sure some existed, but they weren't hanging around my friends and family in Lincoln Park. Most of the Puerto Ricans I knew took long bus rides to work. The Puerto Ricans we knew worked on assembly lines in factories and stacked things in warehouses and drove cabs. If they didn't have a steady job, then most of them were hustling one way or another to make some money; clerking in a store, making deliveries, whatever they could find. One day, I hoped I would meet a Puerto Rican in Chicago who could show me their big, fat government welfare check, but I never did.

Now, every Saturday in San Sebastián, I was paying Puerto Rican men, some of the older ones permanently bent over from hard work. They stood in the sun waiting for their thirty or forty bucks a week. They treated me with respect, unaware that back in San Sebastián I was still the strange, outsider kid from America whose Spanish wasn't so good. As I watched them waiting in line for the envelopes in my box, a word formed that I couldn't get out of my mind. "Peasant." This was a word I hardly understood and had probably never used, but it felt accurate. To witness something right in front of me that fit the word "peasant" seemed unbelievable, surreal. It was like stumbling upon a Viking or a Pilgrim in your backyard.

But I was simply seeing *jíbaros*, the Puerto Rican worker, the man embodied by *la pava*. They were right there, and I was paying them. The whole process seemed like a chapter out of a history textbook. When we drove from site to site, we would see the cutters' houses in the fields. The cutters didn't own any land; they were simply employees of Central Plata. Some had small plots of land where they were allowed to grow food. They lived in small wooden huts with zinc roofs in the fields. Some of the huts were up on stilts, with chickens running around underneath. They had shutters for windows because glass was too expensive; no indoor plumbing, usually no indoor kitchens. Smoke from their fires for cooking swirled above their shacks.

But they did it. Stuck in a job with no future, but resigned to the fact that chopping thousands of stalks of sugarcane was the only way to feed their families. After paying those men, I never again considered for a moment the idea that Puerto Ricans don't work hard.

IF MY FAMILY had arrived in San Sebastián much later, I probably never would have had my Saturday-morning job. By 1970, the Puerto Rican sugar industry was in trouble. It seemed like the Puerto Rican government could never quite decide whether they wanted to give up on sugar and develop other industries or go all in to promote sugar production and preserve the jobs that went with it.

Over time, the US government helped to make the decision for them. Congress passed legislation that established sugar quotas. Congressmen were more interested in propping up sugar producers in Florida and Louisiana than in Puerto Rico. By the time Luis and Tino and I were riding around in our jeeps paying the cutters, production was declining and the government was taking over the mills, trying to hang on to an industry that was once the heart of the island's economy. It was too late.

Today, Puerto Rico imports sugar.

But when the Gutiérrez family came to San Sebastián, Central Plata was still a landmark in the town and one of the biggest employers around. It was huge and dominated the landscape outside of San Juan. Luis's dad had worked there for years. It was a small honor to be associated with this fundamental part of life in San Sebastián, especially for an outsider from the United States. But for me, even though I loved the five bucks, my Saturday-morning trips into the sugar cane fields mattered for a reason much more important than having a job.

I had finally made some friends in Puerto Rico.

OUR FRIENDSHIP might never have happened if Tino hadn't spent a summer visiting relatives in Chicago. He had been to Wrigley Field and wandered up and down Division Street. He asked me questions. He wanted to know more about the Cubs and the Pirates and Roberto Clemente. His familiarity with my hometown made me seem less of an outcast to him. He liked Chicago; he wanted to know more.

And Luis and Tino were pals. They did everything together. Luis was tall and athletic. Tino wasn't much taller than me, and we would try to keep up with Luis at basketball. Luis and Tino were both sharp and articulate and they wanted to get ahead. Luis's dad's job at Central Plata put them solidly in San Sebastián's middle class, but Luis was hardly privileged; far from the doctors' and lawyers' kids who always had plenty of money to spend. In San Sebastián forty years ago, single moms were rare, but Tino's dad wasn't around. His mom worked hard as a cook in a grade school and kept a close eye on Tino at home. I think their backgrounds gave them a sense of sympathy toward the American outsider. They looked at me and saw somebody trying to get by, trying to fit in. They knew it wasn't always easy in San Sebastián.

But while Luis and Tino would hang out with me on the plaza or shoot baskets on the weekends, they couldn't do much to help me at school. Puerto Rican schools were not only tough in their treatment of outsiders but also ruthless about how they stratified the kids. By the time I showed up with my broken Spanish and Chicago pronunciations, the smartest kids had been separated from everyone else and traveled as a pack of all-stars from honors class to honors class, learning more and faster than the rest of us laggards. Luis and Tino were both in the honors classes, so I didn't see as much of them at school as I would have liked. I stumbled through the basic classes, my Spanish improving but not fast enough to really impress anyone.

It was a harsh reversal from my experience in Chicago.

At home, the nice white teachers, beginning in kindergarten, had separated the kids too. Only, in Lincoln Park, it was the Spanish-speakers who were punished. When I started school in Chicago, I had to demonstrate that despite my brown skin and funny name, my English was just fine. Once the teachers decided I could understand them, I didn't have to stay in the corner with the Latino kids who were brought up speaking only Spanish. I remember Latino kids being sent to the back of the room, or even the coat room, to play Monopoly and Parcheesi with one another while the rest of us did our ABCs. I guess the theory was that reading about "free parking" and "do not pass go" would be enough to help them eventually catch up with the rest of the class.

Now, in Puerto Rico, despite always getting good grades, particularly in English, I was the one basically sitting in the corner. I was competitive, and I believed that I could keep up with the advanced kids, except for one little problem: I was still speaking my second language. Math was tough enough without trying to keep up with what the teacher was saying. The teachers, and even some of the kids, were losing interest in mocking me, but I still had a long way to go to catch up with the honors students.

As hard as school was, the weekends were worse. Until Luis and Tino befriended me, the weekends stretched on forever. My strongest memory of my early weekends in San Sebastián is of silence. Chicago was never quiet. My friends yelled. Gang members threatened. People played music. My friends and I schemed and chattered to see who would stay overnight at someone's house. In San Sebastián during my first months there was nothing.

I would get up early to help clean the restaurant for the weekend, scrubbing and mopping with my dad until everything shined. When I was done, there were still hours to fill. I listened to records in my room, over and over again. I knew every lyric, every drumbeat, and every backup vocal to the Rolling Stones and Jimi Hendrix and Smokey Robinson records I had brought from Chicago. Today, whenever I hear the Temptations sing "My Girl," I think of sitting alone on my bed in our apartment on a Sunday afternoon in Puerto Rico.

So when Luis and Tino took an interest in me, I grabbed on to their attention like a life preserver. They thought I was a curiosity, a kind of project for them. I could tell them about the times I saw Clemente play at Wrigley; they could give me a briefing on Puerto Rican customs. But something else bonded us from the start: we shared a real interest in politics. They were genuinely concerned for the Puerto Rican kid from Chicago they assumed was so desperate for friends that he was hanging out with the Young Americans for Freedom—the Statehooders—outside of school.

At the end of the 1960s, Statehooders were a minority in San Sebastián. Most people were "Populares"—supporters of the Popular Democratic Party. Like my mom, most people remembered the Populares government of Muñoz-Marín as the party that brought electricity and indoor plumbing to the people. They also handed out thousands of *parcelas*, small plots of land where you could build a house. For most of the people in San Sebastián, the commonwealth was familiar. It seemed a reasonable compromise between the unlikely goal of becoming another state in the United States or the risky idea of Puerto Rico being on its own as a nation.

This was new to me, the idea that the status of Puerto Rico defined everyone's politics. In Chicago, the dividing lines were far different. There were the law-and-order Daley Democrats of my dad's generation or the young people who sympathized with the anti-Vietnam demonstrators that Daley's police rounded up in Grant Park. The rich, mostly white real-estate guys—the "gentrifiers"—who were moving in and starting to make our neighborhood too expensive or the organizers and activists who wanted to fight for affordable housing and better schools.

In Puerto Rico, the political dividing line was all about the island's relationship with the United States. And in San Sebastián, at least, the Statehooders weren't doing too well. Or at least that's what Luis and Tino told me as they explained why hanging out with the Young Americans for Freedom was such a lonely and losing proposition. My dad's explanation of Puerto Rico's politics was even more direct.

I asked him in the restaurant about all of the competing Puerto Rican political parties. He stepped away from the stove to give me his no-nonsense tutorial.

"Look, here's how it works. There's the good guys. La Pavas. Their colors are red and white and their symbols are bread and land and freedom. They brought electricity and plumbing to the people. That's the Populares. Then there are the Statehooders. Las Palmas. They're OK, but Puerto Rico will never be a state and most people don't want Puerto Rico to be a state. So you don't have to even think about them."

But he saved his most serious guidance for last. He explained it to me like he was delivering a news bulletin that I should ignore at my own peril, warning of a hurricane coming and giving me instructions to get away from the coast.

"There's one last group. They want independence. Their ideas are crazy. The only thing crazier than Puerto Rico being a state is Puerto Rico being its own country. Don't ever associate with them. People will think you are a Communist. They are a fringe group. Hang around with them and you'll never get a job."

My father went back to cooking, pleased that he had delivered his message.

Here's a tip for fathers of fifteen-year-old boys: if you want your son to stay away from something, don't describe it as dangerous and subversive.

I got the message. I thought, Thanks, Dad. The Independentistas sound like a lot of fun to me.

They sounded like fun to Luis and Tino, too. And though my dad didn't seem aware of it, my new collection of friends weren't the only people sympathetic to independence in San Sebastián. My parents' little part of Puerto Rico had a tradition of standing up to their colonial occupiers.

In the fight for Puerto Rican independence from Spain on September 23, 1868, Puerto Rican patriots surprised the Spaniards at Lares, a town about twenty minutes east through the mountains from San Sebastián. The rebels took control of the town and flew the first flag of free Puerto Rico on the altar of the Iglesia de San José. After their success in Lares, they moved west to San Sebastián, ready to spread their rebellion and liberate all of Puerto Rico from Spanish control.

Unfortunately, the Spaniards weren't about to repeat the mistake they made at Lares, where they had underestimated the rebels. They sent reinforcements down from Aguadilla and Mayaguez before the rebels could add San Sebastián to the free republic of Puerto Rico, and the revolt ended in my adopted town. But the Grito de Lares—an annual celebration of Puerto Rico's first steps toward freedom—was still an important event in Puerto Rico, and an independent spirit was still alive in Lares and San Sebastián.

I loved the history I was learning about San Sebastián and our town's champions of independence. Our forebears engaged in house-to-house fighting with the Spaniards, battles commemorated in a huge mural on our church in the plaza. Our history made San Sebastián seem less remote, less foreign. I loved talking politics with Tino and Luis. What they said made sense. The Young Americans for Freedom thought that my proficiency in English and my love of America made me a perfect addition to the statehood movement. "Nobody should make fun of you for speaking English—that should be everyone's goal," they told me.

It made sense to me. Maybe because nobody else was talking to me at all. But the truth was that the Young Americans for Freedom had completely misunderstood my experience in Puerto Rico.

It was Luis and Tino who had it right. I loved America, but things in Puerto Rico didn't look too American to me. I was an English-speaking American kid dropped into the middle of a Caribbean island. I felt lost, isolated, and confused. I didn't look around and think my new surroundings were a lot like Pennsylvania or California or Alabama—a new state where the biggest differences might be a funny accent and where people called Coca-Cola "soda" instead of "pop." I felt that I had been dropped into a new culture, a new experience. It felt like a new country. And I felt that way even though I was Puerto Rican.

It was all so different. Bugs and heat, Spanish and *cuchifritos*, girls who acted like you were committing a crime if you spoke to them at an inappropriate time. Radio stations and television channels that I couldn't understand. Puerto Rico wasn't filled with New York versus Chicago differences that didn't really matter that much. I wasn't comparing stickball in the street with baseball in the park, garbage on the sidewalk as opposed to in the alley. In Puerto Rico, I had trouble understanding what people were saying, what people expected of me, the right way to behave and fit in. The truth was that even a Puerto Rican kid who grew up eating rice and beans could become a gringo on this island.

The point my enthusiastic friend from Young Americans for Freedom was making was that Puerto Rico really wasn't so different and could easily be a state. Tino and Luis simply said, "Look around." They didn't have to say what they really meant, which was: How at home do you feel?

They were right. Unlike the Spanish-speaking kids handing out the flyers with American flags promoting statehood, I was living the contradictions between Chicago and San Sebastián. I knew the United States. It was my home. I had lived there, happily, for the first fifteen years of my life—long enough to know that Puerto Rico was a long way from the United States. In my new home, we had sugarcane cutters and mothers' maiden names tacked on to the end of your name. We had kilometers and street signs in Spanish. We had chopped-up pig parts boiling in big vats. Everything I had seen and heard and experienced reinforced what I thought the moment I stepped off of our Pan Am plane into the searing heat of Puerto Rico and my dad told me to speak Spanish.

Puerto Rico is different.

ONE DIFFERENCE I was desperate to make go away was my inability to get any girls to pay attention to me. Because while I was enjoying my time with Luis and Tino, I was on the lookout for a girl willing to befriend the lost kid from America.

So I was optimistic when Gloria, a girl who was in most of my classes, finally noticed me. She smiled. She never made fun of me. We started talking. I didn't need much help with math, but asking her questions gave us something to talk about. It helped me to practice my Spanish. She was friendly and nice. She didn't correct my use of formal and informal. She at least pretended to understand everything I said. As the year went on, I was becoming less of an entertainment to the school in general. Fortunately for me, high school kids have short attention spans. Talking with Gloria helped me feel like I was becoming more comfortable with Puerto Rican customs—she never shot her hand in the air and asked the teacher to save her from the too-forward kid from Chicago.

One day in math class, Gloria invited me to her house to do homework together. No girls, other than my sister, had paid any serious attention to me since we'd moved to San Sebastián. It was an important invitation to me. I thought, Finally, after nearly a year of being ignored, I might be getting girls to notice me again. I was excited to visit her.

In Chicago, I could visit my friends every day for a week and never see a parent. Their parents were working, or on the bus home from work. A few of them might be at the bar. In San Sebastián, parents seemed to be everywhere. Living rooms were patrolled by watchful parents. Gloria's mom greeted us. Their house was quiet and dark, and there were no brothers or sisters around. I had the feeling that Gloria might be lonely too. We sat across the kitchen table from each other and her mom hovered over us, a combination of welcoming and inter-rogating. She was like a very polite, smiling police detective.

Gloria's mom wanted to know about my family and what they did. Where were they from in Puerto Rico? What did they do in the United States? Why did they leave Puerto Rico? Why did we come back? I thought I had passed the interview successfully, and was ready to pre-tend to concentrate on math while I really concentrated on Gloria—hopefully with her mom out of the room. But her mom had another question for me—a *Columbo*-esque, "one more thing" inquiry that gave me the feeling it was the question she had been building toward the whole time.

Gloria's mom mused that the only Gutiérrez she knew in San Sebastián was the shoemaker. Was I related to the shoemaker? Glo-ria had gone to get something out of the refrigerator and was stand-ing behind her mother. This question immediately captured Gloria's attention, and she decided urgent coaching was needed. She discreetly waved to me and forcefully shook her head, making it clear that I should not tell her mother I was related to San Sebastián's shoemaker.

Odd, I thought, that this would be so important to Gloria. Was the cobbler Gutiérrez that terrible at making shoes? Had he ripped off Gloria's family? My answer was easy, because we *weren't* related to the shoemaker. I told her mom that I didn't even know the shoemaker, and she seemed pleased. Satisfied with the results of her inquiry, her mom finally gave us a few unsupervised minutes.

"What was the big deal with the shoemaker?" I asked Gloria.

She leaned over to whisper to me, to let me in on the secret.

"He's very dark," she said.

Dark. I thought I should invite Gloria to get on a plane with me and go back to Chicago, where white people thought *all* Puerto Ricans were dark. Back home, the shoemaker would have just been another

Puerto Rican—maybe a little darker, but just hanging in there with the rest of us trying to get a break from the white folks who ran everything. But it was a different standard in Puerto Rico. When everyone was Puerto Rican, the amount of skin pigmentation was something to hang on to, to keep some class divisions alive.

I thought it was peculiar, to want to differentiate all the Puerto Ricans from one another instead of all sticking together. But when I thought about it, I had to admit that even in Chicago we weren't entirely immune from ranking the darkness of people we came across every day.

In Chicago, I would hear people admiring a new baby say, "How pretty, she looks just like a little Americanita." My parents were proud Puerto Rican people, but they were not unique in adopting the idea that "American" traits—light skin, blue eyes, light hair—made people attractive. You heard it all the time. Women gossiping about other women might say, "She's really dark, but at least she's pretty." Dark, but . . . You never heard "white, but . . ." White was good enough.

This constant worry about how you looked and acted and spoke, and whether it was good enough for you to fit in and be accepted, affected everyone's life more than any Puerto Rican would ever admit. When I was a kid, in about seventh grade, I started to use hair relaxer. It wasn't uncommon in our neighborhood. You had to go to an African American beauty products store to buy it, but I knew lots of kids who used it. It was a thick, sticky white cream like Noxzema that came in a round jar and you would rub into your hair. You stood in front of the bathroom mirror, applying it carefully, relieved that nobody could see you with this oily, oozing cream all over your head. You could feel it heating up. The stuff hurt—it would sting if you got it on your face, so you would rub petroleum jelly on to protect your skin and keep the burn concentrated on your scalp. You left the cream in for a half hour or so and then shampooed it out. Wearing one of your mom's nylon stockings over your hair at night might help to preserve the effect.

It worked. It straightened my tight, curly hair—for about two days. Nobody said anything, because lots of people were trying it. Curly haired Puerto Ricans would show up in class with flowing, straight hair and everyone would treat it like a perfectly normal occurrence, like a golden-haired Caucasian fairy had come in the middle of the night and tapped your curly hair with her wand. It didn't seem to make any girls notice me, so I quit. If I wasn't impressing girls, it wasn't worth the trouble. But I was not the only Puerto Rican in the neighborhood who looked around and thought, Why can't I have nice straight blond hair like the popular white guys?

I didn't have any hair relaxer in San Sebastián, but my new friend Gloria was relieved that I wasn't secretly related to the too-dark shoemaker in town. I thought I would never be completely prepared for all the new customs I faced every day.

AT LEAST in Puerto Rico I was surrounded by curly hair and varying shades of brown skin. Instead of wanting to imitate the handsome white guys, I was more interested in imitating the successful and rich Puerto Ricans. I'd left Chicago with a typical combination of racial pride and racial self-doubt. Don't call Puerto Ricans lazy and don't mess with us, I would think, ready to back up my friends in a fight. But I still had the worries that go along with every person in power being a different color from you. It affected your expectations. In Chicago, I never heard any of my friends talk about going to college. I had never once heard a Puerto Rican fantasize about becoming a doctor or a senator. We didn't even have any context for thinking and wishing about being a professional, wearing a suit, being a leader. Make it through school. Find a job. Stay safe and meet a nice girl. Make some money. Avoid the gangs. Those were the Lincoln Park Puerto Rican dreams for me and most of my friends.

All that changed in Puerto Rico. In San Sebastián, every leader was Puerto Rican. The mayor, the judges, the doctors, and the lawyers. The Méndez family seemed to own half the town. The Rotary Club was a bunch of Puerto Ricans. The teachers and the mailmen. Puerto Rican policemen wandered up and down Pueblo Nuevo. Some of them might have been hard on me; some of them might have mocked my Spanish, but in San Sebastián it was suddenly clear to me that Puerto Ricans could do anything.

And everyone I knew in school in Puerto Rico was talking about college. In San Sebastián, going to college wasn't a question. The question was which college you would choose. I'd never had a conversation with my parents about college before I moved to Puerto Rico. Not one. But everyone around me wanted to move up. Some wanted to escape the mountains and make it in to San Juan. Some wanted to go to America. And they didn't want to drive a cab when they got there. College was the only way to do it. People took their studies, and their future, seriously.

Luis and Tino gave me the rundown of the most desirable colleges. They wanted to go to the University of Puerto Rico. It was best to go to UPR at Río Piedras, but Mayaguez was OK too. If you couldn't get into UPR, then maybe Inter-American, the private university. But Luis and Tino both were aiming for UPR. It was the best, and it cost a fraction of what tuition was at the private schools, so your parents would be happy. The trick was, you had to get in.

I didn't have the vaguest clue how to get in to college. Why would I even think about it? In Chicago, I loved to watch *Perry Mason* on television. I imagined myself in the courtroom, all eyes focused on me while I made an impassioned defense of my wrongly accused client, revealing in a moving and dramatic twist that the real killer was actually—right there—seated in this very courtroom! But I couldn't have told you the first thing about how to become Perry Mason. My parents didn't know. My friends didn't know. If I ever thought about law school, I considered it a place where white people went.

"How would I get into the University of Puerto Rico?" I asked Luis and Tino, assuming it involved some other ancient Caribbean tradition that would be lost on me. Señor Hernández and his stack of note cards probably had something to do with the decision.

"Just do well on your boards," they told me.

"Boards?"

For them, being around me was something like being around a first-grader trapped inside a teenager's body. I looked like everyone else, but I was still learning to walk when it came to understanding how the world worked in Puerto Rico.

Your college boards, your college entrance test, they said. Luis smiled and told me, don't worry, you're going to do well on your boards.

I thought they were just being nice to me. Why, I asked him, would I do well on my boards? You don't exactly see me excelling here in high school. My goal is to avoid being mocked by my teachers. It seems unlikely I'll do well on a college entrance exam. I'm still struggling with formal and informal.

And then, with words l remember well, words that began to turn the lock on a door to dreams of a better future, he told me how the Puerto Rico college boards worked: "You'll do fine. They're in three parts. Spanish, math—and English."

Hallelujah, I remember thinking. English. One-third of the college boards. Finally, some justice for the Puerto Rican kid from Chicago. One-third English was a test I could handle. Maybe I just might become Perry Mason after all.

CHAPTER SIX

Winning a Medal for Speaking English

CHOSE TO RECITE the Gettysburg Address for English Day for one reason. It wasn't because it's the greatest speech in American history. I chose it because it was short. I wanted something that I could memorize easily. I actually counted the words: 270. Perfect. I knew I could handle that.

During my junior year in Puerto Rico, my class was preparing for English Day at the Lions Club. English Day, I was learning, was San Sebastián's Olympics of the English language. Once per year, in the spring, the students of Manuel Méndez Liciaga High School made a pilgrimage to the Lions Club to demonstrate their best English to the teachers and parents of San Sebastián. The adults and students settled down in folding chairs set up in rows and took a couple of hours to see how San Sebastián's next generation was doing with the second language of Puerto Rico.

All of the junior class competed in poetry and speeches and songs. The winners took home medals for the best performances. Everyone told me that the students coveted those medals. Taking English every year was a real pain for most of my classmates. It wasn't fun. It was a foreign language. The ones who were good at it were eager to take home a medal as evidence of their hard work. The large hall of the

Lions Club had a stage in the front for the parade of young Puerto Ricans to demonstrate their English skills. Oratory was the main category, the marquee event of the day, where representatives of each class were chosen to give it their best shot with an important speech in English.

The kids from the honors class almost always won. They did more than win; they dominated. Why shouldn't they? These were the smartest kids in school, singled out years ago and bundled into the top class. For them, winning on English Day was expected. Second place was a failure. Their junior class designation told the civic leaders in attendance all they needed to know. When the honors kids were announced, they said they were representing class 11-14—junior year, top class of the fourteen in the grade.

This was long before school administrators spent any time worrying about giving anyone an inferiority complex. Every class in my school had a rank, and junior year you stuck with your group all day, moving from class to class together. Tino and Luis were proud, card-carrying members of 11-14. Some kids were stuck in 11-1, or 11-2. I don't believe any of the high school staff worried that maybe it wasn't so great for teenagers to get stuck with a label that put them thirteen levels behind the top kids. It was a tough place. You don't like being in 11-1? Then you should have been smarter.

Like the other 11-14 kids, Luis and Tino were ready to take home some medals on English Day. I was hoping to upset their plans. By my second year in Puerto Rico, I had worked my way into 11-13. It was almost entirely because of my English. The advanced English teacher, Mrs. Badillo, was my antidote to Señor Hernández. She recognized both my struggles in school overall and my ability in English during my first year. She saw that I got decent grades even though I had trouble communicating all of my answers. She believed that once my Spanish improved, I could keep up with anyone. And she liked English-speakers. When I was in her class, she tried to make other kids feel like my ability to speak English was of value, something that everyone should try to emulate instead of mocking.

Mrs. Badillo tipped me off early to English Day. She called me up to the front of her class. I thought I might be in trouble. She told me I might want to start preparing a speech, and that I would be an excellent choice to represent 11-13 in the English Day oratory competition. She told me that nobody from any class other than honors had won in a long time, communicating that fact like it was a challenge. I think Mrs. Badillo liked to make trouble. She was proud to teach English, and she thought it was undervalued at our school in the hills of Puerto Rico. We would diagram and parse sentences on the chalkboard in her class constantly. She was always excited, her chalk flying from subject to predicate to object like an air-traffic controller landing a jumbo jet. Most of the kids hated it just as much as she loved it. Watching how enthusiastic she was about English despite the day-to-day indifference of her class was inspiring. I was glad somebody else liked English.

Though she was too dignified to be blatant about it, Mrs. Badillo wanted me to win. She was a closet subversive who wanted to take the smartest kids off their pedestals. For the Olympics of English, she thought she might have an underdog who could catch one of the heavily favored sprinters at the wire.

English Day helped me feel like my San Sebastián fortunes were improving a little. First, I had college boards coming up that would be one-third English. Now a big-time competition that everyone thought was incredibly important was all about English. The honors kids still thought they were going to win. I had other plans for them that day, but I also felt a little bit like a ringer, like maybe I should raise my hand and remind everyone I grew up in Chicago. But the truth was the 11-14 kids were so busy ignoring anyone who wasn't in their honors group that it didn't occur to them that the skinny kid from America who grew up speaking English might give them some trouble.

It occurred to me, but I wasn't in any mood to be chivalrous and bow out of an English competition. I thought it was time for payback, and not just because I was on year two of being laughed at for my Spanish. By my second year in Puerto Rico, Gloria's mom was not the only person who seemed to look down on me, or my family. My Spanish was getting better, but for all they knew we might still be related to that "dark" shoemaker. In school, I was the kid who had to run home every afternoon during the break to wait on tables and serve factory workers at our little restaurant. It's not like our nameless restaurant was viewed as a prestigious hub of fine dining. My dad didn't join the Rotary Club; he was too busy putting chickens on the rotisserie. We were a long way from San Sebastián's elite.

The doctors' and lawyers' kids at my school didn't run back to their dads' offices to work as secretaries or clean the bathrooms. Most of them didn't run anywhere at all. They drove. My high school was home to nice cars that my much richer classmates drove anywhere they wanted. They weren't hitchhiking; some were going places in their Datsun 280-Zs or Volvos. By my junior year, my sister Ada—who grew prettier every day—was dating the son of a San Sebastián doctor. Ada had a group of male admirers more than willing to overlook her relative poverty. The doctor's son would pull up outside of our home in his new, red Triumph Spitfire convertible, and Ada would be off for the day.

Even in a place that was 100 percent Puerto Rican, people could still find ways to divide and classify one another. In Chicago, nobody ever hassled me because we didn't have much money. Everybody I knew was just this side of broke in Chicago. But in San Sebastián, I met a new class of well-off Puerto Ricans. Suddenly, we weren't like every other Puerto Rican. We were new, and poor. To me, it was inspiring that San Sebastián was filled with so many accomplished, professional Puerto Ricans. I looked up to them. But many of them looked down on us.

We rented our restaurant and apartment from Pedro, who owned the grocery next door. He was huge and friendly—a big, amiable barrel of a man. I thought, if this guy ever hugs me, I'll be dead. Maybe he was friendly because he collected a rent check from us every month. But despite being our landlord, he worked as hard as my dad. He was always in his store, stocking shelves, talking to customers, handling the cash register. He competed with us in soda and liquor and snack sales. He usually undersold us, because his inventory was bigger. It didn't seem to worry him that he was keeping his tenant from making money. Still, I liked him. He was a friendly guy and one more person I could talk to.

Pedro had a daughter about Ada's age who went to school with us.

When I first saw her in the store, I thought that she might be an excellent candidate for friendship in our lonely little town. We would have a lot in common; she helped in the store, I worked in the restaurant. We were young laborers—I thought we would compare customer-service tips. I was wrong. My experience with commerce in San Sebastián involved pouring bleach into a bucket and carrying armfuls of lunch plates. The daughter's experience with commerce consisted of asking her dad for money. I never saw her work a day in the store. She had younger sisters, and together they would stop by with their mom, looking like they couldn't wait to leave and start shopping somewhere. Pedro, jovial as ever, would happily open the cash register and hand over a stack of bills. I wanted to line up behind the girls and hope Pedro wouldn't notice an extra outstretched hand.

The girls excelled in communicating with one look that I shouldn't assume that sharing storefronts side by side in San Sebastián made us peers. They had perfected the "I can't see you" stare. They looked above and beyond and around me, and never spoke to me. Not once— not at the store, not at school. I was their invisible tenant, the kid who swept floors. The floors they owned. It made me feel sorry for their dad. As much as I disliked being chained to our restaurant for a weekly salary of nothing, I didn't expect my dad to do all the work and then hand over the cash. It seemed wrong. But the girls next door had shopping to do. The production of wealth was their dad's job. The distribution of wealth was theirs. I thought about how much fun it would have been to watch them ask my dad, just once, for money.

My dad concentrated on his work and didn't seem to care that we had lost our social standing by moving back home. He knew we weren't among San Sebastián's elite, and he expected me to understand it too. Not long before English Day, I had been asked to a dance at the San Sebastián Rotary Club. I was asked by the younger sister of a girl in one of my classes. She was outgoing and pretty. That she had singled me out and asked me to the dance gave me hope that I was fitting in. My classmates were always talking about the parties at the Rotary Club. They were exclusive, and being invited gave you a chance to mingle with San Sebastián's elite. I thought that being part of that club would send an important message that I was less of an outsider.

At the restaurant, I told my dad I had been invited to the exclusive dance. I told him partially out of pride, and mainly because I needed him to help me figure out how I was going to get this girl to the dance. I hadn't yet been on a date in San Sebastián.

I explained my big Puerto Rican social breakthrough to my dad. He didn't look at me with a sense of excitement, or pride. He said, "You understand that there are financial obligations that come with taking a girl to a fancy dance. You'll need a suit—maybe even a tuxedo, a boutonniere. You'll have to buy the girl a corsage. You need a car to get her there. Have you thought about these things?"

Of course I had thought about them. I worried about it. That's why I was talking to him. I needed his help. I thought maybe one night out wouldn't be too much to ask. In Chicago, for my first holy communion and my eighth-grade graduation, my parents had bought me suits. But now my dad thought the request was unreasonable, that we couldn't afford it. But instead of telling my dad to take the cost out of my nonexistent tips from waiting on tables every day for a year, I stood quietly, mumbling that maybe I hadn't completely thought it through.

His concerns weren't just about the money.

"The Rotary Dance?" he said. "You're not one of them. That is for the *blanquitos*. You won't have any fun. They won't accept you."

For my dad, that was the end of the discussion. He had work to do, and he didn't have the time, or the money, for a Rotary dance. Those dances were for other people, not for his son. The *blanquitos* were the "little white ones," a metaphor for the rich, the privileged ones. Those dances weren't for the son of the owner of a small restaurant.

You don't need to tell me about not being accepted, I thought. I've lived it. But I didn't fight it. What was the point? It's hard to remember my dad changing his mind about anything. I told the girl I couldn't go to the dance with her. She was shocked. Who says no to the Rotary dance in San Sebastián? Especially if you are the kid most everyone ignores. It was probably too late for her to find another date, so she was left out of the dance too. She looked like she was beginning to understand why nobody asked me anywhere.

My dad's concern about the money didn't surprise me. Tuxedos and flowers weren't in his budget. But I was surprised he was so willing to accept that we weren't good enough for a dance at the Rotary. My dad, who a year before was discussing a real estate partnership with a wealthy property owner in Chicago, seemed perfectly content that his place in the world was café owner and short-order cook in a small town in Puerto Rico. Our life didn't include Rotary dances. Our life was about giant vats of rice and racks of pork chops.

I THOUGHT our life could be more than that, and by the time English Day came around, I felt I had some slights to avenge. Maybe the Rotary wouldn't have me, but they couldn't keep me out of the Lions Club on English Day. Mrs. Badillo was preparing me to do battle with 11-14, and I was ready for a little class warfare with the rich and success-ful kids of San Sebastián. I saw it as a warm-up for my college boards, the beginning of an English-fueled run to success. Luis and Tino told me I would never win, but I think their bravado was just high school kids having fun with their friend. They were with me every day. They knew it wasn't exactly challenging for me to give a speech in English. And secretly, I think they were pulling for me.

I read my copy of the Gettysburg Address every day, working to become a five-foot-five, Puerto Rican Abraham Lincoln. I stood in front of the same mirror where I'd once perfected saying Luis Vicente Gutiérrez-Olmedo, and said, "Of the people, by the people, for the people" over and over again. This time, I reversed my practice routine. I eradicated any rolling r's like they were weeds from a yard. I treated any hint of languorous Spanish pronunciations like foreign invaders. I recited the speech over and over again. "Brought forth on this conti-nent, a new nation." The words felt like a welcome reminder of home. I pictured myself on the corner of Halsted and Dickens, talking to Frankie, before any accent marks and island pronunciations made their way to my tongue. It was easy, natural.

What was even better was that in the back of my mind, I also heard the Puerto Rican accents of the smartest kids at school. The too-long r in "proposition that all men are created equal." It felt good to picture the privileged kids up onstage speaking my language for once, under a spotlight, struggling with words that didn't come naturally. And I didn't think Señor Hernández's dignified, disappearing *h* would work so well on "hallow this ground." Allow this ground? How's your silent *h* now, Señor Hernández? I was ready and I knew it. I've got my *h*'s back. I might spend every day peeling potatoes, and I might not be good enough for the Rotary dance, but I was ready to send home the gang in 11-14 one medal short.

English Day was a pretty merciless exhibition. The kids from the lower classes didn't have much of a shot, and as the day went on, we heard some terrible English. I sat with Mrs. Badillo and my class, listening and thinking that if any of these kids had been dropped into St. Michael's in Chicago and been expected to speak only English when they were fifteen, they would have had a tough time too, just like I was having in San Sebastián. Song after song, speech after speech, I was being reminded that it's hard to pick up a second language. With every botched English pronunciation, I felt a little better about my progress in Spanish.

The oratory competition, and my shot at the Gettysburg Address, was at the end of the day. I had the speech down. It took about two minutes. The rhythm of Lincoln's words made it flow like a poem. It wasn't terribly hard to memorize, and I had spent hours on it. In Chicago, nobody would have cared that I pronounced all of the words right. Big deal. But as I moved through the speech, I enunciated every syllable. The gentry of Puerto Rico looked on with curiosity. For once, that I looked just as Puerto Rican as everyone who had gone before me worked in my favor. The audience paid attention to every word, even though some of them barely understood what I was saying. English Day at the Lions Club didn't mean that everyone in the audience was speaking English to one another. All I heard from the audience all day was regular, everyday Spanish.

The more I'd practiced the speech, the more the words gained meaning for me. Not everyone in the room at the Lions Club had exactly lived the words "all men are created equal" when it came to San Sebastián's newcomers. My speech was my introduction to the genius of Lincoln. Reading those 270 words over and over and over, even if you chose the short speech mainly so you could stick it to the rich kids, still drove home his meaning. I felt the truth of the words he had written.

One English word flowed after another, and when I finished my speech, the room was silent for a moment. Then my class applauded like I had just scored the winning run in the big game. They sensed victory. The adults in the room applauded and nodded and were appreciative of my effort. Mrs. Badillo looked proud of my performance, and a little worried that despite my excellent delivery, the honors kids would win out of tradition. We waited for them to finish their oratory.

The honors kids were very good. Their English was excellent, and they worked hard and practiced every pronunciation. They did their best. But English wasn't their native language and everyone in the room knew it. I felt the teachers and the audience and Mrs. Badillo realizing that they couldn't do anything but give the medal to the kid from Chicago. And they did.

Since the day my family plucked me from Halsted and Dickens, put me on a plane, and set me up as a waiter in a Puerto Rican café in the hills of San Sebastián, the only reason I had ever been the center of attention was for speaking terrible Spanish. Now I was the kid who helped our class win on English Day. The kids of 11-13 were thrilled to beat the honors kids in anything. It didn't matter to them at all who had led them to the Promised Land. They didn't care if it took a ringer to do it, or if their champion on English Day was the kid from Chicago everyone had taunted. That day, I had knocked down the kids who won everything. The San Sebastián gentry were impressed, and Mrs. Badillo smiled like a successful coach.

In my heart, I think I knew that winning a competition in English was a little like cheating for me. But my new mentor, Abraham Lincoln, had just reminded the Lions Club that all men are created equal, so I savored my medal. More important, it was another step toward a normal high school life. People paid more attention to me afterward. Kids began to acknowledge that I wasn't just a misfit or an outsider, I was simply someone who grew up somewhere else. Their new calculation of Luis Gutiérrez was simple. He just kicked everyone's ass in English, so how bad can he really be?

Luis and Tino, as I expected, were happy for me. They showed whatever solidarity they had to show with their classmates, and then celebrated. Tino, whose economic status was as far away from the upper class of San Sebastián as mine, looked at my medal with pride. My friends and I had something to celebrate. We were having fun, and I was fitting in.

YEARS LATER, when I was in Congress, I got an urgent call from my friend Luis's wife, Maria. Luis had had a heart attack. They performed open-heart surgery and didn't know if he would make it. Thankfully, he did, and when he was well enough to talk, I reached him by phone. It was a very scary time, and I was thrilled to hear his voice. I didn't know if I would ever hear from my high school co-conspirator again. I was even happier when he came on the line and sounded cheerful, almost laughing.

"Luis, I've been worried about you. How are you feeling?" I asked him.

Better, he told me, though he confessed he didn't know at first if he would pull through.

"I know, it was very serious," I said.

He was still chuckling.

"Not because of that. When it happened, they wheeled me into the emergency room in San Sebastián and I saw the doctor. Do you know who the doctor was? It was Ricardo from high school."

I remembered him, and I knew exactly why Luis was chuckling.

"Ricardo. He was in 11-2—almost the bottom class! I thought I was dead for sure."

I laughed.

"You know what, Luis?" he said to me. "The kid from 11-2 saved my life."

*   *   *

THE SUMMER BEFORE my success on English Day, I did something that helped to improve my outlook about San Sebastián.

I went home.

During my first year in San Sebastián, through the loneliness and the isolation, I harassed my parents constantly about Chicago. I was a teenager committed to spreading my discontent like a plague. Why did you bring me here? There is nothing to do. Nobody understands me. People make fun of me. I was happy in Chicago. I'm sure I told them more than once that they were ruining my life.

My dad's a calm guy. And stubborn. But even he couldn't take it after a while. Eventually, instead of listening to me complain and whine, he did something almost unthinkable for him. He bought me a plane ticket and sent me to Chicago for the summer.

At the end of my first year of school, I counted down the days and planned my return. I would be staying with my dad's sister back in Lincoln Park. My parents had only one condition. I had to find a job to pay for the ticket. That was an easy deal for me. I had already worked for free in the restaurant. I was ready to go back home.

My aunt Wilda and uncle Raul, my godfather, lived right around the corner from our old apartment. Her daughter, my cousin Vildy, was right around my age. I was going back to the old neighborhood.

My uncle picked me up from the airport and we made our way to Lincoln Park. Home. Nothing had changed and everything had changed. I saw the bodega, the Woolworths on North Avenue, the corner where the Harrison Street Gents hung out. It was like walking into the mental picture I had held in my mind for a year.

But this summer would be different. I had to work, so my time to track down old friends came second to tracking down some money to send back home. Some of my friends had moved on. Frankie was gone. I learned that even a year is a long time in the life of fifteen-year-olds. Those last moments in Chicago were frozen in my mind; the way things should be in my hometown, shining with the glow of memory. Everyone else had just kept living their lives.

But even if I couldn't reconnect with all of my friends, I could reconnect with the feeling that everything was familiar. I heard English everywhere I went, and I shopped at the bodega. I listened to Motown on the radio. I met new friends with my cousin Vildy. I walked to the Biograph Theater and watched lots of movies without subtitles.

Finding a job wasn't a problem. I was a restaurant industry veteran. Not too far from Lincoln Park, the Golden Nugget Restaurant, a busy, twenty-four-hour pancake and waffle house, was looking for busboys. Chicago had a million places like the Golden Nugget. It had a big neon sign that said OPEN 24 HOURS in the window; a counter for the older, lonely guys who ate half of their meals there; bright fluorescent lights; Formica booths; and plastic trifold menus. I knew the job would be a piece of cake. There was nothing in a restaurant that I couldn't do. I was so grateful for a job that my interview lasted five minutes. They told me they were paying $60 per week. To me, that was like finding a pot of gold. Within forty-eight hours of returning to Chicago I was employed at an exorbitant salary.

Within one week of returning to Chicago, I was unemployed. And I learned something about job interviews: ask questions. It was true they were paying $60 a week. It was also true that they expected their busboys to work at least ten hours a day, six days a week, before they took home their sixty bucks. And at the Golden Nugget, there was no mercy for the newest busboys. I spent ten hours carrying huge tubs of dirty plates and silverware and cups to their huge kitchen. I refilled ketchup and mustard and salt and pepper on the tables. I loaded the industrial-size dishwasher. I unloaded it. We still washed some dishes by hand.

In Puerto Rico, our restaurant was jammed at lunchtime, maybe for two hours tops. The Golden Nugget was busy *all* the time. There seemed to be an insatiable hunger for pancakes in the neighborhood. Or cheap burgers. Hot, open-faced sandwiches were a specialty too. Thin, salty roast beef covered in gravy thick enough to oil your car engine. Fast, fattening, and cheap could have been our motto. If people in San Sebastián were as hungry as the customers at the Golden Nugget, my dad would be rich. I never stopped running.

I didn't mind working, but I felt like the owner had tricked me with his sixty-dollars-a-week sales pitch. I was making less than a dollar an hour. By the end of my week I had trouble dragging myself out of bed. I had blisters and cuts on my hands from the hot water and the knives. The Golden Nugget made me miss our civilized bar backed with rum and the rotisserie dripping with chicken grease. At the end of the first week I hung up my apron. I knew I could do better. At my next job interview, I would ask how many hours you had to work before they paid you the $60. By the end of my second week back home, I had found a superior restaurant option. I was doing lunch prep and bussing tables at the restaurant at the Carson Pirie Scott department store in the Loop. Fewer hours, more money, and a nicer neighborhood. Once I had the steam and the heat of the Golden Nugget behind me, I thought the rest of my Chicago summer would be fine.

But I didn't know how much trouble I would find.

Vildy's friend Magdelena was a year younger than me, thin, and cute. She was outgoing and friendly in ways that were foreign to the more formal girls in Puerto Rico. Cutting out the constant parental supervision and mysterious cultural rituals of San Sebastián was a relief. I liked Magdelena, and Magdelena liked me. We went out. No problem. I might have been less thrilled if she had told me that her last boyfriend had been a Latin King. When I found out, I thought my return trip to Chicago had probably just become a lot more complicated. I was right.

Magdelena and I were walking on Halsted Street and holding hands when we saw two Latin Kings on the corner up ahead of us. If I had spied them two seconds sooner Magdelena and I could have unclenched our hands and ducked into one of the stores. But the Kings' eyes locked on us. We knew we were in trouble.

They didn't do anything that afternoon, maybe because Magdelena's boyfriend wasn't standing on the corner with them. Or, her ex-boyfriend. That's what she told me, and as far as we were concerned, that relationship was over. But "ex" can have a complicated meaning if your gang-member boyfriend hasn't decided that he's an "ex." I didn't quite understand the unwritten rule, but I was about to learn it. Here's the rule: the relationship is over when your gang-member boyfriend decides it's over.

The next night, I was sitting with Raymond, Vildy's boyfriend, on the stoop of a house at Fremont and Wisconsin. We were just hanging out, laughing and enjoying a Chicago summer night. I thought just maybe I could get away with my romance with Magdelena. Then, out of everywhere, like the D-Day invasion, we were surrounded. One minute we were alone on the stoop, the next minute ten or twelve Latin Kings came out from behind cars, out of alleys, running down the block right at us. This wasn't a group of neighborhood trouble-makers. These were dangerous gang members, guys who hurt people. Magdelena's ex-boyfriend was with them. He was a big guy, muscular and fit. In the neighborhood, everyone knew him.

I hadn't been back a month yet, and I was scared. I knew a lot of them. It was my neighborhood; I had gone to school with some of them, but they had changed. They didn't look like they wanted to talk, or warn me, or negotiate. We were surrounded by Latin Kings, and I was no longer a neighborhood kid. A year before, maybe I could have talked myself out of trouble, reminded one of the guys that I had gone to school with him. In the past year, I hadn't been hanging out in my neighborhood. I had been stirring *cuchifritos* and serving chicken in San Sebastián.

Their leader looked up at us. He stared right at me and pointed and said, "You. I want to talk to you, asshole." Some of his friends were smiling. This was fun for them. Some looked angry, impatient, ready for some violence to break up the boredom of a summer night. Even after a year in Puerto Rico, I knew what they wanted. They were ready for me to come down off the stoop and get my beating. They weren't joking around, and I was scared. The leader continued to look right at me.

Raymond was in the ROTC. He didn't look afraid. He hadn't immediately jumped to his feet, looking for an escape when the Latin Kings appeared. Now he slowly stood up, then reached behind him and pulled a gun out of the back of his jeans. It was a big gun with a long clip. I had no idea he was carrying a gun. I had never been that close to a gun. He pointed the gun directly at the Latin King closest to the house. I thought he might shoot him. I thought the King would pull his own gun, and I ducked. Instead, the gang members turned immediately and ran. They all scattered, running and diving behind cars even more quickly than they had come running down the street. While they were disappearing, Raymond and I jumped down the steps to run to my house. Even with his gun, Raymond didn't want to spend any extra time with ten gang members. We didn't look back. We made it home. I was breathing hard and glad to be off the street, but I knew it wasn't over. Mr. ROTC might have saved us tonight, I thought, but he won't help us tomorrow, or next week, or whenever payback comes.

I was scared—real fear, the fear that comes from being close to a gun and anger and a street full of irrational and hateful guys.

That was the first time I was really scared in Chicago. Maybe it was because I was a little older and the gang members didn't see me just as a kid anymore. Maybe it was because I had been gone a year and had lost twelve months of nurturing diplomatic relations with the gang guys on the block. Maybe I just shouldn't have been holding hands with a gang member's ex-girlfriend. As isolated and lonely and frustrated as I felt in San Sebastián, I was never close to violence. I didn't sleep much that night, and I woke up the next day ready to watch my back, wondering when I would see the Latin Kings again, and just how far away Vildy's ROTC boyfriend would be when I did.

It didn't take long to find out. The Latin Kings didn't like having to run away from a guy with a gun. They wanted revenge.

The next day, I was on the street, walking a different route and being careful, watching and looking over my shoulder, I saw two Latin Kings coming up quickly behind me. I had almost made it home; I was only a block away. I knew the guys following me. It was Dead Eye and Hankie. I knew Hankie was the leader of the Latin Kings. Dead Eye's name didn't have anything to do with his eyesight. It had everything to do with how well he shot a gun. You saw the names Hankie and Dead Eye in graffiti on every blank wall that could be found.

I didn't consider standing and negotiating or fighting for even an instant. I just ran. Dead Eye and Hankie ran too. I'm small and fast—a good flight animal. I ran hard and didn't look back. I made it home, with the Kings right behind me. They stopped at the sidewalk of our building, because my uncle Raul was standing on the stoop. He stared them down, then told them to go away and leave me alone. He didn't back down or hesitate to tell them to get away from his house. He yelled at them, a responsible adult staring down problem kids.

But as soon as he tough-talked the Latin Kings away, he went back inside and called my other uncle—the one who lived two miles away on the other side of the expressway. He said, "Quiro has to leave here immediately." It didn't make me feel any better that inside the safety of his house, away from the stares of Dead Eye and Hankie, my uncle looked scared too. I didn't argue with my uncle. I packed my things that moment, no delay, no discussion, no good-bye kiss to Magdelena. In a half hour, my uncle Ruben pulled up out front. They put me in the car, gave me a wave, and within an hour of making it home a few yards ahead of the Latin Kings, I had a new home for the remainder of my summer, farther away from my old neighborhood.

At that moment, as much as I missed Chicago and was happy to be back, I began to think that maybe my dad was on to something. In Puerto Rico, I was bored. But I was perfecting my Spanish and trying to fit in at school. It was hard to find trouble with a magnifying glass in San Sebastián. A few dollars on the rail at the neighborhood pool hall was as wild as my life ever got. Within a few weeks of returning to Chicago, I was running—literally—for my life from neighborhood thugs.

Both moments—with the Kings on my heels chasing me home and with a dozen of them coming up fast to the stoop I was sitting on—I thought I was in real trouble. If Vildy's boyfriend hadn't been carrying a gun, when I ran for office years later I might have been known as the candidate with the rearranged face. I don't think any of the Latin Kings who wanted to exact revenge on me for holding Magdelena's hand had guns with them. That wouldn't be the case today. If Vildy's ROTC boyfriend pointed a gun at twelve Latin Kings today, shots would be fired. That summer, the shots would have been fired at me, and who knows if I would be telling this story.

After that, the summer flashed by. I had made more than enough money to pay back my parents for the plane ticket. I had some pocket money while I was in Chicago, enough to buy a slice of pizza or a hot dog, enough to go to the Biograph and see a movie—but the truth was after my brush with the Latin Kings, I was on lockdown. I had to be careful all the time.

So despite working and making money and having my aunts and uncles and Vildy around, in only one year away I was already starting to lose my grasp on the feeling that Chicago was my home. I learned that teenagers erase people from their lives quickly. People move on. To my friends, I was gone—thousands of miles away on an island. And I wasn't back for good, so nobody was welcoming me home with a party and a slap on the back as we made plans together for school next year. I was just back for an extended visit, a good chunk of which I spent carrying dishes into the kitchen at Carson's, clearing the tables of well-dressed Chicago ladies who had taken their daughters and grand-daughters out for a day of shopping and lunch. People were happy to see me, like they might be happy to see any guest. But I wasn't good old Louie from the neighborhood, back from exile in the Caribbean. I was a visitor.

The Latin Kings had forced me to flee the old neighborhood, land-ing on a block with an unfamiliar bodega and kids I didn't know. I wasn't staying with Vildy, the cousin closest to me in age. I missed Magdelena. I liked her and I was happy to have a girl to spend the summer with. But I can't say I was gallant enough to think seriously even once about venturing back into gang territory to win her back. Every time I thought of Magdelena, her slim figure and nice smile were chased out of my memory by Dead Eye and Hankie. Not slim. Not nice. Nobody was going to write a love story about me reclaiming my girl that summer. Instead, they might write a survival story about how I managed to make it through the summer.

Despite my scrape with violence, I was happy to get a break from the hills and the heat and Cuchilandia and my cousins and the women complaining about their food in our restaurant. I loved Chicago. But it wasn't the same. As my uncle drove me back to the airport and my flight to San Juan, I didn't feel like I was returning home or leaving home. I felt like I was looking for a home.

* * *

AS MY JUNIOR YEAR went on, as Luis and Tino and I became closer friends, as we paid the sugarcane workers, as I triumphed on English Day, I kept thinking that maybe, just maybe, I would eventually find my home at college.

The college boards were in the middle of the school year. This was long before you could take a test-prep course. Our test prep was to worry. People talked about the test, people boasted about how well they would do, people speculated about how others would do poorly.

Luis was smart. I knew he would do well. He was confident. Luis was always planning ahead, and he already knew he wanted to be a lawyer. As we did homework at his house one day, he surprised me with just how specific his plans for the future were.

"You know, Luis, I'm out of here after this year," he said to me.

I didn't know what he meant. I thought maybe he was moving.

"I took summer school last year, and I'm doing it again this year. I'll have enough credits to graduate. I'm not coming back for senior year. I'm done. I'm going to do well on the boards and then go to UPR." He went back to doing his homework, as if me finding out that my best friend wasn't coming back for senior year was routine news.

"You can do that? Just skip senior year?"

"As long as you have the credits. That's all it takes. You should check. They'd probably give you all sorts of credits for your classes in Chicago. Give it a try. We'll go to UPR together."

I thought about my Chicago classes. St. Michael's was ahead of Liciaga when it came to math and science. I had already taken algebra. I was ahead in chemistry too. It didn't seem possible to me. Just make senior year vanish. It occurred to me that Luis was just playing a prank.

"You're screwing around with me," I told him.

Luis barely looked up from his homework. "Talk to the counselor. Figure it out."

"Yeah, you'd like that. Very funny. English-speaking kid from Chicago asks counselor if he can graduate early."

Luis just shrugged. I thought he was joking, but I also knew I was going to ask the counselor. Any chance of being done a year early was worth the potential embarrassment.

I barely knew the counselor. I asked him. He didn't laugh. Luis and Tino didn't jump out of the closet and yell, "We got you!" The counselor looked up my records. He didn't look very interested in the fact that he was giving me a year of my life back.

"You have all of your math and science requirements. All you need is senior English and senior Spanish. You could do that during the summer. If you do that, you're done."

Summer school was mostly for kids who had failed and were repeating. How hard could it be?

Why had nobody mentioned this to me? I have to study with Luis Águila and have him mention it like it's nothing? I asked the counselor how soon I could sign up for summer school.

Suddenly my path was clear. I was not only keeping up with my class, I was going to lap them. I was going to be done, finished, out of there. I still hadn't talked to my parents about college, or skipping senior year. The key was to present my plan to them when it was complete. And to be able to tell them it was free. Luis told me that UPR cost virtually nothing. He was right; it only cost about $70 per semester. All I needed was good scores on my boards.

I knew I was set for the English. I thought I could handle the math. It was mostly formulas and equations. The challenge was the Spanish. But the truth was, almost without my fully realizing it, my Spanish had become perfectly acceptable. Maybe even good. People in San Sebastián made fun of my accent more than my vocabulary or my usage. It was hard to shake fifteen years of the streets of Chicago completely from my tongue, but nobody had much on me in grammar anymore. I rarely messed up formal and informal now, though the whole idea still seemed a little ridiculous to me. I had no trouble communicating with Tino and Luis. I had felt my progress when I was in Chicago for the summer. Back home in the neighborhood, I had become the best teenage Spanish-speaker in Lincoln Park.

If I could just translate my Spanish progress from my tongue to the little circles of the standardized college boards, I told myself, I could be on my way out of high school. Everyone, including Mrs. Badillo, told me not to worry, that I would do fine on the boards. I worried, and didn't sleep much the night before the test.

I wasn't worried about the English, which came first. I felt confident that I had answered every question correctly. I took a deep breath and thought, I aced it. It gave me confidence for the rest of the test. The math was manageable. I wasn't a great math student, but I was good at memorizing what I needed to know. So far, so good. Now, just the Spanish.

I read the questions like it was my second language, but like it was a second language that I understood well. As I took the test, I thought: Dad might have taken me away from all of my friends, he might have conscripted me to work in his restaurant, but he also make me bilingual. And I might even go to college. None of these things would have happened for me in Chicago. And if I weren't becoming as stubborn as he was, I might have thanked him.

I handed in my test, feeling confident, and waited for the results.

Just like their no-nonsense division of kids by class from 11-1 to 11-14, in San Sebastián, the junior class did not get a confidential notice of our test scores. No nice letter in a sealed envelope about how hard you tried. The scores were posted in long columns, best to worst, for the world to see, right outside the door of the counselor's office.

I made my way through the crowd, some kids looking relieved, some kids celebrating, some looking like they wished their names at the bottom of the list weren't quite so public. I didn't have to scan very far from the top to find my name.

Out of 800, I scored nearly 600 on the math and the Spanish, not great but above average. My Spanish was now officially good enough. I scored a 793 on the English. I missed one question, and thought it must have been a scoring error. I wondered if I should protest, then resigned myself to the fact that I must have simply filled in the wrong circle with my #2 lead pencil. My combined score of over 1900 put me in the top 10 percent in Puerto Rico. The English did it for me. In Puerto Rico back then, there was no special college application process. Schools just looked at your grades and your test scores, rated you on their scale, and said yes or no. Combined with my decent grades, I had my choice of colleges in Puerto Rico, including the best—and very inexpensive—UPR at Rio Piedras.

I wish I could say I was modest and gracious about my success. I wasn't. Kids all asked one another how they did. I told them to look for my name near the top, the one with the 1900. Remember me? The kid you made fun of? The outsider. The gringo? I'm going to UPR, and I'm going next year.

I found Luis. He was happy. He had done well too. We were on our way.

CHAPTER SEVEN

A Declaration of Independence

MY GOAL for our day of coffee-picking was simple. I wanted to pick as many coffee beans as quickly as I could. I wanted to fill my wicker basket with Puerto Rican coffee beans and show the world with my overflowing bounty that our island could provide enough for all of us. My hands flew, beans popped off of the vines and into my basket. At my speed, I didn't have much time to monitor the progress of my fellow coffee pickers, but the few times I glanced up, I saw them moving slowly, carefully examining every plant on the hillside. Obviously, the island natives didn't have the drive and motivation I did to leverage our coffee cultivation into Puerto Rican independence.

The older and very patient Puerto Rican farmer, who flew a huge Puerto Rican flag in the field at the front of his coffee farm, didn't really need fifteen or twenty idealistic supporters of independence for Puerto Rico climbing all over his plants and picking his coffee beans. The architects and lawyers, bus drivers and students were on his property for an "agriculture day" for the Puerto Rican Independence Party, a day to get back to our roots and protect the agricultural heritage of our island—or our nation—as I now passionately thought of Puerto Rico. Gathering and picking coffee beans was an expression of a fundamental belief of independence supporters. We were utilizing Puerto Rico's natural resources. We were demonstrating that we had all we needed right here on our island. With each bean, we were moving Puerto Rico toward self-sufficiency.

By my second year in Puerto Rico, I was an avid disciple of the Puerto Rican independence movement. I had become passionately committed to two key goals. The first was to get all of my credits in summer school classes so I could leave Manuel Méndez Liciaga High School behind and move on to the University of Puerto Rico. The second was to spread my belief in independence for Puerto Rico.

On that plantation in the hills outside of San Sebastián, I grasped one fact right away: picking coffee is hard work. I didn't see anyone on the plantation who reminded me of Juan Valdez. The Juan Valdez of television commercials from my childhood was a cheerful, handsome Latino guy in beautiful, unruffled white work clothes. He charmed suburban moms with a confident smile and a dashing red scarf tied neatly around his neck. His lovable donkey was almost as handsome as Juan. Both Juan and the donkey had gone missing the day I was picking coffee.

I also learned that coffee didn't grow in neatly arranged rows. Juan couldn't have ridden his donkey happily through the field, gathering delicious coffee beans. Coffee likes the shade, and grows on sloping hills. Coffee plants are dense and sturdy. You need to bend over and lean in close to pick the beans. They share their territory with lots of other creatures that like the shade. Like snakes, spiders, and insects like the *abayarde*, a particularly vicious and nasty antlike creature that stings coffee-pickers in Puerto Rico. The footing on the hills is slippery; it's like working on mini ski slopes. After working for an hour, I didn't see any clothes as neatly pressed and clean as those of dashing Juan Valdez. I didn't think that coffee drinkers would have found Juan so lovable if he had been covered with dirt and sweat and constantly knocking spiders off of his arm.

Still, after an hour or so of working in the Puerto Rican sun, I didn't think anyone could challenge me as the fastest coffee picker in our group. My basket was nearly full, and everyone else was still moving in slow motion. My friends' baskets weren't half as full as mine. When I'd filled my basket to the top a few minutes later, I didn't throw my hands up in the air and shout, "Done!" like I'd won a contest on a game show, but that's what I was thinking. Game over, I thought, the kid from Chicago wins. They should have asked this gringo for some coffee-picking tips a long time ago.

When I told the owner of the farm that I had filled my basket, he looked impressed. He also looked skeptical. He looked like a man who had picked a lot of coffee beans and knew about how long it should take to fill a wicker basket. But he was curious. The others stopped to watch as well. They seemed surprised that I could have gotten so far ahead of them. People looked at me like they thought we might be able to patent my coffee-picking technique and save the economy.

The coffee farmer looked in my bucket and smiled. He put his hand deep into my wicker basket and let several handfuls fall through his fingers, checking from top to bottom, turning them over with familiarity. The more he looked in my basket, the more amused he seemed to be. He held up a dark red coffee bean for me to examine.

"When they are ripe, they are red. Deep red, maroon. From now on, only pick the red ones," he said. He smiled at me; a smile of tolerance, a smile that said we can't be too choosy when it comes to our Independentista brothers and sisters. You take what you can get. The others in my party laughed. One woman patted me on the head, like a parent consoling a disappointed toddler. "Stay away from the green ones," she said.

Most of the beans in my bucket were green. At some point before we started maybe someone said, "Only pick the red ones," but I didn't remember it. Maybe the farmer who ran the place thought it was so obvious that even a kid from the big city would understand that if beans are two colors—red or green—you might want to leave the green ones on the vine. But I didn't really understand the whole idea of "ripe." What did I know? I was a city kid. I didn't think too much about food's natural state on the vine. If it was at the bodega, you could eat it.

One of the workers at the farm took my basket away. Instead of helping, I had created extra work for the farmer. His worker sorted out and saved all of the red ones. The green ones were hopeless, a picked-too-soon sacrifice. They depulped the red cherries and laid them out on a large piece of burlap in the sun. They were still drying coffee the traditional way. They saved what they could from my basket and we all went on picking, doing our part for the future of Puerto Rico.

Joining my fellow Independentistas picking coffee was just one way I was showing my commitment to the nation of Puerto Rico. Throughout my second year in high school, I became more educated every day on the history of Puerto Rico and the passion of the Independentistas of San Sebastián, people committed to sustaining the patriotic ideals that had led to overthrowing the Spaniards and establishing the first free and independent government of Puerto Rico in Lares more than a hundred years ago.

It had ended badly for those rebels, but like patriots throughout history, they lost a battle but became role models for generations who came after them. I was now proudly one of them. The education that the independence leaders of San Sebastián gave a kid from Chicago was changing me every day.

MOVEMENTS NEED LEADERS, and our champion was Rubén Berríos. Ruben was young and handsome and had seemingly come out of nowhere to take charge of the Independence Party. He was a lawyer who was educated at Georgetown and Yale and he had blond hair that made him look as much like a Viking as a Puerto Rican. He stood up to the Americans about their use of the Puerto Rican island of Culebra for naval training, leading sit-ins and protests. His knowledge of Puerto Rican and American history seemed endless. And I had never, anywhere, heard anyone speak like he did.

I admired people who spoke with confidence and pride, maybe because my parents were so soft-spoken. I was the inexplicably outspoken and talkative member of a quiet family. My dad was a tenured professor in the school of "only speak when you have something to say." He valued quiet. Berrios valued blunt and beautiful rhetoric about the future and potential of Puerto Rico. The Puerto Rican people could do anything, he told us. Our potential was unlimited, and unrelated to a faraway Congress that didn't even allow our Puerto Rican member to vote. We could only fulfill our potential, Berrios explained, if we could make all of our decisions for ourselves. His prescription for Puerto Rico was self-reliance.

He mocked the nearly universally accepted idea that Puerto Ricans should be grateful to their huge neighbors to the north for all of their generosity and assistance. He would sarcastically run down a list of things we had come to depend on but should provide for ourselves. I heard Berrios tell stories of Puerto Rico's history, of how governments worldwide had colonized and ruled people without their consent, how Puerto Rico—our nation of Puerto Rico—had never been given an opportunity to rule itself, not by the Spaniards, not by the Americans, not by anyone. Rubén Berríos did not come to town to talk about electricity, like the Commonwealthers. He didn't talk about tax policy and public works. He talked about the beauty of Puerto Rican culture and the potential of the Puerto Rican people. Berrios said that it was time, finally, for Puerto Ricans to make all of the decisions about Puerto Rico.

Why shouldn't that make sense to an American kid from Chicago? I loved the Fourth of July, I believed in George Washington. Didn't I get to celebrate and stuff myself at our huge family picnic on the Fourth of July because America wanted to make all of its decisions for itself? Wasn't the holiday actually called Independence Day? When I related Rubén Berríos's passionate rhetoric about independence to the history I knew, I thought of Thomas Jefferson and Ben Franklin. They always seemed like the good guys to me.

In the election of 1972, Berrios crisscrossed the island. This was long before a campaign's effectiveness was judged by how much advertising you were putting up in every television market or by the bottom line on your campaign finance filing. You judged your campaign and your momentum by something much more personal and real. How many people showed up to hear Berrios speak? How enthusiastic were they? How moved were they by what he had to say? What did he make you feel, really *feel*, when you listened to him?

When I listened to Rubén Berríos, I felt Puerto Rico was on the verge of something historic. People I had never seen before poured into San Sebastián to hear him speak. In our town square, I would stand in crowds of flag-waving Puerto Ricans who were just as enthralled and moved by Berrios's speeches as I was. I'd stand shoulder to shoulder with men and women, young and old, who shouted in agreement every time Berrios said that only Puerto Ricans should decide our future.

The first time I heard him in San Sebastián, I was enthralled. I couldn't imagine how any Puerto Rican could vote against him. The second time he came to town, Luis Águila and I commandeered his dad's car and we followed Berrios all day. He delivered his speech in San Sebastián, firing up the crowd. When he finished, Luis and I jumped in the car and followed him to Isabela, flying along the highway to keep up, like Deadheads who didn't want to miss one note from Jerry Garcia. We saw him three times in one day, listening to the same basic speech but cheering just as loudly every time.

I would watch Berrios on the stage, smiling and calm one moment, speaking like a historian. The next moment, he would be excited and angry, wave his arms, hit the podium, and demand that you fight alongside him for change. I thought, I've found my home. Nobody cheering along with me in this crowd questions whether I'm Puerto Rican enough. I knew, listening to Berrios, that I was plenty Puerto Rican. Not just in the way that all of us with funny names and brown skin had to stand up for one another against racist cops or teachers who assumed we were gangbangers or stupid. Being Puertorriqueño wasn't just a defense mechanism against the bigotry and low expectations of a mostly white power structure. It was something to celebrate, to be proud of because we were a special people who came from a place like nowhere else on earth. The Independence Party and Rubén Berríos were teaching me what it really meant to have Puerto Rico in my heart. It wasn't just that we hung out together and ate the same food and stood together when the cops cruised slowly down Halsted and gave us dirty looks.

Having Puerto Rico in your heart was to know that regardless of whether you lived in San Sebastián or Lincoln Park or the Bronx, you had an unbreakable connection to a beautiful tropical island, one hundred miles long and thirty-five miles wide, in the Caribbean. Having Puerto Rico in your heart was to know that we had the ability to govern ourselves—just as the rebels at Lares who risked their lives believed. It was to know and understand the sacrifices and history of your Puerto Rican ancestors, Segundo Ruiz Belvis, Don Pedro Albizu Campos, Ramón Emeterio Betances, and so many others. It was to believe that Puerto Ricans did not need to be ruled like children, overseen by distant, faceless bureaucrats in Madrid or Washington, DC.

It was also believing that our island was a bountiful place of riches. We had sugar and coffee to harvest, fish to eat and export, beaches and rain forests to attract tourists and support our economy. It was knowing that our island was filled with four million people, smart and articulate, capable of building businesses and creating art and harvesting crops. We had resources to consume and sell, arts and culture to celebrate and enjoy, people who could lead and inspire us. My dad was right about the Independentistas. They were troublemakers. They looked at Puerto Rico's fundamental political relationship with the United States—a relationship that had defined Puerto Rico since the turn of the century—and said, "Why?" Why do we need to be governed by anyone? We have all we need right here. We're Puerto Ricans. We can take care of ourselves.

To me, it was an incredibly inspiring message. Puerto Ricans didn't stick together just to get by in a tough world run by people who weren't the same skin color as us. We could join together and excel. We didn't have to settle; we could thrive. We could be self-sufficient. We could be independent.

But the ideal of independence was much more than political to me. It was personal. Leaders and activists in the independence movement took time with me, listened to me, and taught me about our history. I sat down and shared meals with doctors and lawyers and engineers. People who were respected in San Sebastián. These were not the radicals my dad described to me, these were people who cared for sick people and owned businesses. They were thoughtful and committed and organized.

One of San Sebastián's dentists was a strong supporter of independence. Like many of the older leaders and activists, he was intrigued by me. A kid from Chicago, learning Spanish, having a tough time in San Sebastián. The kind of kid who might just pick all the green coffee beans if you let him loose on a farm. Yet I was devouring Puerto Rican history and memorizing the Independence Party platform. I always wanted to learn more. They gave me extra attention and worked to make me feel welcome.

After meetings, the young leaders would pull me aside and tell me a more personal version of what I was reading in the independence literature.

"You're Puerto Rican. You've always been Puerto Rican. Don't let anyone tell you different. Nobody can take that away from you." To be as self-reliant as supporters of independence thought Puerto Rico should be, our little island couldn't afford to shun even one Puerto Rican. When a respected dentist, or doctor, or lawyer said "You're Puerto Rican" to me, what I thought was—Finally! Here I am, surrounded by all these smart people and they think I'm plenty Puerto Rican. They made it clear: Wherever you go and whatever you do, you are one of us. You aren't an outsider—you are an exile returning home. Your Spanish can be excellent or terrible. You can be rich or poor. You can live in Lincoln Park or San Sebastián. But you don't ever have to doubt that you are Puerto Rican. In a poem, Juan Antonio Corretjer wrote, "I'd be Puerto Rican even if I was born on the moon." That's what I wanted to hear.

I had found a home in San Sebastián. And it taught me, for the first time, to think about politics as something exciting and engaging and fun. A topic you could care about, argue about, and connect to your life. I threw myself into independence politics like a drowning man learning to swim. I studied and memorized the party platform late into the night. I attended every meeting, at the high school and with the older leaders in town. I volunteered for everything I could volunteer for.

I even took one of the assignments nobody else wanted. Before long, I was standing on the plaza selling the Independence Party newspaper, *La Hora*. There was no more public way to declare your allegiance to the Partido Independentista Puertorriqueño (the PIP) than to sell *La Hora* in the plaza. Everyone came to the plaza. Selling *La Hora* was like putting your face on an independence billboard. But I was proud to be seen standing at the gateway of the plaza, holding my coffee can with a slot for money cut in the top and my stack of newspapers, shouting to passersby that they could receive the news— the real news—for only a quarter.

With every classmate who looked surprised to see the Chicago kid selling the "radical" newspaper, with every customer at the restaurant who came in and asked why I was for independence, my pride in overcoming loneliness and isolation grew. As I spread the gospel of independence, I wanted to look at my classmates and say, "Who's the gringo—the Americanito—now?" It wasn't me. Not the Independentista, the kid selling newspapers in the plaza.

With every lecture I heard, with every newspaper I sold, I was ready for more. I was insatiable, a devourer of Puerto Rican history and polemics on our future. Fortunately for me, the election was coming up. And I was on the front lines, fighting for our candidates. Rubén Berríos was running for the Puerto Rican Senate, and another man, just as inspiring—Noel Colón Martínez—was running for governor. I was ready.

WITH THE ELECTION of 1972, I had my chance to prove that I wasn't just a kid with a passing interest in Puerto Rican independence.

The Twenty-Sixth Amendment to the US Constitution lowered the voting age from twenty-one to eighteen. It passed in 1971, and in Puerto Rico, the PIP had high hopes that those Puerto Rican young people would turn out and give us unprecedented success at the ballot box.

With every rally for Rubén Berríos and Noel Colón Martínez, it felt like the election was going our way. My generation loved our independence leaders. Our party was on the move. We were united. We were excited.

I prepared for Election Day more like it was my wedding day. My job was to be an Independence Party poll watcher in my polling place.

I wanted to make the party proud. I wanted to find every independence vote I could, and be an honest and upstanding supervisor at my neighborhood polling place. I knew my job. Get my neighbors to vote for independence. And make sure the Statehooders and Populares didn't steal any votes from us.

I quickly learned that the Statehooder and commonwealth poll watchers were happy to turn over all of the main responsibilities in the polling place to me and my friend Jose, the other independence stalwart and my partner for Election Day. The Statehooders and Populares didn't trust each other, so they gave the key to the ballot box to me, the eighteen-year-old who had never been inside a polling station in his life. They might have thought that Independentistas were crazy, but they also thought we were honest.

The party had conducted meticulous training for poll watching. We learned how to handle the ballots, making sure the voter inserted the ballot straight into the ballot box and that none of the poll watchers tampered with any votes. Everything was a simple paper ballot back then, and you marked your vote by hand. We were told to guard the key to the ballot box like it was a matter of national security. I had studied the election handbook like a bible. I was ready.

I needed to be, because in Puerto Rico in 1972, everyone voted. I never met a person who said they didn't vote. No liquor sales were allowed on Election Day. Which meant the night before the election was a celebration, as everyone loaded up on supplies to make it through the dry Tuesday. In 1972, it was impossible to imagine someone saying that they weren't going to vote. It wasn't even practical. What would you do on Election Day? Everyone else was voting and campaigning and dragging their friends out to vote and bragging that they were going to win or taunting you for voting for the wrong party. Nobody was just sitting around playing dominoes. It would be embarrassing to hang out and wash your car while everyone was parading around town shouting at one another about the election.

Our polling place was located in my high school. We didn't even need the whole day. Our voters knew the polling place would open at one p.m. That was the time to vote. Everyone showed up outside and lined up. At one o'clock, I opened the door, and my neighbors filed in, some of them wondering who the new, skinny guy in charge was. And why he looked like he's fifteen years old? At about one thirty, we closed the door. There was no reason to keep it open. Everyone was there.

It didn't take long to mark your paper ballot with your pencil, because virtually everyone voted a straight party ballot. You made an *x* by the *pava*, the hat of the Puerto Rican sugarcane worker and the symbol of the Popular Democratic Party. It was printed right on the ballot. You either voted for the *pava* or the *palma*—the palm tree that was the symbol of the Statehooders. My party had a Puerto Rican flag. It seems like a quaint, admirable time now. Virtually everyone in your neighborhood gathered at one place, at the same time, to make a simple *x* on a ballot. For those couple of hours on our national election holiday, you felt as though your entire community, without exception, was coming together to make an important decision.

After everyone had voted and left, we locked the door. We didn't have to worry about stragglers. There weren't any. They trusted me to unlock the box and go through the ballots. I took out the stack of ballots and placed them on the table. The Populare and statehood poll watchers were ready. I would pick up a paper ballot, look at it, and announce the result. I would then pass it to the other poll watchers, who would verify it and keep track of the tally.

One after another, I carefully looked at the ballots, proud to be at the heart of the electoral process. After about thirty ballots, I wondered where all of the cheering Independentistas I had stood next to in the plaza at all of those rallies had gone. I called out the results, one ballot after another. Statehood, popular, popular, statehood. Nothing for independence. Not one. The Populares were winning. The island had elected its first statehood governor four years before, and my neighbors seemed ready to kick him out. But my team was getting shut out entirely.

I was astonished. The rallies had been filled with exuberant young Puerto Ricans committed to self-governance and living a future without the United States looking over our shoulder. We all felt confident that the lowered voting age would work in our favor. The words of

Rubén Berríos had thundered through the crowd and filled us with visions of a strong, independent Puerto Rico. Where were my allies?

And still, I called out statehood and popular, statehood and popular. This was a time before opinion polls came out every day predicting what would happen. With every ballot I called out, I was more astounded. The other poll watchers were completely unsurprised. They saw it election after election: another young and idealistic Independentista realizing, ballot by ballot, the reality that few of his brethren shared his vision for Puerto Rico.

Finally, I made it to the bottom of the pile. The poll watchers voted first, so I knew we were getting to our ballots. I hadn't called out one independence vote yet, and I knew how I had marked my ballot. Mine was coming up. I picked it up and shouted, "*Un voto por la independencia!*" The others laughed and clapped and cheered. It was funny to them. I turned to Jose and said, "Your vote is next."

I picked up his ballot, ready to proclaim another independence vote. I looked, and looked again, and then I looked directly at Jose, who did not look back at me. "*Un voto mixto,*" I said. One mixed vote: independence for local offices, popular for governor. He voted for Rubén Berríos, against Noel Colón Martínez. That ballot was our only mixed vote of the day, and it came from the other independence poll watcher. The other poll watchers thought this was the highlight of the day. The Independentistas have two party functionaries in the polling place and they can't even get two votes for governor.

I kept staring at Jose. This was humiliating to me. I wasn't laughing, I was irate. "You're a traitor. This will not go unrecorded. You have decided to ruin your reputation, and I am going to make sure it stays ruined. The party will know about this betrayal!" I shouted, the other poll watchers still laughing.

"I've picked coffee and sold newspapers and gone to meetings," I went on. "I ignored my dad's advice. I went to the rallies and campaigned. You have sold us out."

I screamed at him because I was mad, and I kept screaming because I wanted everyone to know that I had voted straight party. I didn't want anyone wondering if I was the one who had flipped that day. I'm sure it never occurred to Jose that his mixed ballot would stand out like that. I'm sure throughout the entire count he was waiting for the cover of another independence ballot that never came. It was down to the end, and it was just the two of us, and our beleaguered candidate for governor couldn't carry both of our votes.

At the end of the day, my job was to take my results to the party headquarters. I ran out of the polling place to the plaza where our office was. My dentist friend was gathering results. I showed him what happened. I detailed the betrayal of Rubén Berríos and Noel Colón Martínez.

"Can you believe he did this?" I asked, still outraged at this defection from within our party ranks.

He gave me the calm look of a lifelong Independentista.

"Luis," he said, giving me paternal advice, "he was not the only one."

I didn't stick around party headquarters that night. I couldn't bear the defeat. My dad was watching the results on TV. When I came home, he didn't congratulate me on my first vote, or on my political activism. Knowing the Independence Party was getting crushed, he said, "I guess all of those thousands of people who turned out for the rallies didn't end up voting for your candidate. I told you the PIP wasn't very good at showing up for elections."

I sat down next to him.

"I showed up," I told him. "I showed up and voted straight PIP."

He laughed. "I'm sure you did. I have no doubt that you did."

Most of the people who were beside me at the rallies did go to the polls and vote. Unfortunately for the PIP, in 1972, they did what fervent supporters of independence have done election after election—what they still do today. They scream loudly for their candidates at the rallies, they are brought nearly to tears by the patriotic words extolling a free and independent Puerto Rico, they campaign sincerely and diligently for their PIP candidates, and then they go into the polling place and worry that a vote for the PIP candidate for governor is a vote that makes it a little more likely that the Statehooders win. I believe a vastly larger number of Puerto Ricans than those who vote for independence are genuine supporters of the idea. But they are also generally appalled at the idea of statehood for Puerto Rico. At the polling place they bite their tongues and shake their heads and vote for the moderate, acceptable, and many times perfectly admirable popular candidate, the party of electricity. We might sing about it in our songs and wave our flag with pride, but in the end, there are only a few willing to risk it all and cast that ballot.

But when I voted independence that day, I thought I was voting for more than a political party. I was standing with my friends. With Luis and the doctors and lawyers, with all of the leaders in San Sebastián who had let me into their club, made me their friend, taught me about history, and never, ever questioned whether I was Puerto Rican enough for them.

WHILE I WAS BUSY learning about independence for Puerto Rico, things were changing at home.

Before the start of my second school year, I woke up one day to start peeling potatoes and mopping the floors. My dad was already up, but he wasn't going through his usual routine in the restaurant. I looked at my mom, who was standing near the counter, looking lost. She pointed to the front door.

There was a new sign on the door. I thought maybe my dad had finally given the restaurant a name.

I opened the door and looked. The sign was simple, homemade, one big word written in pen.

CLOSED.

My dad looked at me and said, "We need to start packing things away and deciding what we want to keep and what we want to take. We're closed."

His determination made clear he didn't mean closed for the day, or week, or for remodeling. He was done.

My first thought was a teenage thought: I won't have to get up so early every day. My second thought was a little more mature. How are we were going to support ourselves?

My dad hadn't said a word to me. From the look on my mom's face that morning, I wasn't sure he had said anything to her. More than a year of cooking and cleaning and arguing with customers and it was over without any warning, no discussion. The regular customers showed up for lunch. We looked at them through the windows and doors as we cleaned and sorted and boxed things. My dad waved them away. They were amazed. People who just the day before had complained about paying because their chicken was too salty couldn't believe we were gone. They looked confused. Where would they eat?

My dad frequently gave credit to customers. Many of them still owed him money. Over the next couple of weeks, many people came by to settle their accounts. My dad wouldn't take their money. It was an act of anger as much as generosity. My mom thought it was the constant complaining and negotiating and bargaining about paying for the food that eventually made my dad give up. Now that he was done with the restaurant business, he didn't want their money. He wanted them to go away.

"He couldn't take it anymore," my mom said. "He built this beautiful restaurant, and nobody appreciated it."

Now that it was almost gone, it did seem beautiful to me. We kept it spotless. He'd bought expensive, brand-new equipment. The kitchen was open to the restaurant and always shined. He arranged the bottles of liquor carefully behind the bar. The bar gleamed. My dad was a perfectionist. He wanted to do things right. But people argued over a nickel or a dime.

I could see the stress my dad was under. For him, it was the same thing every day. The complaining customers during the day, playing dominoes until late at night, trying to coax another beer out of the guys at the table. And nothing seemed to change—our business wouldn't grow. We would see the same workers in the morning picking up a quick breakfast before going to the factory, the same ladies every day for lunch, the same guys for beer and dominoes at night. After a year, it was clear what we were—an inexpensive lunch place for factory workers.

I never once looked at a ledger book or heard my dad talk in any detail about the financial side of the business. Delivery guys came and went, my dad paid them, he cooked, we cleaned, and we ate every meal in the kitchen of the restaurant. But my dad's demeanor told me more than any balance sheet. He was worried. He didn't come home until late at night, after the last domino was laid and the last Lowenbrau served. He was tired and more short-tempered than he had been in Chicago. In San Sebastián, it seemed my parents had switched places and personalities. My mom might not have liked the restaurant hours, but she was happy to be back home. My dad lost his confidence, his strong sense of his place in the world.

Across town, meanwhile, Uncle Keko still had people waiting in line for their paper cups of *cuchifritos* at Cuchilandia. My uncle's fried-pig-parts business was booming, and he never had to buy a rotisserie or new refrigerators or ovens. He had his cauldron, his big paddle, and a few giant knives and he was in business. My dad called Cuchilandia "*la mina.*" The mine. A source of endless money.

My dad also saw the food trucks down by the factory every day, selling paper plates of rice and beans and sandwiches out of the back of their panel vans. Their overhead was the cost of food and gas. No rent check to Pedro to keep his daughters shopping, no bills to repair the stove.

My dad was trying to do more; not just serve *cuchifritos*, not serve people from the back of a truck. I didn't understand it at the time, but my dad really did want our modest little café to be special. But I'm not sure he knew how to make a restaurant work up in the hills in a little town in Puerto Rico. He did his best, and it was hurting him to fail.

In Chicago, he had been a cabdriver, and good at it. We didn't have a lot, but we did just fine. Then he was a building manager, a trusted man who needed to install a phone so the property owner could reach him. He managed his buildings and managed his time, knowing when things were done and he could sit and read the paper or take his son to a baseball game.

In Puerto Rico, he was distracted and grumpy. As the owner of a humble and apparently unsuccessful restaurant, he didn't have time for baseball or the evening news. I watched my dad sweat and work and worry and wondered again why in the world we had decided to move thousands of miles to run a little restaurant in the middle of a tropical island. On the days I felt most sorry for myself, I would think that it served him right. He was getting just what he deserved for his ridiculous plan to abandon Chicago.

On better days, I wanted things to turn around, wanted him to succeed. I looked at my dad, a proud man battling to run his own business and take care of his family. He wasn't happy, and I felt bad for him—I felt bad for us. I missed the dad I had known before San Sebastián, the man I grew up with in Chicago. I wanted to sit next to him at Wrigley Field and cheer for Clemente again.

A few months after he scrawled "closed" on that piece of paper and put it up on the door, it was done. He tried to sell the whole business with all of the equipment. Nobody was interested. He ended up selling most of the food and drinks to Pedro. No more chicken, no more Fanta. There was no eBay or Craigslist for the equipment, so he sold it cheap to whomever he could. Not many people in San Sebastián were looking for commercial refrigerators. We moved out of Pedro's apartment. My mom and dad started looking for jobs. Our brief reign as small business owners was over.

Today, about all that's left of my dad's experiment as a restaurateur are the recipes in our family kitchen. I never knew it until he decided to open a café in the hills of Puerto Rico, but my dad was a great cook. The food that we ate in our restaurant kitchen was delicious. I do my best today, without the help of his giant pot for cooking rice, or his rotisserie, to duplicate it.

One of his specialties was *bistek encebollado*. Beef with onions. I take flank or cube steak, just like he did, and cut it up. I rub garlic into the beef and cover it in salt and pepper. I layer the beef with lots of onions. Then I make a simple mixture of oil and vinegar and pour it all over the beef and onions and let it marinate. "You have to let the oil, vinegar, and garlic cook it for you," my dad would say, standing at the counter, flipping the layers. He was right. You turn it on the second day; you eat it on the third. It tastes great. My kids go crazy for it and ask me to make it all the time.

When they eat *bistek encebollado*, they regularly say, "Dad, you should open a restaurant." And I think to myself, We already tried that.

CHAPTER EIGHT

Puerto Rican Lucky Numbers

G OING TO the University of Puerto Rico a year early felt like an escape. My parents had brought me to Puerto Rico. I had scrubbed floors and washed dishes, learned Spanish, and adjusted to a tropical island. Now I was taking charge of my life. I was getting a twelve-month head start on my future.

Being on my own didn't mean having more money. The tuition was inexpensive, but you still had to eat. UPR didn't have many dorms then, so I found the cheapest rooming house I could. There were five of us in one bedroom of a three-room apartment. Two bunk beds and a single bed covered almost every inch of the floor. We were supervised by a grumpy woman who made us our breakfast and dinner. We were on our own for lunch, which meant I often didn't eat.

I realized quickly that UPR emptied out on the weekends. Most people ran out of money and wanted to go home and get fed by their parents. I didn't have a car. Luis Águila was my ride, but he arranged his classes so he could take off early on Friday to see his girlfriend back in San Sebastián. When I couldn't sneak out of class to ride with Luis, I was on my own. I became an expert at public transportation and hitchhiking. In the plaza in Río Piedras, I could get a public car—a large van that sat and idled until it filled up with people trying to get out of San Juan. It would take me as far as Bayamón. From there, my thumb was the only route back to San Sebastián. I always carried my red UPR duffel bag with me, an advertisement to passing drivers that I was a student and not a potential killer. I never had trouble getting home.

And I didn't have trouble keeping up in school. By the time I made it to UPR, my Spanish hardly attracted a second look. Excelling in English still gave me an advantage. I made it through the academics of my first year easily. I hitchhiked back to San Sebastián practically every weekend. Like everyone in college, I tried to decide where I was really headed, what I really wanted to do. And the truth is that I wasn't quite sure.

A lot of my attention was still focused on San Sebastián. I was still close to my friends in the independence movement. I was still putting up posters and selling *La Hora* on the weekend, learning from older leaders. But I was ready for something different. I was restless. It had been more than two years since my dad loaded us in the Impala and drove us away from everything we knew. I always thought I would return to the United States as soon as possible. But I wasn't sure where home was anymore.

AT THE END of my sophomore year at UPR, a notice went up on the bulletin board in the dormitory for a college exchange program to promote English proficiency. UPR was partnering with the State University of New York. If you were accepted, you could end up anywhere in their system, maybe Syracuse, maybe Binghamton.

My Independentista friends laughed at having an "exchange" program with an American school. The State University of New York wasn't having an exchange program with kids in Wisconsin, or Idaho. These uniquely Puerto Rican contradictions happened all the time. They still do. Call an airline to book a flight to Puerto Rico, and many will put you through to their international desk. You'll pay international rates to ship a package by UPS or FedEx to Puerto Rico. Every four years, we cheer enthusiastically for the Puerto Rican Olympic team. I've never noticed any bursts of enthusiasm for the Tennessee Olympic team.

But after I laughed at the colonial condescension, I considered it. I wondered how my experience would compare to a university in New York. It wasn't Chicago, but it was the States. If you were accepted, the program was all-expenses-paid. I wouldn't have to ask my parents for a nickel.

I filled out the application, which asked questions they could have asked a kid from Nicaragua or Spain. The questions were written by some academic diversity expert with the gallant goal of picking some brown-skinned, Third World child of the sugarcane fields and granting him the opportunity to see the real beauty that is America. I realized that by my second year of college, I had undergone a transformation. I wasn't only responding to the application like a transplanted Chicagoan bemused by the tone but just pleased for the chance to get to a school in America. I read the application like a Puerto Rican, offended that some guy in an office somewhere in New York thought we all needed to be uplifted by the professors in America.

Now I wanted to get back to the States and do well for my island, my people—to show everyone that Puerto Ricans weren't second-class citizens. Not long after I sent away my application, I received a thick envelope back from the University of New York at Albany. The next fall, I would have my chance to show upstate New York just what a Puerto Rican kid could do.

I STEPPED OFF of my shuttle bus from LaGuardia, grabbed my one suitcase, and headed to my dorm—the international dorm, of course— and found my room. When I found it, I was confused. Girls were all around—up and down the hallways, some of them with suitcases. Some were unpacking their belongings in rooms right down the hall from me.

Back at UPR, the traditional structure of Puerto Rican society endured. The girls were stored safely in their own dorms as if in a vault. The dorms were locked promptly at ten p.m. during the week; on Fridays and Saturdays they stayed open until the daring hour of eleven p.m. My sophomore year, I'd moved from my rooming house into the dorms, but spent a lot of time at the apartment of a friend. I managed to get in trouble. I was tutoring—actually, honestly tutoring—a girl I knew in the apartment between classes during the day. My friend found me later in the day and hit me in the back of the head.

"Why did you do that?" I asked him.

"Because our landlord is threatening to kick us out. He said you had a pretty girl in the apartment all afternoon. You know you can't bring girls back to the apartment."

"We didn't do anything—we were studying," I protested.

My roommate laughed. "Well, that's doubly stupid. I should have hit you harder."

On the island, the rules still reflected the belief that nothing but sin was produced by unmarried males and females being together without supervision. There were no exceptions.

At Albany, girls were everywhere, allowed to run free and go wherever they wanted. It was shocking and liberating. We were all trying to grow up, figure out who we were and what we wanted to do. I loved the freedom, and our dorm was a laboratory of cultures and people. Of course, all the Puerto Ricans in the exchange program chose to live in the international dorm, but that wasn't surprising to me. I grew up in America, and then I moved to Puerto Rico. I knew the difference. The international dorm was exactly the place for us.

I had never really been anywhere except where my parents took me. Now I was meeting Jamaicans with Bob Marley posters on their walls, and kids from Spain. I was fascinated by three Israeli guys who were eager to make friends because they wanted to tell you all about their country.

I had never met an Israeli. I never really knew anyone Jewish. The guys were my age but so serious that they seemed much older. They had a reverence for Israel and spoke of it with pride, acting like ambassadors at every opportunity. They described what it was like to be on a kibbutz and talked about the importance of agriculture. They talked in detail about industry and factories and building an economy that could sustain their people. They were eager to make you understand the constant threats to their security, about what it was like to be surrounded by hostile neighbors. The Puerto Rican independence movement was always critical of Israel because they didn't support the creation of an independent Palestinian state. Israel never made any friends with independence leaders because they stood with the U.S. against anti-colonialism efforts at the U.N. Meeting new people was exposing me to whole new points of view.

Halfway through the year, their commitment became much more than talk when they left to go defend Israel in the 1973 war. They were gone about six weeks, and then, all of a sudden, there they were, back in the cafeteria, eating lunch again. Some kids go on spring break, they went home and fought in a war and saved their country. They came back with a golden tan like they had been cutting sugarcane. They never once complained.

The more I listened to them talk about Israel, the more familiar it felt. Their passion for their nation made a tremendous impression on me, and not only because they were young guys who cared about something much greater than the next exam or the next party. Their country was part of them, and they would do anything for it—even leave school and go risk their lives. They loved their home and lived the self-reliance that my independence friends and mentors preached for Puerto Rico.

My natural thought was that if Israel can do it, why can't Puerto Rico? My parents and so many people on the island, even though they felt a deep patriotism for Puerto Rico, had lived with the idea of being Americans—or almost Americans—for so long that the idea of being our own nation simply seemed like a child's fantasy. But why? Puerto Rico had as many or more natural resources than Israel. We had beautiful tourist attractions that could anchor our economy. We had capable and industrious people. Wasn't a kibbutz the logical extension of my agricultural day on the farm picking coffee?

Israel survived and thrived despite the fact that it was covered in desert and surrounded by enemies. Puerto Rico had the sea and beaches and rain forests. The Dominican Republic and Haiti weren't exactly aiming missiles at us. Even if we became independent, the United States wouldn't be our enemy.

For the moment I set aside any concerns my independence background gave me about colonialism. I admired the pride and love my new friends had for their home. I worried about them when they left for the war. And I was never more convinced that carving out our own future, as our own nation, was the right path for Puerto Rico.

IN THE SUMMER, I took the subway from my aunt's apartment in the Bronx all the way down to Wall Street, from the apartments at the top to the skyscrapers at the bottom of Manhattan—a block-by-block pilgrimage from a neighborhood where Puerto Ricans and blacks crammed as many people as possible into crowded bedrooms and hung out on their stoops, all the way to the center of the financial world. I even got a job at a bank. But I wasn't rubbing shoulders with financial titans. I wasn't even counting money or taking deposits. I was giving away toasters.

I needed to make some money for college. I needed to feed myself at Albany. My aunt was happy to let me stay with her during that first summer. I found a temp agency that would guarantee me work for three months.

I couldn't believe my good luck when they started me at the bank. I had never had such an easy job. I learned what "bankers' hours" meant. I didn't have to get to work until nine and nobody even considered staying past five. They gave me my own table in the corner. It was quiet and air-conditioned. I was just the giveaway guy, but you had to start somewhere.

I was smiling and telling Mrs. Smith how happy we were that she had opened her account with us. I would give her a shiny new toaster and make her day. I thought they must have been kidding me. I was getting the same amount of money for sitting around making people happy that I had gotten for bussing tables at the Golden Nugget or chopping vegetables at Carson's.

I didn't want to lose the job. I was so polite and friendly that people probably thought it was chemically induced. I studied the rules. I knew exactly what it took to get a free toaster. I could imagine a career inside of a bank.

Then one day a woman came over to my table with her receipt for opening a new account. You had to open an account with $500 to get one of my toasters. I greeted her enthusiastically: "Welcome, and thank you for opening an account with us. We're thrilled to have you as a new customer."

She wasn't impressed with my joyous greeting. And she wanted two toasters, because she had opened her account with $1,000.

My decision was easy. Just follow the rules. It didn't matter how big your account was. For one new account, you got one new toaster.

"I'm so sorry, ma'am, but we can only give one toaster per account." I kept smiling.

She said she opened it with double the amount. She wanted two toasters.

I was starting to sweat. I was just a 110-pound kid happy to have a temp job in a nice, cool office. I liked my bankers' hours. I wasn't giving her an extra toaster. But I thought maybe I could give her some inside information.

"Ma'am, maybe if you opened two accounts of $500 each, I could give you two toasters."

She looked at me like I was crazy, like I didn't understand a thing about how toaster giveaways worked. But I wasn't going to budge. They weren't my toasters to hand out like lollipops. She marched away. In about sixty seconds, she came back with the manager. The manager had never spoken to me before. It didn't look like he was going to congratulate me for following the rules.

"Young man, could you give this very nice lady two toasters, please?"

And I did. No problem. I gave the demanding lady a smile like I was thrilled to do it. I wondered to myself just how much toast a person could eat. If she had put five grand in her account, would she have expected me to give her ten toasters? She could open up a toast restaurant.

When our wealthy toaster collector was gone, the manager came back. He was nice to me. He said he understood I was just trying to follow the rules. And he told me to make sure every customer left happy.

That was fine with me. I wasn't paying for the toasters. If I could have foreseen my future, I would have given her the two toasters but let her know that in thirty years when I was a subcommittee chairman on the House Financial Services Committee, I would be regulating the industry to make clear that you only get one toaster for one account.

I SHOWED UP at the agency the morning of the third week ready to give away a toaster for every five hundred bucks' worth of deposits. Instead, the temp guys told me to come back at five thirty and wear comfortable clothes. That didn't sound like an office job to me. But I was wrong. It was an office job. Cleaning them.

On week three, I went to work as a janitor. The week before, I had been enjoying a long lunch break. Now I was cleaning urinals. I filled in for old Polish ladies at a huge high-rise building that was mostly investment firms and brokers. I would step in whenever one of the regular janitors was sick, or managed to scrape together a vacation day or two.

It was solitary work. It was quiet by five thirty. Whether I was on the fifth or the fiftieth floor, it all looked the same. Rows and rows of cubicles and desks on the inside, bigger offices along the walls. I would sometimes get waved away by somebody working late, usually a young guy who looked like he might have screwed something up during the day and was frantically trying to fix it. I liked getting shooed away. That was one fewer desk out of a hundred that I had to clean. I moved deliberately from office to office, getting my routine down. I would wipe down the desk—circular motions starting from the middle—and empty lots of ashtrays. Empty every wastebasket and vacuum the floors. I would leave the bathrooms and the nastiest work, cleaning all the toilets and urinals, until last.

After punching in, the only words I would hear in the next eight hours were the unlucky stragglers grumbling that I should come back later. By seven or eight p.m., there was never anyone around. I might as well have been Jack Nicholson wandering through the hotel in *The Shining*. And the routine never varied. Sometimes the toilets were worse than at others; once or twice an office party that the workers left for me to clean up. But mostly it was just work. Sweep, mop, scrub, empty.

I didn't finish until one thirty in the morning. I felt like my own boss, running my little cleaning and sweeping business. There were no Latinos working full-time as janitors in that building. Latino immigrants' turn at cleaning things for wealthy people was just starting. The previous generation of Eastern European immigrants was still holding a lot of brooms. I only saw other janitors at the beginning of the shift, and most of the women didn't speak much English. I was on my own. I just worked my way through, office to office, desk to desk. My cart was my rolling office. I had a large trash can hooked into the middle, my vacuum and mop hooked on the front. All of my cleaning supplies conveniently right in front of me: cheap industrial cleaner, rags, glass cleaner, toilet brush.

I think about that summer when my colleagues or today's Fox pundits talk about all the jobs immigrants are taking away from native-born Americans. Back then, it was just me and a bunch of little old Polish ladies. There was nobody on a waiting list for bathroom duty at the temp agency. They were thrilled to have me. I wasn't cutting to the front of a long line of hopeful urinal cleaners. And I haven't seen any evidence since then that times have changed.

I knew—or hoped—my turn with the toilet brush was temporary. I was cleaning urinals to raise money for school, trying to make sure I wouldn't miss any meals. My older coworkers, however, had done it for years. Thousands—probably tens of thousands—of dirty toilets, desks, and ashtrays. They did it for three or four bucks an hour. Yet they showed up day after day, and every morning the brokers came back to clean offices. Those Polish ladies were cleaning toilets because they cared about something much larger than paying for a hot meal, or maybe a plane ticket home for Christmas. They were doing it for their families. And I'm sure that many of those Polish cleaning ladies eventually landed a son or daughter in an office just like the ones they were cleaning. And just like so many immigrants now—at the end of a long day of scrubbing and mopping—that was the only payment they really wanted.

MY EXCHANGE PROGRAM at Albany was only a year. My family assumed I'd be heading back to Puerto Rico. UPR expected me back. The college sent me a plane ticket back to San Juan.

But I wasn't sure. I missed Tino and Luis, missed the independence politics of San Sebastián. But were those hills, and the dorms at UPR, really home?

I did know that things had grown tense in the Gutiérrez household. After we closed the restaurant, my dad found a job selling cars in Mayaguez. His career as an Opel salesman didn't last long. You had to sell plenty of Opels to make money. My dad was a quiet person, not a gregarious salesman. It was hard to imagine him smooth-talking the customers. It was easy to imagine him telling somebody that saving their money was a better idea than buying a new car. My mom started working at the Hanes underwear plant. She would bring home the irregulars and send them off to me. I was Irregular Louie, the underwear king. I could have given Hanes rejects away to my friends. While my mom worked, my dad searched for his next job.

To my sister's bewilderment, he found it in a program sponsored by the Veterans' Administration. The VA was encouraging veterans to go back to school. They were mostly interested in getting people to college, but they would also help you to finish high school. My dad studied the details of the program. He called the VA and asked some questions. He determined, to his surprise, that his government was offering to pay him to get his high school degree.

My dad had never made it past the eighth grade. School was a luxury. He needed to make money and found his first job as a projectionist. Now the VA was offering him both: an education and some cash. The catch was that it wasn't a GED or correspondence program. To participate, you needed to attend an actual high school. For the Gutiérrez family, that meant Manuel Méndez Liciaga—the same high school as my sister.

High school had been rough for me. But I'm not sure that Señor

Hernández's assault on my Spanish was as rough as Ada being a high school senior alongside my dad. He walked the halls just like any other student. She saw him at lunch and throughout the day. Her friends looked at her like her family was crazy and asked why her father was in algebra class with them. He trailed along behind Ada so he didn't get lost in the building. He wasn't embarrassed. To get his money, he had to go to Ada's school. What was the big deal? He was decades beyond caring what high school kids, including his daughter, thought of him.

My dad ended up liking the classes more than the money. When I went home for Christmas break from Albany during Ada's father-daughter senior year, my dad pulled out his well-read copy of Cervantes to discuss *Don Quixote* with me. I had never seen my dad read a book. He was fascinated by civics and political science. He was even more eager to discuss why he was right to support the commonwealth and I was wrong to support independence. He wanted to discuss Plato and Socrates. My sister rolled her eyes at me and told me she was glad he had someone else to harass about his newfound academic interest. I asked Ada if Mom had agreed to go to the prom with him. Ada was not amused.

My dad wasn't the only one. There were a few other veterans wandering around the high school—guys my dad's age, between jobs or thrilled by the idea of a few bucks from the government. I was happy my dad was getting his diploma, but I also thought about how much his life had changed since Chicago. For our *Don Quixote* discussions, I was tempted to ask him what parallels he saw between windmills and a small café buried in the hills of Puerto Rico. I didn't. I headed back to Albany to decide what I would do next.

At the end of the year, the envelope with my plane ticket back to San Juan sat on my dresser. I avoided thinking about it. My parents wondered when I was coming back for good. Even though I wasn't sure where I wanted to go, I felt like I had options. One advantage of having no money is that you can have no money anywhere. After a couple of days of plotting my future, I headed to the airline ticket office.

I waited in line and told the impatient guy working that day that I wanted to cash in my ticket. He looked at it, looked at the rule book, and told me I hadn't bought it, so I couldn't get the money for it. I retreated outside. I sat on the curb. I thought about my choices. I went back in and stood in the line for another ticket agent. When I made it to the front of his line, I had a different approach.

"I've changed my travel plans," I said. "Can I change this ticket to Chicago?"

He was friendlier. He said that I could. I was thrilled. I booked a flight for the next day to Chicago. I even got some money back. The flight to Chicago was cheaper than the one to San Juan.

I went home and packed. I could still fit all of my belongings into one suitcase. I had one aunt left in Chicago. I called her. My aunt Nilda agreed to let me stay with her. I flew out the next day and took the bus and train in from O'Hare. She didn't have to give me directions, because Aunt Nilda had moved into our old apartment on Willow Street. Her husband, my uncle Joe, had my dad's old job managing the building. After years of missing Chicago, I was moving back home, to the very place where I had grown up, where I stored my clothes in two drawers, where everything seemed so easy before Dad bought the Impala station wagon and packed us off for Puerto Rico. I didn't even have to sleep in the hallway. Aunt Nilda let me share a real bedroom. Once again, two cousins had to make some room for Luis Gutiérrez. I was living in Ada's old room.

I felt like I had traveled the world since I last went to sleep in Lincoln Park. I had left as an angry Chicago teenager. I was a kid who only spoke English, exiled from his home and sent to a place that only spoke Spanish. Now I was back. Close to graduating from college, ready to agitate for fairness for Latinos and independence for Puerto Ricans, able to speak Spanish better than just about anybody in the neighborhood. It was good to be home.

MY CHALLENGE in Chicago was the same as everywhere else. I needed a job to make some money so I could afford to pay for school and finish up in the fall.

Aunt Nilda knew of summer openings at the Helene Curtis factory.

Helene Curtis was a growing shampoo and cosmetics company. They needed warehouse guys to move product in their shipping department. The place was busy, a break from the solitude of being a janitor. I ran a forklift, moving boxes all day long. I was energized by the place. I didn't have toasters to give away, but at least there were other people to talk to.

The first week I was a bit too energized. You were supposed to move about 1,300 boxes per day. I was moving 800 by noon. There were only a handful of summer employees. Most of the guys were lifers. One pulled me aside, a big Irish guy who looked like he should be outside working construction or playing football.

"Kid, you're only going to be here for the summer. We do this every day. Slow the fuck down," he told me.

He didn't look like he was joking. I slowed down. It was hard, physical work, and I'm not sure I could have kept up the pace all summer anyway—especially with the manager yelling at me all the time. He yelled at everyone. He was straight out of Central Casting—close-cropped hair; white, short-sleeve, button-down shirt; pocket protector; and clipboard. He was always watching out for any malcontents or pro-union agitators. He eavesdropped on everyone and reported any anticompany comments to his supervisors. It was clear the morale wasn't very high on the shipping-room floor. All summer, the manager was a tyrant—denying vacation requests, writing people up for small infractions—real or imagined—always berating people. He chased people out of the bathroom the minute break was over. He was always spewing anti-union comments and seeing some sort of Socialist plot behind every conversation. I felt bad for the guys who weren't leaving at the end of summer.

I decided to show some extra solidarity with my coworkers. On the last day of my summer employment, I drove my forklift over toward the microphone system that the manager was always using to scream at us. I grabbed it and turned it on. I shouted that I had an important announcement to make. Everyone stopped. Nobody had ever heard anyone other than the manager on the intercom. I stood on top of my forklift and shouted, "We create all of the wealth for this company, and we get nothing in return."

My coworkers looked at me like I was crazy, but they all listened. "It's time to strike for justice."

The manager's face turned red and he rushed into the middle of the floor. Now my coworkers were amused.

I yelled every leftist, pro-labor slogan I could think of, mostly because I knew that's what would incite the manager's anti-union paranoia the most.

He yelled at me, then turned around and yelled at the other workers to ignore me and said that anyone who joined in with me would be fired. I think he tried to fire me, but I reminded him that my career was already over.

"Power to the worker!" I kept shouting. The manager gave up, which took the fun out of it, so I climbed down. The other guys laughed or shook their heads at the crazy kid as I made my way out. I only wanted one last thing from Helene Curtis. The company was always giving away damaged shampoo, so I grabbed one last armful for Aunt Nilda. She now had enough Helene Curtis rejects that she would never have to pay to wash her hair again.

HELENE CURTIS is still a prominent Chicago company. Not long after I was elected to Congress, the owner called me up. He had noticed that I was a former employee. He said the company would love to have me come down and take a tour, and they would tout their alum to their current workers.

I went down to the plant. They were in a new location. Everything was automated. Nobody was running forklifts, nobody was getting yelled at. It was a good company, but much less interesting. I was disappointed I wouldn't be able to see where I had shouted my leftist propaganda. Still, I was getting the VIP tour. Everyone was nice to me.

"The congressman used to work here," the manager said to the workers. I said hello and enjoyed meeting everyone, but what I really wanted to tell them was that their personnel records must be awfully sketchy, otherwise they never would have invited me back.

* * *

NORTHEASTERN ILLINOIS UNIVERSITY was becoming the school of choice for neighborhood Puerto Ricans. It didn't cost very much, and you could take the bus up Kimball Avenue from my neighborhood to get there. They were starting to reach out to Latinos and had several classes on Latin America. Some of my old friends from the neighborhood were going there. I had chosen my final college, and I only had one year to go.

The first thing my friend Freddie did when he showed me around Northeastern was introduce me to the Union of Puerto Rican Students. Of course I joined. We raised money for Puerto Rican students who needed help, sometimes paying for lunches or clothes or books. We protested that there should be more Latino professors, and more help for Latino students to improve their English.

But at the heart of the union was a political activism directed toward independence for Puerto Rico. We published a newspaper, *Que Ondee Sola*—"may it wave alone"—that said everything about Puerto Rico and our feelings about our flag. I quickly found that most of the students were just learning about Puerto Rican history and activism and the independence philosophy that I had been living and promoting on the island. My time in Puerto Rico gave me an experience that everyone wanted to know more about. I was no longer an outsider—I was an expert. By the end of my second week, I was the vice president of the union, and recruiting new members every day.

Within a year, I was in charge. We were debating whether to have a sit-in at the university president's office because he wouldn't fire the director of the Latino outreach program. The guy who was supposed to be helping Latino students was going to law school full-time and running for alderman. He wasn't spending much time promoting the needs of Puerto Ricans at Northeastern. We all thought he should go, except for the president of our group, who didn't feel like making trouble over it. As a union meeting got more and more raucous and people became more upset, he decided it was time to save this fight for another day. So he declared the meeting adjourned and headed home with all the people who agreed with him.

I looked around the room. There were a lot more people still there than had left with the president. I didn't remember him holding a vote on adjourning. That was when I realized that understanding *Robert's Rules of Order* was a powerful weapon.

I took the podium, reminded them that I was vice president, and asked my friends if they recalled any motion or vote on adjourning. They didn't. I asked them if they wanted to vote on the matter at hand—taking further action about the sit-in and protests. They did. After that resolution passed, I asked them another question. Did they think we should have a committee to impeach the president for dereliction of duties? Not surprisingly, everyone who was still there, most of whom were my friends or people I had recruited, thought that was a good idea. The president never came back to defend his record. Within a couple of weeks, I was the new president.

My coup led to a more active union. It also led to a black eye two weeks later when the angry brother of the deposed president nearly knocked me out. My friend Freddie broke his hand when he hit him back. Within a couple of months at Northeastern, I had one black eye, my friend had a broken bone, and I was a president of the student union, and completely committed to Puerto Rican students and fairness for Latinos.

I HAD JUST FINISHED selling the *Claridad* newspaper on campus. I was becoming proficient in selling the pro-independence, leftist Puerto Rican newspaper. At Northeastern, if you saw me on campus, I wasn't going to invite you to a party. I was going to try to sell you our newspaper, or recruit you for the Union of Puerto Rican Students.

About the only break I took from my activism was to eat. As I came into the warm cafeteria after selling my newspapers on a cold winter day, I ran into Maria and her friend Soraida. I would see both of them around campus, and they would regularly buy *Claridad* from me. Maria headed right toward me.

"Luis, my church is having a Valentine's Day dance and I need to sell tickets. Please, help me out, buy a ticket and support my church. It will be fun." Maria was smiling and being charming while reminding me that she had forked over a few dollars to me that year for my left-wing newspapers.

I immediately saw an opportunity for something far more important.

"Why would I want to buy one ticket to a dance? It's no fun to go to a dance alone. Now, if your friend Soraida will go with me, then you've sold two tickets to the dance."

Maria's economic interest in her church fund-raiser immediately overpowered her loyalty to her friend. She turned to Soraida with excitement.

"Soraida, you should go with him. Then I can sell two tickets."

Soraida clearly wasn't getting any cut of ticket sales. And she didn't seem too excited about going to a dance with the campus radical.

I smiled, and decided to move on before she said no.

"I have to go develop some pictures for the newspaper," I said. "I'll be in the darkroom. Why don't you just let me know?"

I was both a salesman and a photographer for our newspaper. I figured I could wait in the dark to see which was greater—Soraida's loyalty to her friend or her reluctance to go to the dance with me.

It wasn't the first time I had tried to convince Soraida Arocho to go out with me.

The winter before, we performed at a Latino culture celebration sponsored by the Spanish department at Northeastern. It was a night of performances to highlight our diverse Latino—then mostly called Chicano—roots. There were songs and dances and dramatic readings. I wouldn't miss out on a night to celebrate Puerto Rican culture. I wasn't a particularly good singer or dancer, but nobody was more enthusiastic about their Puerto Rican heritage.

I recited a poem that celebrated the African roots of Puerto Rican culture while also acknowledging the hard work of Puerto Ricans. I dressed like a sugarcane cutter, wearing a *pava*, going barefoot, remembering my days as paymaster. I even found a machete. I did a native dance and recited my poem while a friend played the congas. It was as Afro–Puerto Rican as you could get. If camera phones and YouTube had existed in 1975, one of my political opponents would have played the clip back to try to startle white voters at some point in my career. I performed the dance to enthusiastic applause.

But the best part of the night was Soraida's performance. She performed a dance with Maria. It was a parody of politics, which ended with them dancing across the stage holding placards that said VOTEN POR YO. Vote for me. I watched her performance and was impressed that the very cute girl I had noticed on campus many times before also had a sense of humor. And could dance. She had my vote.

Maybe the success of my poem gave me confidence. I found Soraida and told her how much I liked her dance. I hung around. I made myself hard to get rid of. Before she finally got free of me, I left her a note asking her out, and I waited for a response.

A few days later, she couldn't avoid me on campus any longer. She couldn't go out with me, she said.

"You can't, or you won't?" I asked her.

Soraida told me she was moving back to Puerto Rico. Her dad had died, and her mom was moving the family back. I know all about moving to Puerto Rico, I told her. I could give her some tips. She wasn't interested, and she was leaving in just a few months. She didn't need any new entanglements before she left. She wanted to start a new life in Puerto Rico with a clean slate, she said.

After having been clearly told no once, I wasn't optimistic about my second try as I developed pictures in the darkroom and waited. I would take pictures of people as I tried to sell them the newspaper, telling them I would develop the print and give it to them. I was sure I had some pictures of Soraida somewhere. I was looking for them when there was a knock on the darkroom door. I was ready to take my rejection. At least it would save me a few bucks on dance tickets.

It was Soraida. I stepped outside. She only said one word.

"Yes."

I was going to the dance after all.

I NEEDED TO BUY some clothes. All I had was jeans, cheap polo shirts and T-shirts, and an old pea coat that I bought at the Army surplus store. I wanted to impress Soraida, but I didn't own anything decent enough for a church dance.

I made the budget-busting decision to spend twenty dollars on a new pair of dress slacks and a shirt. I should have saved the shirt for a 1970s museum. It was shiny and nylon, with a big collar. It had a design on it like a mural—a picture of dancing women. If you think John Travolta in *Saturday Night Fever*, you would be close, except my shirt was more dramatic. I felt confident it was just what I needed.

After spending the $20, I was eager to protect my investment and make sure the night went well. I wrote down a list of questions to ask Soraida, a cheat sheet for when the conversation slowed. I still remember the bold reminder at the top: "No more bad-ass Puerto Rican"— my shorthand to remind myself to talk about something other than Puerto Rican independence and empowerment. Not everyone likes two hours of conversation about agricultural policy and colonialism. "Talk about movies" was one of the instructions. I was ready to slip off to the bathroom to review my card whenever necessary.

I took the bus over to Soraida's house. I knocked on her door and submitted myself to inspection by her family. It was routine. I had been interrogated by the family of every Puerto Rican girl I had ever known, starting with the mom who was worried I was related to the "dark" shoemaker. But Soraida's mom had already gone ahead to Puerto Rico to get ready for their move, and her father had passed away. I was going to be scrutinized by a grandmother and Soraida's brother Cisco, who was there representing her twelve brothers and sisters. As was standard, Soraida was still "getting ready," so Cisco and Grandma had plenty of time to interview me.

I filibustered about living in Puerto Rico until Soraida came downstairs. She looked beautiful. She looked at me and asked a simple question.

"Where's your car?"

I thought, My dad has a car, and it's in Puerto Rico. Owning a car was not something that had ever seemed remotely possible to me. I had bought a new shirt. A car was asking too much. The church was only three blocks away.

"I thought we would walk," I blurted, to the laughter of everyone in the room. She looked at me like I had suggested we ride motorcycles to Wisconsin, as if it were obvious that girls didn't walk to dances in college.

She got on the phone. Her niece's boyfriend had a car. Chula and Luis would pick us up for the dance.

Once we were delivered at the door, I rebounded. I didn't have to use any of my flash cards, because Soraida and I had plenty to talk about.

Soraida was born in Puerto Rico, in Moca, a town not more than ten miles down the road from San Sebastián. Luis Águila and I chased Rubén Berríos around out there. Her family was poor too. My mom had once been happy to have a spigot at the bottom of the hill for water. Soraida's family took a bucket to the river when she was little.

As their family grew larger, her parents' chances of supporting everyone grew smaller, so her dad packed everyone up and moved them to Chicago. Soraida grew up in Humboldt Park, across the expressway from Lincoln Park, and every story Soraida told triggered a memory from me. She had to learn English in Chicago when she was little; I had to learn Spanish in San Sebastián in high school. Now her mom was taking her back, and she was going to have to start all over again on the island.

Several of her twelve brothers and sisters had already returned. Her mom didn't want to stay after her dad passed away. Stories about her father were a category where I couldn't match Soraida. Her dad had raised a family of thirteen as the neighborhood *bolitero*, the man Puerto Ricans played their numbers with. Soraida didn't remember him ever having another job. He raised a baker's dozen kids on hustle and ingenuity.

His name was Juan and everyone in the neighborhood knew him as "Don Juan." Everyone knew that Don Juan could get you a bottle of Pitorro, or find you a card game, or give you a small loan if you were short one week. Soraida loved her dad, his position of respect in the neighborhood, his friendship with everyone they knew. He was a sharp dresser—the best-dressed guy around. She rarely saw him without his fedora.

"You have to look like a man of means," he would tell her. "This is a neighborhood service. I talk to our friends and neighbors. They come to me with their problems. Your clothes say who you are."

The neighborhood *boliteros* were really the middlemen. They all worked for the big banker outside of the neighborhood and made their money on tips. When you hit your number, you gave the *bolitero* a bit of your winnings—a "little taste." They made their living on charm and trust. If Grandma Perez forgot to play her regular number one week, and it hit, Don Juan would pay her anyway. A gesture of kindness meant more money down the road. When you hit the *bolita*, it was a celebration. You could play for a dime, or a quarter, and you might win $50 or $100. Play a dollar, and you might win $500, and that was real money. Real money for you, and real money for Don Juan.

The police were always hassling the *boliteros*, but they were part of the community, no different from the bodega owner or the barber. The *bolitero* might as well have been the milkman. The police were the outsiders. Soraida said the police would talk to his regulars, guys who played his numbers every week. They would ask them if Don Juan was the *bolitero* and they would tell the cops they didn't have any idea what they were talking about. They had never heard of any Don Juan. When she got older and the police department finally hired a few Puerto Rican cops, even they would play Don Juan's numbers, thinking of it as natural as buying a candy bar at the store.

That still didn't keep the police away from their Humboldt Park apartment. One day Soraida heard her brother-in-law yelling from the upstairs apartment. "*Las cosas están mala,*" he shouted. Things are bad, he said over and over, a warning in Spanish that the police were coming. They didn't knock. They came in, and Soraida's older sister Lucy asked if they had a search warrant. They waved around some piece of paper, told all the kids to sit down on the couch, and then opened every drawer and lifted every cushion. Soraida and Lucy just watched. They couldn't find anything, until they came to a large pad of paper with very long lines for columns on it. There was nothing else written on it. They asked Lucy what it was.

"It's my art paper. That's an art project," Lucy told the police.

"Are you sure?"

"It's for art," Lucy said.

The police didn't take anything away that day, but they kept coming back, looking around, never finding anything. One day, Lucy and Soraida and their mother were at home watching television. They hadn't had any visits from law enforcement lately, but Don Juan kept telling them that the police were watching closely. A promo for the news came on and said they had breaking news about an arrest in the numbers racket.

They watched the news together and Lucy was the first to yell, "Oh, my God. That's Dad!" He and a buddy who drove him around had been arrested, and it led the news. Big break in the Puerto Rican numbers business, the police said. They made it sound like Don Juan was a gangster, a leader in a major organized crime operation. Soraida told me she was worried and scared, but also was impressed by how nice her dad looked on TV. He was dressed up in his long coat and hat and looked handsome. They wondered when they would see him again.

Their uncle bailed him out, and the police confiscated his friend's car as evidence. That seemed to satisfy the police. Soraida doesn't remember him going to court, and he never spent a day in jail. To her, it seemed like it was all made up to make the police look good on television.

All of the police attention made Don Juan particularly careful when he brewed a new batch of Pitorro, his homemade Puerto Rican rum. He was known for the quality and strength of his moonshine. "It was always sold before he even started," Soraida said. He would sell it for $25 per gallon, which was a lot of money—but it took a long time, making a gallon a drop at a time.

You could use yeast and sugarcane and corn to brew it, though being creative with whatever ingredients were available was a necessity of Pitorro production. Don Juan would brew it overnight, putting newspaper up in the windows to discourage inspection by the authorities. He did it in the kitchen so he could control the heat. Soraida could smell it, and fell asleep to the drip, drip, drip of Puerto Rican moonshine being brewed in the house. She said the police scared her far less than the possibility of her dad blowing them up some early morning.

Being a successful *bolitero* required creativity. Don Juan had lots of different jobs. When they first arrived in Chicago, he was a *piraguero*. *Piragueros* were the neighborhood sno-cone salesmen. Don Juan would get out his wooden cart, buy a big block of ice, set up five or six syrups for flavors, and sell sno-cones. He parked on a corner, and people came to him all day. It kept him out in the neighborhood, visible to everyone, making friends and connections.

For Don Juan, being a *bolitero* was a family business. Sometimes he worked with his brother, Soraida's uncle Lorenzo. Together they could cover more territory, see more people. Lorenzo had lost a leg to diabetes, so he made his way around the neighborhood on a wooden leg. They were mainstays of Humboldt Park, Don Juan and Soraida's uncle, her dad dressed like the hero of a romance novel, his sidekick trying to keep up with him on his one good leg. The leg was also storage. Her uncle would screw off his wooden leg and put the numbers and money inside, a nice, safe hiding spot. It worked well until one day the police stopped him on the sidewalk in front of their house, made him take off his leg and hand it to them. They shook it from side to side, and little slips of paper fluttered all over the sidewalk, a snowfall of Puerto Rican lucky numbers.

Even in Lincoln Park, we thought the police should just leave the *boliteros* alone. They were just entrepreneurs. It was part of Puerto Rican culture, no different from the church bingo. But the police kept hassling them anyway, right up until the time the government decided to take over. It wasn't the police who put the *boliteros* out of business; it was the lottery—a state-sanctioned and managed numbers game. When the lottery came to Illinois, I remember thinking that Don Juan was now officially a man before his time, a neighborhood businessman with an idea so good that the state of Illinois was going to use it to fund their schools.

Soraida loved her dad, but respected her mom even more. "She had to be a saint to live like that," Soraida has always said.

Being the *bolitero*'s spouse took patience. She carried trays of coffee down to a basement filled with guys playing poker and a table covered in money. She helped her husband cover up the windows when he was brewing Pitorro. They never knew what the next week would bring. Sometimes Don Juan came home with a large roll of cash. Sometimes, when his customers were having bad luck on the numbers, or he was having bad luck at the card table, or the police were watching too closely, he didn't bring home very much at all.

When business was good, he wanted to share the profits with his mom, who still lived in Moca. Sometimes, Soraida and Lucy would look at each other and one of them would say, "When's the last time you saw Dad?" After the first few times, they knew. "He must be in Puerto Rico," Soraida would say. He would just go; leave the house with Uncle Lorenzo on Friday and return on Monday or Tuesday with apologies and gifts. He would bring home mangoes and *quenepas*—a delicious grapelike fruit that you couldn't find in Chicago—from the island as a way to say he was sorry. Sometimes, Soraida's mom was so mad she would throw the fruit out the window into the backyard, and the kids would scramble to pick it up and eat it. They weren't letting Don Juan's delicious mangoes go to waste.

But now Don Juan was gone, and Soraida's mom was ready to go home. She had four children younger than Soraida, still in high school and grade school. They could all chip in to make it in Puerto Rico. She thought just like my parents. She would go where it was warm and safe and familiar. Soraida would be leaving in just two months.

That first night, the dance went great. The best investment I ever made. I didn't need my conversation note cards once. Everything after the dance went well too. All of our bus rides home after school, and the trips to the movies, and the surprise birthday party her family let me in on. I couldn't believe the girl who put on funny dance skits about politics, who had traveled back and forth from Chicago to Puerto Rico, whose family was even more unpredictable and entertaining than mine—and who was beautiful and charming and kind—was going two thousand miles away from me.

She was about to leave, and I finally got the courage to talk to her about what it meant for us. How would we manage her departure and our separation?

Soraida wasn't worried. She was matter-of-fact.

"You always knew I was leaving. I told you that the first time you asked me out. A clean slate. Remember?"

She said it like she would move on, and I would move on—just like she had warned me.

She didn't know me that well yet. That moment, I knew she was right. I would move on. To San Sebastián, Puerto Rico. Right across the island from Soraida.

CHAPTER NINE

Cabdriver, Exterminator, Spark-Plug Salesman

HAD HARDLY EVER driven a car. When would I have been behind the wheel? I certainly couldn't afford one, and my dad had only ever given me one driving lesson in Puerto Rico. If I had driven fifty miles in my life, it was a lot.

Now I was behind the wheel of a huge City of Chicago Checker Taxi. I would go to the garage on Halsted and check in with the starter to get my cab and within a few minutes I would be out on the street. These weren't the cabs you see today—these were, giant, classic Chicago yellow cabs, big and round and hulking. Think Robert De Niro in *Taxi Driver*. Put a gun and a turret on the front and it was a tank. I weighed about 120 pounds and had a twenty-eight-inch waist, and I was cruising through downtown Chicago traffic behind the wheel of a 4,500-pound vehicle.

I needed money to make it back to Puerto Rico. I needed a plane ticket. And while my parents would let me stay with them, they weren't going to finance my efforts to court Soraida Arocho. I had a mission—I believed Soraida and I were meant to be together. But I had a problem—she was now two thousand miles away on a tropical island and I was broke. I needed cash fast.

My options were limited. Unless a workers' uprising had supplanted the management, I didn't think they would take me back at Helene Curtis. A restaurant job would barely pay my rent. Then it struck me. My dad's cigar box. That paid for a lot of meals when I was growing up. I could go to school during the day and drive at night. I would get my taxi license.

How hard can it be to drive a cab? thought the kid who had hardly ever driven a car. I was sort of right. It wasn't hard to get the chauffer's license. All you needed was a valid driver's license and to pass a test about Chicago geography and street names. I studied. State and Madison Streets are ground zero in Chicago—0 east, west, north, and south. I worked my way out from there. I might have been a bad driver, but I was a good student. One quick street test, and I had my license. I was a Chicago cabdriver.

I soon learned that there is a huge difference between answering questions in a quiet classroom and having a busy businessman bark "take me to Wells and Goethe." MapQuest and GPS were still a couple of decades away. I was frequently lost. I learned on the job, consulting my book of Chicago streets and asking my passengers for help. Fortunately for me, and for the safety of Chicago passengers, I quickly learned that 90 percent of cab passengers travel similar routes. Once I learned how to navigate between the shopping districts on State and Michigan to Union and Northwestern train stations and office buildings in the Loop, I was mostly harmless. I had never driven on an expressway before, so I did everything I could to stay off of the Kennedy and Dan Ryan. People went fast. It seemed dangerous to me.

When I started, if a passenger gave me an address I didn't recognize, I simply turned around in my taxi and told them the truth.

"Ma'am, I'm sorry, I don't know how to get there. I just started. Honestly, I'm only driving this cab to earn money so I can go back and be with my girlfriend in Puerto Rico. I need to get back to her as soon as possible. So if you don't mind, if you could tell me how to get where you are going, that would really help me out."

I said it earnestly. I didn't want to get lost or waste the passenger's money. But pretty soon, I realized that my "just trying to earn money to be with my girlfriend" story was pretty good. Eventually, I could tell with remarkable accuracy which passengers wanted to hear more details about my lost love and how I was determined not to let Soraida get away. Women who were shopping—not hurrying to a business meeting—were the best audience.

"She's been gone almost a month, and she's beautiful, and if I don't make it to Puerto Rico I just know she's going to meet some other guy," I would say while they directed me where to go and listened to my story. I'm sure an income report would show an upswing in tip revenue from the passengers who listened to my story of being separated from the love of my life. Driving a cab was a great classroom for marketing and sales.

The more you listen, the more you learn in a cab. Although I was figuring out that being polite, chatty, and even lovelorn could help my bottom line, I never gave a moment's thought to how I looked when I drove. I dressed like I was going to class at Northeastern. I just pulled on whatever pants were relatively clean and my old green army jacket. I never had much of a budget for haircuts.

One day, after telling my stories of longing for Puerto Rico to a very nice white guy in an expensive suit, he gave me my fare and a decent tip and then hesitated before he got out of the car.

"Can I give you some advice? You seem like a nice guy, but you should invest in a haircut and a shave. I shave every day before work. Why shouldn't you? Maybe think about the clothes you wear when you are driving. This cab is your office, and I'm your customer. If you make a little more effort, I bet business will be better," he said, and he was off to continue his successful life.

I had never thought about it, but it was obvious. I looked like a college kid, so I was getting tipped like a college kid. I invested in a haircut. I shaved before work. I tried a decent shirt. It helped. I appreciated a stranger taking the time to give me sound business advice.

Making money as a cabbie is all about putting in the time. In the early '70s in Chicago, being a cabbie was a union job and you earned a salary. I signed up as a Teamster and I was willing to take whatever hours they would give me. Mostly I came in around four p.m. and took second shift, driving nights all over Chicago. I worked every hour I could, putting every dollar into my Soraida Reunion Fund.

It took me less than three months. Miraculously, I never had an accident. I also had to finish up school. I asked my counselor what I needed to graduate, and was not surprised to find I had neglected my math and science requirements. I looked for easy math and science classes for a liberal arts major—I remember taking a geology class where we mostly looked at pictures of rocks. That did it. I counted my dollars, bought my plane ticket, and I was off to Puerto Rico. Soraida was about to find out just how hard it was to get rid of Luis Gutiérrez.

SORAIDA AND I had written while we were apart, but she wasn't exactly begging me to come see her. I signed all of my letters to her "Love, Luis." Writing back, she signed them "Your friend, Soraida." I wasn't dissuaded. Her family had gone back to Caguas, a town across the island from San Sebastián. If she hadn't returned to be with her mother and the rest of her siblings, I wouldn't have gone back to Puerto Rico. I was ready to build a life in Chicago, but I wasn't ready to build a life without Soraida, so I climbed on the plane and once again made my way to San Juan.

Though my parents had been urging me to come home, and it had been more than two years since I had seen them, when I landed in San Juan, I didn't take the public car to San Sebastián, I went straight to Caguas. I needed to hear an answer from Soraida. The public car took me as far as the plaza in the center of town. My strategy was to find a hotel, store my bag, and then wash up and change to impress Soraida. But there were no hotels in Caguas. A cabdriver told me he could take me to a motel. I thought that sounded great—even cheaper, but when I said yes, he looked suspicious. It wasn't in a very nice part of town. It was rundown. All of the rooms had garages immediately below them. You didn't even have to walk outside, so nobody could see you or your car from the street. When the clerk at the desk asked for how long I wanted the room, I told him two days. He looked confused.

"Kid, this is the kind of place people rent by the hour," he said. Now I understood why the cabdriver had given me such strange looks. I wasn't starting my return to Puerto Rico in a very reputable place. But that didn't stop me. I changed. Finally my cab pulled up outside Soraida's family's apartment.

I really didn't know what to expect. My memory of our time together in Chicago was a memory of falling in love. But when it was time to go back to Puerto Rico with her family, Soraida didn't hesitate. She reminded me that I'd known all along she would be leaving. Now, as I stood at her door, I wondered if I had logged all of those hours in Chicago traffic, telling stories for tips, in exchange for a heartbreaking trip back to Puerto Rico.

Soraida answered the door. She looked wonderful. For me it was like nothing had changed. Certainly one thing that was the same was being interrogated by her family. Before I could properly greet her or tell her how much I'd missed her, I was joined by her grandmother and her mom, her brothers and sisters, looking me up and down and asking me questions in their living room.

I thought to myself, You already know me. We've been through this once. Can't you just review your notes? But now I was the guy who had come all the way to Puerto Rico to pursue Soraida. Puerto Rican families never tire of interrogating boyfriends. If anything, the questions were tougher.

"Do you have a job here? Are you staying in Puerto Rico? You've come all this way just to be near Soraida?"

I said I was looking for work. I tried to avoid the word "cabdriver." I tried not to look too desperate or eager, but the truth was I had come all this way, and I didn't have a job, and I didn't have much of a plan beyond wanting to win Soraida back.

Eventually the questions became too much even for Soraida to bear. She excused us and we went out for a walk. But in Puerto Rico, young couples can't even walk to the corner store alone. What would the neighbors say if they saw two young people alone? Chaperones are attached to you like an ankle bracelet on a convict. Soraida's sister Jeannette was sent out to tag along behind us.

With our supervisor a few steps behind, I could finally talk to Soraida.

"I told you I would show up. I said I would be kind of like an insurance policy—if you missed me, I would be there. If not, I would simply walk away. So tomorrow I'll be going to San Sebastián. Can I come back next week? Do you want to make a claim on the insurance policy?"

Soraida looked like she had thought about this and knew her answer.

"My mother does not really accept the notion of friendship, of a guy coming all this way to see me as friends. To her, you are either a couple or you aren't. So if you are going to come again next week, you need to get her permission. When we get back, you should talk to her and ask to see me again," Soraida said.

I avoided my instinct to jump up and down and cheer. I wouldn't have been shocked if she had said thanks for coming and sent me home. She did the opposite. She wanted to follow Puerto Rican custom and let her family know that we were serious about each other. Tradition can be very helpful to the matchmaking process.

I went back in, concealed my excitement, and tried to say something sensible to Soraida's mother.

"Doña Pella, I have something to ask you. I have saved up all of this money, and I have come all this way." I kept pausing and hesitating. I mumbled. I started over. The gravity of what I was asking seemed too much. But not to Doña Pella, who had six daughters. She had been through this before.

"Stop—you want to see my daughter," she said.

I did, and she gave me her permission, and from that moment forward, I was part of Soraida's family. They immediately rescued me from the by-the-hour motel and insisted that I stay at her sister's house, which would become like a home to me. They wouldn't even think of letting me take a public car to San Sebastián. Now I was their responsibility, and they drove me instead, and the next morning, my parents not only saw me for the first time in two years, they met their future daughter-in-law.

MY PARENTS ALWAYS thought their family's future was in Puerto Rico; that's why they returned. I think they would have been pleased if I had never left, if I had stayed at the University of Puerto Rico and finished my education and started my life on the island. They were glad I was back. My dad, however, was skeptical.

"What do you mean you've been driving a cab?" he asked me, astonished to hear that I was following in his footsteps. He thought he drove a cab so I wouldn't have to.

"I just needed some cash to get back home," I told him, but my cab driving career set off alarm bells for him, like maybe I had just been goofing off in the United States.

"Let me see your diploma," he said to me.

Well, he had me there. The truth was I had left in such a hurry that I didn't bother to pick up my diploma. I didn't need it to court Soraida, so I assumed it was in an office somewhere at Northeastern. But to my dad, I had just confessed to working as a cabbie and couldn't produce a diploma. He was worried about me, and kept asking questions about college, trying to make sure I had actually gone.

But I wasn't worried, because Soraida had taken me back. We became inseparable. Soraida was going to school at the Instituto de Cultura Puertorriqueña in San Juan. She went during the week. My vocation was looking for work during the week and counting the minutes until I could see her on the weekends.

Finding a job wasn't easy. San Sebastián wasn't exactly filled with choices. Eventually, I convinced myself that I shouldn't be working for someone else—this was the time for me to be an entrepreneur—to start something of my own. For my dreams of being my own boss, I had a partner, my old buddy Luis Águila.

Luis was getting ready to enter law school, but he had a proposal for how we could make money before he started. Actually, for years we've argued about whose idea it was, but I'm confident that he was the one who dreamed up the Águila-Gutiérrez spark-plug empire.

At that time, the roads in Puerto Rico were filled with Toyotas. And in the 1970s, Puerto Ricans were always working on their cars; tuning them up, replacing spark plugs. Luis had a brainstorm. Why not sell Nippondenso spark plugs? According to Luis Águila, they were the original spark plugs that were in Toyotas. All the mechanics and roadside shops in Puerto Rico sold NGK spark plugs. But Luis knew that Nippondenso was trying to get a foothold in Puerto Rico. They were looking for salesmen. We were ready to start our business.

To help me look for a job, and to see Soraida, my dad bought a used, yellow Volkswagen Beetle. I thought it was a beautiful car. Luis also had a yellow Volkswagen Beetle. One afternoon, we got in our matching cars and headed to San Juan to fill them up with Nippondenso spark plugs. The new company was happy to sell us as many as they could. They didn't care that we didn't know anything about cars and had never sold anything before. They just knew that they had sold us as many cases of spark plugs as our twin Volkswagens could hold. When the eager Águila-Gutiérrez sales team walked through their door, it was a good day for the new Nippondenso guys in San Juan.

Pretty soon we were out on the road, traveling up and down the hills, through the countryside and from coast to coast in Puerto Rico, looking for every body shop and gas station and mechanic we could find. You didn't have to drive far on the island to find a guy running some sort of garage. Most of them had displays of NGK spark plugs. We would pull up, two guys who looked like kids, driving banana-colored VWs. We smiled widely and carried our boxes of Nippondenso spark plugs up to the owner.

"It's the hottest, newest spark plug in Puerto Rico," we would say.

"How would you like to offer your customers original Toyota spark plugs?" we asked. We would do anything to get a sale—negotiate cost, give volume discount. We told them we would set up a display for them that would guarantee that Nippondenso spark plugs would fly out of the store.

We didn't know much about sales, but people were intrigued by the Toyota pitch. Once we had made the sale, our marketing savvy consisted of building a pyramid of Nippondenso spark plug boxes in their shop windows. We would carefully place our boxes and build our pyramid and then stand back with pride. The owner would look a little skeptical, like it didn't strike him as marketing genius that we stacked up a bunch of boxes in his window. But our enthusiasm and confidence was working. All over the island, we were selling spark plugs. We were certain that we had found our calling. Within a few weeks, our cars, once loaded with boxes, were empty—our stock moved to store windows across Puerto Rico.

When we returned with our empty cars, my dad was so impressed he was ready to invest money in our new venture. We headed back down to San Juan, and the Nippondenso guys couldn't believe we had sold out. They were impressed. We filled up our cars again, ready to head back out. Driving back to San Sebastián, Luis asked me how long it took a garage to sell a box of spark plugs. I thought about it and looked at him, realizing that maybe we hadn't carefully thought through every aspect of our business plan.

"I don't have any idea," I said.

We were about to find out.

We retraced our route, ready to replenish the stock of our loyal Nippondenso dealers. At our first stop, the owner was very glad we had come back. He practically yelled.

"I can't sell any of these things," he said. "Everybody wants NGK. I'm not sure these are even original Toyota parts. You need to take them back," he said. We backed up, saying something about sales being final. We hoped things were better at our next customer. We didn't pull right in at the next stop; we looked cautiously from the road at his shop window, and saw an untouched, beautifully stacked pyramid of spark plugs. Luis and I looked at each other, and at the backseats of our cars, filled with more boxes of spark plugs.

We kept hoping we would see something different, but store after store had windows filled with Nippondenso spark plugs. I told Luis we must be great salesmen. We had just sold mechanics a bunch of stuff nobody wanted. We decided to wait it out, let them sell. We gave it a little time, made another trip to our customers, and saw the same thing: our pyramids standing strong for the ages. We should have built little spark-plug sphinxes next to them. At one of the shops, the mechanic spotted our yellow cars, saw us lurking, and tried to flag us down. We just kept going. We couldn't take any spark plugs back. Our Volkswagens were out of room.

Just like we didn't give our customers any mercy, the Nippondenso guys in San Juan didn't give us any mercy either. "But we can't sell any more of them," we said. They shrugged. Eventually, they did buy our stock back from us at a greatly reduced price, and my first attempt at entrepreneurship ended with Luis and me in debt.

✳   ✳   ✳

OUR SPARK-PLUG DEBACLE didn't cure me of a desire to start my own business. I wanted to marry Soraida, and if I was going to marry her, I needed some money.

Puerto Rico has bugs, as well as plenty of exterminators willing to take your money to get them out of your home. It's tropical, after all. Bugs are everywhere, and they grow large in the Puerto Rican sun. How hard could the exterminating business be? I went to the local agricultural supply store. I looked at the cost of the insecticide they sold in bulk to kill bugs, some sort of deadly mix of chemicals. I went to Sears and found a tank and a sprayer. Even more important, at Sears I found cheap khaki pants and a shirt. I thought the uniform was the key. I had to look like an exterminator.

I bought my insecticide, which smelled foul and dangerous. But the instructions said just mix it with water and it would be effective. I thought that my niche in the business would be to provide the best, most effective pest control to the people of Puerto Rico, so I disregarded the instructions and put in more poison and less water. If the amount they recommended was good for killing bugs, I figured that putting in double would be twice as good.

On one of my weekends with Soraida, I asked her sister to stitch the name of my company on my new exterminator uniform.

"I didn't know it had a name," her sister Nery said to me.

"It does now. R&B Exterminators," I told her. I wanted it to sound American and new. R&B was the name of a clothing store on Milwaukee Avenue in Chicago that Soraida and I liked. I took what money I had and bought an ad in the Caguas newspaper, promising the most innovative exterminating techniques by a great new company—R&B. Then, with my insecticide mixed, and my spray can in hand, I set out to sell my services the only way I knew how. I went door to door.

I had my pitch ready. When people answered the door to find a very small guy with a very large spray can, I had some simple questions for them.

"Have you heard of R&B Exterminators? We're the newest company with state of the art methods."

Shockingly, nobody had.

"You mean you haven't seen our television commercials? How about our new radio ads?" I would ask.

People would say no, because there weren't any radio or TV ads. But then I would pull out my newspaper ad, and ask if they had seen that one. Many people said they had.

"Well, I'll make sure to report to the company that our newspaper advertising seems to be the most effective. And while I have you here, can I offer you our special introductory plan? I'll do your whole house for the special price of $4.99," I said. I chose $4.99 because the number stuck in my head as the wage we'd paid the sugarcane cutters at Central Plata.

It worked. Quite a few people took me up on my offer.

At my first sale, I had pumped up my can of insecticide with too much pressure and when I applied the first amount under the sink a cloud of gas erupted and I nearly suffocated. That didn't stop me. I took in some fresh air and kept going. Given my high bug-killer-to-water ratio, I felt confident my stuff would work. I generously applied my revolutionary product around the house. And I soon felt dizzy and sick.

The smell was overwhelming. A couple of times, I thought I could see the fumes winding their way into the house like a plume of smoke from some chemical spill. I was worried that I was going to pass out, but I was more worried I might kill a customer. I quickly finished. I was pretty sure that I had already killed anything that moved.

"Should that smell be so strong?" my customer asked.

"That's our amazing new product," I said. "Oh, and you might want to leave the house for a while" I told her. I collected my $4.99 and I was off, happy to breathe some fresh air.

After that, I tried remixing my solution, but I could never get it quite right. I had been using so much of the insecticide that I needed a refill right away. I had gone through it much quicker than I planned, throwing off my calculations of how to make a profit. No wonder everyone else put so much water in. My spray cans broke and I had to keep replacing them. I couldn't afford another ad. I kept at it for two months. I had some customers, I just wasn't making any money. Fortunately for my respiratory health, my brief career as an exterminator was over, and I was looking for work again.

MY FALTERING CAREER didn't stop me from planning my future with Soraida. We were spending every available minute together. I would find an odd job here and there for some extra cash. I would arrive on Saturday and we would fill our weekend with movies and picnics. We took long walks. Jeannette, our bored teenage chaperone, trailed behind us.

I think Soraida's family started to wonder if I would ever propose. But I needed some money. I couldn't even afford a ring. Then I discovered that Puerto Rican schools had a shortage of English teachers. They were looking for anyone bilingual with a college degree. I was quick to sign up.

The new regional superintendent of schools was in charge of hiring, and he was a familiar face—the former principal of Manuel Méndez Liciaga High School. The same man who had called me to his office to ask me to stop selling the independence newspaper in front of the school. I needed the job. I hoped he didn't remember.

He welcomed me into his office. "Are you still being a troublemaker?" he asked me. But he was smiling.

"I'm trying to stay out of trouble," I said. I think he was desperate enough for English teachers that he would have taken me even if Luis and Tino and I had organized a revolution and taken over his school. He remembered much more than I would have guessed. He remembered that I had been a good student, and that I had a rough time fitting in.

"You were one of the first of many who came back from the US," he said. He told me their opening for English teachers was in Las Marias, and I could start right away. I was grateful. I could start saving for a ring.

I scraped together $150. I showed the jeweler my money. "Show me what you've got for a hundred and fifty bucks," I said. What they had was a very small ring. But I couldn't wait.

I placed the modest ring in a beautiful box and I put it in the glove compartment of my Volkswagen. After we went to a movie, I told Soraida that I had something for her in the glove compartment. She looked, found the box, and immediately put it back in. She didn't say a word. Her family might have been ready. Soraida wasn't.

My second lame proposal attempt was on a long walk. She gave the box right back to me again. Finally, I thought maybe a Christmas offer would close the deal. I wrapped the tiny ring in a giant box to throw her off. Everyone got together on Christmas Eve. At 12:01 everyone started opening presents. Everyone wanted to know what was in the big box for Soraida. So did she. What was in the very big box was her very small ring, though it was the biggest I could afford.

Immediately, her relatives started celebrating.

"They are getting married!" People hugged and cheered. At some point during the crying and hugging and celebrating, Soraida simply took the ring and put it on. I've asked her many times if she would have said yes if it were just the two of us and we weren't surrounded by a living room full of happy relatives. She always says, "Of course I would have." We've been together thirty-five years, so I'm convinced.

We set a date that was more than a year away, but Soraida's family kept encouraging us to move it up. In Puerto Rico, the chaperones don't go away with the engagement, and I think her family was tired of monitoring us. We were married in Caguas in an old Catholic church on the plaza. I was ready to get rid of the chaperones too. At the end of our wedding and our reception, we said our good-byes to our happy relatives, ready to begin our life as an unsupervised married couple.

As we were about ready to head out to our hotel, her grandmother, Clotilde, stopped us.

"You're leaving?" her grandmother asked. Yes, we told her, we were starting our honeymoon.

"Good. You can take me home," she said. And we did. The newly-weds took the bride's grandmother home and helped her into bed. We gave her the medicine she took every night, went back out to our car, looked around, and realized we had finally run out of chaperones.

* * *

FINANCIALLY, we weren't at all ready to be married. Soraida was a full-time student. I had a very meager teacher's salary. It was the poorest we've ever been. To stay fed, I was basically in the school's free lunch program. The lunch ladies at the school adopted me and piled my tray high with food. I'm sure it was a violation of some federal policy. At home, we could afford eggs but not chicken. Soraida became an expert omelet maker. We regularly showed up at her sister Nery's house around six o'clock. There was always meat at her sister's house. All of our money went to rent and school.

After a while, it was clear how hard it was going to be for us to live on my teacher's salary. We thought about options. Spark-plug salesman and exterminator had been crossed off the list. Like both sets of our parents before us, when we thought about the future of the family we were eager to start, we imagined brighter economic options in the United States. The choices were wider, the jobs paid better. Soraida's sister Lucy was still there, and I had my network of friends from Northeastern. Some things don't change—generation after generation, people have looked to the United States for economic opportunity. Soraida and I headed back to Chicago.

IT WAS GREAT to be reunited with friends and family. I saw some of my old Northeastern University crowd. Soraida was happy to be with Lucy. I was becoming best friends with Lucy's husband, Juan Torres— or Juano to his buddies.

We found a small apartment. But fairly soon I wondered if our economic calculations had been right.

I tracked down every job lead. Juano worked for the Post Office, but he had been in the Navy and his military service had helped him get in. I was way down on the waiting list. I heard Commonwealth Edison was hiring, and went to apply. I would have taken anything. They called me in for an interview, looked over my application, and wondered why I was willing to be a meter reader for an electric company when I had gone to college.

"I just need the money," I said.

"You're overqualified to be a meter reader," they told me.

"Then put me in customer service," I said.

"Then where will we put our meter readers when we promote them?" they asked.

The gas company told me the same thing, banks as well. I was overqualified to be a teller. I just wanted to be qualified enough to pay my rent and eat. Fortunately, Soraida found a job, and went to school at night. I mulled over my options. I knew one thing I was qualified to do. Soon, I was back in my cab.

Now that I've been in Congress for twenty years, finding out that I once drove a cab for a living surprises people. But to me, a kid struggling to find a job and support my new wife, it seemed like the most natural thing in the world. It had paid for my trip to go to Puerto Rico to win Soraida back. If you were willing to put in the hours and learn the tricks of the trade, driving a cab was good money. Once I made the decision and I was back behind the wheel picking up fares, Soraida and I felt like we were rich.

I would go down to the cab office and clock in around six thirty or seven a.m. so I didn't miss the morning rush. At first, I wondered why some of the other guys always drove off in the nicer, newer cabs, or why they always got the ones with air-conditioning. I asked around. Of course, I thought, I should have known the capitalistic answer to that question. You need to take care of the starter. I started giving him an extra five bucks, and pretty soon I was hitting the streets in an air-conditioned cab.

At the start of the day, you need to get into a rhythm. The train station to an office building to another office to a hotel, up and down Michigan Avenue and State Street and Clark and LaSalle. City Hall to North Michigan, back down to the Loop. On a good day you feel like a pitcher on a sunny afternoon with his best fastball, picking up one businessman after another, raking in good tips from frequent cab customers. I was always friendly. If someone wanted to talk, I talked. If they wanted to be quiet, I sat and drove. Smart cabdrivers realize they are part of the hospitality industry. A waitress keeps refilling your coffee cup, you give her a better tip. Be pleasant, be efficient, drive a clean cab, give a tourist a helpful suggestion, and pocket extra tip money as well. And I took a lesson from my dad: I always had a newspaper in my cab.

By nine thirty a.m., the morning rush was over. I looked for a cab stand and parked and waited at a busy hotel or the train station. I always liked cab stands. Better to sit in park for a half hour and wait for a fare than drive for a half hour empty while burning gas. Every minute driving up and down Dearborn Street in an empty cab cost me and Soraida money. Things picked up at lunch again, and for as long as you were willing to work, you were a small business owner, collecting fares and putting money in your pocket. It was much better than I would have done as a meter reader, and way more than I made as an English teacher in the hills of Puerto Rico.

To be a successful cabbie, you had to avoid getting ripped off. You never knew who would try to scam you out of a fare. Early on, I took a fare to a huge office building in the heart of the Loop. He was a well-dressed guy in an expensive suit carrying a fancy leather briefcase. He said he was just dropping off a document and then needed to go to O'Hare. "Just keep the meter running," he said, and he was up and out of the cab, and I never saw him again. You learn quickly to get the cash, or hang on to that expensive briefcase, whenever someone says they are coming back.

I picked up a young, attractive woman at an expensive Lake Shore Drive apartment building one morning. She looked like a rich Gold Coast socialite. She had on high heels and fancy clothes and some sort of fur scarf. If she had been carrying a small poodle, her outfit would have been complete. When we made it downtown, she suddenly realized, to her shock, that she didn't have a bit of cash. She apologized and told me how embarrassed she was and said nothing like that had ever happened to her. She looked like she might cry.

I assumed she was probably telling me the truth. It looked like she was wearing a couple of hundred dollars' worth of clothes. She needed to scam me out of five bucks like Donald Trump needs to scam a free hotel room.

"Don't worry, I'm not going to call the police or anything," I said.

She looked relieved. Then she realized she had her checkbook. She happily wrote me a check for double the fare and thanked me profusely for understanding. The next day I took the check to the bank. Account closed, and another lesson learned about guessing who is trying to hustle you and who isn't.

I soon realized that I looked at potential fares differently from most of my cab-driving colleagues. Back then, a lot of the cabdrivers in Chicago were older white guys. They had been on the job for a while. It wasn't an immigrant business yet. It also meant that I saw African Americans and Latinos get bypassed all the time on the street. I was more keenly attuned to racial slights and fairness than most of my coworkers. I knew I wouldn't like to stand on a corner waving at passing taxis just to watch them stop at the next corner to pick up the handsome white businessman in a suit. After all, a pretty blond woman in hundred-dollar shoes had written me a bad check—so how can you tell who's going to rip you off?

I knew my fellow cabbies. Some of them just didn't like blacks and Latinos. But an even bigger part of the hesitancy to pick up minority fares was pure capitalism: you were likelier to get taken to a neighborhood outside of your regular path through the Gold Coast or the Loop, a place where you couldn't pick up a fare coming back. A trip to the West Side of Chicago meant you came back empty. That didn't stop me, but dead-heading back without a fare cost me a few bucks.

I was working Christmas Eve—a great day for cabbies because everyone is shopping and trying to make some last-minute stops before Christmas. I was heading down Michigan Avenue, and two blocks up I saw an older African American woman with two little children and an armful of packages hailing a cab. I saw her and I knew exactly what was going to happen. All of the cabs in front of me drove right by her like she was invisible. It was about four p.m., and it was snowing. If she took a cabbie to the West Side or South Side, in afternoon traffic, it was at least an hour out and an hour back. Two hours during prime time for one fare took a chunk out of your bottom line. Nobody stopped for her, and when I pulled over she looked grateful. Who knew? Maybe she was going to a Loop hotel.

She wasn't. She was going home, to around Seventy-Ninth and Stony Island, the far South Side of Chicago. I knew my booming Christmas Eve was done, but if I hadn't stopped for her, she would have spent more of her Christmas Eve standing on Michigan Avenue. She couldn't have been nicer, and she was appreciative. I'm sure she always had to wait longer to get a cab in the Loop, and I'm sure she knew why. She gave me a nice tip, and I called it a day. I headed home to Christmas Eve with Soraida.

Of course, the decision to pick up everyone didn't always work out. I picked up an African American lady at a grocery store one afternoon. She got in and said, "Cabrini–Green—do you know where that is?" I sure did. The roughest public-housing development in town. Maybe in all of America. She was friendly, and we talked the whole way. When I pulled into the lot, and navigated around the burned-out cars and the litter to find a spot near her building, I remember exactly the fare I told her.

"That's one-dollar and fifty-five cents, ma'am," I said.

She looked shocked. "A dollar fifty-five," she repeated, as if I had asked for a million bucks.

She got out of the car and looked up at the building. "Tommy! Tommy!" she shouted a few times.

Tommy finally stuck his head out of a window on the third or fourth floor.

"This guy says his cab costs a dollar fifty-five!" she yelled.

Tommy looked down at me and slowly repeated the amount of the fare. Tommy was a big guy. Tommy didn't appear to be a friendly guy. Tommy gave me a look that suggested he was not convinced that a dollar fifty-five was a reasonable price for my services.

I weighed about one-half of what Tommy did. I figured the elevator probably wasn't working at Cabrini–Green, so I had a minute to make a decision. I quickly helped the woman unload her groceries, and then I told her to keep her dollar fifty-five. I made my way out of the parking lot as fast as I could. Part of being a successful cabbie was sensible risk management.

I came home late most nights, but I came home happy. When I'd started driving a cab to earn money to make my way to Puerto Rico, I hardly knew my way around. Now I was a veteran. I knew the business. I knew the streets and how to get places quickly. I returned home with cash in my pocket and Soraida to welcome me.

But still, I hadn't exactly dreamed of becoming a cabdriver. During my days in San Sebastián, during my study for my college boards, at the University of Puerto Rico and Albany and Northeastern, I thought of a different future. One day, I was waiting at a cab stand by Continental Bank. It was a slow time, and I had probably been waiting a half hour. Finally I made it to the front—the moment to make some money after thirty minutes of nothing.

I looked in my rearview mirror and saw the fare approaching. It was a Puerto Rican guy I knew well from Northeastern. He had been in the Union of Puerto Rican Students—he was a member, I was the president. He was dressed in a suit, carrying a briefcase. He was a few steps from my cab. I sat up, hit the gas, and drove away, leaving behind my fare and the entire reason I had been sitting and waiting. I'm sure he wondered what was wrong with that crazy cabbie who pulled off without him, but I just didn't want to explain to him why I was driving a taxi, particularly when he looked like he was doing so well.

Eventually, I started looking for jobs again. I found out the state of Illinois needed social workers. Soraida and I had found a nice little house on Homer Street. With a little work on our part, and with the money I had saved from driving cabs, it might just make a nice place for a young couple with a little girl on the way. Being a social worker paid a little more than half of what I was making in the cab, but I was ready. I parked my taxi.

CHAPTER TEN

Neon-Orange Campaign Signs

W E BOUGHT the house on Homer Street, and we sanded and scrubbed and painted and built, young homeowners determined to show all of our nice white neighbors that the world wasn't ending just because another Puerto Rican family moved in on their street. Omaira came into our world and we focused on making a great life for her. Soraida and I were both happy as social workers. We loved it there.

And then Dan Rostenkowski's precinct captains knocked on my door with a very simple request. I understood exactly what these guys wanted—just a little help making sure a black guy didn't become mayor of Chicago. I suppose I'm someone who has difficulty tolerating calm and contentment. When I chased Rostenkowski's guys down the street, even I thought I was probably just blowing off steam when I yelled at them and told them I would take them on. But when they left I didn't really calm down. I wanted to do everything I could to help Harold Washington. I made a decision. Not only would I get my neighbors to vote for Harold, I would teach Dan Rostenkowski a lesson.

* * *

I MADE GOOD on my promise to try to beat the captains at their own game. I had sold newspapers and put up signs and agitated for the Puerto Rican Independence Party and the Union of Puerto Rican Students. I understood how to organize, but I had never done any actual campaigning. Still, the fact that one of the most powerful Democrats in America had asked me to support a Republican for mayor got me out of my house and into my precinct.

To help Harold Washington, I organized my friends and family and knocked on doors and learned what "pluses" and "minuses" and "zeros" were in the world of Chicago elections. I was taking on the Chicago machine and was proud of it. We took our poll sheet—the list of every registered voter in the ten square blocks that made up the 2nd Precinct—and went door-to-door talking to every voter we could find. Most of the Puerto Ricans we talked to, and every single one of the African Americans, supported Harold. They became pluses. We wanted to make sure they voted on Election Day. The Epton voters were almost all white. They were our minuses. We wanted them to stay home.

Then we worked on the most important group—the zeros. They were the undecideds.

The undecideds were Puerto Ricans who weren't sure they wanted to disappoint the precinct captains pushing so hard for Epton. They were whites who weren't buying the argument that Chicago shouldn't have a black mayor. Even a few of the machine regulars were a little bit on the fence. A lot of them weren't crazy about the black guy, but the unknown Republican also happened to be Jewish. They had to sort out their racial and religious fears and decide which was stronger. We stalked the zeros and tried to sell them on Harold Washington every moment we could. Every now and then we would turn one more zero into a plus.

Still, the guys who came to my house had been confident. They knew their precinct. They had done almost everyone in the neighborhood a favor. They never lost. Epton's slogan—"Before It's Too Late"—communicated precisely the fear and panic they wanted their mostly white voters to feel. The captains laughed at us. They never for a moment thought they would lose the precinct to a bunch of political rookies supporting a black guy for mayor of Chicago.

But they did. We beat them by 60 votes in their own backyard. In the 2nd Precinct of the 32nd Ward, Washington beat Epton 280 to 220. The captains were shocked. They didn't look too eager to report to Rostenkowski that they had just lost to the friends and family of the little Puerto Rican guy who had chased them down the street. We celebrated, then we plotted our next victory over the machine.

My plan was simple. If I could help Harold beat Rosty's people for Mayor, why couldn't I beat Rosty for Democratic committeeman? We thought Rostenkowski deserved the punishment. We thought we were fighting for much more than a local party post. We were fighting racism. We were taking on a political machine that excluded Latinos and African Americans.

I knew my neighborhood was changing. Rosty was Polish. His alderman, Terry Gabinski, was Polish. Myron Kulas, his state representative, was Ukrainian. Yet when I walked down North Avenue in the heart of the 32nd Ward, I could choose among several bodegas to buy café con leche or play the *bolita*. The 32nd Ward was still a working-class neighborhood, and while there were plenty of Poles and Italians who had lived there for generations, it was people who looked and talked and spelled their names like me who were moving in. You were as likely to find a plantain as a pierogi. The 32nd Ward was filled with white people who were too old or not quite affluent enough to move out to the suburbs, and Latinos with just enough money to afford to move in. The old, white, and male power structure wasn't exactly bending over backward to welcome the newcomers. Latinos and Puerto Ricans had helped to make Harold Washington mayor; I thought they were ready to finally start electing their ward leaders too.

Still excited by our victory in one precinct, I reunited my hearty group of volunteers. All we had to do was repeat what we had done in the 2nd Precinct in the fifty-three other ones of the 32nd Ward. It was like franchising a successful hot-dog stand. One neighborhood likes your hot dogs, how hard can it be to sell them somewhere else?

Even now, it's hard for me to explain to other members of Congress the importance of the position of Democratic committeeman. In Chicago, people understood "Democratic committeeman." For years, it was shorthand for "tough guy who runs the neighborhood." He's the guy who controls neighborhood services, because he has a direct line to government jobs. City jobs, county jobs, state jobs. Chicago dreamed up new arms of government just to give Democratic committeemen places to put their captains. You might meet a captain who worked at the Cook County Board of Review or the City of Chicago Bureau of Motor Vehicles or the Cook County Recorder of Deeds. I would regularly meet people with a government job title that sounded like it must be made up. I would think to myself, What in the world do all of these people actually do? I was about to find out. They knock on doors and ask their neighbors to vote for Dan Rostenkowski.

But none of these facts kept me from running. I wanted to be Harold Washington's loyal lieutenant, standing beside him and crushing both the machine and racism. That was our motivation. We knew if we just met people and told them the truth about our plans for a better neighborhood, we would win.

I made it official. I was a candidate for Democratic committeeman of the 32nd Ward, and for months, we felt great. We thought our insurgent campaign was moving right along against Rosty. I didn't see much evidence of his captains. It almost felt like we had the neighborhood all to ourselves. I actually believed I had a national Democratic leader, the powerful chairman of the Ways and Means Committee of the US House of Representatives, on the run. Time and history and momentum were on my side, I told myself. The winds of change were blowing in Chicago; I was on the way in and Rosty and his old-style way of doing things were on the way out. Then, on Sunday morning three weeks out, I left my house early because I wanted to visit a couple of churches. I had been everywhere. Knocking on doors, going to block parties, handing out my homemade flyers at the entrance to the El. I was going to add some new congregations to the Gutiérrez crusade.

The signs were everywhere. On my home block. Were they neon? Rosty's campaign signs were the brightest orange I had ever seen. The background was a dark navy blue that made his name jump out like you were about to be surrounded and captured by attacking fluorescent orange letters. It didn't have a slogan or even the name of the office he was running for. Just ROSTENKOWSKI. The signs were up and down my street and in the windows of my neighbors' houses. To my casual glance, it looked like they didn't miss anyone. I felt like a bank robber who thinks he is getting away with millions and then looks up to see a hundred FBI agents pointing their guns at him. My neighbors had just cast the first vote of the election, and it was a landslide for Rostenkowski.

I was humiliated. Where had all of my Harold Washington voters gone? I was astonished that my neighbors could, in unison, turn against me. They knew I would have to walk right by signs, on my block, for my opponent every day. Apparently none of them cared. It was like they had all just put up signs in their windows saying "Our neighbor Luis Gutiérrez is a loser."

We were good friends with our next-door neighbors. They were among the first to befriend us when we moved in. They had a daughter Omaira's age, and our kids played together, riding trikes up and down the block. On any weekend, you could find our kids together on one of our front stoops, dolls or toys in hand, having fun. Soraida talked with the other mom all the time. They had a Rostenkowski sign in their window.

For a minute, I hoped it was some sort of joke—a misunderstanding. Maybe my neighbors didn't know I was running. But I couldn't fool myself. They knew. Everyone knew. I was friendly with these people. I had convinced a lot of them to vote for Harold Washington. They liked me. Some of the older white folks might not have been crazy about Puerto Ricans moving in, but I seemed pretty harmless. I had a job. I took care of my house. My wife and daughter were polite. They all knew I was taking on the machine, that I was reforming Chicago government, that I was punishing the establishment for supporting a Republican. And that Sunday morning I learned that they were all with Rostenkowski.

I hurried inside. I started calculating the money I had spent on my campaign. I wanted to say to Soraida, "Honey, I'm sorry; I've made a terrible mistake. I don't know what I was thinking." Instead, all I could manage to do was sit down at the kitchen table and say, "Everyone on the block has a Rostenkowski sign in their window."

Soraida was surprised. She had been receiving my regular updates on how well my campaign was going. A less patient and kind woman would have said, "Don't complain to me. I didn't tell you to run against one of the most powerful people in the country." She didn't. She tried to make me feel better. She told me to keep going, not to worry about a few signs.

But nothing could console me. Dan Rostenkowski might as well have stamped his campaign signs on the inside of my eyelids. I would lie down in bed, close my eyes at the end of another long day of knocking on doors, and his signs would still be there, glowing, penetrating my brain like a virus. They never went away. I dreamed about them, and they were the first thing I pictured when I woke up.

The orange and blue illuminated my folly. I had been stupid, arrogant. I was too busy with my dreams of running an underground, insurgent guerrilla campaign to notice that there was a counterinsurgency brewing all around me. While I was hunting votes with a little popgun of complaints about Rosty not being a real Democrat, he was mobilizing his army of city and county and state and federal workers. His army was better trained and much better equipped, and they were just waiting for the right time to teach me how the machine really worked.

I felt like I couldn't breathe. I begged my neighbors to take the signs down. I started with our friends next door.

"Hello, Donna. I see you have a Rostenkowski sign. Look, it's embarrassing. Our kids play together. Even if you don't vote for me, I was hoping, as a favor, that you could take it down. It makes me look bad to have so many Rosty signs here in my own neighborhood, and we're friends. Do you think you could take it down?"

They told me that a captain for Rostenkowski had come weeks ago. He had told them how disappointed Chairman Rostenkowski—everyone always referred to Rostenkowski as "chairman"—was that they had signed my petitions to get on the ballot. That the captains had helped them before with city services. Could they just sign an authorization that would allow them to put a sign in the window? It would only be up in the window for a few weeks.

They seemed sorry, and a little embarrassed, but made it clear they had signed the form. It felt official to them. Rosty's guys had been smart enough to make them sign on the dotted line, and for our friends, that was that. They had the authorization to put a sign up. They hoped I wasn't mad. But they weren't taking the sign down.

I tried the same approach with some of my other neighbors. My pitch was a forlorn plea not to embarrass me. Some people were much more direct than my friends. They said, "We support Rostenkowski." Some people talked about favors the precinct captains had done for them. Eventually I succeeded in getting a couple of my neighbors to take the signs down. But after a half hour or so of mostly futile efforts and awkward conversations with neighbors who basically told me to stop causing them problems, I understood that it was time to give up. I went home.

I looked up and down my block one more time. My block was Dan Rostenkowski territory.

UNTIL THAT SUNDAY morning I had believed everything was going great. Like supporting Puerto Rican independence or courting Soraida or fighting for Puerto Rican empowerment in college, I couldn't do things halfway. So my first decision was that to beat Dan Rostenkowski, I had to be a full-time candidate. I couldn't beat him if I spent all day as a social worker.

I did what any first-time candidate for office running against a nationally known, powerful, and well-financed twelve-term member of Congress would do. I quit my job and cashed in my pension fund.

I quit in October. The election was in March. When I told my supervisor at the Illinois Department of Children & Family Services that I was leaving to run against Dan Rostenkowski for committeeman he looked at me like I'd told him I was leaving to try out to play quarterback for the Bears. He said, "Good luck," trying as hard as possible to sound sincere. My pension savings amounted to about $3,000. I took it and paid our mortgage ahead for six months—up to Election Day, plus one additional month.

With Soraida working, our family would probably have just enough money to make it through the campaign. But how would I buy signs and print flyers? How would I pay to have petitions printed? Rent a campaign office? I needed to fund our assault on the Chicago machine.

So I turned to my reliable money-making option. I went downtown, renewed my chauffer's license, and got back behind the wheel of a cab. I couldn't seem to leave my taxi days behind me. But I never felt like I was going backward. Driving a cab to me was always a reliable moneymaker, an emergency savings account that was always there. Now it would fund my door-to-door battle against racism. I was ready.

We had learned our Chicago campaign basics in Harold's campaign, but none of us had any idea how to franchise that very limited success. My campaign wasn't much more than my family and a few close friends. Soraida, as always, stood by my side. Her sister Lucy and Lucy's husband Juano, who was also my best friend, were with us all the time. Ada was enlisted, happily joining her big brother in another questionable project. Together, we did all the things we thought a successful campaign should do.

We found an office that I could afford on my cab-driving budget. It was a dirty storefront with one big room and a tiny bathroom. It had peeling tile on the floor. You could have pulled up every square in an afternoon if you felt an urge to redecorate. It had a metal accordion gate to pull closed and lock over the door and big front window. Without the gate, in that neighborhood somebody would have smashed the window, even though we didn't have anything to steal. The office didn't have any heat, so I bought a space heater and put a pan of water on top of it as a humidifier. The bathroom was the kind you might find in a nearly abandoned gas station if you left the interstate and got lost. You used our campaign bathroom only if it was essential. If you could wait until you got home, you were thrilled. The paint was peeling off of the walls, so I bought some white paint—white was always cheapest—and my good friend Felipe Najar and I painted the place. We had one phone because that is all we could afford. The security deposit for the phone line almost busted our budget, so we decided that one telephone was plenty for taking on Dan Rostenkowski.

The tallest hurdle in any local race, particularly in Chicago, is getting your name on the ballot. Democratic committeemen like Rosty excelled at running unopposed. The ballot rules required not only a minimum number of signatures from registered voters, but also a maximum. That made it much harder. If you needed 1,900 good signatures from actual registered voters to get on the ballot, one way to do it was to get a signature from every person with a pulse you encountered, and hope that of your 5,000 signatures, 1,900 of them were actually telling the truth when they told you they were registered voters. Not in Chicago. I needed 1,900 signatures to get on, but I couldn't turn in more than 2,500.

It was a brilliant machine trick, designed to protect the incumbents. I had to find almost two thousand actual registered voters, but I couldn't go over the limit. And I needed to convince them to sign for me. And I had to do it by December, when it was cold and people weren't too crazy about opening their door, especially to talk to some Puerto Rican stranger. It wasn't a coincidence that Illinois had one of the earliest primaries in the nation. We voted in March because the incumbents who controlled elections knew that very few rational humans want to campaign in Chicago in December, January, and February.

But I was determined to get on the ballot. I would drive my cab for three or four days, make enough money to print more petitions and pay the office rent, and then go door-to-door for three or four days, asking people to sign my petitions. Before I started, I knew I had to dress the part of an elected official. That was a problem, because I didn't own a suit, and a new suit wasn't in my campaign budget. So I pulled out my JCPenney credit card, headed into the men's department, and came out with a blue, 100 percent polyester suit. It couldn't have been more than $100, but it felt like the outfit of a winner to me. It wasn't like I had a lot of choices. I didn't have a hundred bucks. I owned two credit cards, Montgomery Ward and JCPenney, so my suit was going to have to come from one of those places. I went upscale and chose Penney's. I was ready to go door-to-door.

I didn't have any campaign consultants to tell me that as long as I was trying to look like a respectable candidate, I might also want to cut my hair. To go along with my new navy-blue suit I sported a kind of half afro. It was the afro of a thirty-year-old who was just beginning to lose some hair. It was long and wavy, higher in some places than others. But the afro was overshadowed by my mustache. I definitely wasn't losing any hair from my upper lip. My mustache was wide and thick and impressive. I still only weighed about 130 pounds. That my body weight could support that hair and mustache defied some law of physics. But Soraida liked my look, and it wasn't much different from most other Puerto Ricans in the neighborhood, so I never considered a trip to the barber. I just put on my suit and headed out with my petitions to talk to all of the little old Polish ladies in Dan Rostenkowski's neighborhood.

When I talked to white voters, I said I would stand up for Democrats and Democratic principles, and quite a few people signed. Some, I'm sure, just wanted to get the Puerto Rican with the giant mustache off their porch before he stole something.

With Puerto Ricans, my message was clear. I would talk about empowerment and fairness.

"It's our turn. We need Puerto Rican leaders who understand the Puerto Rican community," I would say over and over again, and it was an easy sell. I might not have understood all of the mechanics of campaigning yet, but I understood that Latinos were being ignored. I understood that Latinos were mad, just like I was. People responded, just like they responded when I talked about Harold Washington the year before. I would go up and down blocks that were almost entirely Puerto Rican in the 32nd Ward and talk with family after family who had never once been represented in any elected office by a Puerto Rican. Their alderman was Polish. A few blocks west, in the 26th Ward, all of the Puerto Ricans were represented by Michael Nardulli, an Italian. The Puerto Ricans to the north in the 33rd Ward were represented by Dick Mell, who was Polish and German. These were not leaders who were thinking of ways to reach out to their growing

Latino constituency. They were thinking of ways to make sure all of the Italians and Poles kept voting for them. Puerto Ricans were ready for change.

What surprised me was that I was having a tough time getting African Americans to sign my petitions. I couldn't even get most of them to open the door. They'd loved me when I was going door-to-door for Harold Washington. Then I was one of them, a minority standing up to the white guys in power. I knew that to have a chance with Rosty I would have to do well with my African American friends. But apartment after apartment, house after house, I was left standing in the hallway or on the porch. Or doors would open and I would say, "I'm Luis Gutiérrez and I'm running for Democratic Committeeman," and people would look annoyed that they had gotten up to walk all the way across their living room for such nonsense.

I spent a night thinking about my African American strategy. The next day, I abandoned the "Gutiérrez for Committeeman" approach.

Harold Washington was now mayor of Chicago, but that didn't mean he was running Chicago. Almost all of the white aldermen had formed an unmovable bloc of opposition to Harold. The leader was Ed Vrdolyak, who symbolized exactly what all of us who supported Harold wanted to put an end to in Chicago. "Fast Eddie," a nickname he didn't mind, wore expensive suits and gave bombastic speeches. He ignored minorities. He was driven around in a black Cadillac with "Eddie V10" on the license plate—his nickname and the ward he represented. If Harold wanted to declare a day honorary "Chicago Likes Puppies Day," Vrdolyak opposed him. Council wars were on, and Vrdolyak was the perfect villain, Harold Washington's very own Lex Luthor.

So the next day, when I started door-to-door in the black community, I didn't say a word about my campaign. Instead, I knocked on the voter's door and shouted "Committee to fire Ed Vrdolyak!" People answered the door when I said that. One guy who looked like he was just back from lifting weights at the gym answered the door, looked at my petition, and said, "This doesn't say a damn thing about firing Ed Vrdolyak. It says Luis Gutiérrez."

I looked up—way up—and told him, "That's right. That's me. Vote for me, and I'll vote to fire Ed Vrdolyak."

It was true. The Democratic committeemen elected the Cook County Democratic Party chairman, who happened to be Alderman Ed Vrdolyak. If I were committeeman, I would vote to fire him. The bodybuilder looked skeptical, but like almost every other African American voter who heard my "fire Eddie" pitch, he signed my petition. Once I explained why it would matter to have a committeeman who was loyal to Harold, more and more people were happy to sign up.

In the end, I had 2,400 signatures—hundreds more than I needed, 100 under the maximum. They were quality signatures. I knew, because I collected most of them myself. Usually, the machine challenges them. But I had the right number. I found the right people. My petitions were good. I was on the ballot.

THAT NEARLY SIXTY PERCENT of the ward had voted against Harold Washington for mayor didn't really deter me from making support for Harold the center of my campaign. In the African American precincts, I continued to talk about firing Vrdolyak. I took some of my cab money and printed up signs that matched Harold's campaign colors. More prominent than my name was IF YOU WANT THINGS FIXED, PUNCH 266, my ballot number displayed under a picture of Harold Washington.

When I was out collecting signatures, I made sure I went to every precinct in the ward, even if it was just to get a few signatures from a block. I wanted Rosty's people to think we had people everywhere, that the insurgent Luis Gutiérrez campaign had soldiers combing the countryside and leaving no village untouched. It was really just me, driving around in my VW.

Next, I decided to use the US Mail to help me seem omnipresent. The Rosty campaign was years before direct mail became a staple of every election. I don't believe I had ever heard the phrase "bulk rate." I thought I would drive Rosty crazy by mailing thank-you letters to all 2,400 people who had signed my petition. This was an expensive decision that meant more hours in the cab. Mine was a campaign that couldn't even afford to buy buttons. Instead, we borrowed a button-making machine. We sat in our cold campaign office, hand-stamping "Vote Gutiérrez" buttons out of plastic, thrilled when we had fifty buttons to give to our supporters. Deciding to buy 2,400 first-class stamps was a major investment.

I wrote a letter talking about fairness and social justice. Juano, Felipe, Soraida, Ada, and Lucy and I spent a week in the office folding the letters and addressing and stamping the envelopes. I would look at one of the 2,400 names on the petitions and then rewrite the address on the envelope, name after name.

Into our second day of addressing, my hand started to cramp and all I could think of was my long days after school at St. Michael's, writing, "I will not talk in class," or "I will not chew gum in class." Sometimes two hundred times, sometimes five hundred times. The fastest way to do it was to break the phrase down: write "I will not" over and over again down the left-hand side of the chalkboard, and then "talk in class" down the right-hand side until you were done. Trust me. I did it enough to know.

But there was no shortcut on the envelopes. These days, candidates write a large check to a direct mail consultant, who buys micro-targeted lists and sends out a glossy piece, complete with photos, that looks good enough to have been sent by Ralph Lauren or Chevrolet. Back then it was just me and my family and friends, addressing and stamping. It was less efficient, but much more fun. With each completed envelope, we thought we were guaranteeing chaos in the Rostenkowski campaign. "My God, this Gutiérrez guy is everywhere," Rosty would say when my letters covered the ward like a Chicago snowstorm.

When we finally finished, we didn't even know enough to take our letters to the central Chicago post office for faster delivery. We just carried big boxes down to the corner and dumped them in the neighborhood mailbox, waiting for the Gutiérrez tidal wave to spread by letter carrier across the 32nd Ward. All of us who worked on the project were proud. We ate our chips, drank our soda, sealed our envelopes, and felt as connected to a political campaign as you could. Of course, there was no tidal wave. I don't recall one voter ever saying a word about our letter, but we still thought the work was worth it.

My letter was in the mail. I was moving door-to-door, my Penney's suit was getting regularly dry cleaned and becoming a little shinier every time. When we needed money, I drove my cab. I invested the money in campaign flyers that my friend Slim Coleman had printed cheap at a leftist print shop called Justice Printing. But I needed money for more signs. That meant more hours in the cab.

So I did what any sensible candidate would do. I gave Soraida an early celebratory kiss and headed to the Gold Coast of Chicago to drive my cab on New Year's Eve. That's a huge night for cabbies. People are drunk and happy. Usually that means generous tips. And they aren't just a little tipsy in the way they are on a regular Thursday night when they stop off after work and decide they can make it home just fine. Most of them are drunk enough to look hard for the closest cab.

I hung out around the bars on Division Street, the center of nightlife in Chicago. I ran from Mother's Bar to big fancy parties at hotel ballrooms downtown and back up again. Mother's to the Palmer House, the Drake up to Rush Street, my cab filled with celebrating, grateful people. Some of them were sober enough to feel sorry for me for working New Year's Eve. I always made sure to mention my wife and daughter, celebrating without me at home. I drove and drove, laughing at every drunken joke, wishing every drunk a great New Year. When I made it home around five a.m., I handed Soraida the money. Chicago's partiers had paid for more campaign signs for Luis Gutiérrez.

With our petitions submitted and our letters in the mail, I was ready to utilize the New Year's money on blanketing the ward with signs. I had put a few in people's houses. I had one in my window. But my experience in San Sebastián for Puerto Rican independence had taught me that the easiest, quickest way to put up a sign was to find a blank wall, run out from your car, put up the sign, and then jump back in to look for the next empty space. A hit-and-run Gutiérrez sign strategy also fit the spirit of our campaign. We were everywhere and nowhere. Yesterday, a blank wall on an abandoned building; today, transformed by the magic of our campaign into a Gutiérrez billboard.

We had one essential tool in our efforts to blanket the ward with Gutiérrez signs. Wheat paste was a thin glue mixture that you could buy for next to nothing—perfect for my budget. All you needed was wheat paste, water, a bucket, and a few paintbrushes, and you were a sign crew. We mixed our paste, put it in the back of Juano's Buick station wagon, and headed out. At every stop, we would quickly dip the brush in the bucket, paint the back of the sign, and it was ready to post. Those signs really stuck. They didn't peel off.

It was cold, just after New Year's, and we wanted to ring in 1984 with signs everywhere. The viaduct on Fullerton and Western? Hit it with signs. Every space in the ward that already had an advertisement for a band or a bar or another political candidate? We wheat-pasted over it. The tantalizing side of a building with the large Post No Bills sign? Thanks for the tip, we nailed that one too. Post No Bills signs were like targets directing us to great locations. The empty blue side of the neighborhood mailbox? Too tempting to resist.

After a few weekends of laughing and pasting, always watching for cops just in case Rosty had his guys looking for us, the public spaces in the ward were screaming "Gutiérrez." Not too many years later, Chicago would ban political signs in public spots and charge you a hefty fine for every one you put up. It's a good law, and unfortunately, I think Juano and I did more than our share to move that law toward reality. But in that campaign, we were thrilled with the results of our hard work.

Some days, campaigning door-to-door, or driving around the neighborhood, I would look at all of the signs and think that there really was a Gutiérrez campaign juggernaut, almost forgetting that each and every one of the signs had been put up by my brother-in-law and me.

BUT ALL OF those actions were before Dan Rostenkowski flipped the switch to start his campaign machine. We might have been fooling ourselves. But we weren't fooling him. On Sunday morning, his signs went up, the cannon shot that started a three-week barrage that taught me exactly what machine politics meant.

Before I ran for office, I had a very basic understanding of the Chicago "machine." Precinct captains would come to your house and ask you to vote for the candidates the committeeman was supporting. The guys I chased down the street when they asked me to support Epton had been to my house before, and I had never argued with them. A lot of the time, they were pushing candidates for offices that didn't mean much to me. Did I really care which old white guy was elected Cook County clerk? I would mostly nod agreeably and they would be on their way.

You had a reason to pay attention when the committeeman's guys came to your door. In Chicago in 1984, paying your income, property, and sales taxes wasn't enough to guarantee that you received all of the services those taxes should buy. The machine created a middleman between your tax bill and your garbage pickup or your property-tax appeal. In Chicago, you didn't buy your government service wholesale, you bought it through a broker, and that broker was your committeeman.

The precinct captain wasn't some idealistic volunteer for Dan Rostenkowski, a man who wanted to knock on his neighbors' doors in January because he was thrilled with Rosty's latest speech about investment tax credits. Rosty's captains, just like those in every other ward in Chicago, were employees who owed their jobs to Rosty. The desire to keep their job, or get a promotion, or a transfer, or get their son or brother or best friend a job, provided very tangible motivation to help him. It also put them in a position to provide the services.

I told voters I would be a fighter. I told them I would support Harold Washington's agenda for change. I told them I would speak out for Democratic ideals. Rosty's guys told voters they would take care of their parking tickets. They would get their trees trimmed. I was competing with 150 Rosty volunteers who had conversations like this every day:

CAPTAIN: We hope you can vote for Dan Rostenkowski for
    Democratic committeeman. Can I count on your support?
VOTER: Well, we've had a pothole right in front of our house
    for a month. Can you help take care of it?
CAPTAIN: Absolutely. Chairman Rostenkowski would be happy
    to take care of that. Can I count on your vote?

VOTER: Thanks. Sure, I'll support him, and I'll be checking on the pothole.
CAPTAIN: Just remember who took care of it for you.

Then the first captain would tell another captain who was a deputy superintendent in the Department of Streets and Sanitation that he needed a pothole filled on Wabansia Street. And before Election Day, the voter had a nice, smooth surface in front of his house and Rosty had a vote.

There was no better time in Chicago to get out of jury duty, or have a building-code violation dismissed, than before Election Day. That winter, the 32nd Ward was a flurry of workers responding to a list of requests taken door-to-door, all placed with a captain, all ending with a voter saying, "Sure, I'm for Dan Rostenkowski."

I thought the success I had in selling Harold Washington to my neighbors would translate to a committeeman's race. But people were much likelier to vote their conscience for mayor. They usually voted their garbage needs for committeeman.

Most of these captains had lived in the neighborhood for years. They had been doing favors forever. Once they started putting the squeeze on their voters, I had trouble getting people to open their doors. Even people who had signed my petitions started hiding from me. I talked to one older Puerto Rican guy who had enthusiastically signed my petition but now was peering out at me from a door he would only open a few inches.

"I just wanted to make sure you were still supporting me. Remember, you signed my petition?"

"I know," he said, shaking his head. "I heard all about it. They came and talked to me about it. You got me in a lot of trouble. Please, you're a nice guy. I don't want any more trouble. Leave me alone." And the door was closed. It became the daily refrain during the last three weeks: "You got me in trouble." Most people didn't dislike me, they just didn't want grief from the guys who made sure they could get a city permit to close their street for the block party.

I should have listened to the guy who ran a popular bodega in the neighborhood. He was well known on his block and a proud Puerto

Rican. Early on, I asked him to put a sign in his window, and he smiled at me and invited me into the store.

"Are you hungry?" he asked. I said I was. He took me to the back and asked an employee to make me some sandwiches.

"When you're hungry, I'll feed you. You need some food for volunteers, I'll give it to you. If you are thirsty there's the cooler. I'm glad you're standing up for Puerto Ricans. But I'm never putting your sign in my window. You know why? Because you're going to lose. And after you lose, I don't need Rostenkowski's guys and their city building inspectors making my life miserable. What are you going to do for me after you lose?"

I thought he was behind the times, not willing to take a risk for his people. But by Election Day, store after store on the business strips— many of them owned by Puerto Ricans—were displaying Rostenkowski signs in their windows.

The Rostenkowski sign blitz didn't include just houses and businesses. It included city utility poles. I wheat-pasted some of my signs at the bottom. Rostenkowski had crews with trucks and ladders who covered up my signs and put two-sided signs at the very top, stapled together and secured with rope, up and down virtually every street in the ward. In the last three weeks, they bought every billboard in the neighborhood. I had sad, homemade-looking signs that Juano and I pasted on the sides of mailboxes. He had 20-by-40-foot billboards at the busiest intersections in town. I could almost hear Dan Rostenkowski laughing and saying, "Hey, Luis, you wanted to put up some signs? Watch how it's done."

The sea of orange and blue wasn't limited to signs. Other Rostenkowski swag infiltrated every aspect of daily life in the neighborhood. If you went to the grocery, half of the little old ladies were carrying Rostenkowski shopping bags, or wearing Rostenkowski rain hats. You wrote with a Rosty pen, combed your hair with a Rosty comb, did your dishes with a Rosty sponge. His name was embedded into daily life like a soundtrack accompanying your every step through the ward.

Rosty bothered to print only one piece of literature, but it made his point. It had his picture and detailed his accomplishments. The big headline asked a simple question. "Do you want the Chairman of the

Ways and Means Committee or a cab driver?" I had a pretty good idea how most people were going to answer that question.

Their blitz and their cabdriver literature accomplished their main goal. I was demoralized. I knew it was over. I knew it had never really begun. Soraida would encourage me at the end of the night. "You're doing the right thing," she would say. "You might be surprised at how well you do." My wife was hanging in there with me despite the money I had squandered. She was still with me, even though she lived on a block where the only window with a Gutiérrez sign was our own.

But it was clear to me what was going to happen. I was a political dead man walking. I was just waiting for Election Day so Rosty could tighten the noose. Mostly out of gratitude for my family and my volunteers, I kept going. I would talk to anyone who would still answer the door. We counted up our pluses, and I counted the days until it was over.

I worked hard on Election Day, greeting voters and counting the minutes until the polls closed. I decided I wanted to be at home with my wife at the end of the day.

Soraida was exhausted too. She had worked a precinct all day. Finally, we were in our kitchen, listening to the transistor radio we always kept on the counter. At seven p.m., the all-news station tolled its hourly bell and the announcer said, "It is now seven o'clock, and the polls are closed."

Soraida looked at me and saw a tear running down my cheek. I didn't know the last time she had seen me cry. She felt bad.

"Luis, don't cry. You should be proud. There is no reason to be sad."

And I told her the truth.

"I'm not crying because I'm sad. These are tears of happiness. I'm just so glad that it's over."

I HAD ASKED our volunteers to call me at home with their results as they got them from their precincts. Anita called from Wicker Park, from a precinct that was nearly all Puerto Ricans.

"We won!" she shouted. I was shocked and she was proud. A couple of other people called with good news too, all from the Puerto Rican neighborhoods.

"We almost beat him," my friends said, telling me that they lost their precinct by just a few votes. In Noble Square, the heart of my "fire Vrdolyak" campaign, we beat Rosty. The African Americans who had elected Harold Washington mayor had come out and voted for me.

People weren't as quick to call with the bad news, and there was plenty of it. Where there were fewer Puerto Ricans, we were getting crushed, losing 6 or 7 to 1. A lot of precincts came in with numbers like 180 to 25, 210 to 40. My quick calculations told me that ward-wide, I would get 20 percent of the vote, maybe 30.

To me, it didn't add up to much of an election-night party. We couldn't afford a ballroom or a restaurant. Not even a bodega. We were gathering in the basement of my friend's moving company. He was willing to risk Rosty's wrath by hosting the party. It wasn't very big, and it wasn't exactly festive, but it was all we had. We set up a few folding tables and chairs. We bought cheap beer and wine, some chips and pretzels. We were out of signs.

Soraida gave me a hug and a kiss and we were ready to go greet our volunteers. I appreciated their work, but to me it felt like a wake. I could sell newspapers and advocate for Puerto Rican independence, I could organize Puerto Rican students, but I didn't really know how to run a campaign. I had wasted a bunch of money, wasted my friends' time.

As we drove down to the moving company, I had already decided I would never, ever do this again. This was my last campaign. I thought about how sad everyone would be hearing the final, lopsided results, and how depressing the chips and soda at the moving company would be. I had let everyone down.

We made it to the party. Soraida and I held hands and walked down the narrow steps to the basement. You had to duck your head to make it into the room.

As we stepped off the bottom step, the room erupted in applause and cheers. Every single one of the forty or fifty people who had ever addressed an envelope or knocked on a door or put up a sign had turned out, and they were celebrating. Juano and Lucy were drinking my cheap beer and smiling and laughing. They had been in one of the Puerto Rican precincts and almost won. Ada was thrilled. She was a winner, beating Rosty at her neighborhood school. Every person had a story of a Rostenkowski precinct captain who was mad at them because we had gotten a few votes more than they expected.

People couldn't wait to see me, to hug me, to congratulate me, to thank me for working so hard.

I thought, Congratulate me for what? We got our asses kicked. Rosty is laughing at us. But nobody else felt that way. One person after another said, "We'll get him next time," or "I know how to do better in the next election." One by one, I saw that people weren't kidding, they weren't just trying to make me feel better. Somebody was playing music on a cheap tape player. It was a real party, a celebration. The basement was small enough to be crowded, filled with excitement. People compared stories. They wanted to know what was next.

At first, I smiled and just said thanks. I didn't want to be impolite, remind them that we lost, tell them that it was over. Then, person by person, I listened. The people in that room believed. They believed in Harold Washington. They believed Latinos should have some power. My friends and family, who had gone out and knocked on doors in the cold for me and had just lost by thousands of votes, wanted to go out and do it again. They believed a campaign was about more than just getting your trees trimmed. We had actually beaten Rostenkowski in a few precincts, and done pretty well in several more. Puerto Ricans—a lot of Puerto Ricans—had stood up to the machine and voted for Luis Gutiérrez. It didn't matter that I was broke, or inexperienced, or that I was driving a cab. They believed, and they were ready for the next campaign.

I looked around that room, at Soraida and Juano, at Lucy and Ada and Felipe and all of my friends. I was proud of them. I was grateful to them. I thought, If they are ready, then I'm ready. My retirement from politics lasted sixty minutes.

CHAPTER ELEVEN

Learning to Beat the Chicago Machine

MY NEW OFFICE looked like an interrogation room, the kind of place where two tough Irish guys might do a good-cop, bad-cop routine on me. It was a big corner office, but all it had was one metal desk, one metal filing cabinet, and a lone lightbulb hanging in the middle of the ceiling.

A few months before, the closest thing I had to an office was Juano's beat-up station wagon. I had a mortgage I was paying with my cashed-out pension fund. The day after I lost to Rosty, all I had was my 24 percent of the vote and my cab. But about four months after my losing campaign, Mayor Washington decided that Luis Gutiérrez—the reckless Puerto Rican kid who thought he could beat Congressman Dan Rostenkowski—should work for the city of Chicago.

Now I had my own office. I also had my own driver.

My driver was Carlo, an ancient Italian guy who looked like he was just over from Sicily. Carlo was a very round, very short guy with a bald head. We were a good pair, both about five-foot-six—but he had about 100 pounds on me. He drove a Ford Crown Victoria as long as a boat. He couldn't have been friendlier. The first day he picked me up, he told me he had recently been released from prison. I asked him what he was in for.

"Some activities that my associates and I had been up to," he told me, cheerfully continuing down the road toward my new place of work.

I was curious. "What kind of activities? Who were your associates?"

He just smiled. He suggested in his Italian accent that if he had told other interested parties more about his associates, he might not have been sent to jail at all. I might be his new boss, but that didn't mean he was going to share any secrets with me.

Carlo picked me up at the house on Homer in the morning, got me to work, and then sat and drank coffee with his son, waiting for me to ask him to drive me someplace else. His son worked for me too. They both came with the job. They spent a lot of time talking about what to have for lunch. I had advanced from driving people for money to being driven around. I had employees that included a father-and-son team.

My new job was as a supervisor at the sprawling work yard and office space around Northwest Incinerator in Chicago. Northwest Incinerator had been burning about 20 percent of Chicago's garbage since the late 1960s, and the two huge smokestacks that towered over it were Northwest Side landmarks. It was supposed to be the solution to Chicago's garbage problem, but in reality environmental groups were about six or seven years away from shutting it down. It was surrounded by huge trucking and maintenance yards. It served as a warehouse for parts and supplies. There was a whole world of city workers surrounding the place that I never knew existed.

As assistant superintendent in the city of Chicago's Bureau of Equipment Services, I suddenly had one of those mysterious jobs I always heard the precinct captains talking about. I had been hired by Ernest Barefield, Mayor Harold Washington's chief of staff.

During my campaign, the mayor had avoided me. He didn't send me a check or attend a rally. When he was asked about me at a campaign event for other reform-minded candidates, he said, "I like Luis too," as he quickly walked away from the podium. Harold didn't like Rosty, and Rosty didn't like him. But that didn't mean the mayor was going to support a cabdriver with no chance of beating the powerful congressman who was bringing in hundreds of millions of dollars for his city.

But once I was no longer Rosty's opponent, things changed. The mayor needed allies. He apparently thought my kamikaze effort showed some initiative—a senseless determination. I was learning, to my surprise, that my unsuccessful campaign made me someone to know in Chicago politics. I was like the puny kid who straps on a helmet and charges as hard as he can toward the other team's all-pro middle linebacker. I might have gotten knocked unconscious, but it made people think maybe I was a good guy to have on their team.

It wasn't long before Barefield called me to his office.

"The mayor needs help, and he's looking for young, talented people for his administration. He is looking for people who want to put his plans in place. He would like to see what you can do for the city," Barefield said.

I was in City Hall, being offered a job working for Harold Washington. I didn't even have to think about it.

"I will do anything for this mayor. I'm going to do a great job. I'll be his eyes and ears and you can count on me," I said. I shook his hand and I was ready to leave.

Barefield smiled and asked if I was interested in knowing how much the job paid.

It hadn't even occurred to me. Working for Harold Washington was enough for me. That was like winning the lottery. When Barefield offered me the job, Soraida and I were broke. I barely cared how much it paid, though I remember today to the dollar what Barefield told me—$29,844. It was nearly double what I was making as a social worker.

WHEN I REPORTED to Northwest Incinerator, another guy showed up and told me he was my assistant. I asked him what he meant. He just shrugged his shoulders and told me it meant he would do whatever I told him to do. I told him I didn't need an assistant. Within an hour, the only other Puerto Rican guy who worked there told me he heard I was firing my assistant and that I should hire him. Puerto Ricans should stick together. I told him I still didn't need an assistant, even if it was a Puerto Rican assistant.

Northwest Incinerator seemed to collect people who were some-body's "guy," but their sponsor didn't know quite know where to put them. My supervisor was an older Irish guy. I expected an orientation, or an assignment. Maybe a work plan. He just looked at me in my shiny JCPenney special that had barely survived the campaign and said, "So you're the mayor's guy?"

"That's right."

It was hard to get used to that idea, but I liked the sound of it. My new boss didn't look like he was the African American mayor's guy. He looked more like a Jameson guy.

He simply said, "Just let me know what you are up to."

Nothing more. No job description. No "Welcome to the City of Chicago" training video. What I was up to was trying to figure out what I was up to. The mayor had given me a lot of responsibility. All of the motor truck drivers reported to me. I had an office and a title and the mayor had my back.

I had just run a whole campaign against patronage. Now I was seeing it up close. One of the results of the dysfunctional city coun-cil was that Mayor Washington, to keep the city running, needed to hire people who would actually carry out his orders. City departments were staffed mostly by guys just like Rosty's captains who had come to my house and asked me to vote for Epton. The mayor was running a city brimming with four decades' worth of political workers hired by Irish mayors named Daley and Byrne. Most of them hated Harold Washington. It didn't make it easy to carry out a reform agenda.

I looked around the warehouse and the yard, filled with guys sitting in trucks reading newspapers and studying take-out menus like they were treasure maps. Teamsters seemed to move vehicles around aim-lessly like they were playing some sort of game of tag with their trucks. This was where tax dollars went to die. Barefield wanted to see what I could do. I decided my assignment was to make as much mischief as I could get away with.

I told my boss that I didn't need an assistant.

He looked annoyed. "You know, that's just more work for me. It means I need to find another place to put him."

I told him I was trying to save the city money. Then I started asking guys questions about how all of the purchasing worked. At first, people looked at me like I was crazy. I just showed them my badge that said ASSISTANT SUPERINTENDENT and kept asking. How did they give notice to the contracts? How did they decide who would bid? What constituted an emergency? It didn't take me long to figure out that they had a lot of procurement "emergencies," which made it easier to give out a contract without a prolonged competitive bidding process. The same vendors would always get the "emergency" business. You could make a fortune if you knew how this worked. Nobody wanted to talk to me, but nobody really wanted to get on the bad side of the mayor, either, so they usually told me just enough to make me go bother someone else.

I started reporting back to the mayor's office. Ben Reyes, Harold's deputy mayor who helped me get my job, seemed impressed about the reports, but more pleased that I wasn't just sitting in my office sending my assistant out to get coffee. I felt like I had passed his test.

Before I knew it, I was driving down to Hyde Park for a different kind of meeting. The only reason I had ever gone to Hyde Park before was to drop off a fare. Now I was on my way to the mayor of the city of Chicago's condo.

Harold Washington liked to hold political meetings at home on the weekends. I was invited to talk politics with him. On Saturday, his condo would fill with people like me. Some of us had helped in his campaign, some of us had taken on guys like Rostenkowski. All of us thought we were part of a crusade to change Chicago. We would do anything for him.

His condo struck me as the kind of place somebody just out of college would have, simple and functional. He would move around a few chairs and seven or eight of us would sit and talk about how we could overcome Alderman Ed Vrdolyak and his opposition to the mayor's policies. He would ask questions about Latino priorities and how he could expand his Latino vote.

For me, it was like being in the presence of a celebrity. Mayor Washington was big, nearly six feet tall, carrying thirty or forty more pounds than he should have. He looked like a former football player who had stopped working out. He had a booming baritone voice. The smile that had charmed Chicago worked in private as well. He liked to laugh and have fun. And he could talk. He would talk politics until he tired out everyone in the room. The televised debates had been huge in making him mayor. People tuned in to hear Rich Daley and Jane Byrne—the two real candidates—debate, and it was the practically unknown black guy who was funny and smart and articulate.

He was even more entertaining in private. He seemed to have no life or interests outside of politics and government. He didn't play golf. He didn't go to the theater. His hobby was politics. The mayor would vent about the latest city council outrage or his difficulty getting the army of city workers who were loyal to Daley and Rostenkowski and Vrdolyak and twenty other guys just like them to do anything for him.

Every meeting was an education. He knew firsthand that minority neighborhoods had been ignored by the machine. The more I listened to him, the more convinced I was that he was the beginning of something new in Chicago. Eventually, he started calling me to City Hall. I met with commissioners, suggested other Latinos he could hire, ways the city could help our neighborhood. I talked about our need for affordable housing. I told him we had to tow away the abandoned cars that littered our neighborhood like hot-dog wrappers. He listened. I took away simple marching orders from those meetings. I should find ways, in my humble corner of Chicago at a giant garbage incinerator, to help put the mayor's agenda in place.

My annoyed Irish boss noticed how much I was gone. He thought I was up to something. He called me into his office.

"I've given you a lot of freedom here. Now I understand you're out running around City Hall. You can't leave your workplace without permission. You need to check with me, and you need to put together some reports on exactly what it is you're doing all of the time away from the office," he told me.

He looked pleased that he was finally putting me in my place. But I had a simple thought: I was the one meeting with the mayor, not him.

"Just so I understand, when the mayor calls me, I should tell him that I need to get permission from you first before I meet with him. And after the meeting, I need to report back to you and let you know everything the mayor has told me. I want to make sure I have this right—I'm supposed to report all of my private conversations with the mayor to you—that's what you're telling me?"

We looked at each other for a while. He was probably cursing silently that Chicago was now a city where a skinny Puerto Rican kid could tell him to go take a leap.

He smiled at me and said, "That won't be necessary."

Not long after that, my boss was happy because the mayor's people transferred me. I moved to the Bureau of Electricity. I didn't know AC from DC. Beyond my ability to plug in a toaster, I knew nothing about electricity. The mayor's people didn't care. They just wanted me to cause trouble. They kept getting complaints about how long it took for the bureau to finish basic jobs. Linemen would go out to fix a streetlight and it would take all day. Now my office was my car, and Barefield unleashed me to follow city crews around and figure out what they were actually doing.

Right away, I realized that the first thing crews did in the morning after reporting to their jobsite was go to breakfast. I would sit in my car, wait for the trucks to show up, and then follow the crew into the diner, where they were ordering eggs and short stacks. Linemen are big guys. I weighed about 130. I was the last person they expected to interrupt their morning coffee. I asked them how they could take a break before the workday had even started. They looked at me like I had just flown in from Jupiter. I was tempted to bring along a recording that played the words "Who the fuck are you?" just to save the guys the trouble of saying it every time. I kept showing my ID, and eventually, word spread that there was a crazy new superintendent out causing chaos. A guy who didn't answer to any of their political patrons—a guy who was doing the mayor's dirty work.

That didn't stop guys from taking extended breaks. I went to the Southeast Side, where it was taking forever to wire new stoplights. There were two or three city trucks, and orange caution cones diverting and slowing down traffic where the street was torn up. But nobody was there.

I rapped on the window where one lonely driver was sitting in his truck drinking coffee. I showed him my city ID. He didn't look too pleased.

"Where is everybody?"

"I'm here."

"I see that. Where's everybody else?"

"All I know is that I'm here."

"Well, I'm sure they'll be back soon."

I sat in my car across the street from him. He looked like I was keeping him awake. I figured the crew couldn't disappear for long. I was wrong. We sat all afternoon. The driver didn't have any way to escape. I was bored too, but at least I ruined his day.

Just before quitting time, the door to the bar on the corner opened and three city workers came out and walked across the street, ready to get back in their trucks and go home. I introduced myself, told them I had been sitting there for hours. I headed back to City Hall to write them up for spending the afternoon in the bar instead of fixing the streetlight. I did this over and over again—chasing down workers, sitting in trucks, writing people up, and then negotiating with the union over punishment. I wish I could say I upended a culture of city workers who were more committed to getting their committeeman re-elected than filling potholes or trimming trees. I didn't, but I did convince Mayor Washington and Ernie Barefield that I was a guy they could count on.

FROM THE BEGINNING, the mayor was really testing me for one task. He needed a few more loyal aldermen to overcome Eddie Vrdolyak. He thought his chance was coming. Civil rights groups had sued the city over the last city council map, which was drawn after the 1980 census to specifically limit minority representation throughout Chicago.

Nowhere was their creative mapmaking more obvious than in Puerto Rican neighborhoods. Humboldt Park was the heart of Chicago's Puerto Rican community. The intersection of North Avenue and Western Avenue was close to the epicenter of the Puerto Rican population in Chicago. The white aldermen who drew the map put their compass at North and Western and used it as the starting point for three different wards—splitting the Puerto Ricans into different voting blocs for different white aldermen. Close to 100,000 Puerto Ricans were conveniently divided in thirds so they wouldn't outnumber the Poles and Ukrainians, the Irish and Germans. The old bosses understood coalition building—with one another. They just didn't want anyone in their coalition with any skin color darker than a suntan.

The city under Jane Byrne had been fighting the voting rights lawsuit, pretending the ward boundaries were perfectly fair. They weren't. They were an obvious violation of the voting rights act, but the legal fight had held up the suit for years.

When Harold Washington was elected, he sent the city attorney to court to say "We surrender—guilty as charged." Harold's lawyers said they agreed that the boundaries were discriminatory. They wouldn't fight it, and urged a remap. Even in a Chicago filled with judges sympathetic to the machine, it was hard to beat back a lawsuit when the defendant said they agreed with the plaintiff.

For Harold, there was much more than fairness at stake. He was stuck with an unbending, intransigent city council led by Ed Vrdolyak. They had taken over the committees and made it hard for aldermen loyal to the mayor to even put up a new stop sign in their ward.

The deadlocked Chicago City Council was so dysfunctional it was a national joke. Every city council meeting was a new piece of Chicago political theater, usually ending with the passage of legislation by Vrdolyak's majority. The mayor would veto it. Vrdolyak didn't have enough votes to override the veto. The meetings consisted of three or four hours of yelling that led to virtually nothing.

The *Wall Street Journal* called it "Beirut on the Lake." Comedian Aaron Freeman coined the phrase "council wars." He cast Harold as "Luke Skytalker." Vrdolyak was "Darth Vrdolyak," a menacing villain who spoke of the power of the "clout." There was no limit to the antics, and the anger and animosity was very real, and ugly. In one city council meeting, Vrdolyak questioned the mayor's sexual preferences.

The competing city council factions didn't argue just over big issues—they couldn't agree on basic appointments to boards and commissions. There were fifty members in the city council. Vrdolyak controlled 29 votes. They opposed the mayor's bond issue, which he was going to use to repair streets and sidewalks all over the city. They couldn't agree on contracting regulations, so projects to expand O'Hare Airport and fix mass transit lines almost shut down. In candid moments, white aldermen openly admitted that their strategy was simple: make sure Harold couldn't get anything done and elect somebody else next time.

Cartoonists had a field day. In one, a newspaper editor asks his reporter if anything has changed since Washington became mayor. The reporter says, "Nope. He's still black."

It was that simple, and Harold knew it. Harold was articulate and forceful and he understood completely the dynamic that was keeping him from actually running the city. He said it all the time. Irish voters could elect an Irish mayor and that's just smart ethnic politics, but when black voters elect a black mayor, somehow that's a threat to all white people.

The only way to slay Darth Vrdolyak and declare peace in the council wars was for the mayor to have a loyal city council. Everyone believed that when they threw the old map out and drew a new, fair one, Puerto Ricans would have a new ward in Chicago. And the mayor just happened to have a Puerto Rican guy working for him who had already convinced a bunch of Puerto Ricans to vote for him. We were just waiting for the new map. I was on the campaign trail already.

This time it wasn't so lonely. I wasn't just some unknown tilting at the unmovable windmill of Dan Rostenkowski. I was the guy who just might be able to give control of the city council to Harold Washington.

Instead of begging my family and friends to campaign for me, I had strangers asking me how they could help. Word traveled that I was working for the city. I wasn't shy about telling people I had been meeting with the mayor. I wasn't naïve. I knew that most of the supporters I met every day weren't Luis Gutiérrez fanatics. They were Harold Washington fanatics. So was I. We had a common interest—delivering the city from the stranglehold of the Vrdolyak Twenty-Nine.

The only problem was we didn't have a map, or a ward, yet. So I started the West Town Independent Political Organization. I applied every skill I had learned from the Puerto Rican independence move-ment and the Union of Puerto Rican Students, as well as my Rosten-kowski failure. We published a newspaper. We formed an organization with bylaws and elected officers. We started a garbage-can fund to buy garbage cans in areas that Mike Nardulli, our old Italian alderman, had completely ignored. We even stenciled my name onto some of the garbage cans.

It's hard to convey just how neglected some parts of the Puerto Rican neighborhoods were. The white leaders had started abandoning Humboldt Park when Puerto Ricans started moving in. The Hum-boldt Park neighborhood had always been an immigrant magnet, and it thrived for a long time. The two-hundred-acre park at the center of it was a showplace. The neighborhood was home to Scandinavians, then Poles, then German and Russian Jews. Division Street, at the south end of Humboldt Park, had nurtured Saul Bellow and Nelson Algren and Studs Terkel. The changing immigrant groups elected changing immigrant leaders.

Until the Puerto Ricans came. Then the last wave of white immi-grants worked hard to stop the clock and hang on to their power. Just like Harold saw happen with blacks, the white power structure worked harder and longer to stay in charge when Humboldt Park turned Puerto Rican. They split up our population, and focused their resources on the dwindling white neighborhoods. When I came back to Chicago from college at Albany, I was shocked at just how much Humboldt Park had changed. My old neighborhood of Lincoln Park was improv-ing so much that Puerto Ricans couldn't afford to live there anymore. Wealthy families, mostly white, were buying old houses and starting to renovate and rebuild. There was construction everywhere. Fancy restaurants were replacing corner bars. Lincoln Park was becoming home to the very wealthiest Chicagoans. My old Latino and black neighbors were out of luck.

In Humboldt Park, things were going in the opposite direction. Everyone referred to the heart of the neighborhood as "the pit." In the pit, entire sides of many blocks were nothing but abandoned houses and empty lots. Puerto Rican families lived on the other side, dealing with the gangs and drug dealers who took over the shells of houses.

Whole blocks became garbage dumps. Companies that didn't want to pay garbage fees at private dumps would send their dump trucks and unload right in the middle of a lot, their drivers idly looking around and smoking cigarettes while they poured garbage and building debris across the street from where kids were playing. This "fly dumping" was routine. Lots were littered with abandoned cars. You could collect a wheelbarrow full of empty beer bottles in ten minutes. You could fill up a bucket with hypodermic needles.

Nardulli didn't want anything to do with the pit. He pretended it didn't exist. For the city of Chicago, it was a ghost town of sporadic garbage pickup, busted-up sidewalks, broken streetlights. It seemed beyond repair.

We saw opportunity. And voters. Just being willing to walk up and down the street in the pit was a novelty for candidates. But it didn't stop me and Juano and Felipe. Or any of my friends from the West Town Independent Political Organization. We registered voters, we wrote down complaints. We pounded in giant stakes all over the abandoned lots to help keep out the fly dumpers. We talked about affordable housing. Nardulli didn't want any low-cost housing. That would just mean more Puerto Ricans.

I felt at home in the pit. I had lived around poor Puerto Ricans my whole life. I survived the Harrison Street Gents and the pool hustlers in San Sebastián; I could survive here. But I still thought, This neighborhood is bad—worse than any Puerto Rican neighborhood I could have imagined while growing up in Lincoln Park. The way Chicago's machine had let Humboldt Park crumble was a crime.

Plenty of people agreed with me. The West Town IPO was an organization of organizations. We had black nationalists and white radicals looking to make trouble. We had somebody from every left-leaning, Marxist-sympathizing, radical organization in the city. We had Puerto Rican Independentistas. Members of the Puerto Rican Socialist Party. Housing advocates. Environmentalists. But we had one abiding interest—there was an aldermanic election coming up, and every single one of us wanted to take control of the city council away from Ed Vrdolyak.

We needed money to keep the organization going. I hadn't convinced anyone to give me money to run against Rostenkowski. The only money I raised came from passengers in my cab. This time, I was determined to be more professional. We rented a hall on Milwaukee Avenue for a fund-raiser. I swept and mopped it myself. I carried the kegs of beer up the stairs. They were heavy, but I got them up the steps and put them on ice. Soraida and Lucy and Felipe and I made phone calls inviting people. There was excitement about our organization. But the real excitement was about the one special guest who was coming—Mayor Harold Washington.

The night of the event, the place was packed, and when the mayor arrived I finally had a chance to introduce him to Soraida. I told him that she was not only my wife but also our organization's treasurer. He took her hand and Harold gave Soraida a long, slow look from the top of her head to the tips of her toes, and said to me, "My, my, my. I see the secret to your success. A beautiful and smart woman. It's good that you let her control the money."

Harold was like that—charming enough to get away with a little flirtation without offending anyone. That night, after the event, Soraida said to me before we fell asleep, "Even the mayor knows I'm the reason for your success." Harold created a fan for life in Soraida.

When Harold spoke at the event, he couldn't have been clearer about his plans for Latino neighborhoods: "How can our city have so many Latinos and no representation? It's not fair. It's not right. But we can fix it. We can draw a fair map, and we can elect Luis Gutiérrez to the city council."

People roared, people hugged me and patted me on the back. Harold had made it official. I was Harold's guy, and we were going to put the city council on his side.

WHILE I WAS raising money, civil rights groups were negotiating the settlement to the redistricting lawsuit. I studied possible alignments of the new wards. I knew the machine would protect Rostenkowski and keep all of the Poles in the 32nd Ward. My guess was the predominantly Puerto Rican ward would be the 26th Ward. I also figured that I didn't currently live where the new ward would be. I had to move.

Soraida and I hated to leave our house on Homer. We had survived the fire and rebuilt our home. We had raised Omaira there. But I didn't think Homer was going to be part of the new Puerto Rican ward. I moved to the most Puerto Rican, centrally located block I could find, figuring it would be the hardest to keep out of the new ward. We opened our campaign office on Division Street. I placed my bets and hoped for the best.

When the maps were announced in October, my wager paid off. My house was in the 26th Ward. Most of Humboldt Park was in the 26th Ward. Wicker Park, where I had run against Rosty and convinced most of the Puerto Ricans to vote for me, was in the 26th Ward. I started with a base. The mayor sent in some of his best political strategists. Every day, people like Slim Coleman, a transplanted Texan who was one of the mayor's key citywide organizers, would help turn our idealistic volunteers into a precinct army.

Vrdolyak and the machine studied the map too. Even they knew they couldn't run a white candidate in this ward. They needed a Puerto Rican. Vrdolyak's ally, Alderman Dick Mell, helped him find one. Just a year before, Mell had one of his precinct captains, Manny Torres, appointed to the Cook County Board when the incumbent was convicted of extortion. Manny was Puerto Rican. He was a big, tough guy who was a body builder. And he was a loyal machine Democrat—exactly the guy they needed to keep the 26th ward loyal to Darth Vrdolyak. They had their candidate.

To beat the machine in Chicago, you needed to keep down their votes from people who don't exist. My volunteers and the mayor's experts looked at the voter rolls in Rostenkowski and Nardulli's old areas. The lists showed a lot more Polish families than you saw when you actually walked down the street. We kept knocking people off the voters' list, one after another. People you just couldn't find when you went to the address on the polling sheet. Kids who had moved away years ago. People who were dead, and had been for a while. Voters who seemed to keep their voting rights longer than their breathing rights.

I was amazed at how quickly we became an efficient political operation, and how far I had come since my homemade effort against Rostenkowski. We kept calling Manny Torres the machine candidate, and it drove him crazy.

"Look at the Gutiérrez campaign!" he would yell, his muscles bulging. "He has all the mayor's people. He has all of the mayor's money. He has the mayor's organization. Gutiérrez is the machine candidate," Manny said again and again.

In some ways, he was right. Even in a city where your archenemy controlled the city council, being the mayor gave you political power. But we were still running against decades of control by a Democratic machine that Harold was trying to dismantle. They matched us worker for worker in the precincts, and raised more money than we did. They had experienced precinct captains, a bunch of guys who worked at Northwest Incinerator and a hundred other city jobs. We had affordable-housing advocates and teachers, immigrants' rights agitators, professors. Our team looked ragtag, but we became organized and disciplined. We knew much more than one seat in the city council was at stake. It wasn't just about a city job for us; it was about changing the city.

With the mayor's help, I finally had some money to spend. Instead of wheat paste, we could afford billboards. I remembered the feeling of drowning in a sea of orange and blue Rostenkowski signs. The first thing I did was buy all the billboards closest to my campaign office and my house. I never wanted to look out my front window at my opponents' signs again. I thought about my sign strategy some more, then I went back to the sign company and bought the billboard directly across from Manny's campaign office. The first thing he saw every day was a giant GUTIÉRREZ FOR ALDERMAN billboard. The colors, of course, were bright orange and blue.

Our campaign strategy was simple. Take the 26th Ward away from the machine, and give the city council back to the people. We talked housing and neighborhood cleanup, our fair share of services and respect for Latinos. We said the name Ed Vrdolyak almost as much as the name Luis Gutiérrez—especially when we were talking to African American voters.

Manny's strategy was simple too. He called me soft on crime, a dangerous radical, a terrorist.

That people called me a terrorist without thinking twice about it says a lot about how minorities are treated as political candidates. It's true that I had always been an activist and a progressive. When I was running against Rostenkowski, I was active in the Puerto Rican high school in the neighborhood. It was a community center and a haven for progressive Puerto Ricans who believed in Puerto Rican independence. During my time at Northeastern, the Puerto Rican Student Union agitated constantly for leftist causes. So Manny Torres got copies of the newspaper we published and waved them around, quoting from stories that promoted Puerto Rican independence and bashed the United States for being colonialists. Even on the island, people had been suspicious of independence supporters. Our opponents always tried to portray us as anti-American. A few months of independence activism in San Sebastián moved me quickly from being called the "Americanito" to being called anti-American. It didn't make any sense. I missed America, I loved America. But living on an island in the Caribbean, standing with a giant paddle stirring a cauldron full of bubbling pig innards and listening to all of my family and neighbors speak Spanish, it didn't make any sense to me that America should be in charge of Puerto Rico.

But the idea that you could love America but hate America's relationship with Puerto Rico was too complicated for people to understand. The more time I spent in Chicago, the more I saw that the people who understood this feeling best were people who had lived in both places. They understood that America's relationship with the island was fundamentally one of ruler and the ruled; an English-speaking world power enforcing its will on a very different society and culture simply because it could.

But Manny Torres had never lived a day in Puerto Rico. Manny, just like Rostenkowski, looked at me and my "radical" friends and saw danger. But politically, he saw opportunity. To Manny and his supporters, many of whom were nervous white voters, my campaign embodied the stereotype of scary Latinos. I had been a student activist. I led sit-ins that shut down the president of the university's office. I had wild, curly hair and a giant mustache. My campaign was filled with a bunch of African Americans who supported Harold Washington and a bunch of white liberals who looked like they were disappointed the '60s were over.

Many minorities who've run for office know how this works. Just ask Barack Obama. Who could be less threatening to white voters than Barack Obama? He was president of *Harvard Law Review.* He's handsome, articulate, and soft-spoken. By nature, he's a conciliator. Still, despite those credentials, 70 percent of white men in America voted against him for president in 2012. And what is the go-to trick of his opponents when they really need to attack him? Obama's a scary radical. His name rhymes with Osama. He's secretly a Muslim. He's an immigrant. He hung around with Bill Ayers. His pastor is a black nationalist. And—horror of horrors—he likes Saul Alinsky.

I've faced this resistance from my first election. Fox News would have found my 1986 campaign ten times more horrifying than anything Obama's ever done. Most of my white supporters were huge Saul Alinsky followers, and some of them carried around his book, *Rules for Radicals.* I was a Puerto Rican nationalist. In 1980s Chicago, if radical meant you thought it was time to throw out the machine, I was as radical as they came.

So it wasn't a surprise when a reporter showed up the Saturday morning before the election and asked me to comment on the unexploded pipe bomb that had been found on the front steps of Manny's office. I always had plenty to say, but that one stumped me. So I said the first thing that came to my mind. Manny probably put it there himself. He was setting me up. They always wanted to prove I was a terrorist, what better way to do it?

That's the kind of campaign it was. Two weeks before the primary, Cook County state's attorney Rich Daley announced a crackdown on gangs in Humboldt Park. Most of the time the state's attorney acted like Humboldt Park didn't even exist, but this man, who would one day be mayor, was supporting Manny, and their campaign was a law-and-order campaign. They arrested a bunch of Puerto Ricans. I'm sure some of them deserved it. I'm sure some of them didn't. But I know the crackdown wasn't fooling anyone. City officials had neglected Humboldt Park for too long for anyone to think that the arrests were anything more than a campaign stunt. People knew it was political, and even more Gutiérrez signs went up in the pit, which Manny tried to spin by telling people all of the gangs were on my side.

We felt momentum moving our way. Every day, finding Puerto Ricans who wanted to register to vote was easier. But there were still plenty of white voters in the 26th Ward, and Vrdolyak and Mell had the ward blanketed with workers. Every day was like a parade of campaign volunteers, going up and down blocks, knocking on doors, giving the other guys the evil eye from across the street. The media covered it like a street brawl.

The Sunday before Election Day, we thought we were done with bombs and arrests and charges of terrorism. But then reporters showed up at one of our campaign events in a frenzy. Did I want to comment on the shots that had been fired at Manny Torres?

When Manny and his wife left his campaign office for a Sunday-evening event, they said they heard three gunshots and then heard bullets hit the building behind them. The first thing Manny did after making sure he wasn't bleeding was talk to reporters.

"The supporters of Luis Gutiérrez are shooting at me," he said. The police found bullet casings. Whether they were real or whether somebody put them there, I'll never know. He certainly didn't have any evidence we were shooting at him, because we weren't. He couldn't say who, exactly, among my supporters was shooting at him. That didn't stop the Chicago reporters from covering his charge. They came to see me, and I answered with a charge of my own. After all, what are you supposed to do when a reporter asks you if you are trying to have your opponent killed? I said we were about to win this election, so why would I want to risk it all by committing a felony? Obviously, Manny was exaggerating and lying when he said we were involved.

The reporters ran back to Manny. This time his wife answered. She was more emphatic.

"If you find the bullets, you'll find Luis Gutiérrez's fingerprints on them," she said.

How was I supposed to answer that one? That I had never touched a bullet in my life? You can't answer it. You just keep getting ready for Election Day. Nobody was ever arrested, and I don't think anyone looked very hard. It was easier to let Manny keep telling people I was shooting at him.

ELECTION DAY was cold and gloomy. I knocked on doors and rounded people up all day. Two years earlier, against Rosty, Election Day had been like a death march. Heading from one polling place to another, my relatives and friends outnumbered five to one, six to one, by Rosty's people. This time we matched them person for person. Nobody was lonely, nobody was intimidated. We were taking back Humboldt Park and Wicker Park and all of our neighborhoods. We were fighting for our mayor.

The night before the election, Mayor Washington appeared live, on the early news, on a split-screen interview with Vrdolyak. Harold's message was clear—we're deciding control of the city council tomorrow, and I need you to support Luis Gutiérrez.

He called me after the interview. He was in a good mood.

"How are we gonna do tomorrow, Lou?" he asked.

I told him we were going to make it. And then I said he didn't have to appear with Ed Vrdolyak to help me. It was beneath him. Vrdolyak didn't deserve that respect. He didn't have to do that for me.

Harold just laughed.

"Lou, I'm just letting my people know who my champion is in the election tomorrow. We're going to make history."

That's what I thought about all day long. We couldn't let the mayor down. At the end of the day, one celebrating volunteer after another came back to the office. They felt confident. As the votes started to come in, I thought, The mayor is right—we are going to make history.

CHAPTER TWELVE

I Would Cut My Throat
from Ear to Ear
Before I Count Those Ballots

I F I BEAT Manny Torres, Darth Vrdolyak and his unmovable bloc of twenty-nine aldermen would finally have to surrender the power they had usurped from the rightfully elected mayor, Harold Washington.

Election night was up and down, joy and sorrow and back again. It looked good early. Then it looked like we were in trouble. At midnight, Manny was up by 35 votes and it seemed all of the precincts were in. At his party, Manny was already up onstage, giving his victory speech. The news that Vrdolyak and Manny were celebrating had traveled to our campaign party. People were crying. They couldn't believe we had lost.

But my captains in the 7th Precinct told me that their precinct wasn't counted yet. There had been trouble with the machine that counts the votes, so they took the ballot box directly to the Board of Elections. At his victory celebration, Manny seemed to be ignoring the fact that we hadn't counted all of the votes. The election now depended on one precinct.

The captains in the 7th Precinct were great volunteers. I knew how hard they had worked. They had been door-to-door in the neighborhood for months. After they told me that their precinct hadn't been counted, they pulled out their hard card to show it to me. The hard card was a fundamental campaign tool. It was a piece of cardboard the size of a newspaper. A sheet with the name of every registered voter in the precinct, arranged by address, was glued to the card. Virtually every name on their hard card had a plus or minus or zero next to it. They had talked to about 90 percent of the voters in the precinct. They knew who was with me and who was with Manny. They had just spent the last thirteen hours dragging all of our pluses to the polls. One of our volunteers sat in the polling place and crossed off every person who voted. They didn't need to wait for the votes to be counted. They knew exactly who had voted and whom they voted for.

"So give me the news," I said to them.

"We won by fifty votes at least."

I believed them. I hugged them both. I jumped onstage. I said it wasn't over. I said not only was there one more precinct to count, but that when they counted it, we would be winners. People didn't know whether to believe me. Candidates always say stuff like that, have one last moment of glory before reality sets in and they go home losers. I told everyone to ignore Manny's victory speech. Reporters were waiting for me to concede. I refused. I said we were waiting for the last precinct to be officially counted.

The Board of Elections said they would count the 7th Precinct's ballots one by one. Every TV station in Chicago was there. The Board of Elections officials—loyal to Vrdolyak—let them all in. They called out every vote. I had made a lot of progress since my lonely vote-counting for the Independentistas in Puerto Rico in 1972. In that election, we'd had one solitary vote in my precinct—mine. But this time, one after another, they called out "Gutiérrez." I stood next to my loyal captain. Every now and then, when they counted a few in a row for Manny, I would check with her: "Still confident?"

"Don't worry," she told me, looking happier every time the increasingly glum election officials called out the name Gutiérrez.

She thought we'd won the precinct by 50 votes. She was wrong. We did even better. We had to wait until the day after the election, but by 20 votes, I was the alderman of the 26th Ward.

In two years, I had gone from being a guy annoyed that Rosten-kowski captains wanted to put an Epton sign in my window to being the Chicago alderman who would deliver control of the city council to Harold Washington.

All that was needed to make it official was for the Board of Elections to certify the vote. I had 5,245 votes, Manny had 5,225. Vrdolyak's machine operatives had knocked a school crossing guard named Jim Blasinski off the ballot because they didn't want any of their little old Polish ladies to get confused and vote for him instead of Torres. He refused to go away completely, and running as a write-in candidate he'd received 11 votes.

Winning by 20 votes out of 10,481 votes cast is an incredibly close election. The Vrdolyak-controlled Board of Elections delayed and debated certifying the results. Manny filed lawsuits questioning my absentee ballots. He filed for a recount. In response, I filed my own lawsuits. Virtually every day one of us had lawyers in court. Still the Board of Elections wouldn't certify the results. The press called it the campaign that wouldn't end.

I didn't wait for the Board of Elections. We had a victory parade down Division Street. Puerto Ricans lined the road and I shouted thank you from the back of a convertible. We turned my campaign office into an aldermanic office. I started taking requests and working with all of the mayor's friends in city government to deliver services. We went to court to have Mike Nardulli, who no longer lived in the ward but was still representing us until the Board of Elections acted, thrown out of the city council. I printed business cards that said LUIS GUTIÉRREZ, ALDERMAN, 26TH WARD. We answered the phone "Alderman Gutiérrez's office."

My lawyers kept moving from court to court, demanding that the results be certified by the Board of Elections. The court would agree, and then Vrdolyak and his crew would appeal to buy more time. I showed up at a city council meeting and demanded to be seated. "I am the people's alderman," I said to anyone who would listen. I brought fifty campaign workers with me, shouting "Nardulli must go!" Mayor Washington delayed the start of the meeting by two hours, hoping the board would fold under the public pressure and agree to seat me. They didn't, and the mayor had to sit through yet another meeting controlled by Vrdolyak and his allies.

"You win and you still can't take your seat. This is insanity," I said at the meeting. But my parades and press conferences, my aldermanic office and business cards didn't deter Fast Eddie Vrdolyak. When they thought they had the votes, they were immune to the media, or public opinion, or conventional wisdom.

They might have been 20 votes short of electing Manny Torres alderman, but Vrdolyak still thought he had the votes that really counted. The Municipal Officers Canvassing Board of the Board of Elections, the panel that would decide to certify the results, had five members. Three of them, including the chairman of the board, were loyal to the Vrdolyak Twenty-Nine. Two were allies of the mayor. Vrdolyak did the math. He believed those 3 votes were worth more than my 5,245.

The courts were taking their time. Nearly a month had passed since Election Day. Manny and I had filed seven different lawsuits. The Cook County Circuit Court and the Illinois Appellate Court ruled that the Board of Elections should certify the results. The case went all the way to the Illinois Supreme Court. I thought it would be the last stop. Manny and Vrdolyak were finally out of appeals, and out of time.

But as I sat in my make-believe aldermanic office fielding requests for new garbage cans and sidewalk repairs, their team concocted a brilliant plan to save Manny Torres. It didn't involve a recount or a lawsuit. It involved a do-over.

Aldermanic elections in Chicago are nonpartisan. You didn't run in Democratic and Republican primaries. Why bother? There weren't any Republicans anyway. So everyone who wanted to run was put into one primary. If any candidate received more than 50 percent of the vote, the election was over. If nobody received more than 50 percent, then the top two vote-getters went into a runoff. It's still that way in Chicago municipal elections.

Manny and I had been fighting in court for so long that the scheduled city runoff election was less than two weeks away. But given that there were just two of us running, nobody, including me, ever considered a runoff in the 26th Ward. It was a winner-take-all primary. I was the winner, and I was ready to take it all.

But all of us who thought that the drama would end at the Illinois Supreme Court had underestimated the creative genius of the Chicago machine. Ever since that election, I've imagined Vrdolyak waking up in the middle of the night, sitting straight up in bed, smiling to himself, and whispering, "Blasinski."

As the lawsuits and appeals moved toward the Supreme Court, Eddie and Manny changed tactics. They knew a court would eventually force the Board of Elections to certify the results, so they just came up with a different result.

I had 20 votes more than Manny. Blasinski, the crossing-guard whom nobody had heard of and who didn't campaign, had somehow come up with 11 write-in votes. If Blasinski had gotten just nine more votes, I would still have more votes than Manny, but I wouldn't have the required 50 percent plus one to win. Blasinski's 20 votes would force a Gutiérrez-Torres runoff.

On April 2, less than two weeks after the primary, the Board of Elections announced that they had discovered 9 additional write-in votes for Blasinski in their post-election voter canvass. The votes were discovered in the basement of a Board of Elections warehouse, where the ballots were being held for "safekeeping" after the election. Nobody from my campaign, and no independent poll-watchers were present when these write-in votes were discovered. The write-in ballots appeared to have been moved from a big box in the warehouse to a smaller box that was brought to the Board of Elections. Somebody had handled them—which is never supposed to happen with write-in ballots. Nobody could explain how they had been overlooked. They were just there somehow; just enough Blasinski votes, waiting to be counted. Torres immediately asked the Board of Elections to count the write-ins and certify the vote. Counting the write-ins would leave me short of a majority of the vote. We would be in a runoff.

It seemed too ludicrous to believe. Our campaign still thought if we could get the courts to demand certification, we would be fine. Even

My dad combs my hair in our apartment on Willow Street in Lincoln Park. Neighborhood "barbers" who operated out of their basements did most of my hair-cutting for a buck or less.

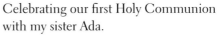

With my mom in Chicago, returning home after church in our Sunday best.

Celebrating our first Holy Communion with my sister Ada.

My Aunt Nilda with my uncles in Gary, Indiana. Gary was filled with Puerto Ricans, just like the extended Gutiérrez clan, who worked in the steel mills.

I'm in the front row, second from the left, with my Newberry School
fifth grade classmates. In just over four years, my family would leave
Chicago for Puerto Rico.

With Soraida on one of our first dates.
Soon she would leave for Puerto Rico, and I would follow her.

With Soraida and Omaira in the living room of our house on Homer Street. About two months after this picture was taken, the Molotov cocktail came through the window behind us and burned down much of the home.

Leading a march during my campaign for alderman in 1986. We are carrying signs that say "Re-elect Alderman Gutiérrez" to remind voters that our win in the primary election had been stolen from us.

Holding Omaira and campaigning with Mayor Washington. I've never met anyone who brought as much joy and enthusiasm to politics as Harold Washington.

One of our tree-planting days when I was alderman. Every day was a battle to provide services to a neighborhood the Chicago machine had ignored for decades.

With Omaira and my family at a neighborhood festival in Humboldt Park.

NELSON ALGREN AV

When I was alderman, we dedicated a street in Wicker Park as honorary "Nelson Algren Avenue." My neighborhood has always been home to newcomers to Chicago.

With Soraida, Omaira, Jessica, and my niece Maritza on the steps of the capitol the day I was sworn in as congressman in 1993.

I'm filling out a citizenship application form at one of our early citizenship workshops in Chicago. The crowds have always overflowed our capacity, and we've now helped more than 50,000 people start on the road to citizenship.

With my much taller friend Senator Bill Bradley after a presidential debate in Iowa. Al Gore and much of the Democratic leadership in Congress weren't too thrilled that I endorsed Bradley for president in 2000.

Talking immigration on Air Force One with President Bush. *Courtesy of the White House Photo Office*

An early meeting with President Obama on Air Force One.
Courtesy of the White House Photo Office

Speaking at one of countless immigration rights rallies.

An immigration rights rally sponsored by the Center for Community Change, one of our nation's leading pro-immigrant advocacy organizations.

I am led away after being arrested for refusing to leave the White House in protest of President Obama's record on immigration and deportations.

My friend the president pulls me aside in the State Dining Room and tells me to "get off his back" after an early meeting at the White House with the Congressional Hispanic Caucus. *Courtesy of the White House Photo Office*

An Oval Office meeting where my friends Bob Menendez and Nydia Velázquez continue our push to curtail President Obama's record-breaking pace of deportations and fight for comprehensive immigration reform. *Courtesy of the White House Photo Office*

the *Chicago Tribune*, hardly a friend to progressive candidates, called the sudden discovery of the ballots "highly suspicious." The *Tribune* helping Harold Washington and me is like Rush Limbaugh calling Obama's health-care plan "kind of a neat idea." Everyone else thought that the discovery of just enough write-in votes for an unknown candidate to throw the election into a runoff to be so outrageous that even Vrdolyak, even in Chicago, couldn't get away with it. I held press conferences and complained. We filed a lawsuit to prevent the write-ins from being counted. We said they had been tampered with. Vrdolyak just stuck with his game plan, still confident that he had the only 3 votes that counted—his guys on the election board.

Finally—twelve days before the scheduled runoff—the Illinois Supreme Court ordered the Board of Elections to certify the results.

I thought Torres and Vrdolyak were out of options. I was ready to be sworn in. I arranged for Omaira to take the day off from first grade to watch. Almost one hundred of my volunteers were going downtown with me to celebrate. I hired a band to play traditional Puerto Rican music. Reporters followed us as we headed toward City Hall. I stopped at the liquor store and asked for nonalcoholic Champagne.

"I don't want to have too much to drink and get arrested on my first day in office," I told the crowd. Everyone laughed and cheered.

We arrived downtown just as the Board of Elections was convening at the Cook County Circuit Court, in the Daley Building. The Supreme Court order to certify the election was handed to them. They quickly agreed.

The chairman of the board called for a vote to certify the election. Immediately, a member of the canvassing board moved to include the absentee ballots found in the warehouse in the final count. Spectators in the room gasped, then yelled and jeered. That didn't slow the board down. It voted. To make things absolutely clear, the Vrdolyak allies voted first—one-two-three—to include the absentee ballots. It was time for Harold's allies to vote. One of them was a big African American guy with a voice as deep as Harold's. He looked at the other members and said, "I would cut my throat from ear to ear before I count those ballots."

It didn't matter if he cut his throat or not. He was still in the minority. The vote was three to two. The mysteriously discovered Blasinski ballots would be counted. The election was certified. I was now one vote short of a majority.

The Chicago TV stations were live on the five o'clock news. For nearly a month, everyone had thought it was just a matter of time until Mayor Washington was finally in charge of the city. Now, in a move that was breathtakingly bold even for the Chicago machine, we were going to have a runoff in twelve days.

Reporters were scrambling for interviews. The mayor's people were outraged, yelling "They stole it!" and promising legal challenges. Vrdolyak's people made clear that they would abide by the board's ruling, as if they were simply ordinary citizens following the orders of an impartial governmental body. The reporters really wanted to hear from me. They were ready for exciting live television featuring an outraged Luis Gutiérrez. In the primary, I wasn't exactly shy and soft-spoken. I had accused Manny of planting a pipe bomb on his own front steps. The Chicago media probably thought I might set a new record for decibel levels reached in a press conference.

I finally stepped up to the microphones to face the bank of cameras that were on live Chicago television. I shook my head, and I spoke as quietly as I could while still being heard.

"I don't know what I'm going to do. They've broken us. My campaign's broke. I'm out of money. The machine has all of their dirty, filthy money and they will just get more of it. I spent all of mine. I don't know how I will get more. I'll do the best I can, but I don't know how you beat this machine."

The reporters kept asking about the decision and how angry I must be. I didn't take the bait. I just looked sad, defeated. I stepped away from the microphone and Ben Reyes, my campaign manager, looked at me like I was crazy.

"What's wrong with you? You look like you've given up. People will think you don't have a chance."

"You'll see," I said, and we climbed in his car and headed back to my campaign office.

The only flaw in my strategy was not having people ready at the office to collect the donations. By the time we made it back to Division Street, the office was surrounded. It looked like a run on a bank. When they saw me getting out of the car, a loud roar went up. People chanted "Gutiérrez." One after another, people yelled and pleaded, "Don't give up!"

These were folks from the neighborhood, people without much money. They were lining up to volunteer and to hand over whatever they could, whatever they had. Some gave a dollar or two. They gave us five-dollar bills, ten-dollar bills, fifty bucks that they had collected from their friends. They knew we had been robbed, and they were investing in the rematch.

I wasn't exaggerating when I talked to the reporters. We were worse than broke. We were about $20,000 in debt. Between the campaign and the lawsuits, we didn't have a nickel for the runoff. But within an hour of the outrageous action of the Board of Elections and my heart-broken plea, we were working our way back up.

People were mad. How could they not be mad? An anonymous election panel had just counted the precise number of ballots needed to put the election into a runoff. Ballots found in a basement. I decided I didn't need to turn up the heat—I needed to appeal to people's hearts. Puerto Ricans knew what I was doing. It was the *"Ay, bendito,"* routine—poor me. Nobody will help me. What am I going to do?

I knew what to do. People were already angry. What we needed was money.

Within a few hours we had it. People came by the office all night with modest checks and cash. The next day, an African American guy showed up at our office. I had never seen him before. He said he had taken up a collection from all of his African American coworkers at their factory on the south side. "We're not going to let them steal this one from Harold," he told me. Then he got in his car and drove away. He gave us $800. *Ay, bendito.*

We had money coming in. People were fired up. We had so many volunteers we were running out of places to put people. We spent some of our fresh money on new campaign buttons and gave them out. When our volunteers and supporters saw them, everyone laughed and cheered. The buttons said RE-ELECT ALDERMAN GUTIÉRREZ.

* * *

BY THE TIME we collected our money and went back to work on an election we knew we had already won; the machine guys had already collected eight hundred absentee ballots. The machine lived on collecting absentee ballots. Chicago was home to more voters who somehow couldn't make it to their polling place on Election Day than any city in the world. Shockingly, these shut-ins always voted for the machine. Some of the addresses on the absentee ballots were empty lots. Before we knew it, we were nearly 1,000 votes down. But I knew public opinion was on my side.

Re-elect became our battle cry, our shorthand for "Don't let them steal it again." We had our billboard company add the word "re-elect" to our billboards, and asked them to change the one across from Manny's office first. It drove him crazy. He held a press conference just to announce that I hadn't been elected to anything.

"He's lying to the voters," Manny said. "He didn't win anything. You can't re-elect him."

Most of the reporters just shook their heads and then covered the entire issue of the phantom basement write-in ballots again. Every time Manny complained, it just reminded voters that we had been cheated. It was an important political lesson to me. When your opponent is hitting you hard and scoring points, don't defend yourself. That's the time to attack your opponent and change the subject.

Eventually, Manny did change the subject, back to the only one he had really felt comfortable talking about all along—that I was a dangerous terrorist.

Every day Manny held a press conference accusing me of something outrageous. A week before the runoff, he stood in front of Cook County Jail, pointed toward the imposing brick building, and said, "This prison is filled with inmates who are voting for and supporting Luis Gutiérrez." Manny's strategy was clear: convince white ethnic voters that I was soft on crime and I would go easy on the gangs. The white voters were his base, and he would say anything to keep them afraid and motivated.

By the time of the runoff, I knew that Puerto Ricans were tired of hearing nothing but a law-and-order message. But Manny was so entranced by his tough-guy rhetoric that he didn't understand he was running to represent a neighborhood filled with Latinos who were fed up—just like I was. Puerto Ricans were tired of being represented by distant aldermen who had never set foot on their block. They were sick of gangs too—but they were also tired of being treated by white police officers as if every Puerto Rican was a Latin King. They had the crazy idea that the 26th Ward—even the poorest, most Puerto Rican parts of the 26th Ward—should get its fair share of city services. They were ready to stand up to the machine and fight for Harold Washington.

Finally, I couldn't take the constant accusations of being a criminal and terrorist anymore. I pictured the Chicago media as being connected at the hip to a pulley system that took them back and forth between Manny and me several times a day, to his office and then to mine, to ask one of us about whatever wacky charge the other one had come up with that morning. They would find me on the street campaigning, or crammed into my packed office, which was overflowing with volunteers waiting for an assignment. I would talk to them in some cluttered corner.

After the "inmates for Gutiérrez" charge, I said to the reporters, "Manny says this ridiculous stuff to you every day because he's a coward. He would never say any of these things to my face. He's too afraid. So today I challenge Manny to a series of debates so that the voters can hear the truth and see us face-to-face. I know what he'll say. He won't do it."

I saved my most important point for last.

"And we should debate both in Spanish and in English, so all of the voters of the Twenty-Sixth Ward can understand us."

The reporters hooked their belts to their pulleys and sped back to Manny's office.

"Gutiérrez says you're a coward. He says you won't debate him. And he says you should do it in English and in Spanish. Will you debate him?"

They must have caught Manny without any of Vrdolyak's handlers around him. His handlers didn't have any interest in a debate. Manny wasn't television friendly and they knew it. I was unpredictable and outrageous, but I always had something to say. The mayor's people sometimes worried about what it might be, but they knew I would say it with passion.

Manny wasn't running for alderman because he had the most detailed policy proposals, or because he looked like an anchorman. They chose him because he was a good precinct captain. He was big and looked tough, more like a security guard than a politician. If one of Vrdolyak's people had been around that afternoon, they would have laughed at my debate challenge. But Manny was not going to be called a coward.

"I'll debate Luis Gutiérrez anytime, any place, and in any language he wants. I'll debate him in Spanish, Russian, and Chinese," he told reporters.

It was the most important moment of the campaign. Manny had swallowed the bait, and we were on.

I didn't study talking points and position papers to prepare for the debate. I just went over a few of my main points, which mainly boiled down to this simple fact: I'm for Harold Washington and Latino empowerment, Manny Torres is for Ed Vrdolyak and the status quo. We made a tour of the public-affairs shows around town. We spent a lot of time yelling at each other. I reminded people I had already been elected once. He would call me a liar, his face turning red and insisting that I had never been elected to anything.

By the time we made it to our last English-language debate the Sunday before the primary, Chicago political reporter Carol Marin scolded us, saying we had been too negative and had made one unsubstantiated charge after another. She asked if we wanted to tone down our rhetoric or apologize for the things we had said. I think she was worried we might actually hurt each other.

Things had been nasty. Even Soraida was telling me to tone it down.

I looked into the camera and said, "I have said some things I regret and I'm sorry. The voters probably deserved better." I thought a little humility the last weekend couldn't hurt.

Carol seemed pleased that she had extracted a mea culpa from the unpredictable Luis Gutiérrez. She turned to Manny with the same question.

Manny gave his best body-builder glare, like he was challenging Carol to disagree.

"I don't regret a thing. He's a terrorist and a criminal. Everything I've said is true."

And with that, our debates were over. Except for one. On Monday night, the day before Election Day, Manny had agreed to debate me in Spanish on Channel 44, the Telemundo affiliate and most-watched Spanish-language station in Chicago.

While Manny was holding press conferences in front of prisons and accusing me of shooting at him, our campaign had been spreading our own little rumor.

As my captains went door-to-door to Spanish-speakers in the Puerto Rican neighborhoods, especially in the pit, they delivered a very specific set of talking points: "We'll clean up the neighborhood—no more abandoned cars, no more dumping. We'll get your trash picked up every week. We want to build more affordable housing, not keep it out."

And then, almost as an afterthought, like it was something that just occurred to the captain as he was about to leave the voter's house, he would say, "And I hear that Manny Torres doesn't even speak Spanish. I don't know for sure, but that's what everyone tells me. Don't know how he's going to communicate with you if he can't speak Spanish."

We said this over and over again at the end of long conversations in Spanish. A little parting aside, said like we were curious. "Is it true that Manny doesn't speak any Spanish?"

I didn't know for sure. Like every other Latino politician, Manny told people he spoke "some" Spanish. But I had never heard him say *adiós,* or *gracias*—not once.

My unscientific guess would have been that Spanish was the first language of about one-quarter of the residents of the 26th Ward in 1986. A fundamental theme of my campaign was that the Latino community was being neglected and ignored, that for decades we had been represented by guys with last names like Kulas and Rostenkowski who were uninterested in the needs of Latinos. When you're running on a Latino-empowerment platform, speaking the first language of your constituents is essential. When I went door-to-door, I spoke Spanish all the time. When in doubt about the language of a voter, I would try Spanish first. It didn't offend Puerto Ricans who spoke only English, and it helped to make my point that I was different and committed to treating Puerto Ricans fairly. I had learned my lesson in San Sebastián—nobody was going to out-Spanish me.

There weren't any Spanish-speakers making any decisions in Mike Nardulli's office. If you lived in the 26th Ward and only spoke Spanish and needed help from your alderman, you were out of luck. We thought just planting the seed of doubt in voters' minds that even if they elected Manny Torres they wouldn't have a Spanish-speaking alderman would get us some votes. We never dreamed Manny would actually give us a chance to prove it, but on Monday night on Telemundo, we were about to get an earful of Manny's Spanish-speaking ability. Our captains went door-to-door and blanketed the pit with flyers, telling everyone to watch. The week before Election Day, our daily message to Latinos was simple—watch Telemundo, Channel 44 on Monday night.

I think Manny agreed to the debate the night before the election because he thought it was too late to matter. But every day in our campaign was another day in the circus. We were the top story in Chicago. The Telemundo studio was packed with people, and reporters from all the other stations were covering it. Manny entered, accompanied by his usual entourage, none of whom looked comfortable at a Spanish-language television station. All of the station's employees were nice to us. My supporters watched and liked Spanish-language television. We felt at home.

The debate was only a half hour long, maybe short enough for Manny to get by. Before we started, I thought for one panicked moment, What if his Spanish is great? We just told thousands of voters to check it out. Maybe this joke will be on me.

The production assistant miked us, and we took our place behind podiums in the studio. I had the first opening statement, in which the

Puerto Rican kid from Chicago, who had felt alone and outcast in San Sebastián because his Spanish was so bad and longed desperately to go home and speak English to his friends, delivered a glowing tribute to the beauty and importance of the Spanish language.

"I'm so glad that we have the opportunity to speak to the people of the Twenty-Sixth Ward in Spanish tonight. For months, we've discussed the issues in English. We've debated all week in English. I'm so pleased that our TV station, Channel 44, has given us a half hour to speak Spanish with you. I want you to know that in my aldermanic office, Spanish will be welcome, and every Spanish-speaking person will have a place to be respected and be served."

My ode to Spanish was limited only by my time. After a while they made me stop, and the camera turned to Manny.

I realized right away that I didn't have anything to worry about. His Spanish was awful. Not awful in the way mine was when I tried to talk to Señor Hernández on my first day of school; someone trying to improve their second language. His Spanish was awful in the way of someone who doesn't speak the language. He sputtered through three or four sentences that he had clearly practiced all day in his Chicago accent. My Polish was as good as his Spanish.

Still, at least he was trying, and a lot of Latinos might give him credit for the effort.

We started the questions. Manny sputtered through his answer to the first question. He looked unhappy to be stuck there, like he had been dropped into a torture chamber.

I went again, and then the Telemundo reporter asked him another question in Spanish. But Manny was done with Spanish for the night. He had memorized an opening statement. He tried one question. He wasn't going to mess around with any language other than English for the rest of the half hour.

After the reporter's question, Manny looked directly into the camera and said, "I'm going to speak in English for the rest of the debate. English is the language of the Chicago City Council. That is the language I will need to be alderman of the 26th Ward. Everyone deserves to understand what we say here tonight."

He told an audience of Spanish-speakers that he was not only unwilling to speak Spanish to them, but that their language didn't really count in the city council anyway. And he kept his word. For the rest of the half hour, you didn't hear another *hola* out of Manny Torres. You saw an animated, Spanish-loving Luis Gutiérrez, rolling my r's and stretching my Spanish vocabulary as much as I could next to a nervous guy speaking English to a television audience who didn't understand a word he was saying.

The phones started ringing immediately. Telemundo had sent their receptionists home for the day. The only employees still there were production people and reporters covering the debate. But I had plenty of people there. I had volunteers all over the office, waiting and watching. There was nobody there to keep them from answering the phones, so they started picking them up.

Callers were angry. They thought their calls would make a difference. "Tell him to speak Spanish. We can't understand him." People had tuned in, on the very last day, to finally hear a debate in Spanish. Instead, it was the same old English. People pleaded, "Why isn't he speaking Spanish?"

"He doesn't speak Spanish," my volunteers said. "If you're angry, vote for Gutiérrez. He speaks Spanish." It was like we were running a Gutiérrez for Alderman phone bank. "Of course he should speak Spanish—make sure to vote for Luis tomorrow."

I kept answering questions in Spanish, adding comments wondering how people would receive service if Manny Torres didn't respect his constituents enough to speak their language.

By the end of the debate, Manny was sweating and eager to leave. The English reporters chased him out, asking him why he didn't speak Spanish. But the truth was they didn't realize the size of Manny's problem. It wasn't that his Spanish was terrible. It was that he was dismissive, just like all the Polish and Irish and Italian machine guys had been dismissive for decades. He turned his back on us.

That Manny didn't speak the language was bad, that he didn't respect the language was unforgivable. I knew. It wasn't that long ago that I landed in a strange place where not speaking the language made me an outsider. My only salvation was to learn it as quickly as possible. It was a lesson Manny had never learned.

That night, on the way home, I stopped at a gas station to fill up my Celica. A Puerto Rican guy was next to me. He was excited to see me. He yelled out to me, "Hey, you're Gutiérrez. That other guy *nos faltó el respecto.* I'm voting for you." He'd switched to Spanish midsentence just to emphasize that Manny didn't respect our language.

Manny didn't know that our volunteers had been going door-to-door for weeks like covert operatives, spreading their "Manny doesn't speak Spanish" gunpowder all over the ward. The air was thick with it, and that night on Telemundo, Manny lit the match.

Telemundo started with their election coverage first thing in the morning. They asked people standing in line at polling places who they were voting for.

An elderly Puerto Rican lady said, "I'm for—I forget his name—the one who speaks Spanish."

I heard it all day long in the precincts. People proud of their culture, proud of their language, people ready to elect a Puerto Rican to the city council. People shouted to me in Spanish all day long. "Way to go, Gutiérrez—you showed him last night!" Puerto Rican flags filled the air. We had our cars with loudspeakers, driving up and down Division and the side streets, blasting salsa music.

I think Vrdolyak knew when he saw the weather report that Manny was in trouble. It was an eighty-five-degree April day. People were coming out of hibernation. I walked up and down the streets and people were sitting on their stoops, hanging out of windows.

"Did you vote?" I asked people over and over again. Guys would be sitting on their porches drinking beer, and I would bother them until they got in line at their polling place. We ran through the empty lots that we had been cleaning for months, racing toward some house where a captain said there was a family who hadn't voted yet. For thirteen hours straight, we talked to Puerto Ricans, out enjoying a spring day. At some polling places, Puerto Ricans stood in lines that stretched around the corner, waiting an hour to "re-elect" Luis Gutiérrez.

Most working people vote at the end of the day. The lines kept getting longer and longer in the late afternoon. At North Avenue and Maplewood at five o'clock, the line of African Americans went all the way around the block. I waved. They cheered. Manny's people scowled, and our volunteers told us later that Manny's captains had called the line of voters "the Hershey train."

Later that day, a captain who had friends in Manny's campaign passed along some intelligence about Manny's debate strategy.

"His captains were telling all the white voters to watch the debate. They kept telling white voters to watch Channel 44, and see which candidate respects the English language." Even on election eve, on a Spanish-language television station, Manny was playing to Vrdolyak's white base.

It was a mistake.

The night of the primary six weeks before, every precinct that reported was like another round in an Ali-Frazier title fight. In the Puerto Rican precincts, I would surge ahead. A couple of mostly white precincts would report, and I would be behind. An African American precinct would put me on top again. It had been like that all night, until finally, we had to march over to the Board of Elections the next day to count the ballots one-by-one.

The runoff wasn't a fifteen-round decision. It was a three-round knockout. When the first precinct came in, I knew we were going to win. It was a largely white precinct in Mell's base in the former 33rd Ward. We'd lost nearly 2 to 1 in the primary. I lost it again, but we were closer this time. Then Puerto Rican precincts started to report. It wasn't even close. It wasn't just the margin, it was the sheer volume. No Puerto Rican wanted to be the one who stayed home and kept Ed Vrdolyak in power. People voted like it was their patriotic duty. The turnout was huge, and the numbers kept coming in. Big wins in Latino precincts, closer losses in white precincts. We were never behind all night.

Our election-night party was in a ballroom on the top floor of a Russian Orthodox church. We had a band, and lots of food and liquor. People wanted to bring more food than we could fit in the place. When I showed up, it was impossible to get up the stairs. People were on the street. Television trucks lined the block, ready to go live. In two years we had moved from chips and pretzels in the basement of a moving company to the hottest party in town.

The salsa got louder, and people got happier, and every TV station in town wanted to talk to me. At our party after the Rostenkowski campaign, I hardly had anyone to hug other than my wife, my close friends, and Juano and Lucy. Now I could barely find my family because the place was so packed. We watched Manny Torres at his very quiet party. He went to the stage and refused to concede. The blank look on his face said far more than any speech. We kept counting, and it looked like we were going to win by 1,000 votes.

I knew that not even Ed Vrdolyak could find 1,000 write-in ballots in a basement this time. It didn't take long before Eddie himself made it official. He was already adjusting to his new reality. He said to reporters, "I look forward to working with the mayor on projects that are helpful to the people of Chicago." Manny Torres didn't have to concede. Darth Vrdolyak did it for him.

It took lots of court cases, and mysterious ballots in a basement, and a do-over election. In the end, it took me being saved by my Spanish-speaking skill—a skill learned in the pool halls and sugarcane fields and strict classrooms of San Sebastián, the little town my dad took me to against my will. But finally, it was over. I was the alderman of the 26th Ward, and Harold Washington was in charge of the city of Chicago.

CHAPTER THIRTEEN

A Soldier in
Harold Washington's Army

THE BOARD of Elections didn't delay certifying the results this time. Within one week of my "re-election," the Board voted unanimously to certify. Harold Washington didn't waste any time either. Soraida and I went down to City Hall, and I stood in front of the mayor's office with my hand on the Bible, ready—finally—to be sworn in as alderman of the 26th Ward. Charles Freeman, the first African American Supreme Court Justice in Illinois, administered the oath. Harold Washington stood behind me and beamed his unmistakable smile.

Harold had been elected Mayor in April of 1983, but for nearly three years, twenty-nine aldermen had prevented him from truly being in charge of the city. Chicagoans had endured thirty-six months of city council arguing and threatening, of grandstanding and gridlock. The next city council meeting was less than a week away. After I was sworn in, Harold gave me a hug. "I've been waiting for this for a long time," he told me.

On May 9, Harold gaveled the meeting to order. City council meetings are held in a cavernous room on the second floor of City Hall, with sections set aside for press and spectators. The room was even more packed than usual. Since Harold was elected, the opposing factions went at it from the long tables that served as desks on the floor while spectators cheered or booed. This meeting felt like a party. Aldermen who supported Harold, many of whom had campaigned with me, greeted me like a liberator; smiling, laughing, slapping me on my back. We felt like our time had come.

Our mayor didn't wait to start winning votes. He had a shopping list of appointments that needed to be filled. He had city departments with acting directors and commissioners, and he hadn't been able to place any new leadership in Chicago's affiliated agencies. From the Chicago schools to public housing, key leadership positions had been filled by enemies of the mayor.

Some of the leaders had been around since Harold was a teenager. From the day he was elected, the mayor had been trying to get rid of Ed Kelly, who ran Chicago's Park District. Kelly had started with the parks in 1947. He turned the Park District into a factory for political patronage. Welles Park, in Kelly's home neighborhood, had more full-time workers than Humboldt Park. Humboldt Park covered 207 acres, Welles Park covered about 15. Kelly had been the first Democratic committeeman to endorse Epton, the Republican, for mayor. Now that Harold had a majority of the city council, however, Kelly, and a hundred guys like him, were headed toward the unemployment line. It was like a Chicago political earthquake, a seismic shift in power.

Harold called for votes right away, just to test whether he was dreaming about controlling the city council. It couldn't have been closer—Harold didn't even have a majority. My election, split the council 25 to 25. When the clerk called out, "The vote is tied, twenty-five to twenty-five," after the test vote, Harold smiled over his new city council, said "not anymore," and cast the first of a day's worth of tie-breaking votes. For a year, Harold couldn't leave a city council meeting to go to the bathroom. Without his own vote, he didn't have a majority.

We approved appointment after appointment for Harold. It was the most orderly and composed city council meeting that Chicago had seen since Harold became mayor. Ed Vrdolyak—the animated, talkative, combative Ed Vrdolyak—the man who had thwarted Harold Washington for three years, sat quietly. On my first day as alderman of the 26th Ward, I don't remember Vrdolyak saying a word.

I cast every vote with the mayor. I celebrated with Soraida that night. Just a few years earlier, I never would have guessed I would be an elected official. Being an elected official was very public, and the political process seemed slow. I wasn't much for negotiating and compromising. I wanted to cheer and march, to be the person demanding change.

Even back when I'd listened to Rubén Berríos or Noel Colón Martínez on the plaza in San Sebastián, I didn't imagine being them—I imagined fighting as a soldier for the things they believed in. The most radical pro-independence Puerto Ricans didn't even believe in US elections. They thought voting was legitimizing the colonizing power. During the aldermanic campaign, I would see them going up and down the block, telling Puerto Ricans not to vote for anyone.

But watching Harold changed me. Even though Vrdolyak had snatched control of the city council away from him, he never gave up, and he didn't cut any deals with him. In almost three years of hand-to-hand combat with the Vrdolyak crew, I don't remember Harold ever giving in on a key point.

He had proven to be exactly what he seemed when I first attended one of his campaign speeches in our neighborhood in 1983. I'd sat next to Soraida, with Omaira on my lap, as Harold spoke to a packed room at Northwest Hall on a freezing night. He reminded me of Rubén Berríos. He said things I didn't think any politician would say. He talked about the recent shootings of two Puerto Ricans by police in Humboldt Park and said the crimes should be investigated. In Chicago, I had never heard an elected official suggest the police had done something wrong. He said that the current police superintendent should be fired. He talked about hiring Latinos at City Hall. I bounced Omaira on my knee and wondered, Where did this guy come from?

Once I really knew him, it became clear that there was nobody quite like him. Nobody enjoyed politics and campaigning more than Harold. When I ran for alderman, he came to rally after rally. Every time he came, I would try some new campaign speech, testing what would get him most excited. I wanted to impress him. Not long before the primary, at Northwest Hall again, I tried out a new line. With Harold sitting behind me, I yelled, "When I get to city council, and cast my first vote, and the clerk calls the roll, we'll see if there are still twenty-nine other jackasses who want to vote against you."

Harold jumped out of his seat, rushed up to the podium, and hugged me. He held my arm up over my head. He was dying to beat Vrdolyak. At that same event, after he finished his remarks, he took a Puerto Rican *pava*—the straw hat of the sugarcane workers and symbol of the Puerto Rican *jibaro*—and happily put it on, smiling to a crowd that chanted and cheered. At other events, he put on my "Gutiérrez for the 26th Ward" baseball cap and campaigned with me. Politics with Harold was not remotely as scripted and staged as it is today. Every Barack Obama event I've attended looks like a movie set, with every moment planned and directed. Harold's events were more like old-time revivals.

Like Rubén Berríos and Puerto Rican independence leaders, Harold believed in the power of a speech—of standing with people and talking until you convinced them to be on your side. Harold loved to play with words. He never said "guess" if he could say "prognosticate." He always bypassed "fast" for "expeditiously." Commentators, mostly white, would make fun of him for it. I thought he just wanted to blow up the notion held by far too many voters that a black man couldn't be the most articulate guy around.

He was gregarious and made you feel like politics was joyous, something to celebrate. His enthusiasm was part of the reason that everyone who supported him simply thought of him as "Harold." I hardly remember an African American calling him "Mayor Washington." How could you call a guy who jumped up and hugged you at a rally, someone who would gleefully wear a funny hat, "Mayor Washington"? On the night he upset Byrne and Daley, his overflowing crowd of supporters chanted "We want Harold" over and over again until he finally took the stage and accepted the nomination.

"You want Harold? You got Harold!" he boomed, in a moment that none of us ever forgot. And that's who he always was—Harold. Harold, who never gave in to Vrdolyak; Harold, who smiled and inspired hope no matter how nasty the fight. Harold, who was finally in charge.

He was brimming with ideas. The excitement of his new power bounced around City Hall like lasers had been let loose. The city council met once per month and at each meeting we worked to make Chicago more progressive. He proposed a tough ethics reform package. He put in Freedom of Information Act reforms that made more information about the city available to reporters. He could finally pass bonds that put much-needed money into infrastructure improvements for Chicago neighborhoods. He recruited academics and community activists and put them in charge of city departments.

I was busy voting with Harold and trying to keep my promises to the people of the 26th Ward. We had made a lot of promises. Being a Chicago alderman is the definition of grassroots American politics. Your constituents don't watch you on TV, complain to their coworkers, and wish things were different. They come down to your office, wait outside your door, and demand that you fix the pothole in front of their house. I held "ward night" every Monday, where people lined up to tell me about problems that had been ignored and requests that had been denied. I had a year's worth of campaigning door-to-door and listening to people talk about problems in their neighborhood. I had long lists of priorities—vacant lots, broken streetlights, corners where gangs gathered every day.

We went to work on sidewalks, streets, and alleys in Humboldt Park. Funding bonds for capital improvements was like breaking two dams. The first was that Nardulli and the gang didn't care about poor people in Humboldt Park. The second was that Vrdolyak wouldn't give Harold any money. But now we had money, and we started digging and paving and cleaning. When city crews showed up in the pit to repave blocks, people came out of their houses and sat on the stoops and watched, amazed that Chicago had discovered that people actually lived in their neighborhood. It was like the United Nations was airlifting in supplies.

Help was needed in business areas as well. Division Street had vaulted sidewalks—a Chicago historical oddity. Most of the city was built on a swamp. Because it flooded all the time, the city raised buildings and streets in the late 1800s, creating new sidewalks that were sometimes six or seven feet above the old ones. Division Street, the heart of Puerto Rican Chicago, had ancient, decaying vaulted sidewalks with craters that opened to a six-foot drop onto the street level of 1880. If you weren't careful, you could walk down the block and disappear through a hole back into the nineteenth century. It was dangerous, and nobody had done anything about it. We rebuilt the sidewalks block by block, and businesses slowly started taking a look at Division Street again as a place to open up.

I felt like the Mayor and I were a team. Not long after I was elected, Harold planned a trip to New York to talk to the credit-rating agencies, investors, and businesses that might want to come to Chicago. His goal was to convince bankers and the bond market that he had brought peace to Beirut on the Lake, that council wars were over and he had won. What better proof of victory than bringing along the alderman who finally made Vrdolyak wave the white flag?

Harold was taking care of his twenty-fifth vote. It was true that he needed all of us, but when you are the key that finally picks the lock, you get some extra attention. He made one of his security people switch seats with me on the plane so I could fly first class. I had never flown first class before. The mayor told me about our strategy for the meetings. He was going to point to me and say, *See that guy—he won, and now I'm in charge.* I spent a day as the mayor's mascot, telling bond guys in the most expensive suits I had ever seen that I was with the mayor. Harold worked them like they were voters. We went from investment house to investment house, and before we left, Chicago's reputation was rebounding with the guys who made decisions about our credit rating.

It was a long day of meetings, and a long party at night with elected officials in New York, where my future congressional colleagues like John Conyers and Charlie Rangel celebrated our triumphant mayor. I left the party early, because as much as I love politics, I was learning that Harold never slowed down or stopped. His life was one long parade of government meetings and political rallies, interrupted by as little sleep as possible.

We had an early flight back to Chicago the next day. I dragged myself onto the plane. Harold was happy and alert, reading three newspapers. He had finished one Bloody Mary and was starting on a second one.

"You've got to keep up, son," he said to me.

I wondered how he did it. He was thirty years older and a hundred pounds heavier than me, but he was awake after me and up before me. He was already studying the papers for ideas. I ordered a Coke, perked up, and tried to learn as much as I could.

HAROLD WAS MAKING progress on appointments. He was putting reforms in place. But he needed money to run the city. The Council Wars had starved the city of money. The mayor was going to take a political risk and raise property taxes.

He called me to his office to discuss the property-tax vote. I knew something unusual was going on when I saw Walter Knorr, the book-ish budget expert who was city comptroller. This wasn't going to be just another political strategy meeting.

The mayor was in a good mood, ready for the fight. He wanted my help.

"Lou, the truth is that taxes have gone down for most people because Vrdolyak didn't want me to have any money to spend. It's not the taxes that bother Vrdolyak—it's that I get to decide where the money goes."

I wasn't sure why the mayor was telling me this. I supported him. I didn't need a pep talk.

"I was thinking that the best way to show the people of Chicago that taxes are lower since I've been mayor is to show the property-tax bills of Vrdolyak and the aldermen who oppose me. Walter's got the records right there."

Knorr was holding a stack of papers. Apparently the property-tax records for all of Vrdolyak's guys. Anyone can find tax records. It's pub-lic information, but not too many Chicagoans would take the time. Knorr had it in a convenient bundle.

"After we pass the budget, I was hoping you would rise and ask to enter into the record the tax records for the aldermen. Maybe give an example or two. Let's make clear to the people of Chicago the facts about taxes."

At first, I was flattered. It was always nice to be asked by the mayor to fight for him. Then I thought, This is probably not such a good idea. As nasty and bitter as the city council had been, this move seemed personal even by Chicago standards. Vrdolyak wouldn't sit quietly while I told everyone in Chicago what he paid in property taxes.

I also wondered why the mayor was asking me to do it. I guessed that I hadn't been Harold's first choice for this assignment. Somebody had already turned him down and he was just working his way down the list to me. Or maybe Harold simply thought I might be the only one of his allies crazy enough to do it. Maybe I shouldn't have been so flattered.

I sat quietly for a minute, Knorr looking like an impatient accountant, and Harold smiling. Who was I kidding? I loved being Harold Washington's co-conspirator.

"Of course, Mr. Mayor, anything you want."

I went to the council meeting with my manila envelope of personal property-tax records of my twenty-five adversaries on the Chicago City Council. I had Vrdolyak's on top.

As the meeting went on, and the debate about the tax increase got angrier, I was happy I had decided to play my part. One after another, the white aldermen, who had seen their property taxes go down under Harold, complained that the mayor was mismanaging the budget by asking for more money from taxpayers. They were already lining up for the re-election fight. They had starved the city of money for three years, and now they were anti-tax crusaders. I thought their hypocrisy deserved to be exposed.

After we passed the tax increase, I rose and asked to make my material public. I understood what he was doing. The mayor didn't want this fight before the vote, when someone might change their mind. He just wanted to rub it in a little after he won.

"Mr. Mayor, I have some information I would like to enter into the record. We've heard a lot about property taxes today. I have here the tax records of the aldermen who opposed your budget. Is it true, Mr. Vrdolyak, that you pay less in taxes under Harold Washington than you did under Jane Byrne?"

Vrdolyak looked shocked. He shouted it wasn't true, that my facts were wrong.

"Well, I have the numbers right here. You paid $5,926 last year, and $6,846 in property taxes under Jane Byrne."

Vrdolyak jumped to his feet. I just kept going, although the rest of the machine guys were starting to scream. With all of them talking at once, it was hard to make it out, but I heard lots of "How could you?" and "How dare you bring my taxes into this?"

"You're unappreciative," I said. "You should be thanking Harold Washington for his good management." I thought I was carrying the day, making a serious budget point. I hadn't noticed that all of my allies were sitting quietly while Vrdolyak's guys were pointing and yelling at me.

Vrdolyak decided to play the victim.

"This is my home. You have made a mistake. Are you so vile? So petty? So venal? I will never address you directly or indirectly on this council floor," he yelled at me.

By this time, a lot of Vrdolyak's allies were on their feet and screaming. They had been bullies for three years. Many of them hated me. They were eager to look like they were being mistreated because I would be so small as to divulge personal information about their taxes.

By this time I was flustered. I looked around for help. Tim Evans, the mayor's floor leader, was looking down, shuffling through papers. Everyone on my team suddenly seemed preoccupied, studying their desks.

I thought, Harold's a smart guy. He knows what he's doing. This must be a good idea. I went from Vrdolyak's taxes to the next ones on my pile. After Vrdolyak, Knorr had arranged them by ward. The alderman of the 1st Ward was Fred Roti.

"You're not alone," I shouted at Vrdolyak, waving the tax records in the air. "Here's what Alderman Fred Roti paid in taxes," and I read the numbers, although by this time there was so much chaos, nobody could really hear what I was saying.

Roti's best friend on the council, Alderman Bernie Stone, who was in his sixties and had a heart condition, started screaming at me. "I paid the taxes each and every year. I never asked anyone for a break. How dare you come in here, you little pipsqueak!"

Stone's face was red. He looked like he wanted to hit me. David Orr, the alderman next to him, stood up to try to calm him. He thought Stone was about to drop dead from his heart condition. Stone pushed him back in to his chair. The TV reporters loved it.

I looked around for help again. None was coming. Stone was still out of control. You couldn't hear anything anymore, so I stopped reading the numbers. Finally, with Stone still yelling at me, the mayor gaveled the meeting adjourned, and said the material would be entered into the record. I looked up toward the mayor, but he was already headed out the back of the council chamber, eager to leave the chaos.

I wasn't sure if this was what the mayor had had in mind, but I knew I had made one mistake—reading Roti's taxes. First, I liked Fred Roti. Of all of Vrdolyak's allies, he was one of the few who was nice to me. He was an affable old guy who looked kind of like George Burns. He acted like he didn't have a care in the world. If Knorr hadn't put Roti's taxes on top, I never would have read them.

But it was more than friendship that made me sweat about reading Fred Roti's taxes. What really concerned me was that Roti wasn't just any alderman. He was nice to me because he didn't care what Vrdolyak thought. He answered to a much different authority than Ed Vrdolyak.

Roti grew up in Chinatown and represented downtown and the Chinese and Italian neighborhoods around it. His father was Bruno Roti, who ran a grocery a few blocks away from Al Capone's headquarters. His dad was also known as "Bruno the bomber" for his work in the same line of business as Capone. It was alleged that Fred had inherited his father's business interests and that Fred Roti was the elected official who got things done for the Chicago mob.

But Fred was such an easygoing guy that it was hard to know

what to believe about him. He always laughed off the unofficial campaign slogan that a reporter had suggested for him: "Vote for Roti and Nobody Gets Hurt." Fred had been alderman of Chicago's 1st Ward for twenty years, so if he was fronting for the mob, he was good at getting away with it. Still, I didn't care about offending Vrdolyak. He deserved it. But I couldn't believe that of the twenty-four other guys I could have attacked, I had chosen a guy whose dad was nicknamed "Bruno the bomber."

When the chaos subsided, I tried the same escape route around the press that the Mayor had used. But I couldn't avoid Fred. He walked straight toward me. He was the only guy on the council shorter than me. He pulled me aside, looked up at me through his coke-bottle glasses, and said, very slowly, "Lou, ward boundaries change. They come and go. But one thing that never changes about the First Ward— it always has the Chicago River." Then he turned and shuffled away.

I headed back to my office, trying to decide if he had just quietly threatened to kill me. I was pretty sure he had. He didn't sound like he was joking. My house had already been bombed. I didn't want to take any chances.

I went home and watched the news that night while I kept an eye out the window. I thought about putting Omaira and Soraida in a hotel. The television coverage proved that the mayor was brilliant. Instead of focusing just on the property-tax increase, reporters were giddy about the renewed chaos in the city council. I saw Bernie Stone calling me a "pipsqueak" on every channel. I knew I had inherited an unwanted nickname. Soraida looked at me, wondering how I had gotten myself into such a mess. I thought about what to do next. I stayed up late watching the street and decided that Fred didn't really want to hurt me. He just wanted to make sure I never said anything personal about him again.

The next day, I got up and went into my ward office and read the word "pipsqueak" in all of the papers. Then my staff told me Mayor Washington was on the phone for me. His voice boomed through the receiver.

"That was wonderful. I loved it. Those hypocrites. Thanks, Lou."

And with that, I stopped worrying. I was a soldier in the mayor's army. Every now and then you took some shrapnel.

Eventually, the furor about the property taxes died down. Even Fred Roti forgave me. Before long, Fred was his friendly self and we were getting along again. I had always hoped that not everything I'd heard about Fred was true, but in 1990, just before I ran for Congress, Fred was indicted for racketeering and extortion. The jury acquitted him on the most serious charge—that he'd bribed a judge to fix the trial of a mob hit man—but he was convicted on most counts. He spent most of the rest of his life in prison. It was a sad ending for a guy I felt some gratitude toward for not throwing me in the river.

I MET WITH HAROLD all the time, sometimes at his home in Hyde Park, often in his office. Increasingly, he was happy and confident, a man who had earned the right to believe that he would be mayor of Chicago for a long time.

I went to his condo one day with a grand plan for Harold's future. I wanted to make sure he was always strong among his Latino constituents. I urged him to convene a group of Latino leaders and have them publicly come up with a "Latino agenda" for the city of Chicago, a blueprint that would help the mayor and give him goals for his second term.

"This way you don't have to constantly listen to suggestions from different aldermen and community groups and other elected officials. You will have a master plan," I told him. I was confident Harold would like my idea.

Harold pondered it for a minute, rearranging his growing bulk in his chair.

"Lou, it means a lot to me that you are thinking of me," he said. "But what you should be thinking about is you. Don't worry about me. I'll be fine. But I need you in the city council. Today, let's talk about what I can do to help you."

I couldn't believe it. I had come with a grand plan to help the mayor, and instead he wanted to help me.

"Tell me one thing I can do for you," the mayor said.

"Anything?" I asked.

"Anything. I want to help you," the mayor told me.

I knew what I wanted. Harold was using his bond money to buy new plastic garbage carts for every ward in the city. But we weren't getting them all at once. It would be more than a year before every ward got them. Aldermen were fighting over them like they were pieces of gold. They were bigger than the metal ones we had been using for years, and the carts and lids were all one piece. I cannot overestimate the appetite of a neighborhood that had been overrun by rats and debris for years for shiny, new plastic garbage cans.

I told him, and Harold called the commissioner of the Department of Streets and Sanitation.

"My friend Lou is getting the carts," he said into the receiver. I was elated. I was getting huge garbage carts for the people of the 26th Ward.

I told Soraida that night. "I'm getting the carts." I wasn't shy among my colleagues, either. "Wow, in the Twenty-Sixth Ward, people really like the new garbage carts," I would say to other aldermen, smiling a little because I knew how badly everyone wanted them.

It took me a while to realize what Harold had done. I wanted him to have a citywide Latino agenda. I thought I was saving him the trouble of everyone always coming to him with problems and suggestions. But Harold wanted to be able to solve the problems and distribute favors himself. He could set his own agenda. With a well-timed promise of new garbage carts, he changed the topic and I left happy anyway.

BY 1987, a few more Chicago voters were getting used to the idea of an African American mayor. Harold was fixing streets and building schools. But in this mayoral election, he wouldn't have the benefit of Jane Byrne and Rich Daley splitting the white vote. In the Democratic primary, he would face Jane Byrne one-on-one.

Meanwhile, I thought I would be having a rematch with Manny Torres. But times had changed. In the 26th Ward, people were getting things fixed, streets repaired, affordable housing built. Puerto Ricans were united solidly behind me and our mayor. Manny decided not to run. His wife ran instead. Instead of fighting for my political life, I spent most of my time campaigning for Harold. When Jane Byrne called Puerto Ricans "aliens," I criticized her nonstop. It's a common trap for Anglo politicians—they forget Puerto Ricans are US citizens and call us immigrants or aliens. They almost always pay for that mistake at the ballot box.

Harold defeated Jane Byrne in the Democratic primary, with 52 percent of the vote. Four years earlier, he'd only received 36 percent in the primary. Reporters barely paid attention to my race, but I beat Manny's wife 2 to 1. We elected three other pro-Harold aldermen, giving the mayor some cushion in the city council. If he could get re-elected, he would be able to leave the council chambers occasionally to go to the bathroom. But before he could declare victory, Harold had to overcome a few more white candidates in the general election. Darth Vrdolyak ran as a third-party candidate. So did Tom Hynes, an ally of Rich Daley.

Not long before the general election, I was meeting with Harold in his office. I wasn't sure I should keep my scheduled meeting with the mayor, because it was the day after his debate with Vrdolyak and Hynes. I watched the debate on television and was mystified by my mayor. He was not himself. He was subdued and cautious. No colorful phrases, no attacking his opponents. He was even nice to Vrdolyak.

Of course, the first thing he asked me in our meeting was how he did in the debate. I was meeting with him because I needed a favor. One of my best volunteers was up for a promotion in his city job. I knew that his wife was pregnant. I wanted to help him. When Harold asked me how he did, I had a dilemma. Tell him the truth and risk offending my friend? Or tell him he was great, and ask for the promotion?

"Mayor, I have to tell you. I watched the debate—and it just wasn't you. Not your usual fire. Not your usual inspiration. It seemed like Vrdolyak got away with a lot of bullshit."

I was resigned to trying to find my guy a job somewhere else.

The mayor laughed and put his arm around me.

"Lou, you just made my day."

I was puzzled. "Why is that?"

"Because I went into that debate with eighteen percent of the white vote, and I was determined to come out of that debate with eighteen percent of the white vote. I was going to make damn sure I didn't lose one white voter last night. If you think I didn't do too well, then I must have accomplished my goal."

The mayor was happy. My volunteer got his promotion. And the mayor was re-elected. He only received 52 percent of the vote against Vrdolyak, but defeating him after defeating Byrne, and electing more allies on the city council, seemed to close the book on council wars.

AS THE MONTHS passed after Harold's re-election, it seemed like you could feel the city slowly exhaling after years of battling. Vrdolyak had left the city council to run for mayor. And I thought it was clear that things were improving. Harold was putting his people in place, finally making Chicago's leadership look as diverse as the city.

Eventually, most of the complaints about who was getting jobs weren't coming from whites. They were coming from blacks who felt Harold wasn't exacting enough revenge on his enemies, not giving African Americans enough. There was a group of African American aldermen who regularly looked at Harold's Latino supporters in meetings and said that we were getting too much.

But Harold had a saying that he used in speeches all the time. As mayor, he was going to be "fairer than fair." He said it to calm white fears, but he also meant it. Harold knew that he was going to be held to a higher standard by everyone. By the media, by white voters, by his political opponents. An Irishman named Daley could stack City Hall with white employees for twenty-five years and hardly be criticized anywhere other than the West Side and South Side of Chicago. But Harold knew that *he* would be constantly watched for any sign of favoritism toward blacks.

The greatness of Harold Washington was that it was his natural inclination to be fair. At heart, he was motivated by the civil rights movement. He wasn't interested in revenge; he was simply interested in what minorities had deserved all along—fairness. In private, more than once, he said to me, "You can't use government to settle old scores." And he didn't. He hired blacks. Lots of them. He did it because Chicago was home to a million black people. But he hired Latinos and whites too. Because that's the way he felt it should be.

Because he was fair, I believe Chicago made progress on racial issues while Harold was mayor. On Palm Sunday in 1983, at the height of the Epton campaign, Harold went to St. Pascal's Church on the Northwest Side with presidential candidate Walter Mondale. Angry white residents surrounded the car that Mondale and Harold were riding in, jeering and taunting them. People hung from streetlamps and cursed at them. "Nigger die" was spray-painted on a door to the church. It made national news.

The hatred and the anger was so intense that day that I'm not sure anyone believed that Harold could defeat Epton, but he did. Four years later, Harold was visiting block parties and festivals in white neighborhoods not far from that church. Most whites hadn't fully embraced him yet, but the taunts had pretty much stopped. And at the end of most of those festivals, Harold had found, one-by-one, a few more white supporters.

AT A COUNCIL meeting in the fall of 1987, about five months after he was re-elected, Harold motioned for me to come up to the podium. He had a policy question. Something about housing, I think. Then we talked while the meeting went on. I told him the big news I had been sharing with everyone. Soraida was pregnant and we were expecting our second child. He was happy for us.

"I haven't seen Soraida for a while. Bring your wife down to the office. Let's just sit down and talk for a few minutes."

Harold always asked me about Soraida and Omaira. I learned over time that a good politician will always remember a few key facts about your family or your accomplishments. I was an early supporter of Bill

Clinton, and when he ran for president we shook hands with commuters at the train station in Wicker Park on a very cold Chicago morning the day before the Illinois Democratic primary in 1992. For years, whenever I was with President Clinton, he would talk about that morning. I appreciated the memory and admired Bill Clinton, but I also knew that in Clinton's voluminous mental note file—the Gutiérrez index card in his brain was imprinted with "cold morning, train stop."

My relationship with Harold was different. When he invited us over, I knew he was looking forward to seeing us.

We went down to City Hall the next week. When we went into his office, Harold had flowers waiting for Soraida. He hugged her and congratulated us. Just the three of us sat and talked. He was at ease. He finally felt like he was winning.

"Another beautiful Gutiérrez for the world. And have you picked out any names for that lucky child?"

Soraida and I looked at each other. We had thought about surprising him, but we couldn't keep it a secret.

"Well, Mr. Mayor, we have picked out a name. If it's a boy, we're going to name him Harold."

At first, the mayor looked like I might be pulling his leg. Then he smiled.

"You're really going to name your son Harold Gutiérrez?" he asked, laughing.

"That's exactly right. That's what we're naming him. Not Geraldo— Harold. And we hope he'll be just like you."

He saw we were serious. He paused. "Well, that's a beautiful name."

"If it's a girl, we'll have to be a little more creative. I'm not sure Harolda works, but we'll figure something out."

The mayor was surprised. For a man who lived his job, I think it reminded him, for a moment, that what he'd done for Soraida and me went way beyond politics. He saw beyond the kid who chased around precinct captains and was crushed by Dan Rostenkowski. He gave me a job and a chance. He practically made me an elected official. The mayor of the third largest city in America has a lot to worry about. He had been through more than most mayors, fighting every day, winning some battles, losing some too. I knew I was important to him, but his world of friends and allies and enemies was so much bigger than mine. I think that afternoon, he finally understood just how important he was to me.

We talked a little bit more, about family and politics, about our plans for the holidays. It was early November, just a couple of weeks until Thanksgiving. Before we left, he hugged us both. He thanked us.

"That's a wonderful gift you gave me today, Lou," he said. Our news had made him happy, and for all he had done for me, and for all he had done for the people of Chicago, I thought Mayor Harold Washington was a man who deserved to be happy.

IT WAS RIGHT before Thanksgiving, and I was taking some time away from City Hall. Nothing much was happening. The city was quiet. Soraida and I were at home together, cleaning the house and getting ready for the holidays. We were hosting our family for Thanksgiving. We were making plans when the phone rang. I answered it.

"Luis, it's Alderman Dick Mell. Now, don't get angry, and don't get excited. We have an important decision to make. Listen—he's dead. One of my guys was the paramedic. On TV they are going to say he still has a chance, but I'm telling you, he's dead."

I didn't know what he was talking about.

"Who's dead?"

"Your mayor. He's dead. Now, we have to decide some things, and I'd like your help. I want to be mayor of the city of Chicago. I'm going to get the votes. I'd like you to keep your options open. Don't make any hasty decisions."

I told him that I didn't believe him. I hung up the phone. I felt sick. I told Soraida what Mell had said and asked her to turn on the television. There was nothing at first, just regular weekday programming. We flipped around. Nothing. Could Mell possibly have been joking?

Then the special reports started. Reporters standing outside City Hall. Reporters standing outside Northwestern Memorial Hospital.

Nobody was sure what was happening, but within a few minutes, the words "massive heart attack" were being used. He was at his desk when it happened.

I held Soraida as she cried. I cried too. My phone started to ring. I ignored it. I didn't want to talk to Mell again. I didn't want to talk to anyone on the phone. I needed to see people who cared as much as I did. I sat with Soraida, and then I went to my office at City Hall.

Nobody knew anything definitive yet, but everyone assumed he was gone. I had chosen the wrong place to go to find fellow mourners. Many of my colleagues were following Dick Mell's lead, talking and plotting. The city council would choose the next mayor, and the campaign was already under way.

Mell wasn't the only white alderman trying to collect 26 votes. Terry Gabinski, Dan Rostenkowski's ally, was working on it too. They were looking for me, trying to line up Latino support.

What was clear immediately was that all it took was the rumor of Harold's death to end African American unity. There was always a group of six or seven African American aldermen who supported Harold only because they wouldn't dare to oppose him. They were just waiting for a return of African American machine politics, a return that was never going to happen while Harold was mayor. At City Hall, one of them looked at me, seemed puzzled, and said, "Don't take things so hard, Gutiérrez."

But I did. Before the doctor even announced Harold's death, there was already black bunting being delivered to City Hall. I sat in my office. The political world was continuing to spin outside it. In fact, it was spinning faster than ever. In Chicago, politics stops for nothing. That afternoon, watching the jockeying and lobbying and promising, seeing some black aldermen just as eager to turn Harold's death to their advantage as the white aldermen were, it was clear to me that we were losing more than Harold. We were losing everything we had fought for.

Harold was the reason I was in politics. And he was gone.

CHAPTER FOURTEEN

Cockfighting in the Basement of Your Business Is Strictly Prohibited

HE MOURNERS stood in a line that went out the doors of City Hall and wound around the corner, waiting to say good-bye to Harold. His body was in the first-floor lobby, the casket covered in a city of Chicago flag and surrounded by flowers. I stood for a long time by the memorial, standing to the side as Chicagoans filed quietly by. Many were heartbroken, shuffling forward as if their grief slowed the function of their legs. I went through the doors and followed the line all the way to the end, then doubled back inside again. Chicago's citizens were sharing in my sadness much more than Chicago's politicians were. I felt better being around them.

The mourners were incredibly diverse. A lot of African Americans, but plenty of Latinos. And white people too. Harold told me he was thrilled to have hung on to 18 percent of the white vote against Vrdolyak. I wondered where everyone came from, all the people who were standing in line, solemn and sad, ready to martyr Harold in death but who had never quite embraced him in life. I thought, Harold, you would have loved this sight. It made me proud of him, because the line of mourners reflected what Chicago politics might have become if Harold had lived.

While Chicago was mourning, the Chicago City Council was

busy dousing itself in gasoline and lighting matches. The city that had earned the name Beirut on the Lake was like a vacation spot compared to post-Harold Chicago. It was more like Pompeii. With his death, all the old rivalries, all the stifled ambitions and animosities exploded to the surface like a volcano.

The Vrdolyak supporters did everything possible to elect one of their guys. Mell told everyone he needed just one more vote to be mayor. He was promising the world for a twenty-sixth vote. If he could have promised immortality, he would have. The rumor was that he offered progressive white aldermen the finance committee chairmanship, or that he had convinced law firms that were friendly with him to offer high-paying jobs to aldermen who would support him for mayor. But nobody was budging.

Then the white guys turned to us, the four Latino aldermen. Ray Figueroa, Jesús García, and I were loyal supporters of Harold. Only Juan Soliz had voted with the Vrdolyak guys. Two days after the mayor died, Soliz asked the Latinos to meet with him. Juan told us the Vrdolyak faction would support him for mayor if he could bring just one of us over to support him. He told us to think about how powerful Latinos would be—but mainly how powerful he would make the person who voted to make him mayor. He seemed to think his offer was irresistible. The meeting was brief, and he left to let us decide. He figured one of us would crack, tempted by whatever riches Juan would deliver to us. As soon as he walked out, the three of us looked at one another and asked, practically in unison, "Is he crazy?" The one Latino who opposed Harold Washington was the last person we wanted to be mayor.

The real negotiating about who would be mayor was happening among the black aldermen. Under Harold's leadership, Chicagoans had almost forgotten that plenty of black aldermen had made it to the Chicago City Council through old-fashioned machine politics. But those aldermen didn't forget. They began scheming to choose the next mayor the minute they heard Harold had been taken to the hospital. For five or six or seven African American aldermen, it was a chance to finally peel off the progressive masks they had been forced to wear under Harold.

They had been pretending to be something they weren't for almost five years because their constituents would have crushed them if they'd opposed Harold. The coalition of black aldermen who supported Harold in lockstep wasn't held together by principle, it was held together by the unstoppable force of Harold Washington's personality and popularity. There's no other way to say it: some black aldermen who were old-style machine guys were glad he was gone. They were ready to make up for years of standing quietly in line and getting no more than their fair share while Harold remade Chicago.

Bob Shaw and Bill Henry, the oldest of the old-style machine politicians, led the charge to elect one of their own. If you called Central Casting and asked them to send over a couple of Chicago politicians, they would have sent over Bob and Bill. Shaw was tall and broad, with a booming voice and a toupee that stopped fooling people long before I made it to the city council. Henry was short and round and always wore flashy clothes and a pinky ring. For a while, he owned part of a soda company and tried to make his brand, "Soul Cola," the official drink of city festivals like Taste of Chicago. They'd been perfectly content when Jane Byrne was mayor. They were getting jobs and contracts. They were for empowerment—as long as they were personal friends with the people being empowered. But they didn't think they could get away with replacing Harold with a white guy. They needed to partner with the white guys to support a willing black candidate.

Our pro-Harold coalition didn't have any votes to spare. From the minute I walked through the doors of City Hall and saw the different factions scheming and plotting, I knew we were in trouble. What could we offer somebody like Bob Shaw to stay with us? Loyalty to Harold's memory? He didn't like him when he was alive.

Vrdolyak's guys weren't split. They were united. With Harold's death, their future brightened in an instant. On one very sad day, they went from waking up in the morning and imagining three or four terms of serving—virtually powerless—under Harold, to going to bed that same night trying to decide which one of them should be mayor.

With insider politics moving against us, we tried to rally the people. We warned everyone that some black aldermen might make a deal with Harold's enemies. At a public memorial at the University of

Illinois at Chicago Pavilion, thousands of people packed into the basketball stadium. One after another, we spoke and called for the people to rally around Harold's memory. When it was my turn, I said the only thing I could think of that would help.

"We must surround City Hall because it is ours!" I yelled, not really sure if I meant it literally. People screamed and cheered. When I finished and sat down, Reverend Jesse Jackson, who had returned from his campaign for president, leaned over and said, "You should be more careful about what you say," apparently worried that my suggestion was too dangerous even for him.

Chicago needed a mayor, and the Vrdolyak guys were pushing for a vote. Especially when it became clear that the African Americans who weren't loyal to Harold had chosen their candidate.

Eugene Sawyer was the longest-serving African American in the Chicago City Council. He was quiet and easygoing. He didn't look or act anything like Shaw or Henry. I always liked Gene. While he had been a loyal machine vote before Harold came along, he was the first African American alderman to endorse him. While others were constantly whining that Latinos were getting too much from the mayor's administration, I never heard Gene complain once.

Gene was more respected than the rest of the machine African Americans. He looked mayoral. For a while, all he said was, "The most important thing is unity." He said it several times. He said we needed a consensus candidate. It turned out that he thought he should be that candidate.

When Gene announced for mayor, he knew that most of us were supporting Tim Evans, Harold's young, articulate, African American floor leader and finance committee chair. Everyone liked Tim, even though before Harold came along he had been a machine guy too. Many of us would have preferred Danny Davis. He had defeated a machine alderman on Chicago's West Side to get to the council. Harold's supporters were split from the beginning, but Evans seemed the best compromise.

I will never know if Gene somehow thought he could be a compromise choice of our coalition. I would like to think that was part of his motive. That he could broker a peace between the black machine guys and the rest of us. But it was too late for that. We were sticking with Evans.

The white aldermen knew they could work with Eugene Sawyer. He had worked with them for years. They had tried electing Mell, or Gabinski. That wasn't going to fly. None of the Latinos would support Juan Soliz. They were out of choices. The best they could do was elect a black mayor they could tolerate, one they could play nice with before they dumped him for a white guy in the next election. The deal had already been cut. Gene Sawyer had the votes to be Mayor: all of Vrdolyak's allies, plus five or six—he claimed more—of his African American colleagues.

I was surprised. I thought Gene must have understood what a betrayal it would seem to his constituents—and to everyone who'd loved Harold—if he partnered with the people who had opposed him at every turn, who had mocked him, had supported a white Republican against him and done everything they could to defeat him.

But at some point, Eugene Sawyer realized that all he had to do was say yes and he could be mayor of the city of Chicago. He didn't have to convince even one ordinary voter to support him. He didn't have to raise millions of dollars. It was right there for him. All he had to do was cut the deal. He had likely never before considered seriously the possibility that he could be in charge—get the big office on the fifth floor, the limo and the driver, all the jobs and the contracts. Suddenly, there it was. Power, tied up in a package with a bow on top, was right in front of him. He just had to unwrap it.

The vote was scheduled for the afternoon of December 1, less than two weeks after Harold's death. At City Hall that day, we were looking for Gene, hoping to talk him out of his decision. We would occasionally get a glimpse of him, moving between offices surrounded by his supporters. Politicians attract hangers-on like Kardashians attract paparazzi. You could see Gene floating through the halls inside a gaggle of suits—men sizing up the chief of staff's office, men imagining how they would divide up the patronage. He insulated himself from reality with a wall of people telling him not to worry about the bad press, about the outrage, about the angry crowd at City Hall calling him Judas.

Jesse Jackson was right about the crowds at City Hall. People were more than mad—people were livid. Since news broke that a group of African Americans were going to vote with the Vrdolyak faction, City Hall had been packed with people. African Americans were demonstrating at the offices of Aldermen suspected of supporting Sawyer. Pretty soon, Gene's claim of 10 to 12 votes was down to a handful of aldermen who were hiding from their angry constituents.

The police had to direct traffic around the Chicagoans circling City Hall. Inside, the hallways were packed with people. Police were up and down every corridor, trying to keep a passage or two clear. You couldn't move inside the council chamber. The dismay had turned to anger and could have easily turned to violence. Without the presence of most of the Chicago Police Department, we might not have been able to meet at all. The night we held the vote would have been an excellent time to rob a liquor store. The police had their hands full keeping Gene Sawyer safe.

On the news, reports stated that Gene was wavering. We delayed the start of the meeting. Time ticked away. We delayed it some more. Nobody seemed to know what was going on. People shared rumors.

"Sawyer has fainted. He's not going to do it."

"Gene is sick; they are taking him to the hospital in an ambulance."

"He's dropping out. We have to start all over."

Nobody knew what to believe.

Finally, someone found him. He wasn't in the hospital, but he did look terrible. We convinced him to meet with us. One by one, in Tim Evans's finance committee office, we asked him to reconsider. He looked like a man who had made a mistake and was pulsing with regret. He looked a little like a character from a zombie movie—somebody who had left his former body and brain behind. Did he want to be mayor? Well, what politician doesn't want to be mayor of the third largest city in the country? But the chanting crowds were beginning to make him understand the price he would pay to sit behind that desk.

I asked him to simply wait.

"Gene, we don't have to do this today. Let's just take a break. I'll make a motion to adjourn, and we'll put off the vote. We'll take some time and figure it out. We've always been friends. This isn't you," I said to him. I thought it was the right thing to do. Maybe we needed a brand-new candidate. It wasn't like Harold had a last will and testament that bequeathed the mayor's office to Tim Evans. I told Gene maybe we could all compromise. He barely spoke, but I felt like we were making progress.

As Gene seemed to consider our pleas, the door opened. We all looked up. We hadn't invited anyone else.

It was an angry white alderman. He didn't look at any of us. He wasn't interested in talking to anyone except Gene Sawyer. He looked directly at him.

"Gene, this can work two ways. You can come down to the city council and we will elect you mayor, just like you promised us." He emphasized "promise" like it was a threat. "Or you can stay up here like a coward and I'll nominate you and we'll elect you mayor without you. Either way, at the end of the day you're going to be mayor. You should come talk to your supporters instead of talking to these guys." The alderman then stood and waited, like his puppy was going to follow him.

I'm not sure I had ever seen a member of the Chicago City Council talked to like that, except maybe me when I read everyone's property taxes out loud. I thought he had gone too far, that Gene would tell him to go screw himself. Instead, he followed him out. At that moment, I thought we were done. It was like Gene Sawyer was in a trance. A couple of us tried to follow him, but he was out the door and down the hall.

Day had turned to night, and the protesters were angry, hungry, and impatient. But apparently Gene was ready to become mayor. I saw him with his crew going to the council floor. He had added some ministers to the group, who were praying over him, trying to give him comfort that he was doing the right thing. Even churches can use city contracts.

The Vrdolyak loyalists had one last hurdle to electing Gene Sawyer mayor. The acting mayor was David Orr, the alderman who had tried to keep Bernie Stone from having a heart attack when I pulled my property-tax stunt. He had been Harold's ally. David controlled who was allowed to speak and who could make a motion to nominate the mayor.

For hours, past midnight and into the early morning, David bypassed the machine guys who were screaming to be called upon. They were invisible. One Harold ally after another was recognized by David Orr. We couldn't adjourn, or elect Evans. We didn't have the votes. Instead, one after another, we made speeches sanctifying Harold Washington and vilifying Eugene Sawyer.

Gene sat motionless. The white aldermen kept taking turns forming a shield around him to protect him from the taunts and jeers of the crowd. Early in the meeting, the people in the gallery began throwing things. Eventually they decided the best thing to throw was change— pennies and dimes and nickels. All night long, machine aldermen dodged coins. The police kept throwing people out, but another enraged Harold supporter would just replace the evicted spectator. It was like a Whack-A-Mole game populated by Harold fanatics.

It felt dangerous. People said Bill Henry was wearing a bulletproof vest under his suit. Without a line of police in front of the gallery, I don't think Gene would have been safe. The jeers never stopped. When we spoke, you had to scream to be heard. I was even harder on Gene than most people.

We were outraged. We should have been. For years, the people who were now electing Sawyer as mayor had done everything possible to stop Harold and the progressive changes he wanted for Chicago. We'd overcome them. Now, with one vote, we were losing everything. It seemed like something out of Shakespeare. We were fighting among ourselves while our enemies laughed at us.

Still, I wish I hadn't berated Gene Sawyer that night. I wish I had said the same things I told him in private. I should have said, "Let's take a break. Let's try for peace." I always believed, down deep, that Gene Sawyer was a good man. We should have appealed to the man he was before he decided to be mayor.

But there might have been no reaching him. If a black man can look pale, that's how Gene looked throughout that meeting. He sat slumped in his chair, lost—gone. One after another, we yelled at him. Spectators screamed at him. Still he just sat, surrounded by a human wall of colleagues who hated Harold Washington and were going to make him mayor.

Eventually, all of Harold's supporters had taken turns pummeling the Gene Sawyer punching bag. Dick Mell was tired of waiting. He climbed up on top of his desk and stood there, waving his arms and demanding to be recognized.

Eventually, David Orr couldn't hold out any longer. What else could you do? Have the meeting go on for days? Orr recognized a machine alderman. They nominated Sawyer and praised him in speeches. The clerk called the roll. It was four in the morning. In the time since I had been elected alderman of the 26th Ward and delivered the city council to my mentor, we had won vote after vote. Now Harold was gone, and we lost the only vote that mattered. Eugene Sawyer was mayor of the city of Chicago.

I THOUGHT ABOUT all those hours walking up and down the blocks of the 26th Ward, all the miles logged to coffees and community meetings and block clubs. I'd wanted to be alderman, but my main motivation was helping Harold. His control of the city council had lasted two years. Harold was my political compass. Now he was gone. I felt adrift. The new bosses were busy reorganizing the city council. I was chairman of the Special Events Committee. They were purging the leaders of the most important committees first. I figured it would take a little time before they got rid of me. I decided to take a break and try to clear my head.

I headed to Iowa. It was my first trip to the vast Midwest to campaign for an African American candidate for president out among the cornfields. I was there for Jesse Jackson. I didn't have the personal relationship with Jesse Jackson that I'd had with Harold, but it was reinvigorating to go campaign for someone I believed in. We went door-to-door, looking for Latinos to convince to caucus for Jesse. They were hard to find. It was my first experience with politics outside of Chicago. It reminded me that the dysfunction of the Chicago City Council didn't exist from coast to coast. It reminded me that there were still things I wanted to get done for my ward. It was just going to be a lot harder. As I've learned in Congress, getting things done when you are in the minority is like trying to push a boulder uphill. Harold had always helped me, had always been good to the people of the 26th Ward. Gene Sawyer wasn't going to do me any favors.

AT HOME, I had a much more important distraction from my sadness and disappointment. Soraida and I were expecting our second child. Omaira, who was now eight years old, was excited and ready for a little brother or sister. We turned our extra bedroom into a nursery, occupying our time with painting and preparing for the new addition to our family.

The day before Valentine's Day, Soraida delivered a beautiful baby girl. We had debated the name, and then settled on what seemed right. When I told the nurse what to put on the birth certificate, she was a little confused.

"But your last name is Gutiérrez, right?" she asked.

"That's right. Trust me. I'm giving you the full name," I said. Pretty soon, Chicago welcomed her too. A reporter for the *Chicago Defender*, Chicago's African American newspaper, asked me the name of our daughter, and then reported it.

In a few days, we started receiving cards and letters.

Person after person wrote, "Thank you, Alderman. Harold deserves to be remembered."

The one I remember most said "You made a smart choice. I know your daughter will be a fighter, just like Harold."

The cards made us think of Harold, and they made us proud. Our daughter is still proud today. She is always telling people her full name, and every time she fills out a form that asks for her name, she writes it out, her middle name included: Jessica Washington Gutiérrez.

*   *   *

I KEPT WORKING, doing the best I could. If you do your job as alderman right, your residents view you as one-stop shopping for all of their needs. Their congressman seems distant. Their alderman is their neighborhood, go-to guy. Sometimes, though, you wish they weren't quite so eager for help.

I regularly stopped into a neighborhood bodega owned by an older Puerto Rican guy named Pedro. He always supported me and was thrilled when I won. He was one of many Puerto Rican businessmen in the neighborhood who had either been harassed or ignored by Mike Nardulli and City Hall. He was ready for somebody who spoke Spanish and would help him if he needed it.

I went in one day and he was excited, eager to talk to me. He had a crisis, a mystery for me to solve that he explained in rushed Spanish.

"Alderman, the city wants to suspend my liquor license. That will kill me. I'll go out of business. This is totally unfair."

I asked him why.

"An inspector came to the store and says he wants to look in my basement. I take him down the stairs. I don't care. What could be wrong with my basement? Well, you can't believe what he finds. I can't believe it either. I don't know how it happened."

I'm thinking maybe spoiled food, maybe unclean conditions. But Pedro's still talking fast.

"In my basement, there is a bunch of chairs arranged in a circle. And in the corner of my basement, a bunch of cages. And you know what's in some of the cages? Roosters! Some of the cages have roosters in them. Can you believe it? How could these animals get in the basement of my store? The inspector, he says they are for cockfighting. They make the roosters fight each other! This is terrible, I told him. I don't know how any of them got there. Luis—somebody is setting me up. I'm going to go out of business because of these roosters. I need your help."

I looked at him. He didn't smile. He didn't wink. I knew him. I had been buying bread from this guy for a year. He held my gaze. He wasn't going to crack. I was shaking my head. But Pedro had a story and he was sticking to it. Somehow, someone had smuggled roosters and chairs and cages into his basement.

"Wow," I said. "How do you think it happened?"

"I don't know. It's awful," he said. "I would never allow it."

I expected him to give me a conspiratorial nudge with his elbow. Cockfighting is legal in Puerto Rico. You've never had to drive far in Puerto Rico to find an arena for cockfighting. Some of them have signs out front of fierce-looking roosters. Outside San Sebastián even today you can still find a bar that holds cockfights. It just didn't seem possible to me that Pedro was clueless about what was going on in his basement.

But Pedro wasn't using the "I'm Puerto Rican, I didn't know it was illegal" route. He just figured he would go all-in with ignorance. He thought this was why he voted for a Puerto Rican alderman. He helped elect a man who would stand up for his fellow Boricua.

I heard constantly from Puerto Ricans who had been ignored or hassled for years and figured their time had come to get something from city government. They were right, of course. Our community had been totally overlooked, but the right to run cockfights out of your basement wasn't on my list of priorities.

"Pedro—what happened to the birds?"

"The city took them away."

"OK. Good. You're aware that you can't allow this to happen in your basement, right? It's wrong. It's against the law. Even if somebody snuck them in under the cover of night," I told him.

"Of course." He still looked completely serious.

"And you'll make sure this never happens again? Maybe you need a better lock on your door. If it happens again, I can't help you."

He told me it would never happen again. I thought, if I were the mayor of San Sebastián, I wouldn't have to deal with these problems. I used to chop up pig stomach in my backyard and nobody cared. But I called people I knew in City Hall. I said maybe closing Pedro's store was a little extreme. Pedro had never been in trouble before. Maybe a fine and a suspension? Pull the license if he ever does it again. The city agreed to suspend his license for a couple of months.

You learn a lot of political lessons being alderman. Like how sometimes you can't win. Nobody else would have tried to find a compromise for a guy who had allowed cockfights in his basement, but Pedro ended up mad at me because his license was suspended even temporarily. I had to go to another bodega for a while until his liquor license was restored and he was happy again.

WE WERE ALWAYS working hard to reach out to the white residents of the ward who had mostly supported Vrdolyak and Manny Torres, and I felt like we were making real progress when they started coming in for help.

One afternoon an older Polish guy who owned a deli on Chicago Avenue in the mostly Ukrainian part of my neighborhood came in with a crisis. The city wanted to shut him down, just like Pedro. His problem was that he smoked the meats for his deli using his own smoker in the back by the alley. I knew his place. It was popular. You could smell smoked Polish ham all around the neighborhood. But his building wasn't zoned for smoking meats. He said he would go out of business if he didn't do it himself.

Despite what you hear from Tea Partiers, just because I'm a progressive it doesn't mean I'm anti-business. I wanted all of the businesses in my ward to succeed. With the exception of cockfighting. Nobody had ever complained about the smoked meats. The deli owner told me he had just come to America from Warsaw a couple of years before. He brought me a giant envelope stuffed with all of his business and bank documents. He spoke in broken English and clearly didn't understand the rules. I could imagine my dad making the same mistake. I wanted to help him.

I negotiated for a while with the zoning department and went back to the deli owner.

"Can you smoke all of the meats in two days? I could get you a zoning variance that gives you two days per week to smoke the meat," I told him. He was thrilled. He gave me an enthusiastic handshake. Of course he could smoke everything in two days. "You have saved my business," he said.

The next day he came back. I figured he had another problem. Instead, he smiled at me and gave me a thick envelope.

"A gift for you," he said in his Polish accent.

The gift was an envelope overflowing with hundred-dollar bills.

"It's five thousand dollars. For you, for your trouble. You kept me in business," he said, still smiling.

Five grand is a lot of hundred-dollar bills. I took a glance at what that much cash looks like, and gave it back to him.

"I can't take that. You'll get us both in trouble," I told him.

He frowned. He seemed genuinely disappointed. He was confused, like maybe he misunderstood me. He looked at the envelope and he looked at me.

"You don't want it?"

"I'm just doing my job."

He put the envelope back in his coat pocket.

"You know, I was worried I might insult you, because in Warsaw, five thousand dollars would be cheap for what you did for me. The Communists would have wanted much more. This is a bargain." And with that, he was off. He smoked his meats and ran a successful deli the entire time I was alderman.

SOMETIMES, as alderman, you felt great because you helped people and made a difference. Sometimes, you spent your day on problems that you couldn't fix. Some requests seemed insane. People would move in down the street from a bar and complain about the noise. People would move around the corner from a church and complain that there was nowhere to park on Sunday. I tried to help. But Gene was moving my friends out of City Hall, and conspiring with Vrdo-lyak's guys to take power away from all of Harold's allies. I was in Puerto Rico visiting my parents one week when I got a call from Alder-man John Madrzyk.

"I'm taking over your committee next week," he told me. "I thought you might want to give your people a heads-up."

I told him he might want to consider giving the people who worked for me on the committee a few months instead of a couple of weeks. He laughed at me.

"Why would I do that?" he asked.

"Because without me you won't be able to find the extra $30,000 in my committee budget. It's hidden in a line-item you'll never find," I told him.

When Vrdolyak was in charge of the city council and controlled the committees, they were always hiding money. They hid it in obscure line items in the budget and padded their committees with so much mystery money that we probably never found all of it. But with Walter Knorr's help, I found thirty grand that had been hidden by Vrdolyak's guys for the Special Events Committee. I used it to help start the first Latino film festival in Chicago. I knew Madrzyk wouldn't find it. Vrdolyak was Houdini when it came to hiding the taxpayers' money.

Madrzyk wasn't so convinced.

"If there is that much money, I'll find it," he told me.

"Good luck," I said.

A couple of days later, he called me back. "All right, your people can stay two months. Where's the money?"

I told him. Unfortunately for Madrzyk, he used some of that money to pay people who never showed up for work, and a few years later went to jail for running a ghost payrolling scheme.

Gene Sawyer and his allies were taking away my ability to help people. It was time to think about my life after the Chicago City Council.

I liked helping people smoke their meats or keep their bodegas running. Still, I wanted to do more. Reporters had always asked me about running for Congress. They figured I was crazy enough to run against Rostenkowski for committeeman, so why not run for Congress? I told people I was thinking about it. It was the end of the 1980s, and a new decade would bring aldermanic redistricting and congressional redistricting as well. The Latino population was growing, and any fair map would give Latinos a chance to elect a member of Congress.

The more I dealt with trash cans and liquor licenses, the more I wanted to work on public policy. Our greatest accomplishment in Humboldt Park was building affordable housing. We had attacked the empty and abandoned lots one by one. We transferred lots with delinquent taxes to Bickerdike Development Corporation, led by Bob Brehm, a nonprofit that built affordable housing. Where gangs had been selling drugs and companies had been dumping garbage, we were building hundreds of beautiful town houses. We pounded railroad ties into the lots we couldn't sell or develop so the fly dumpers couldn't use them as garbage dumps. I wanted more time to work on issues like housing. Congress seemed like the place to do it.

BEFORE I FIGURED out my political future, the city of Chicago needed to choose a new mayor. Sawyer was only elected to fill the last two years of Harold's term. We had another election coming up.

Tim Evans was planning on running, maybe as a third-party candidate. A white progressive, Larry Bloom, who had always supported Harold, was going to run. A new and supposedly improved Rich Daley was running. A few Harold loyalists wanted to support Sawyer against Daley in the Democratic primary and then support Evans if Daley won. Some wanted to just sit out the primary and support Evans's third-party candidacy. Everywhere I looked, I saw the Harold Washington coalition breaking apart or in disarray.

I wasn't crazy about the third-party idea. Third parties were losing parties. In Chicago, people vote for Democrats. Democratic nominees win. Just ask Bernard Epton. Or Ed Vrdolyak. Or Tom Hynes. Every third-party candidate in the past decade had gone down in flames.

Plus, turning their backs on the Democratic nominee is what had outraged me about Rosty's guys in the first place. It didn't feel quite right that we could be outraged when white Democrats abandoned the party yet feel morally superior when we did it. I was for Tim Evans over Gene Sawyer, but the third-party campaign was dangerous territory. I wanted to talk to Tim Evans about the campaign. I set up a meeting. He canceled it. We tried again, but soon it became clear that we weren't going to get together.

While Tim Evans and I were busy missing each other, another political leader was working hard to reach me. I was in my district office when I got a call from Tim Degnan, Rich Daley's political right hand.

"Alderman, I wonder if we could get together? And I'd like to bring along Bill Daley, Rich's brother," he said.

"His brother? So you've got a Kennedy thing going?" I asked. He laughed. We agreed to meet at my house.

I told Soraida we would have some visitors that Thursday. Having two Irish guys, one named Daley, visit the Gutiérrez household was not a typical afternoon. She wondered what I was up to. I gave Soraida specific instructions for how I wanted the meeting to go. She was puzzled, but agreed to play along.

Degnan and Daley showed up that Thursday. I served my very Irish visitors pastries from the best Puerto Rican bakery in the neighborhood. We talked in our living room. I had never met Bill Daley before. He did seem to be playing the Robert Kennedy role. He was a smart, measured guy who asked a lot of questions—more businessman than politician. His brother was always mocked for his troubles mastering the English language. Putting together articulate sentences was not Rich Daley's strength. Bill didn't have any trouble at all.

They weren't slow about telling me what they wanted.

"We would like you to support Rich and want you to be a cornerstone of our campaign. You have demonstrated that you are a leader. We want you to be a leader for Rich Daley in the Chicago City Council."

I listened. I knew our meeting's clock was ticking, but they were just getting warmed up.

Their emphasis was on making peace—on putting together a coalition from throughout the city that could work together and get things done. Not a return to Beirut on the Lake.

"We want to stop the fighting and bickering, show that Chicago can put that behind us," Bill said. "I can't think of anything that would send a message that Rich Daley wants to bring the city of Chicago together more than you standing next to him."

I understood their point. If they could disarm the person much of Chicago viewed as one of the biggest bomb-throwers in the city council before the war even started, Daley would look like a peacemaker. I did a lot of thoughtful nodding. They looked like they still had a lot more to say.

As Daley and Degnan were making their pitch, Soraida came out of the kitchen, right on time. She was carrying their coats. She handed them to our Irish visitors less than a half hour after the start of our meeting. They looked astonished. I had hardly said anything at all. They looked at me like maybe they had said something wrong, or maybe we had gotten the time of the meeting mixed up. Or had just wandered into the wrong neighborhood.

"I'm sorry, gentlemen. We have a very busy day today. We'll stay in touch and keep talking about this," I told them.

They took their coats and headed out, wondering if they had blown the deal. When they were gone, Soraida told me she thought we were being rude. Why did we have to be so abrupt with them, she wanted to know.

"Because if there's any chance I'm going to be with Rich Daley for mayor, they need to know it won't be easy. It's like wine. You have to let it breathe. We'll go sip by sip," I told her.

They called again the next day. We scheduled another meeting. They said they would meet anywhere but my house. I thought about what to do. Evans was definitely running as a third-party candidate. African Americans were still livid at Sawyer, making a Daley victory over him in the primary almost certain. Daley was refining his message of making peace in the city. He had hired a smart, young team of progressive political consultants, including David Axelrod and Rahm Emanuel, who were busy remaking the son in a very different image from his father. Richard M. Daley seemed to understand that Richard J. Daley's time had passed. He didn't want to be another machine guy, out of touch with the black and Latino neighborhoods in Chicago.

His strategy was working. On Chicago's lakefront, white progressives were tripping over one another to endorse Rich Daley. It seemed easy for progressive whites to leave the Harold Washington coalition. But if I did it, I knew many of Harold's most dedicated followers would consider me a traitor.

I talked to people in my political organization, as well as other Harold loyalists. "You have to be with Evans," they would say, as if there was simply no other choice.

"Really?" I would ask. "Tim Evans is Harold Washington? I wish he were, but he's not."

I talked to as many voters as I could. I was always out in the neighborhood. People were talking about Daley. They seemed to like him. I took my own kind of poll early on in the mayoral race. I went to a Puerto Rican barbershop, one of the busiest places in the neighborhood. I sat quietly and listened. Puerto Ricans love to talk politics. You can pick up a lot while you are waiting for your turn in the barber's chair.

"I don't like Sawyer. I don't like what he did to Harold Washington," men were saying. That wasn't surprising. They had no reason to like Gene Sawyer. Then I heard the same thing again and again: "Alderman, what do you think of Daley? He might not be too bad. I'm not sure people would be too upset with you if you were for Rich Daley." Some of the old guys even liked Daley's father.

I listened. Puerto Ricans weren't that different from the African Americans and the white liberals on the Chicago City Council. It was more than progressive politics that had made them Harold Washington loyalists—it was Harold. More and more people I listened to in my neighborhood were thinking about Rich Daley.

I thought about it. I fully believed that Daley was going to be the next mayor. Sawyer was dead politically the day he cut a deal with the white guys. Evans had the hopeless task of running as a third-party candidate. I could try to help my people either by throwing rocks at Daley from the outside or working with him from the inside. And I wanted to believe he was going to be different. Rich Daley, the candidate who finished third behind Jane Byrne and Harold Washington, looked like a man who had experienced an epiphany. Whether it was a political makeover or a genuine turnaround, he knew he had to change.

At my next meeting with Daley and Degnan, we talked more seriously. I emphasized the affordable housing we were creating in the neighborhood, things that I thought would help Daley make clear that he was going to be a different, inclusive mayor. I told them they needed more Latino department heads, that Latinos needed more schools built in our communities.

Then we ended with a clear Chicago political agreement.

"Alderman, we want the same things you want for Latinos and people of the Twenty-Sixth Ward. Why don't you make a list of what it would take for you to be with us for mayor?"

Simple enough. A shopping list.

One thing I've learned about negotiating in politics, whether it's about an endorsement or comprehensive immigration reform: to get what you want, you'd better ask for a lot more.

The following week, I delivered my list to Degnan and Daley. They looked at me like I was crazy.

"We can't possibly do the number one thing on your list. There's no way. We can't even discuss it," Degnan said.

I looked outraged, disappointed, shocked. "How can we reach an agreement if you can't do the first thing on the list?"

"We want to be helpful. Really we do. Listen, we can do everything else on the list. Everything."

I still looked as if I had been wounded. I looked like I was bitterly disappointed, but might be willing to compromise. "You'll do everything else?"

They said they would.

"All right, then let's elect your brother the mayor of the city of Chicago," I told Bill Daley.

The first item on my list was "Support me for congressman against Dan Rostenkowski." The Daleys went back thirty years with Rosty. Bill said, "He's my friend, we can't do this." Short of Rosty burglarizing their house or kidnapping their dog, there was no way they could ever support me for Congress against him. I knew they couldn't do it, that's why it was on the list. It made everything else seem so reasonable, including being their point person on affordable housing and becoming chairman of the Housing Committee if Daley were elected. Also on the list were continued resources for the 26th Ward, including a new library for Humboldt Park and new schools for Latinos. They were so stunned by the Rosty request that the rest of the list was easy.

I learned something else valuable about the Daley family that day. They underestimated me. To believe that I really thought they might endorse me over Dan Rostenkowski for Congress showed me they thought I was naïve. They should have said, "We know you're just kidding about that first item, Luis. Let's negotiate what you really want." They didn't. Instead, they gave me everything else on the list. I've learned this again and again in nearly thirty years in politics—being underestimated is an asset.

They were ready to talk about making my endorsement public. Not so fast, I said.

"I have an agreement with you guys, but you two aren't running for anything. I don't have an agreement with Rich Daley. His name is on the ballot. When he's elected, he's the one who will be in the mayor's office. I'm used to walking into the mayor's office and talking to a friend. Rich and I need to meet before this is final," I told them.

It's amazing how much people think they can get done in politics without involving the candidate. But the next day, Rich and I met—for the first time in our lives—in Bill Daley's law office. As I looked over his shoulder, I thought to myself that this was going to be a very interesting partnership. Hanging on the wall, right behind Rich Daley, was a picture of Dan Rostenkowski.

Throughout the meeting, Rich was cordial and likable and excited about my endorsement. We talked about housing and schools. We shook hands and talked about a bright future of working together. Twenty years earlier, his father had walked out of his mayor's office and given me five bucks—a fortune—as my Christmas tip for delivering his newspaper. Now I was going to help his son follow in his footsteps.

THE DALEY TEAM treated my endorsement like a major moment in the campaign. Reporters were surprised and treated it like a huge deal. Gutiérrez and Daley together—it was a like an Arab-Israeli summit meeting. Some reporters thought it was nothing more than a political deal. So did some of my supporters. But nobody thought it wasn't news.

I had one very simple final request for the Daley team.

"Will Rich's wife and kids be coming to the endorsement? I want to bring Soraida and the girls," I said.

Degnan looked at me like I was crazy.

"Rich doesn't involve his family in this type of political announcement. It will just be the two of you," he said.

"Well, then there's no endorsement. I guess we've wasted our time," I told him.

Having our families there was very important to me. I wanted this to be more than political. I wanted my endorsement to make a statement that we needed to find some peace, some common ground in the city of Chicago. We'd had a great African American mayor who had stood up for Latinos and built bridges with our community. I wanted people to know that I was with Rich Daley because he could do the same. I thought that having our families there—the very white, very Irish family of Rich Daley, standing next to the very brown, very Puerto Rican family of Luis Gutiérrez—would send a much more powerful message than having two politicians together.

And it did. Soraida and Maggie, Rich's very gracious wife, got along very well. We all talked before the endorsement. Maggie couldn't have been nicer to us. In the media, we didn't merely look like political allies. We looked like partners—families from two very different parts of Chicago coming together and getting along. The coverage was beautiful. Rich Daley had an important new ally—a Puerto Rican who had once delivered the city council to Harold Washington.

IF YOU WANT to feel lonely in a Chicago City Council meeting, be the radical Puerto Rican Harold Washington fanatic who has just endorsed Rich Daley for mayor. Most of my African American friends thought I had betrayed them. The white guys had never liked me, and now they were jealous on top of it. Their view was that the guy who got everything he wanted from Harold had somehow scammed a way to get everything he wanted from Daley too. It wasn't chilly for me—it was ice cold. I looked around the room at hostile city council members and had one simple thought: Daley had better win.

I campaigned all over the city with him. Just as I'd been Harold Washington's walking symbol of control of the city council for the New York bond traders, I was Rich's walking symbol of coalition building in Chicago. I'd never spent so much time in white ethnic neighborhoods. In neighborhoods where they'd resented me before, voters saw me with Daley and thought that maybe Daley trying to get along with everyone was a good thing. In Latino communities, there was a genuine enthusiasm for Daley. He learned to talk about more than law and order, and said the police department would continue to be diverse and reach out to minorities. He talked about housing. He talked about building schools. He talked about everyone getting their fair share. Puerto Ricans were excited.

Ted Kennedy came to town to campaign with Daley, and I met the man who would one day be my steadfast partner on comprehensive immigration reform. I resisted the urge to tell him I'd grown up with a picture of his brother hanging on our dining-room wall. Kennedy was having a ball campaigning with Rich Daley and his new team of diverse allies. We had hugely enthusiastic receptions everywhere we went, and ended the day at a rally packed with Puerto Ricans.

Finally, as Election Day came closer, Daley was headed to a major public forum in the Latino community, right in the 26th Ward at Roberto Clemente High School.

The Harold loyalists in the neighborhood, my old friends, some of whom were sticking with me and some of whom didn't want to be anywhere near me, had organized the forum. Daley's campaign had made the mistake of accepting the invitation without knowing who was in charge. I knew it was a setup. For Harold, I used to make sure rooms were packed with fans who would be for Harold and me instead of Vrdolyak and Manny. The organizers of this event assured Daley that the event would be impartial because they were distributing tickets only to community groups and advocacy organizations.

I know how that works. Most community groups view the world through some political lens: through the lens of elected officials who give them money, or issues they are passionate about, or political candidates they want to defeat. I knew what kind of groups were going to get tickets to this event—groups committed to Tim Evans. It wasn't like the organizers were inviting the Salvation Army. They were inviting advocates, but only advocates who hated Rich Daley.

They made one mistake, though. When they printed the tickets for the event, they didn't number them. And I knew the printer they'd used. It's hard for neighborhood printers to say no to the alderman when he phones in an order for more tickets. A week before the event, I had two new rolls of tickets, perfect counterfeits, to give away to other community groups and activists—ones who, as political coincidence would have it, had a very *positive* opinion about Rich Daley.

Still, Daley was worried about the event.

I met up with him at his office to accompany him to the event. As we walked out, he looked at me with a serious question.

"Are you sure this is a good idea? I had a really bad experience at Roberto Clemente High School when I ran in 1983."

The son of the man who was mayor of Chicago for twenty years, the Cook County state's attorney, the frontrunner to become mayor of the city of Chicago, was worried about a neighborhood forum in the Puerto Rican community.

"Rich, it's a good idea because I'm not in the audience leading the booing from all of Harold Washington's people," I told him. "Believe me, it's under control." I wanted to add that if I hadn't printed a few hundred tickets for our people, he probably would have been right.

To the astonishment of the organizers of the event, Luis Gutiérrez and Rich Daley fans kept showing up, tickets in hand. They asked one another who had given tickets to all of the Daley and Gutiérrez supporters. Daley was scheduled to go first because they expected their partisan crowd to hassle him. Instead, he gave his remarks to a cheering, enthusiastic audience, people with my tickets, waving Daley signs. When he left the event, all of our people streamed out behind him, cheering and celebrating. On TV that night, the story was that Rich Daley had won the debate in the Latino community.

Throughout the campaign, Daley kept asking how he would do in the 26th Ward. I had beaten Manny Torres in a tough fight. We had carried the ward for Harold Washington, but nobody was quite sure if Puerto Ricans would really support Rich Daley. They kept pushing me, telling me that we needed to do well in the Latino community.

On election night, I was watching live TV coverage of the Daley campaign's party. Ward-by-ward totals flashed on a big screen in the front of the room, and people cheered every time Daley was ahead in a ward. Then they came to the 26th Ward. Daley was leading Sawyer 2 to 1. The room exploded. If Rich Daley could win in the home ward of Luis Gutiérrez, everyone thought he was about to become mayor.

They were right. Daley carried 55 percent of the vote against Sawyer. Daley still didn't get any support among blacks, but Latinos strongly supported him. In the 26th Ward, he received 72 percent of the vote.

Two months later, running as a third-party candidate, Evans didn't fare any better. The numbers were nearly identical. We beat Evans almost 3 to 1 in the 26th Ward. Daley carried Latino votes throughout the city again. Chicago had another Daley as mayor.

THE DALEYS were good about keeping their word. At the first city council meeting under our new mayor, they reorganized all of the committees. The Housing Committee was given more power to acquire land and build affordable housing. They combined two committees into one to accommodate my suggestion about how to make housing development more efficient. I was named chairman of the new combined committee.

Not long after that, as council reorganization continued, I was named president pro tempore of the body, the number-two guy to the mayor, the one who would run meetings in his absence. Vrdolyak's guys smirked and shook their heads.

Bob Shaw, the tall, broad, toupeed African American machine alderman who had helped make Sawyer mayor after Washington, rose to be recognized.

"Mayor Daley, I just have one question: Is Luis Gutiérrez going to get anything else, or are you done rewarding him?" My colleagues laughed. Mayor Daley laughed too.

"No, I think that's it," our new mayor said.

To this day, I have a few people who'd knocked on doors for me against Manny Torres, who'd fought alongside me with Harold Washington, who can't quite forgive me for being with Rich Daley for mayor. It doesn't matter to them how many things Daley did for Latinos while in office. Or how often I'm recognized by the AFL-CIO or NOW or the LGBT community as one of the most progressive members of Congress. They can't get over the idea that it wasn't right for me to be with Rich Daley, that somehow things might have turned out differently for Tim Evans if I had been with him.

I understand their feelings, but they have my motivation wrong. I think they also have their politics wrong. I didn't lead Latinos to Rich Daley. It would be nice to be that powerful, but I'm not. Latinos would have stuck with Harold Washington, just like I would have. But Harold was gone and people were ready to give Daley a chance. He went on to win five more elections for mayor. None were ever close, and Latinos supported him overwhelmingly. I didn't lead Latinos to Daley. They led me to him.

As for Bob Shaw and my skeptical colleagues who thought I endorsed Rich Daley just so I could stay powerful at City Hall, they didn't understand. I would do some good things working with Rich Daley as mayor, but endorsing him wasn't a way to remain a player in Chicago. It was a way to strike out on my own and create my own path.

I wanted to fight, and win, for the things that Rubén Berríos and Harold Washington had inspired me to believe in. I knew my time in the city council was nearing an end. It was hard to make a difference as one of fifty voices in City Hall. Harold Washington had shown me what a real leader could do for people. I wanted to be one.

CHAPTER FIFTEEN

Congressional Pay Freeze, Congressional Pariah

MY DAD LOVED talking to all the reporters. Back when I was elected alderman, he had talked to a couple of local guys from Chicago and Puerto Rico. That was different. To my dad, an alderman was really just another local politician. Being alderman felt like a hobby, something you could do in your spare time. But when I was elected to Congress, reporters lined up to talk to him.

Most of my family came to Washington, DC, for the party we had for my swearing-in. I was surrounded by all of the Puerto Ricans who had given me places to sleep or jobs to do, my support network through years of finishing college and trying to make ends meet. Aunt Nilda was there to see the kid who hoarded damaged Helene Curtis shampoo bottles for her become a US representative. Aunt Rose, the sister with the bad leg who my mom helped to raise, was there. Juano and Lucy and a few friends had once stood nearly alone eating chips and pretzels in the moving company's basement after Rosty had crushed me. Now they were standing in a ballroom in the Hilton Hotel on Capitol Hill, surrounded by hundreds of donors, friends, and family.

That I was elected to Congress was almost unimaginable for my family members back in Puerto Rico. The island didn't even have a voting member of Congress. Puerto Rico's representative—the resident commissioner—could only vote in committee. He had to sit back and watch everyone else make the decisions when issues finally came up for a vote on the floor. Now he would be watching the son of Luis and Ada Gutiérrez of San Sebastián.

My dad attended every event in Washington, DC, during the week of my swearing-in. He was proud, telling anyone who would listen that he always knew I was destined for great things. I didn't recall him always telling *me* that, but I was glad he remembered it that way. Reporters kept asking him to explain what it felt like to have a son in Congress.

"Wonderful," he said. "I am so proud of him. I am so glad he's not driving a cab anymore," he would finish, making clear he wasn't just proud, he was also relieved.

We bought Omaira a beautiful new lavender dress for her trip to the house floor for the swearing-in. Jessica was only four years old, and I held her against my chest as I raised my right hand and repeated the Congressional oath of office, promising to support and defend the Constitution of the United States against all enemies, foreign and domestic.

I looked up into the gallery and waved at my mom and dad and my sister, aunts, and uncles. They clapped and cheered. The Puerto Rican kid from the neighborhood was a member of Congress—the first Latino outside of New York and California, Texas, and Florida to be a congressman. One of only three Puerto Ricans. Then, I looked toward Speaker Tom Foley, the man who had just administered the oath that made my entrance into Congress official. If my family knew how things were going between me and Foley and his friends in leadership who ran the place, they might have stopped clapping and started worrying about my congressional future.

I HAD BEEN elected to Congress in a campaign not remotely as close as my aldermanic contest. In the primary, I defeated my old city council colleague Juan Soliz, the man who was one vote away from being mayor. He ended up thousands of votes away from being congressman. In every campaign I had run before, I'd gone door-to-door, talking to voters and making plus and minus counts with my captains. I'd made every decision myself. Congress was different. The district was too big to talk to everyone personally. I hired professional consultants and was surrounded by people who ran campaigns for a living. I sent out mailer after mailer, and did lots of Spanish-language television and radio. It wasn't as much fun, but it worked.

With strong support from Puerto Rican and white voters I swept through the primary and general election. Mexicans mostly stuck with my Mexican American opponent, a problem I would have to address: working on uniting Latinos would have to be a priority for me as a new congressman.

When I won, my campaign team told me the biggest advantage of winning the March Democratic primary—which made me a lock to defeat the Republican in November unless Chicago's political poles reversed—was that I would have months of a head start on my incoming Democratic freshman colleagues.

"Head start for what?" I asked my campaign manager. "I already won. What am I competing for in Washington?"

"Meeting the leadership. Hiring staff. And getting a good committee assignment."

He emphasized that last part. Getting on the right committee in Congress was a little more complicated than it was in the city council. Under Harold, I'd just accepted whatever committee he wanted to give me because I never wanted to cause him any headache. With Daley, I made clear from the beginning that if he wanted my endorsement I had to be in charge of affordable housing and the Housing Committee.

In Congress, it wasn't quite so clear cut. I had never met Speaker Tom Foley before. He would have eighty other freshmen asking him for choice committee assignments. He didn't owe me a thing. I had never even been to Washington before running for Congress. I could play and win the inside game in the Chicago City Council, but this was different.

I studied the arcane rules and rituals of committee assignments. Head start or not, this wasn't going to be easy. Committee assignments were a mysterious Washington, DC, game. Rule #1: there aren't any rules. Assignments are made by a committee that nobody outside of Washington knows—the Steering and Policy Committee, a panel made up of people appointed by the leadership and elected by regions of Congress. They make the committee assignments based on instructions from party leaders and committee chairmen, personal preferences, regional loyalties, and whim.

Before my election, I never thought of plotting to get on a good committee as part of the deal in getting to Congress. I was thrilled to be elected at all. But I'm competitive. If I had an eight-month head start on landing a great committee, I wasn't going to wait for everyone else to catch up. I followed the advice of my experts and began regular pilgrimages to Washington.

If you aim high, the influential committees to target are Appropriations and Ways and Means. It made sense to me; in the Chicago City Council, the action was in the Finance Committee, the domain of Alderman Ed Burke. In government, to control the money is to control the world. In Congress, you could either control how we got the money—Ways and Means; or how we spend the money—Appropriations. Normally a freshman member wouldn't have a prayer of ending up on either committee. But there were so many of us coming to Washington on the tide of the Clinton Democratic sweep that the leadership had quietly put out the word that maybe a few of the right freshmen could end up on these exclusive committees.

My post-election committee campaign began with meeting the people who ran the place. In May, I sat down to lunch with the man third in line to the presidency, Speaker Tom Foley of Washington. My lunch with Foley was the first time I had ever walked through the doors to the Capitol Building, where 535 of us would be making the nation's laws. I was surrounded by tourists who had spent vastly more time under the capitol dome than I had.

For this lunch, it was just me and two other freshmen in the Speaker's dining room. The ceilings were thirteen or fourteen feet high. The walls, painted in dark, dramatic colors, had portraits of past Speakers who solemnly watched us eat on china that my family would have referred to as the "Christmas China," with crystal, on a table covered by a linen tablecloth.

Two gray-haired African American waiters, wearing dark suits and dark ties and white gloves, attended to us. They brought us our food, refilled our drinks, asked us unobtrusively if we needed anything, and then stood quietly at attention while the Speaker introduced me to the ways of the world in Washington, DC. When a waiter talked to me, he called me "sir," leaning over my shoulder respectfully to fill my water glass. I had a hard time concentrating on what the Speaker was saying. I couldn't stop glancing at our waiters, standing, waiting to be summoned, invisible except when we needed something. It's the white gloves I remember most. I had never been served food by anyone wearing white gloves. I had hardly ever been called sir. City council members mostly didn't behave in ways that encouraged anyone to address us as sir. I thought of Washington, DC, as the South. Didn't it occur to anyone that having white-gloved, African American waiters serving us might send the wrong message about Congress?

I don't know what message Speaker Foley was trying to communicate, but what I was learning was that life in Congress was going to be different from life in the real world. Being a city council member might have come with a parking place at City Hall, but it also came with strangers yelling at me because the city hadn't trimmed the tree in front of their house. Being in the city council might mean getting a corner booth at the neighborhood Puerto Rican restaurant. Congress was going to be like having a private room at the finest country club. Congress was going to take a while to get used to.

Speaker Foley talked to us about the "institution." People who had been in Washington a while used the word "institution" a lot when they talked about Congress. The "institution" was something to be honored and protected. It was something to be revered. Apparently, nobody worried that anyone would hear "institution" and summon an image of a place for the mentally ill.

I was definitely honored to be there, but Foley's ode to the institution stood in contrast to what I had just heard from voters back at home. I wasn't disrespectful of the institution, but I was respectful of voters' desire to see some changes in the way things were done in Washington. In my campaign, I had adopted the slogan "Closer to the people than the backrooms of Washington, DC." In my campaign, nobody ever said, "Hey, Luis, stop criticizing the institution." Now I was sitting in one of those backrooms. It was even more opulent and privileged than I had imagined.

In great contrast to the great comfort inside the Speaker's dining room, Congress was taking hits all around the country. Republicans were pushing term limits, with success, from coast to coast. Democrats hadn't felt any pain at the polls yet, mainly because people were tired of Bush Sr. and the recession. Latinos had larger concerns than reforms to Congress, but voters in the 4th Congressional District looked at Washington and saw a remote place, insulated from the real world. Most Latinos I talked to in my campaign had never even thought about what a congressman could do for them. How often did any of them see Dan Rostenkowski? When was the last time he hosted a community meeting about transportation or education or immigration? He didn't have to. He had been overwhelmingly re-elected seventeen times in the district. Just like when I went to the city council, I wanted to make people in the neighborhood realize that government could actually do some things for them.

I wondered what it would take for the Speaker to notice the voter unrest bubbling out in the real world. I didn't dislike Tom Foley, but I thought he acted like a chairman of the board protecting the great legacy of a bank his family had run for generations. He definitely wasn't a rugged sea captain preparing to navigate the good ship Congress through rushing rapids of angry voters. I left lunch and wondered how many more guys like Foley I was going to have to convince to put me on a good committee. I was pretty sure I would have better luck if my target audience were the waiters wearing the white gloves.

Still, I kept working. It was an education. I introduced myself to my new colleagues. I met Kika de la Garza, a Latino member from Texas who was chairman of the Agriculture Committee. He had so many gifts and knickknacks jammed into his office that he hadn't unwrapped them all. His shelves were lined with presents with paper and bows on them, as if every day were Christmas. It must be nice to be a committee chairman, I thought. I made visit after visit to the members of the Steering and Policy Committee, telling them about my experience in the city council, and explaining to them that I had decided what committee—with their support and approval—I would like to be on. I had decided on Ways and Means. The committee chaired by Dan Rostenkowski.

You can't campaign to get on a committee without talking to the chairman. I had run against Dan Rostenkowski for Democratic committeeman but barely ever had a conversation with him. I had never liked his politics, but I hardly knew him personally. I was trying to set aside past differences in my new life as a member of Congress. So was he.

Our peace process had started almost a year before, once I announced I was running in the new Latino-majority district. His district had been moved north, which meant I would be running in half of his old district. Mayor Daley started making clear to his allies that he was supporting me for Congress. I think Rosty was glad to be rid of his growing Latino constituency and to have Luis Gutiérrez out of his district. It didn't take long for me to get a phone call at my City Hall office.

"This is Dan Rostenkowski. I have a check for five thousand dollars for you. You know, I might draw some attention to your campaign that you don't want. Would you like me to send you the check now, or do you want to wait until after the campaign? Either way, you've got five grand from me," he said, his Chicago growl familiar to me through the phone.

I thought about it. Dan Rostenkowski wanted to give me $5,000. It was generous—the maximum amount he could give. When I was talking with Rich Daley about supporting him for mayor, the number-one item on my list had been that he support me over Dan Rostenkowski. Now Rosty wanted to become a Luis Gutiérrez donor.

Rostenkowski asked me if I wanted the donation now or later

because rumors were starting to float around about an investigation of Rosty's office budget concerning how he used official funds. Still, running for Congress is expensive. I told him I would take the money. I put down the phone and I laughed. That was a check I had never expected to get.

Now that I was almost a congressman, if I wanted to be on the nation's tax-writing committee, he was the person I had to see. He seemed ready to forgive me for running against him. I was ready to forgive him for being Ronald Reagan's right-hand man in rewriting the tax code.

Just like the Speaker of the House, the chairman of the Ways and Means Committee has more than one office. He has a little alcove right off the House floor, a big office in the Capitol, and another big office in the House office buildings. Powerful committee chairmen collect offices like tourists collect T-shirts. He seemed to do most of his work out of the Ways and Means office in the Capitol.

At our first meeting we pretended we had never been political enemies. He never mentioned, even as a joke, that I'd once run against him. He sat behind a huge desk and told stories about Congress. Dan Rostenkowski is a big guy. He reminded me of the Bureau of Electricity guys I used to chase around to coffee shops, trying to get them to fix streetlights. You could fit about three Luis Gutiérrezes into Dan Rostenkowski. He looked and sounded like a guy who should never be too far from a big steak and some good bourbon. I mostly listened politely as he spoke. I looked around his fancy office and wondered how I ever thought a cabdriver who had never run for anything could be the guy to defeat him. He didn't promise anything about Ways and Means, but he didn't tell me to stop trying.

After checking in with Rosty, I kept making my rounds. By congressional standards, I was very young—under forty years old. I looked even younger. My future colleagues were usually surprised to meet this wiry Puerto Rican kid who had somehow navigated the tough world of Chicago politics to make it to Washington. It helped my case. If I could survive Chicago, people figured, I must be fairly shrewd. Most of the other Democrats were still running hard in competitive districts out in the real world. I was running up and down the halls of Congress, trying to make friends and allies.

Before long, I was getting a reputation as a freshman to know. I met with Mayor Daley and asked if he could put in a good word with Rostenkowski. He did. In the fall, just before the general election, I sat down for another meeting with Rosty.

I was gaining momentum. In our meeting, I was very clear.

"I would like to count on your support for being on the committee. I know in the end it's up to you. I would like to be a fellow Chicagoan working with you on the Ways and Means Committee," I said.

Looking at me from the end of his long conference table, he asked the only question that mattered.

"Here's what is going to be very important to me in making my decision. The new member will be a long way away from where I am sitting. He'll be the lowest ranking. I want to make sure that I can rely on that member to support their chairman—particularly a chairman whose benevolence put him on the committee. I need to know I have that support," Rostenkowski said, expecting a very simple and clear answer.

At that moment, my campaign for Ways and Means stopped being fun. Suddenly, the merchandise I was trying to buy had a clear price tag. I had spent a lot of time negotiating something that was too expensive for me to afford. I answered the best I could.

"Let me put it to you this way, Mr. Chairman. I look forward to being helpful. I look forward to being cooperative. But I'm leaving the Chicago City Council in great measure so that I can get away from following the dictates of the mayor or any other leader. I am looking forward to a measure of independence. But I will be as helpful to you as I can," I said, thinking I had walked the line fairly well. I had promised him all that I could.

He didn't have much more to say after that. He never directly replied to what I said. I wasn't trying to blow up my chances. I was just being honest.

As I walked out, I thought maybe I had built up enough goodwill with Rostenkowski and other members to survive my answer. Then, waiting in the Ways and Means reception area, I saw Congressman Mel Reynolds. It took Reynolds three tries, but he had just won the Democratic primary in the 2nd Congressional District on Chicago's South Side. He was African-American, a Rhodes Scholar, and ambitious. Rumors had been around that he wanted Ways and Means as well. I said hello, and then I almost laughed out loud. I realized that Mel and I had been invited to the chairman's office for a final exam for the committee seat. I had just taken my test and failed miserably. I looked at Reynolds. I had absolutely no doubt that he would pass the test. At that moment I understood that I would never be on the Ways and Means Committee.

I had a few more meetings with other members, but my heart wasn't in it. I had believed that I might make it onto one of the most exclusive committees in Congress based on my charming personality and some Chicago connections. I was never interested in giving up anything in exchange for it. I had come to Congress to do things, to change things. If Rosty wanted to bury the hatchet and put me on his committee, that was great. I wasn't going to give up my independence for him.

Of course, I also thought to myself—why didn't I just say yes when he asked me and then vote exactly the way I felt like voting once I got there? But as I flew home to Chicago that night, I was glad I didn't. I wanted to go to Congress to be free. My honesty had just liberated me.

TWO MONTHS before I was sworn in, right after Rosty nodded silently at my disappointing answer and waited patiently for someone like Mel Reynolds to tell him exactly what he wanted to hear, the Democratic leadership of the US House of Representatives held a briefing for freshmen. They decided the incoming freshman class, the group that was sweeping Bush Sr. and the Republicans out of power and Bill Clinton into Washington, was too big to handle all at once. They divided us up into three bite-size morsels for orientation. Carved into one-third of the incoming Democrats, we were a small enough group to be supervised, but not so small that they had to spend much time listening to us.

The Midwestern chunk of eager newcomers had campaigned mostly on fixing the sagging economy of the early '90s. Some of us had thrown in a little dose of Congressional reform—a theme our Republican competitors were hammering. We were happily arrayed around a large square table in a sterile conference room at a hotel out by O'Hare Airport. The leaders brought in a few speakers, gave us a preview of a seminar that would be made available to us at the Kennedy School at Harvard, and handed out briefing materials on congressional procedures and ethics. It was a little like day camp.

Many of the leading Dems in Congress had flown in from DC. Speaker Foley was there, and so was Majority Leader Dick Gephardt from Missouri. Key committee chairmen were there to let us know how things worked in Washington. Sitting almost directly across the room from me, eye-to-eye, was my old friend Dan Rostenkowski.

We had a long day of briefings. Mostly, we listened. We all had a lot to learn. Still, it wasn't unlike a high school orientation. That wasn't an accident. Part of the point was to remind us that Congress was a top-down place.

The unwritten briefing point in our book would have come under the heading "knowing your place." Foley wanted to make clear that our vote totals at home might have earned us our seat in Congress, but that everything else we earned inside the place would be harder, and much of it would be determined by the six or seven members of Congress who had flown in from Washington. Just like high school, these guys were the captains of the team, the president of the student council. They couldn't keep us from coming through the door, but they could keep us from the head of the class.

I wasn't surprised. There had been a tough hierarchy in Chicago too. I had been near the top because my election delivered the council to Harold, and because I'd helped make Daley become a more inclusive mayor. In Washington, I knew I would have to work my way up, and I knew I had blown it with Rosty. I had some ground to make up.

At the end of the meeting, they opened the floor for final comments and questions.

I raised the one point that I thought they had missed.

"I want to say thank you. This is a great chance to learn about opportunities that are available to us. I have just one suggestion. I see on this schedule for the upcoming orientation in Washington that there is no specific meeting that is just freshmen. Maybe at that meeting we can find some time for all of us to get together. It's a large class that has been sent here with a clear message from voters to make some changes. I think we want to put our imprimatur on things. Give the next Congress a sense of who we are and what we want to do," I said.

I wasn't angry, and I didn't mean it as an attack. I just figured that if we had eighty freshmen coming in, we should be able to make some time to talk, organize ourselves, and come up with some ideas of our own. It was a sincere attempt at a constructive suggestion. While I clearly was suggesting that the freshmen be able to get together without the adult supervision of the Congressional leadership, it was still nicer than just about anything I had ever said out loud on the Chicago City Council floor.

But it was met first by silence—not just quiet, but the stillness that comes from none of your compadres—the twenty-five or so other freshmen—even nodding. I glanced around and saw a lot of eyes looking down at the table. Except for Rosty, who was smiling and looking right at me. I heard his growl again.

"He doesn't even know where his office is. He doesn't even know where the bathroom is, but already he wants to put his 'imprimatur' on this Congress," he said, laughing and shaking his head.

All of my freshmen colleagues nodded at that. Several looked like they wanted to raise their hands so they could agree with Rosty. They might have agreed with me that all of the freshmen should get together, but they weren't going to speak up in this setting.

Speaker Foley gave everyone the talking point for how to react to my statement.

"We're a Democratic caucus. We need to work together and stay united. We can't have anyone trying to cause division," he said.

The stillness had been broken. Suddenly it was a conference

room full of enthusiastic agreement, murmurs of "united," and "stay together" traveling throughout the room.

Mel Reynolds, the ambitious Congressman who'd met with Rosty after I told him I would not be the rubber stamp he was looking for, was the first freshman to make a specific response to my heresy.

"Mr. Speaker, I don't agree with Gutiérrez. Sometime in April or May, after we've had five or six months, we might come back to you. But it seems to me that you are doing an excellent job by holding this meeting. You've asked us for our opinions. I think you are doing it just right," Reynolds said, cementing his spot on Ways and Means just in case Rosty was having any second thoughts.

John Lewis, the historic civil rights leader who was now a congressman from Georgia and a part of the Democratic leadership, was sitting next to me. People were so busy assuring the leadership that they didn't agree with me that Lewis felt sorry for me and gave me a comforting rub on the shoulder, a "This is tough, but maybe you'll do better next time" gesture.

I knew Lewis was trying to be nice, but the only thing worse than being attacked by a room full of my new colleagues was somebody I admired taking pity on me. When everyone was running out of the breath necessary to distance themselves from me, I made clear I wasn't done speaking. It would have been uncharacteristic of me to allow a room full of people to tell me to go screw myself and not respond.

"Let me just say that it is clear to me that things will operate very differently once we get to Washington, DC. Until then, let me remind you that you are all in the city of Chicago, and I am the president pro tempore of the Chicago City Council, so until we're in Washington, you're all visitors in my jurisdiction," I said.

Rosty had no response to that. What could he say? People looked at me like I was crazy. I had essentially ended the meeting. They knew they had all been ganging up on me, and when I spoke again they expected me to retreat or apologize, to start by saying, "What I really meant was . . ." I didn't have any interest in apologizing. I knew I didn't have any jurisdiction over anyone in the room. That wasn't my point. I just wanted them to know I wasn't afraid of any of them.

My chief of staff picked me up to take me back to the office.

"How did it go?" he asked.

"I think we should get ready for the Agriculture Committee," I told him.

WORD HAD TRAVELED around our congressional class about the crazy freshman from Chicago and the fireworks at O'Hare. I figured there was no reason to be nice now. I mailed every freshman a copy of the book *Adventures in Porkland,* by *Washington Times* reporter Brian Kelly. He detailed some of the most egregious examples of federal waste and perks. The book's tone was pretty straightforward: Congress is full of assholes. I sent it around with a nice note telling everyone I looked forward to working with them to improve things.

Pretty soon, Mayor Daley called me. He was laughing.

"I hear you had an exciting meeting with Rostenkowski and the other new members. Can I give you some advice? Try to get along with people," he told me.

Mayor Daley might have been one of the first to say it, but "Try to get along with people" is advice I've been getting now for twenty years in Congress. I do try. I'm often successful. But I don't mind the fight. I know lots of politicians, particularly those who have been in Congress a while, who do almost everything they can to avoid conflict. I think conflict is part of the fun, and it's often the best way to get things done for your constituents.

I tried to get along with people when I headed to Washington to get sworn in. Of course, it's easy to be congenial when you are mostly alone. Foley stopped taking my calls. Nobody else on Steering and Policy was talking to me, and most of my freshmen colleagues were finding less controversial members to befriend. I had never made a committee request beyond Ways and Means. I knew I wasn't getting that. I couldn't get a return call about putting in a second, or third, or fourth choice.

When assignments finally came out, I had trouble finding anyone to tell me where I ended up. I saw the Ways and Means list. Congressman Mel Reynolds was the first freshman in years to make the committee. Finally I asked one of my few freshmen friends, Bob Menendez of New Jersey, if he could check on my committees. He called me back in a minute.

"Financial Services and Veterans," he said. So few people wanted the Banking and Financial Services Committee that they couldn't even fill all the seats. Veterans' Affairs wasn't the most sought-after committee in Congress either. But I was just glad I wasn't on Agriculture. I was glad the orientation nonsense and the chase for committees was over. We could all stop acting like kids competing for homecoming court. It was time to get to work.

I QUICKLY REALIZED that most of the time there are only a handful of members on the House floor. A few relevant committee members are paying attention and debating whatever bill is up at the time. There are usually a few members hanging around the cloakroom. The Congressional cloakroom is like the clubhouse at an exclusive golf course—a long L-shaped room with private booths to make phone calls, comfortable chairs, and a lunch counter. Young pages and employees are constantly delivering messages and making sure nobody misses a vote. On the floor, C-SPAN tends to only show the person speaking, so you get the idea that the orator actually has an audience. Usually, the speaker doesn't. More people are in the cloakroom having a sandwich.

That members actually show up is one of the many things that set the State of the Union Address apart from day-to-day life in Congress. You sit with just about every one of your colleagues. Very few miss it. Members are so excited that they arrive early and save seats on the aisle, like they are camping out on the lawn for a Springsteen concert. Members with enough seniority will just put up a sign: RESERVED FOR MEMBER X. Some people can get away with just leaving a coat on a chair. Sitting on the aisle means the president might shake your hand. Everyone wants the folks back home to think that the president of the United States, after giving his key speech of the year, has sought them out to shake their hand on television because they are so important.

Many of the members shaking hands might not see the president for another year. It really means they didn't have anything better to do than hang out on the aisle all afternoon, waiting around like a groupie.

But the competition for seats doesn't lessen the spectacle. The Supreme Court Justices file in, robes flapping like relics from some ancient Roman tribunal. Cabinet members all attend, a parade of successors to the president should something terrible happen. I was excited and proud to attend my first State of the Union speech as a member of Congress. I was ready to hear the young ex-governor of Arkansas tell us exactly how he was going to fix the economic mess America was facing in 1993. It was time to convert "It's the Economy, Stupid" into real policy.

One of his themes that night was that we all had to do our part. Bill Clinton had been crisscrossing America for a year. He understood the power of change. He understood that the American people wanted Washington to make some sacrifices. We sat and applauded as Clinton laid out his agenda.

One item got my attention: Clinton was freezing federal pay. From the White House to federal agencies, no raises for any employees.

I looked around at all of my colleagues standing and applauding. They seemed very supportive, Republican and Democrat alike. I thought, That's good—nobody seems a bit concerned that our new president just froze our paychecks. We're all in this together.

When I returned to the office after the speech, I asked my chief of staff and my legislative director if I had understood the president correctly.

"That pay freeze that Clinton just announced—does it apply to the salaries of members of Congress?"

They researched what Clinton was proposing. It didn't take long to find the answer. The spending freeze did *not* apply to members of Congress. We had an automatic cost-of-living raise that could only be changed with legislation. It applied to the white-gloved waiter who had served Tom Foley and me. It applied to janitors in federal agencies. It didn't apply to me. Or my colleagues.

Standing and applauding rules that did not apply to us seemed ridiculous to me. Members of Congress were well compensated. I had never been paid more. But I didn't think it was a question of sacrifice by members. I thought it was a question of equity. If we were freezing salaries—including those of waiters and janitors—then why shouldn't it apply to us? My sense from my constituents was that the clublike atmosphere in Washington annoyed them. They thought that we lived in a bubble, isolated from real problems. What demonstrated isolation and indifference more than not taking a pay freeze when we asked people who made a fraction of what we did to do it?

I drafted a "Dear Colleague" letter, suggesting to all of my peers that the pay freeze should apply to us, and asking them to co-sponsor my new bill. From senior members, the initial reaction was silence. The spirit of reform was not entirely dead among freshmen, though, and some of my colleagues jumped on the bill. But not too many— there were fewer than ten of us.

The media loved it. I was all over talk radio in Chicago. I talked to NPR, one of my first appearances on national media. My congressional pay-freeze legislation was getting mentioned everywhere from the *Today* show to the *Washington Post*. Reporters loved the irony of everyone standing up to cheer Clinton's pay freeze—as long as it didn't apply to their own paychecks.

My colleagues' reaction wasn't chilly. It was subarctic. It cemented my reputation as a troublemaker.

Plenty of members were happy to tell me what they thought.

Just like a political Disneyland, members of Congress can ride a little monorail between our offices and the Capitol. When votes are being held, the train is just for us, transporting us back and forth on our own exclusive railroad. After I introduced the pay-freeze bill, I was riding back after a vote and a congressman stared at me throughout most of the trip. I was still new, learning everyone's names, but I knew who this was. It was Congressman William Ford, chairman of the Education Committee. He had never said a word to me before.

As our train pulled into the office building, he stood up and looked right at me.

"Are you Gutiérrez?" he said.

I told him I was.

"Don't you ever put your hand in my pocket again," he said, and slowly climbed off of the train.

Ford wasn't alone. Bill Richardson, who was trying to help me navigate out of the freshman wilderness I was in, took me aside and said I had to stop doing crazy things like supporting a pay freeze. I was making it hard for him to help me.

What really made the leadership mad was that they were being forced to respond to reporters' questions about whether they would support the pay freeze. Other members started getting calls in their offices. Constituents asked the same thing I did: "You can't possibly be planning to take a pay raise when everyone else has their paycheck frozen, can you?"

They would have if they could have gotten away with it. But they couldn't. Within a week, they decided to cut their losses. The House leadership decided freezing their pay was a good idea after six quick days of Luis Gutiérrez in the media and angry constituents on the phone. Of course, they didn't pass my bill, or give me any credit. They attached the pay freeze as a rider to another bill and passed it quietly by voice vote. Then, leaders talked about the importance of shared sacrifice. Tom Foley and Republican leader Bob Michel put out a stirring statement that said "parity of treatment in respect to salary" should apply to government.

I might not have been getting along with people, but within a month of arriving in Washington, I had a legislative victory. Uncredited, but still a quick win.

I believed the pay freeze was fair. It was the equitable thing to do. I also admit that I enjoyed sticking it to my tormentors. I had basically been shunned. At the meeting at O'Hare I was mocked. I was given a slot on a committee that was so unpopular it still had openings to be filled. From the moment I had told Rosty I wouldn't be a yes-man on his committee, and suggested in Chicago that the freshmen have some time to organize themselves, it had been made very clear that I was on the outside. If I was banned from the club, I'm not sure why anyone thought I would follow the rules of the club. I was also saving some of the taxpayers' money. And standing up for janitors and waiters. It was fun.

But enjoying it didn't mean it was always easy. Just like high school, members eventually decided that it was open season to make fun of me and my bill. After all, I had cost them money. "Hide your wallet, here comes Gutiérrez," people would say. John Murtha of Pennsylvania, a high-ranking member of the Appropriations Committee, would see me, laugh, and say, "There's Gutiérrez. That's a complicated name. If we could only remember how to spell Gutiérrez, I'm sure we could get him on a better committee. I just can't seem to spell it."

One day, in the cloakroom, a long-time Democratic member wouldn't stop. "Look, it's the king of reform" and other comments, one right after the other. The cloakroom was crowded, and other members were laughing. I decided to try to end open season on Luis Gutiérrez. I stood eye to eye with him.

"Tell you what, I'm going to take my right hand and tie it behind my back," I said. I was being loud, making sure everyone heard me.

"My right hand is my good hand. I'll just have one hand. You want to go to the gym and prove something? I'll whip your ass with one hand. Since you're so funny and badass, let's go settle this right now," I said, nearly shouting.

He looked stunned, and then quickly walked away without looking back. If you want to shake up the country club of Congress, act like a street-corner thug. I knew the part. Just act like a Harrison Street Gent. Nobody was treating me with respect, or like I deserved to be there, so I thought I would get everyone's attention. I know they thought I was crazy, but word traveled fast, and everyone left me alone after that. I needed to do something, or I would have been a punching bag my entire first term. My tirade ended most of the Gutiérrez jokes.

I KEPT LOOKING for new reforms to introduce. When I flew into National Airport, I noticed that there were parking spaces right up front for members of Congress. At such a busy airport, it didn't seem to me that we should have the best parking spaces. I introduced legislation to take away the spots. Symbolic, I know, but I thought a few symbols that showed we were trying to be more like our constituents instead of different from them was worthwhile.

Next I studied our budget and thought about the amount of money we could spend on franked mail and how close to Election Day we could send it. Franked mail was supposed to be an official update on what we were doing in Congress, but it could cover just about anything we wanted. Members would routinely send it out not long before Election Day at taxpayer expense. I introduced a bill to extend the ban on franked mail to ninety days before the election. I kept looking. I supported a limit on Political Action Committee (PAC) contributions.

Instead of getting mocked, now I was getting angry looks. But my constituents were paying attention to the news reports that I was trying to shake things up. Which committee you are on, and where you rank on your subcommittee is of extreme importance to people in Washington, DC. But people back home only care if you are getting things done, providing service, and talking about issues that matter. They saw me on TV, they read good editorials about my efforts.

I kept introducing reform legislation. One afternoon, my press secretary came into my office looking both worried and excited.

"60 Minutes just called and asked for a bunch of information about what you're doing. They may want to talk next week," he said.

I smiled. I didn't think there was any reason to be worried. I hadn't been running a Ponzi scheme or bilking the federal government out of money. I was just busy talking about reform, and I assumed now 60 Minutes wanted to talk about it as well.

I knew I had tapped into the national sentiment when I started talking to Morley Safer's producer. They weren't just following my work, they were reflecting a national conversation. Newt Gingrich and the House Republicans were out talking about their "contract with America" and hammering away at the idea that Congress was isolated and out of touch. Foley and the Democratic leadership kept acting like I was making it up, and if maybe I would just shut up about congressional reform, the issue would go away.

But *60 Minutes* wasn't going to go away. I spent several days with their producers following me around the Capitol. My colleagues had grown accustomed to seeing me with the media. But they were surprised when they saw me with Morley Safer. People did double-takes. Eventually, they just shook their heads. None of the leadership could imagine anything good coming out of Luis Gutiérrez wandering around the Capitol with *60 Minutes*.

Being a freshman congressman on *60 Minutes* probably should have made me nervous, but it didn't. Safer couldn't have been more personable and engaging. The first words he said to me were simple: "I bet you're not too popular with your colleagues right now."

"You have no idea," I said. He laughed. Taking on the establishment was his kind of news.

He enjoyed coming to Chicago and walking around my district more than the interviews in Washington. My constituents who saw me walking down Division Street with a famous guy from TV thought I must have been doing something right. Some of my district staff asked Safer for his autograph. None of the questions were tough. How does a street-smart Chicago politician end up making so many enemies among his colleagues? And what is it really like in the backrooms of Washington, DC?

Tell us about the meeting at O'Hare, where you suggested the freshmen get together to make some plans of your own, he asked.

I just told Safer the truth.

"They basically told me to shut up," I said, and he laughed. We had fun together.

After a couple of days of shooting in Chicago, the crew wrapped. My chief of staff still looked nervous. It was *60 Minutes*, after all, not usually the best friend of elected officials. But I knew our biggest concern was simply how much angrier my colleagues would be with me when they saw it.

The week before it aired, they started teasing my segment. "Learn about the education of a freshman member of Congress," was the theme of the promos, with lots of pictures of me. I was on an airplane when it aired on Sunday night.

My chief of staff reached me when I got in.

"You were right. Our only problem is how good it was," he told me.

Safer and the *60 Minutes* team prominently played my quote, where I called Congress the "belly of the beast." Safer called me a "congressional Don Quixote, tilting at sacred windmills."

I talked in detail about the meeting at O'Hare, and I even got my mom mentioned on America's highest-rated show.

"My mom always said, 'Show me with whom you walk, and I'll show you who you are. Well, some of the people I'm walking with, people don't think so highly of right now." I knew about how well that quote would play with the few friends I had left in Congress.

What I wasn't prepared for was how well it played with everyone else.

My office wasn't at all equipped to handle the response. Today, we would have lit up social media and built huge Twitter and Facebook followings. In 1994, my staff struggled to answer the phones and take messages.

When we got to the office, our answering machine was full. At some point in the afternoon, everyone who called simply received a busy signal. We couldn't keep up. We scribbled down the names of supporters and fans from coast to coast. I enjoyed talking to callers. In a couple of days, we started getting money in the mail—small checks, five-dollar bills. People kept calling, people wanted to know what they could do to be supportive.

"Call your congressman, and tell them to support congressional reforms," we said. A lot of people did.

Under the capitol dome, I was as unpopular as ever. There was some talk of an official censure by the Democratic caucus for what I had said. But I think they figured if they punished me, I would just put out another press release and get even more attention. Most members just ignored me, but all it took was one-third of an hour—and Morley Safer—and suddenly I had friends all over the country.

AFTER MY SEGMENT of *60 Minutes* aired, I was in the cloakroom, and Dan Rostenkowski, who apparently hadn't heard that I'd challenged one of his friends to a fistfight, thought he would take his turn having fun with my new notoriety.

"Hey, Louie, did you get the signs taken down at National Airport yet?" he asked.

I didn't know why Rosty was in a joking mood. By this time, it was widely reported that he was under investigation by the federal government for misusing his office funds. It was looking like he might be in real trouble, and he probably should have known how I would answer him.

"No, I'm leaving them up, because I understand that making things like license plates and signs is an important part of the rehabilitation process. I want to make sure that you have something to do while you're in prison," I said.

We didn't talk much after that.

While I continued to tilt at my windmills, Republican challengers out in the real world were talking about congressional reform like it was the antidote to a national epidemic of Washington self-interest. Inexplicably to the House Democratic leadership, Newt Gingrich and his "Contract with America" and the Republican campaign to shake up Washington were making progress. The Democrats had been in control of the House of Representatives for forty years. It never occurred to anyone, including Tom Foley, the protector of the "institution," that we could possibly lose control of the House.

But the headline in DC's political newspaper *Roll Call* the week after the election said TSUNAMI. Democrats were out. Almost sixty new Republicans were in. Newt Gingrich was Speaker of the House. Tom Foley wasn't just out as Speaker. He was all the way out. Voters sent him home, the first sitting Speaker of the House defeated for reelection in more than a hundred years. Rosty was out as well.

One after another, my new Republican colleagues sought me out. "We loved you on 60 *Minutes,*" they said.

"We showed it to our campaign staff to fire them up," they told me. Conservative guys from Alabama and Mississippi would tell me how entertaining I was, how much they wanted to help.

I had no interest in making Newt Gingrich Speaker of the House, and I knew I had little to do with it. I knew that my new conservative friends would quickly realize that outside of congressional reforms, we wouldn't find much to agree on.

But their success, and their accolades, made me wish that Democrats had listened a little sooner. That year, we paid for treating Congress like a country club.

That fight, in my first term, defined how Congress and I would treat each other. Looking back, maybe I shouldn't have threatened to hit someone. But when the pay freeze was the biggest news in town, and members thought they could simply ignore me, mock me, or pretend that I didn't exist, I had to do something. The reputation I acquired that first term has stayed with me for twenty years: Gutiérrez is difficult. Gutiérrez is unpredictable. Mostly, Gutiérrez isn't quite like other members of Congress. He doesn't seem to understand how we are supposed to act.

That's not true. I completely understand how we are supposed to act. I'm just not very good at doing it.

CHAPTER SIXTEEN

Why Don't You and Your People Just Go Back Where You Came From?

AT AGE FOURTEEN, Omaira decided to take a long bus ride to Washington.

She wasn't riding sixteen hours on a crowded bus just to see her father, though. She was traveling with a group of Puerto Ricans coming from Chicago to Washington, DC, like others from across the country, for a celebration of Puerto Rican history and culture. Omaira and her cousin Maritza, Juano and Lucy's daughter, were two happy pilgrims ready to wave Puerto Rican flags and show their pride. That Omaira's dad happened to work in Washington was just a bonus.

But I was thrilled that Omaira was headed to Washington. I had learned quickly that serving in Congress is lonely. I spent three or four days per week, thirty or forty weeks per year, nearly seven hundred miles away from Chicago and my family. Instead, I was surrounded by hundreds of competitive colleagues, most of whom weren't embracing the paycheck-cutting guy from *60 Minutes* as their best pal. Soon after I was elected, I bought a small townhouse in the Capitol Hill neighborhood. I painted and sanded and renovated. Within two years I gave it up. It was expensive. It came with all of the headaches and hassles of home ownership. By 1996, my fourth year in Congress, when we were in session I was sleeping on the couch in my office and showering in the House gym. That's not too uncommon now, but fifteen years ago, there weren't too many other members who always took the first plane out of Washington and back to their families and their constituents as soon as Congress adjourned for the week—and who were also too cheap to pay for a second home.

Soraida was working and caring for the girls, so she didn't make the trip out very often. When Omaira came in, it was like a small vacation. I was thrilled my daughter was in town to keep me company. We enjoyed the festivities together. We attended events at the Korean War Memorial and Vietnam Veterans' Memorial. Quite a few Puerto Ricans were seeing the Vietnam Veterans' Wall for the first time. Many headed back to the buses carefully holding pieces of paper with the etched outline of the names of lost mothers and fathers, brothers and sisters. We had also participated in a tribute to the veterans of the US Army 65th Infantry Regiment. The 65th Regiment, who called themselves "The Borinqueneers," was an almost entirely Puerto Rican regiment that served in WWI, WWII, and saw extensive combat in the Korean War. More than seven hundred Puerto Ricans died in the Korean War. Puerto Ricans made up 2.5 percent of all of the Americans killed in Korea—more than double our share of the US population.

All of the Puerto Rican members of Congress spoke, and the tribute was a reminder of how much Puerto Ricans have sacrificed for America. When it was done I walked back to the Capitol with Omaira and Maritza. The festivities were over and they were going to head back home. After they had stopped in my office, their quickest way back to the buses was through the Capitol Building.

That day, all of our fellow Boricuas had been taking in the sights and filling up the Capitol. When we walked into the main entrance to the Capitol on our way to the buses, the line to get in through security was long. One person after another was slowly taking things out of their pockets and placing their keys and pens and money clips on the conveyor belt of the metal detectors at the entrance. In Congress, your workplace is one of America's top tourist destinations, and you are always elbow to elbow with visitors who have made the pilgrimage to see how their country's government really functions.

As a member, I don't have to wait in security lines. Capitol police officers are trained to recognize us, and we can bypass the lines and the metal detectors. You can walk right by and usually a deferential police officer will greet you, almost always addressing you as "sir" or "ma'am." But I frequently stood in line with everyone else. I stayed away from the elevators that were reserved for members only. I was the reformer, the guy who had told Rosty he was going to be hammering out "Member Parking Only" signs in jail. I figured it was prudent for me to avoid some of the perks that were offered to us.

Also, we were with hundreds of our fellow Puerto Ricans. We had just listened to stories of Puerto Ricans who had given their lives to defend America. I wanted to show some solidarity with my people. As we walked into the Capitol, and Maritza and Omaira gazed at the murals on the wall around the main entrance, I told them we would wait in line with everyone else. We stood and waited our turn, laughing, talking, and recounting the morning's events.

The girls were still carrying small Puerto Rican flags from the events. There are strict rules about what you can do with flags in the Capitol and in the congressional office buildings. You can't unfurl them, and even though our flags were small, I told the girls to wrap them up. When we finally made it to the front of the line, the girls put their rolled-up flags on the conveyor belt in the metal detectors. But they unrolled as they moved through, and they came out the other end open. My daughter and niece picked them up.

Immediately, a young Capitol Hill security aide moved directly toward us. Right away, she was in our face. She had instructions for us, and she didn't say please, and she certainly didn't say "sir."

"Those flags cannot be displayed," she said. She was close to yelling.

I didn't want to make a scene. I knew she was right about the rule.

"I'm sorry. We're going to take care of it," I said.

"I don't want to see those flags," she said. Now she was shouting.

They were small flags.

I told her I understood the rules. I turned to the girls. "You know the rules, just roll them up," I said.

The officer turned right back to me.

"What makes you such an expert on the rules?" she asked me,

apparently offended that I thought I knew enough to be giving instructions in the US Capitol.

"Well, I'm a member of Congress," I said.

She smirked. "I don't think so," she said to me, adding some sarcasm to her anger. She looked like she was trying to stifle a laugh.

I didn't say anything more, just reached into my wallet and took out my Congressional identification card. I handed it to her. There were only 535 of those cards in America. She looked at it. She looked like she couldn't decide whether to laugh at me or start yelling again. She handed it back like I had shown her my Blockbuster rental card.

"That must be a fake," she said.

I felt like I was doing battle in the old neighborhood with one of the cops who didn't like Puerto Ricans.

I could see a supervisor heading over to us, but the security aide wasn't done yet. She wanted to prove that I wasn't fooling her.

She looked right at Omaira, Maritza, and me. "Why don't you and your people just go back where you came from?"

And then, the other police officer arrived and pulled her away from the crowd. If he hadn't arrived, she would have kept talking. She had a point she wanted to make. A third officer walked with me and the girls.

"I'm sorry, Congressman, we're going to take care of this." He recognized me, but it was too late. Her instructions, *Why don't you go back where you came from*, felt like they were reverberating through the Capitol.

When that security officer told me to go back where I came from, I don't think she meant the corner of Willow and Halsted in Chicago. She wasn't reflecting on the history of Puerto Rico's relationship with the United States, and neither would she likely have correctly answered a question about whether every single Puerto Rican born since 1917 is an American citizen.

Her response was simple—I was brown-skinned and curly haired, surrounded by some other brown-skinned people making her day a little more taxing than she liked. She had probably heard some Spanish being spoken that day. It seemed absolutely impossible to her that this outsider, this obvious foreigner, could be a congressman.

That the girls were with me helped me to react responsibly. I told myself more than once not to make a scene in front of my daughter. I was calm, almost apologetic. But that Omaira and Maritza had to see this happen made me irate.

We hurried away from the entrance. The girls needed to get on the bus. I put my arm around my daughter.

"Look, it can happen to anyone," I said, eager to comfort my daughter and niece. You can't let things like this define you. Just shrug it off. We've had a wonderful day."

Omaira looked at me with a calm expression that reminded me that she was growing up.

"Dad, don't worry about it. Just because you are a congressman it doesn't mean that people aren't going to be bigots. It isn't the first time I've heard 'Go back where you came from,'" she said.

And I thought about it. No matter how much I want to, I can't always protect my brown-skinned daughter from being mistreated. Not even being elected to Congress and carrying a fancy congressional ID card closes the books on discrimination.

The girls were champions. They were mad on my behalf, but by the time we made it to the bus, they were done being consoled.

"We're fine" was their attitude. And they were. Because as a minority growing up in America you either learn to roll with some punches or eventually you get knocked out. I know that they remembered the good parts of that weekend—the Puerto Ricans touching names on the Vietnam Wall, listening to stories of the Borinqueneers. They hugged me and got on the bus, ready for the long trip home.

I didn't publicize the incident, but a reporter found out and called me. The Capitol Police were conducting a review and I think they wanted the paper to know that they were going to discipline the security officer. I wasn't looking for coverage. I wanted the police to deal with it and move on. *Roll Call* published the story, and media in Chicago began calling.

Omaira has never been afraid of talking to reporters. My daughter, I'm proud to say, has never been afraid of much of anything. She told them the same things she told me. That it wasn't acceptable for anyone to be treated like that. It didn't matter if you were a member of

Congress. Nobody should be disrespected. She was eager to remind reporters that all Puerto Ricans are American citizens, even if most Americans aren't aware of that fact. She stood up for what was right, and made me proud.

I know Omaira still remembers that day. It was a lesson. She spent hours hearing about a Puerto Rican army regiment that fought the Chinese regular army in the Korean War. The Borinqueneers were awarded 256 silver stars and more than 600 bronze stars in Korea. But when we returned to the Capitol with the rest of our Puerto Rican friends and neighbors, in the eyes of at least one person working for the US government, we were just a bunch of outsiders. Omaira's dad had made it from an apartment on Willow Street to Congress. That didn't make him immune. It's an experience we both tucked away to carry with us as we go on with our lives—that discrimination or unfairness in never far away.

Eventually, the Capitol Hill police apologized. The woman who'd harassed me and my family was not a police officer—she was a security aide who helps at busy times. We encouraged them to discipline her but said we hoped they wouldn't fire her. She didn't lose her job, but she was suspended for more than a month without pay. Later, she called me and apologized. We talked for a while. I wished her well, and I think we both benefitted from the conversation.

I never saw her again around the Capitol. And I stayed right in the country I came from.

I COULD FIND one silver lining to my nasty confrontation with that angry security guard. It confirmed for me that the new path I was traveling in Congress was the right one. Even before I was singled out in the Capitol as a foreigner, I had begun making immigration and citizenship my crusade.

In 1992, just as I was elected to Congress, millions of undocumented immigrants were becoming eligible for citizenship as a result of the 1986 Immigration Reform and Control Act. IRCA increased penalties for businesses that hired undocumented immigrants, but also allowed millions of undocumented immigrants who had been living in the United States to adjust their status and become citizens. Many immigration opponents today would have blown out their vocal cords screaming "amnesty" about IRCA. They would have knocked their heads off from jumping up and down and warning America about this colossal giveaway to "illegals."

So, who signed this massive, pro-amnesty fraud into law? The Gipper, as I remind people all the time. Ronald Reagan saw the inherent political logic in not alienating an already fast-growing segment of the population. He also thought it was the right thing to do.

Ronald Reagan, for all of the many things I disagreed with him about, was not a conservative who used the finger-pointing and divisive language on immigration that propels so many Fox News talking heads and many of my colleagues today. He fought for IRCA, and when he left office and talked about that "shining city" he mentioned so often, he said that city should be "teeming with people of all kinds living in harmony and peace; a city with free ports that hummed with commerce and creativity. And if there had to be city walls, the walls had doors and the doors were open to anyone with the will and the heart to get there."

That kind of crazy talk would get Ronald Reagan a Tea Party opponent in a Republican primary today. But back then, quite a few congressional Republicans joined him in supporting comprehensive immigration reform. Most Republicans don't really like to be reminded of that fact today. With Democratic support and Reagan's push, IRCA passed in 1986, and the immigrants who took advantage of it had to wait about five years to be eligible for citizenship. That meant that all across my district and throughout America, immigrants were ready to become citizens just as I was entering Congress.

At the same time, Reagan's eventual successor as governor of California, Pete Wilson, acted like he was overseeing a contest to see how many immigrants and Latinos Republicans could offend. If Wilson had said to his advisers, "I'm looking to lay the groundwork for a policy that will guarantee that the Republican Party angers and alienates the fastest-growing population in the United States," they would have devised Proposition 187.

With a ballot referendum that denied access to virtually all social services—including health care and education—to all undocumented immigrants, Wilson fueled a political and policy strategy that pretty much killed the Republican Party in California. After decades of Californians voting mostly for Republicans for president, our party's nominee doesn't even have to campaign in California anymore; we just put the 55 electoral votes in the bank and move on. As a Democrat, I should say thank you to Pete Wilson. As a person who likes to see everyone treated fairly, I see Proposition 187 as the first cannon shot in an increasingly ugly Republican barrage on immigrants, an intellectually lazy and fundamentally dishonest strategy for addressing the challenges of California and America: blame all of our problems on Mexicans from across the border.

Latinos perceived Pete Wilson as a street-corner bully. His rhetoric drove immigrants into the arms of anyone who was willing to help them. The panic caused by Proposition 187 created waves of fear among immigrants all across America. In Illinois, I believe more immigrants probably knew Pete Wilson's name than the name of our own governor. With leaders like Wilson lighting a giant bonfire of anti-immigrant paranoia, immigrants were even more inspired to protect their rights and become full-fledged Americans.

The challenge was that the process for becoming a US citizen has never been simple. Once you are eligible, you need to fill out enough paperwork to make a bureaucrat giddy. You need to get fingerprinted and have your photos taken to prove who you are and that you are not a criminal. There were few organizations to help immigrants through this confusing process. Virtually none would provide the help for free. The IRCA rush made it even worse.

Every day, my district staff received the same request again and again: I want to become a citizen and I need your help. They also received very simple complaints: I'm trying to become a citizen and someone is ripping me off. We heard it all the time: people worked hard to scrape together enough money to go to a neighborhood lawyer—or in some cases a con artist pretending to be a lawyer or expert on immigration. People told us that they would be asked for more and more money, that their application was always delayed, that they couldn't get any straight answers from the person who was supposed to be helping them.

Community groups tried to help. My friend Danny Solis and his community group, UNO, were holding citizenship workshops where they would provide help for people who wanted to become citizens. I sent my staff to the workshops to get trained, and attended them myself to learn more.

In every neighborhood, the need was obvious. We learned from the work Danny and UNO were doing. It didn't take long before the number of immigrants sitting in my office waiting for help far outnumbered the veterans and seniors and students combined. I saw the same thing out in the neighborhood. At least once per month I held a "Congressional Community Office." I usually set up a table in a local grocery store, and once people overcame the shock of seeing their congressman sitting in the corner surrounded by avocados and oranges, they would come over and ask me questions. Virtually every inquiry was about immigration and citizenship: about brothers or sisters who couldn't adjust their status, about a spouse who was in danger of being deported, about a citizenship application that was taking forever to be approved.

I attended a huge swearing-in ceremony for one of the early groups of IRCA applicants. They had paid their fee, completed their paperwork, passed their test, and become American citizens. Four or five hundred people raised their right hand, recited the Pledge of Allegiance, and were transformed in one moment by a federal judge into Americans.

We should make attending a citizenship swearing-in an educational requirement for every American. Watching so many people from different backgrounds stand together and share the excitement and pride of becoming an American citizen might slow some of the anti-immigrant demonizing we hear. Most applicants who take the oath have already lived and worked in America for years. A lot of them hold entry-level or low-income jobs and are still striving to get anywhere near the middle class. Every day, they work and contribute to a nation that is sometimes downright hostile to them. Since they are all legal permanent residents, most could continue to live here indefinitely with minimal risk of their day-to-day circumstances changing.

And yet—they want something more. They want to be Americans. There is something that makes it worth all the cost and hassle, something permanent and fulfilling about making that promise to our nation—that you will protect it and uphold our laws—about receiving the protection of our nation in return. I felt it that day. I was born an American citizen, and because of my last name and the color of my skin have been treated like an outsider at times, and yet I shared these newly minted citizens' pride and their excitement at what they had achieved.

But my pride was mixed with confusion about how the ceremony was conducted. Mayor Richard Daley attended and was featured prominently. So was Illinois governor Jim Edgar. It wasn't held at a federal facility. I had the feeling I was the first member of Congress to attend a citizenship swearing-in for a while, yet naturalization is a federal responsibility. Nobody was becoming a citizen of Chicago or Illinois—Mayor Daley can't grant citizenship rights to anyone. Only the federal government grants citizenship. I looked at the faces of the people in attendance; mostly Latino, but also Indians and Pakistanis. Ethiopians, too, and Irish and Polish. A fundamental fact of my service in Congress became clear to me. I was the federal representative of a hugely immigrant district, and I wasn't doing enough to help people become citizens.

I left that workshop and realized that I needed to do more than simply provide citizenship and naturalization services at my office. I thought about the citizenship workshops that I had attended with Danny Solis and others. Those workshops were supplying a service that the federal government should be providing. If a well-run community organization can help people through every step of the citizenship process, then why couldn't a well-run congressional office?

I found out the answer. While a community group like UNO could be authorized by the Immigration and Naturalization Service to handle every aspect of naturalizing legal permanent residents—from accepting the money to turning in the completed application forms—

no congressional office had ever been authorized to do it. From what I could tell, no office had even asked.

Within a few weeks of the citizenship swearing-in, I was sitting across from INS commissioner Doris Meissner, a serious and practical woman who oversaw the nation's immigration policy for Bill Clinton. Most members of Congress like to summon federal officials to come to see them. I had trekked over to the Department of Justice and found my way to the less-than-glamorous INS office. I wanted Doris Meissner to know how important this was to me. She seemed a bit puzzled about what I was asking, or why a Congressman would want to bother her at all about the nuts and bolts of citizenship applications.

I had to explain myself a couple of times: "You authorize community groups to handle citizenship applications. They can conduct workshops and turn them in directly to you. I want to do the same thing. Authorize Congressman Luis Gutiérrez and my office to hold citizenship workshops and turn in applications directly to the INS. It's a federal responsibility. Why can't I do it?" I thought my request was entirely reasonable.

It was clear to me that no member of Congress had asked her about this before. She struggled for a minute to come up with an answer. I knew the typical bureaucratic response. We don't do it this way because we've never done it this way. Finally, she settled on politics as her explanation.

"If congressional offices are involved, it politicizes citizenship. Community groups are nonpartisan and nonprofit."

I thought about that for a minute. Would many of these citizens become voters? Probably. Was I registering them to vote? No. Was it good for me politically? Well, maybe, but then again helping a family whose daughter was having trouble with her federal student aid might be good for me politically as well, but nobody ever suggested I couldn't do that.

"So if a veteran comes into my office with a question about his veterans' benefits, I should send him to the VFW for help? I should send a senior to the AARP? Civil rights complaints go to the NAACP? I run a government office. I'm supposed to help people. My constituents need help with immigration and citizenship. I can't just send them away," I said.

This slowed her down, but she still seemed concerned about making it political.

"If it's a concern about politics, then we can't serve anyone," I said. "You are telling me a community group can do this, but a Congressman who votes on your budget every year can't?"

That was a dilemma for her. Along with 434 of my colleagues in the House, I did vote to authorize her funding every year. As she thought about it, I made my position clear.

"Commissioner, government doesn't really work this way. Agencies don't tell Congress what to do. We fund you and give you direction. I want to make people citizens, so what's the problem?"

I thought if my staff could meet the standards she made community groups meet every year, she didn't really have any justification for not letting me run citizenship workshops. She thought about it some more. The secretary of Veterans' Affairs would never tell members of Congress not to help veterans, so why would the commissioner of the INS tell members not to help immigrants? To Doris Meissner's credit, she said yes, as long as we met the standards. That seemed fair to me.

We trained our staff and they were quickly approved. But this decision was bigger for me. Commissioner Meissner thought I was being political. Some of my friends and advisers thought I was being stupid. I was a Puerto Rican congressman about to help lots of immigrants—mostly Mexicans—become citizens.

I understood the logic. The Mexican population in my district was growing quickly and the Puerto Rican population was standing still. Mexicans were still coming to Chicago, but the great Puerto Rican movement from the island to Chicago had peaked forty years earlier with my parents. Most of the people we made citizens would eventually become voters. Would they be Gutiérrez voters? Some people told me I was signing my political death warrant.

The 4th Congressional District of Illinois was almost unique among majority Latino Congressional districts in the country. In Florida, Cubans represented Cuban-majority districts. In California and Texas, Mexican-Americans represented Mexicans, and in New

York Puerto Ricans represented Puerto Ricans. My district was different. To adhere to the voting rights act, the district had been drawn to include two very distinct Latino communities. With some creative mapmaking, the largely Puerto Rican communities in neighborhoods like Humboldt Park and Logan Square were connected to the Mexican communities of Pilsen and Little Village and Back of the Yards on the Southwest Side. The two Latino communities, which are about three miles apart at their nearest point, are essentially connected along a string of highway and forest preserve and river through the western suburbs. If you walk along the congressional district boundary in the suburbs, and you trip and fall over, you'll end up in my friend Danny Davis's district.

Whenever anyone writes about the evils of political "gerrymandering," they always describe the map of the 4th Congressional District. We're exhibit A. I get calls from reporters about the shape of our district all the time. "Earmuffs" is the favorite description of the shape. Fox News types and conservative commentators usually express outrage and show the district as proof that liberals will stop at nothing to elect more minorities to Congress.

It is true that the district looks strange. It's also true that for a couple of centuries districts were drawn in whatever shape worked to keep minorities *out* of Congress. I never hear Fox News's outrage at the longstanding American tradition of splitting up majority Latino or African American populations, just like the Chicago City Council mapmakers once did to keep a Puerto Rican out and keep the Italians and Poles in. To some, the shape of a district only matters when it gives minorities a fair shake. I'm never apologizing for the overdue ability for Latinos to participate in a fair election, no matter how closely the district resembles a pair of earmuffs. Those earmuffs look just right to me, cozy and warm.

Still, serving the entire district was a challenge. In 1992 and 1994, I ran for Congress against Juan Soliz, the alderman from Pilsen who thought Harold's death might just make him the mayor of Chicago. He couldn't have looked or sounded more Mexican. His parents were migrant farm workers from Texas. He wore cowboy boots and spoke Spanish with a clear Mexican accent. In both elections against Juan

Soliz, I won comfortably among Puerto Ricans, white voters, and black voters—and he crushed me in Mexican neighborhoods.

In my first congressional campaign, I marched through the Mexican neighborhood of Little Village in the Mexican Independence Parade. The event was just days before a huge boxing match between Julio "César" Chávez, a hero to the Mexican community, and Héctor "Macho" Camacho—a Puerto Rican born in Bayamón, Puerto Rico, but who grew up just blocks away from my grandmother's apartment in Spanish Harlem. Puerto Ricans and Mexicans had been trash-talking each other for weeks before the fight. As I walked down the street, holding my Mexican flag and trying to win over Mexican voters, people looked at me and chanted "*Chávez, Chávez, Chávez,*" making sure I knew where their Puerto Rican-Mexican loyalties were.

One man yelled, "Hey, Gutiérrez, let's make a bet on the fight."

I yelled back. "I'll take that bet. I got Chávez."

He looked shocked. "Wait a minute, Gutiérrez—you're Puerto Rican. Why you betting on Chávez?"

I looked at him. "I'm Puerto Rican, but I'm not stupid," I said.

Chávez crushed Camacho a week later, not unlike Soliz crushed me among Mexican voters.

But that didn't stop me from working for votes in the Mexican community.

I remembered what it had been like to be ignored by other ethnicities or races that were clinging to power. Puerto Rican frustration at being ignored forever by the Poles and Italians was a big part of the reason I was elected alderman. Humboldt Park was turning Puerto Rican, and the white guys had tried—unsuccessfully—to stop it. Chicago's Latino community was becoming increasingly Mexican. I wasn't stopping that. You can't stop the rising tide of history. But you can try not to get swept away.

I told my skeptical friends, "You can either be the engine or the caboose. People need help becoming citizens. Helping them is the right thing. It's what I want to do. I can be the engine and lead the way, or I can be the caboose, and follow other people who are doing it. You know what happens to the caboose? It gets cut loose, and the train keeps going. Nobody misses the caboose."

I committed to immigrants for another, more important, reason. I felt deep down that the challenges our Latino community would face in the future would not be determined by our country of origin. Proposition 187 might be directed toward Mexican immigrants, but it was clearly going to increase discrimination toward anyone who looked like they might be from south of any border. Latinos might be able to look at the straight black hair and cowboy boots of Juan Soliz and know he was Mexican. And they could look at my curly hair and listen to me speak Spanish and know I was Puerto Rican. But angry whites blaming immigrants for all of their problems? We all looked the same to them. Just ask that Capitol Hill security officer. She didn't have any idea where I was from, but she was damn sure it wasn't America. Proposition 187, and the two decades of anti-immigrant intolerance that followed, wasn't going to be a Mexican problem. It was going to be a Latino problem.

So the choice was easy. It's a pretty good rule in politics that whenever you have any doubt about a strategy, just do the right thing. If you lose, at least you won't feel guilty about it.

Pretty soon, we were preparing for our first citizenship workshop at a huge field house in Piotrowski Park in Little Village. We trained volunteers. We brought in a photographer. We enlisted Spanish-language television to run public-service announcements promoting the event. We bought water and snacks. Off-duty police officers were ready to take fingerprints. We rented a giant copying machine for all the applications, bought pens and clipboards, put all of our volunteers in T-shirts. We had so many people lined up at long lunch tables inside the gym at the field house ready to help applicants become citizens that we couldn't imagine being overwhelmed.

We weren't very imaginative.

When I arrived at eight a.m., the line of people who wanted to apply was out the door and around the building and down to the end of the block. Working families brought their children. It was important to them. It was cold and snowing, but nobody looked at the line, got back in their car, and went home. People just kept going to the back of the line. The park opened all the doors early so we could get people inside the field house out of the cold. People still kept coming. We filled up rows and rows of chairs until we had to start putting people in the bleachers, with still more people filing in and taking their places, ready to do battle with the bureaucracy.

I had nearly a hundred volunteers. They looked stunned, like I was throwing them before an invading army. By the time the workshop was supposed to start, we already had more than five hundred people waiting, and the lines were getting longer.

"I hope nobody made plans for tonight," I told everyone.

It was chaos, but we looked just organized enough that people trusted we could take care of their applications. Before I was elected, the nearly 100 percent Mexican neighborhood of Little Village had been represented by a Polish congressman for decades. They rarely saw him. The people who came that day didn't care whether I was Polish or Mexican or Puerto Rican, they were just glad I was there.

I talked to family after family, and their reaction was the same, one after another—thank you for doing this. Everywhere I went all day, people followed me, asking questions about their applications, wondering which station to go to next. I think they expected me to say hello and hit the road, to have subcontracted the real work out to someone else. But there wasn't anyone else. It was just us. I didn't want Commissioner Meissner ever to think she was right—that a congress-man couldn't handle the work.

One older Mexican man who had patiently trailed me for a while acted like he had something important to ask. I asked him what his question was.

He told me, in Spanish, "I don't have a question. I just want you to know something. I never, ever expect the government to help my family. When I think of the government, I think of agents who want to deport people. Thank you for being on our side." He shook my hand and went back to his family, satisfied that he had gotten his message across.

I've heard that again and again at workshops and from my constit-uents. Immigrants firmly believe in the power of the US government. They just don't always expect it to be used to help them. Almost every immigrant knows of a friend or family member whom the government has deported—a cousin or coworker, or sometimes a spouse or brother, the government sends away. To that man, I was a very different face of the US government, a friendly face, an ally in his tough daily battle to stay in America and take care of his family.

The Piotrowski field house was filled with energy all day long, almost like a sporting event. I worked all day with my good friends and cosponsors of the event, State Senator Jesús García and Alderman Ricardo Muñoz. People felt empowered. They were finding their way through the system. They were ready to wait, all day if they had to, and they trusted us with their $100 application fee and their photos and their fingerprints. They trusted us with their future.

We were there until almost ten o'clock that night. To serve everyone, I went up and down the long lines and gave people appointments to come back another day to see us in our office. When people looked skeptical, I used a line I've repeated a hundred times since then at crowded workshops. "See this line—you're in the emergency-room line. What happens at the emergency room?"

"You wait," everyone answered.

"That's right. Pretend I'm the doctor. I'll give you an appointment at my office. You won't have to wait. If you want care today, you'll get it, but you're going to be here a while." Lots of people ended up taking an appointment, or we would have been there until one a.m.

That first citizenship workshop was much more than a successful community event to me. Congress had been hard on me. I was proud of the reforms I was pushing, that people were always telling me they had seen me on the news or on *60 Minutes*. But I knew it was going to be tough getting things done if I was always alone, the outsider.

I looked at that packed field house, filled with people not just from Little Village but from all over Chicago, asking me and my staff questions, waiting in line patiently, hanging on to their envelopes filled with the documents that proved they were eligible to become Americans, and I thought, This is it. This is why I'm in Congress. I've found it. This is why I chased Rosty's captains down the street. We're going to make thousands of people citizens.

CHAPTER SEVENTEEN

Fifty Thousand New Citizens

CAME INTO a Hispanic Caucus meeting late. Latino members have always met regularly to exchange notes and review our priorities. Most of the other members were already there, listening to Steny Hoyer of Maryland. Steny has always been a party leader and is now Nancy Pelosi's minority whip in the House. He noticed when I arrived.

"I would like to take a brief break to direct my colleagues' attention to Luis Gutiérrez. You know, we've recently given Luis an award— most improved member of the Democratic Caucus. Of course, he was at the bottom, so he had nowhere to go but up. He was the obvious choice. Welcome, Luis, we have high hopes for you," Steny said, smiling and laughing.

My colleagues laughed too, but it was a different kind of laughter from the smirks that made me want to punch someone or threaten Dan Rostenkowski. I was laughing along with them.

One of the immediate benefits of our citizenship push in Chicago was the opportunity to listen regularly to immigrants describe the challenges they were facing, many of which could only be fixed legislatively. Newt Gingrich and his crew had taken over the House of Representatives, and they were coming up with Proposition 187–like proposals that made it harder for immigrants to adjust their status, to reunite with their families.

The mantra from the people filling up the field houses at the workshops was "I'm just trying to keep my family together." I soon became aware of the problem many young people were facing. They crossed a border with their parents before they were old enough to walk or talk. They had grown up in the United States but had no way to become legal residents of our nation. They lived under constant fear of deportation to a country they had never known, a Mexico or Colombia, an Ireland or Poland that was as distant to them as Australia.

My focus on the nuts and bolts of immigration policy changed my relationships in Washington, DC. Instead of constantly assailing my colleagues on reforms that many of them didn't want any part of, I was proposing immigration policies that made sense to most Democrats. It gave me a substantive issue to fight for that didn't involve putting my hands into my colleagues' pockets.

So when Steny said I was the most improved member of the caucus, he wasn't just going for a laugh. He meant it. He also meant it when he said I had started at the bottom. He was glad I had found something to occupy my time other than congressional reform. Other members felt the same way. John Murtha, the chairman who had told me my "hard-to-spell" last name made it impossible for me to get on a good committee, called me over to him in the corner of the House floor one day. Murtha spent a lot of time in the back corner of the floor, holding court and sharing wisdom that came along with thirty years in the House.

"You know, Gutiérrez, you take a lot of shit, but I have to hand it to you. It took some balls to do what you did," he said. That was high praise from John Murtha, a former Marine and Vietnam War veteran, a guy who'd survived lots of tough Pennsylvania elections.

He wasn't alone in his forgiveness of the reform guy. The Democratic Caucus was changing. Gingrich's Republican tidal wave swept away some of the most intransigent Democrats. Guys like William Ford retired. Instead of being an arrogant party that had spent forty years in the majority, we were learning together how to reinvent ourselves as a feisty opposition party, doing everything we could to help Bill Clinton swat away whatever terrible idea Gingrich was peddling. My niche was keeping my eye on anti-immigrant legislation. Others were fighting on spending and tax and education fronts. We all had a battle to fight against the new Republican majority. I was showing my colleagues I could punch and counterpunch right along with them.

Moving up in seniority also made my colleagues more likely to work with me. Seniority matters to Congress the way that water matters to fish. After I was re-elected a few times, it started to sink in that the former cabdriver and current reformer might be sticking around for a while. After defeating Juan Soliz twice, in the next three elections I had only token opposition. Members start to figure one another out. Instead of yelling at me, people were more likely to talk to me, member to member, trying to convince me to stop messing around with their paychecks.

A colleague approached me one day and said, "Luis, I have an important question for you." He seemed serious. I asked him what he needed to know.

"How many times have you been married?"

"You've met Soraida. She's the only one," I said.

"Once. You're lucky. I'm happy for you. You know how many times I've been married? I'm on number three. Three wives, two ex-wives. It's expensive. Can you please stop screwing around with our pay increase? I need the money."

I WAS GLAD to be making a few friends in Washington, because I had been busy making things harder back in Chicago. At home, none of my political allies cared if I was offending William Ford or some other committee chairman who thought he was royalty in Washington but was anonymous to 99 percent of the American people. But plenty of them cared about whether I was getting along with Mayor Daley.

In my second year in Congress, President Clinton decided the North American Free Trade Agreement was an urgent national priority. Clinton needed most of the Democrats to vote with him if he was going to get his trade agreement. I thought the decision was easy.

NAFTA was a bad deal, another American trade giveaway in which we provide access to our markets and don't get enough in return. My friends in organized labor and the environmental community were against it. I thought I faced more complicated, harder votes regularly.

Lots of other Democrats looked at it just the way I did—doubtful about all of the promises of new jobs, confident about job losses in areas like manufacturing. Pretty soon, it was clear that Clinton didn't have the votes. Ross Perot was running around spouting a ten-gallon hatful of homespun Texas wisdom about the "giant sucking sound" of US jobs going to Mexico. Protectionist Republicans and progressive Democrats were staying miles away from NAFTA. Suddenly, it entered the ugly realm of vote-by-vote, hand-to-hand combat in Washington.

In almost every session there is an issue that quickly moves beyond fact-filled committee analysis of the pros and cons directly into the "What do I need to do to get your vote?" area in which politicians thrive. On these issues, Congress is just a bigger, more prestigious Chicago City Council, with smarter and more devious arm-twisters.

Bill Richardson, who was leading the charge for Clinton among Democrats, came to see me in my office.

"The president wants to know what it will take for you to vote for NAFTA," he said to me. They sent the right person. Bill was smart, and always my friend. He was a member's member, and I'm sure he took a lot of grief from our colleagues for looking out for me, no matter how radioactive my latest reform pipe dream.

"Well, I have environmental concerns. I have workers' rights concerns. There is a lot that needs to be fixed," I said.

Bill sat back in one of the big old leather chairs that congressmen receive for their offices. He smiled at me like I was a little slow.

"That's not what I asked. I asked what you need to vote for it. I'm leaving here to meet with the president. When I talk to him, I need to be able to tell him what you need."

Now I understood.

"What do you think I should need, Bill?" I asked, figuring he already had an offer.

"Well, what if we make you Mr. Citizenship in the United States?" he asked.

They had done their homework. They knew exactly what would tempt me. Good politicians understand the self-interests of their colleagues. I thought about it—a fairly new member of Congress, running around the country deputized by the president of the United States to help immigrants become US citizens—not just in Chicago, but everywhere.

Because that vision was so tempting, I answered before the idea could overcome me.

"I don't think I can do it, Bill. I just don't support it."

We went back and forth for a while. I told him I would think about it, but what I really thought was that I'd better start telling my friends that I was taking a tough vote. If I was going to be making powerful people mad at me for voting no, I'd better make some other powerful people happy by voting no. I called Mayor Daley to tell him I was voting against NAFTA. I got him on the phone from Washington.

"It's just a bad bill, and I think it will cost us jobs. I'm against it," I told him. He acted like I was bothering him. Why would I take up his time with such a trivial matter?

"Fine," he said, ready to get back to running the city of Chicago.

I thought, politically at least, maybe it wasn't such a big deal after all, at least to Mayor Daley. I told my local labor leaders I was sticking with them. They were grateful.

Then President Clinton, who was still having a tough time securing votes, put Bill Daley, my old friend from Chicago and the mayor's brother—his Bobby Kennedy—in charge of the war room that was managing NAFTA. Rahm Emanuel, another tough Chicago guy, was his lieutenant in the battle. Great, I thought. Clinton couldn't have picked the mayor of *New York's* brother to run his NAFTA operation?

It wasn't long before Mayor Daley called me back. He wanted to meet in his office in Chicago. I had hardly been up there since being elected to Congress. When Harold was mayor, the fifth-floor office was my home away from home. This time I was being summoned. I felt like some loafing tax collector who was being called in to meet with the king because revenues were down.

Mayor Daley sat me down across from his huge desk. He didn't waste any time.

"I need you to vote for NAFTA," he said.

"You told me that you didn't care," I said, pretending like maybe he had just forgotten.

"Now Bill's in charge of rounding up votes. It's embarrassing. The president called me personally. It's just one vote," the mayor said.

I sat uncomfortably across from him.

"I'm a Democrat. This is a bad deal. Bad for Chicago, bad for workers, bad for Mexico. These are my principles. It's why I went to Congress. I'm sticking with them," I said respectfully to an increasingly impatient mayor.

Whenever Mayor Daley became excited, his voice would go up an octave, making him sound like an angry kid.

"Principles?" he said, his voice rising. "Principles? I'm a Catholic. I'm supposed to uphold my Catholic principles. Sometimes you have to make a decision against your principles. I have a health department that gives out condoms and where people have abortions. We have a government to run. Now, let me call President Clinton and tell him you are with him." He looked like that should have settled it and he was ready to make the call.

It was tempting. The mayor really wanted my vote, and Richardson's citizenship czar offer was still out there. Mainly, I just wanted to get out of the mayor's office. But I couldn't say yes.

"Mr. Mayor, this is difficult. I think I'm going to go have a cigarette and think about it," I told him. I was trying to quit smoking by then, but I knew there was no smoking in the mayor's office. I thanked him and got up to go. Mayor Daley got his secretary on the intercom.

"Get the congressman an ashtray," he said.

"I thought there was no smoking?" I said.

"You can smoke in here if I tell you that you can smoke in here," he said.

So I did. I stalled. I told him that I needed to talk to some people. I smoked and filibustered until he got tired of waiting. I wanted out of the room. In a district that was still filled with voters who loved Mayor Daley, I didn't need to add him to the list of all the people who were mad at me. I had plenty of those in Washington.

I called my chief of staff and asked for two things. I needed to meet with a key Illinois labor leader, and I needed to schedule a press conference to announce my final position on NAFTA. He told me the president wanted to meet with me as well. I told him to put it on the schedule. Who can say no to Bill Clinton?

The next day, I went to my meeting with the head of organized labor in Illinois, a very nice Irish guy who had always been supportive of me. I was clear with him.

"Look, I'm way out on a limb with NAFTA. The president and the mayor are promising me the world to be with them on it."

"But labor will be with you forever if you are against it," he said.

"That's why I'm here. Here's my problem. You're Irish. Daley's Irish. Daley has lots of unionized city workers. You need him, he needs you, and you guys are friends. Right now, you're not getting along, but pretty soon you two Irishmen will make up, and I'll be the lonely Puerto Rican standing out in the cold. I'm like the guy who sides with one spouse when they split up and who nobody talks to ever again when they get back together. I need to know you will really be with me."

He laughed. He liked a good analogy.

"We'll always be with you Congressman," he said to me. He called union leaders together who sent a very clear message to the mayor that they would support me.

That week I held a press conference in Chicago announcing that I was against NAFTA. Workers and environmentalists stood with me. In a climate where every vote counted, it was national news. I climbed on the plane back to DC.

When I got back to the office and asked about my upcoming meeting with President Clinton, my chief of staff just shook his head.

"He canceled it," he said.

One more ally to cross off the list.

ALL OF MY troublemaking made my immigration efforts that much more important. Congress is an insider's world that thrives on committee assignments and fund-raising and connections. But if you stay in touch with your constituents and carve out a niche on an issue you are passionate about, you can find ways to get things done.

I learned right away that immigration policy wasn't the sexiest issue in Washington, DC. To gain some leadership on the issue, I didn't have to hustle and work to beat out a caucus filled with immigration-policy fanatics. If I had wanted to become the go-to guy on education issues, most of my colleagues would have said, "Get in line." If I had wanted to take the lead on environmental protection, or defending a woman's right to choose, experienced members who had owned those issues for years would have told me to get out of their way.

Immigration was different. While there have always been members of Congress who have worked hard on immigration issues and care deeply about it—leaders like Howard Berman of California and my good friend Bob Menendez of New Jersey—it's a tough issue for people to get engaged in and stay engaged in. The reasons are very practical. Very few immigrants write big campaign checks. Legal immigrants who aren't citizens aren't voters yet, and undocumented immigrants might never become voters. I have about 700,000 people in the district I represent now, but at least 200,000 of them cannot vote for me. They are working their way toward voting rights. Some may never get there. It's just much easier for an elected official to respond to voters than to potential voters.

Early on, the members of the Congressional Hispanic Caucus were organizing ourselves into "task forces" for different policy areas. There was a lot of back and forth for education and jobs and the economy. The arts and culture task force was popular because it gave you a leg up on hanging out with Latino stars and artists at Hispanic Caucus parties and events. As I remember it, we had never had an immigration task force. When I said, "Hey, let's do an immigration task force," nobody raced me to the front to put their name at the top of the list.

Pretty soon, I wanted to build on my local success with the citizenship workshops. I was thinking about my missed opportunity with Bill Richardson and President Clinton on NAFTA, the offer of national leadership on a citizenship campaign. The truth was that nobody else was trying to take the citizenship effort national. Lots of community groups were trying to help across the country, but I was still the only member of Congress who was authorized by the INS to turn in applications directly to them.

I took my plan to the Hispanic Caucus.

"National Citizenship Day," I said. I told my Latino colleagues how we did it in Chicago, recruiting volunteers and enlisting photographers and off-duty policemen.

"That sounds like a lot of work" was the general reaction.

It was, but I walked through what it would take for all of us to work together and have citizenship workshops in our districts across the country. Enthusiasm for the idea began to build. Several non-Latino members wanted to participate. My friend Gene Greene of Houston still holds workshops today. Then, everyone had IRCA-eligible immigrants waiting to become citizens. We all ended up working hard to make it a success. We had our first workshops on the Fourth of July weekend. From Dominicans in New York to Guatemalans in Los Angeles to Mexicans from Chicago to El Paso to New Jersey, we made people citizens—thousands in one weekend.

WHEN YOU HAVE been in the US Senate long enough, you inherit one of the nice little cubbyhole offices near the Senate floor. They are convenient but hidden away. You need to know where they are and be invited to find them. Ted Kennedy had one of the best ones. It was just one big room with a smaller reception area. It looked like it was more appropriate for a ship's captain than a US Senator. There were beautiful model boats and all sorts of nautical souvenirs and knick-knacks and paintings, all mixed in with great historical pictures of Ted and John and Robert Kennedy. It was like an incredibly upscale Red Lobster, but only if the owner of Red Lobster also happened to be the brother of a beloved US president.

Talking with Ted Kennedy about the comprehensive immigration reform bill we were working on was one of those experiences that sent me home at night thinking about how far I had come from Willow and Halsted, from Pueblo Nuevo. I sat in his office looking at pictures of Ted Kennedy with his brothers, his private pictures. It seemed a little familiar. I had looked at John F. Kennedy's picture at dinner every night growing up—the admired, and then martyred, great man who shared my dining-room wall with Jesus Christ.

"Kennedy was a good man," my dad would say. That he was Catholic was important to our family, but it was more than that. He was a people's president, he was for the little guy. He stood for fairness for everyone. I learned what a leader should be like because my parents responded when they felt John F. Kennedy stood up for the common man. That the United States was a place where he could be killed was one more reason my dad thought it was time to return to the island.

Now I was walking the same halls he did when he was a US senator. Growing up with admiration of his family made me take my work in Congress that much more seriously. How could I let down the brother of the man who watched over our dinner table every night? This was an opportunity I couldn't waste, one that all of my experiences had made possible. I had been taught right and wrong by my mom and dad; befriended by good, decent people like Luis and Tino; inspired by leaders like Rubén Berríos and Noel Colón Martínez and Harold Washington; and outraged by people like Dan Rostenkowski and Bernard Epton. All of those experiences, and a lot of knocking on doors and carrying petitions and fixing potholes and completing citizenship applications, had swept me along to this small office right off the US Senate floor, working out details of a comprehensive immigration reform proposal with Senator Ted Kennedy.

I quickly learned that Ted Kennedy was a great guy; generous with his time, fun to be around.

He didn't have to spend time with a junior member of the US House of Representatives working through a very progressive immigration reform proposal. He knew it would be very difficult to pass. But it was important to him, the right thing to do. He thought it was part of his responsibility as a leader on the Senate Judiciary Committee. He also thought that fairness for immigrants was a natural continuation of his family's lifetime commitment to civil rights. In all of our meetings, I never once had to make an argument based on fairness or equity. Those instincts came naturally to him.

An undocumented immigrant who has never been in trouble and

works hard? That person should have a reasonable path to becoming a citizen of the United States. A woman who has no papers but is caring for her US-citizen son and daughter? That person should be helped. Migrant farm workers in California who are the only people US farmers can find to pick their garlic? A laborer who picks grapes in Napa Valley for a fine glass of Chardonnay? They should be able to continue working without fear of deportation. He understood that we were talking about vulnerable and fundamentally decent people, and he wanted to help them. We put together a bill that did.

Of course, we were also more than willing to include enforcement provisions that discouraged illegal immigration and punished employers and immigrants who were breaking laws. My comprehensive immigration bills have always included reasonable enforcement and border security provisions. Ted Kennedy wanted our bill to have a chance, and he wanted Republican cosponsors. So did I.

Ted found his lead Republican cosponsor in a guy who was willing—then, at least—to be a maverick. John McCain worked closely with us, looking through every provision, trying to find a bill that he could support and sell to Republicans. I would go back and forth from Ted Kennedy's nautical office to John McCain's Southwest office, decorated with photos of the desert.

"You have a challenge and I have a challenge," McCain would say. "You have to convince all of your friends in organized labor to accept a guest-worker program. I have to convince all of my Republican friends that there is no way we are going to deport ten million people," McCain said to me more than once.

He was right. A lot of Democrats weren't crazy about the guest-worker provisions, and some labor leaders were worried about "cheap" immigrant labor. But the truth was that Democrats mostly believed in immigration reform and could support something that helped people legalize their status.

It was harder for Republicans. Many of them—fueled by rhetoric from the Glenn Becks and Lou Dobbses of the world, were becoming convinced that immigrants really were the biggest problem facing America. With his own show on CNN, Dobbs made bashing immigrants his crusade. You couldn't predict what crazy accusation he would come up with each night. He blamed an American outbreak of *leprosy* on immigrants. Not only were immigrants not at fault, but there was no leprosy outbreak. Dobbs and others refused to use any word other than "illegals" to describe immigrants without papers, even though entering the United States without permission is a misdemeanor. That doesn't make it OK, but it's hardly the felonious assault on our judicial system that many immigration opponents want you to think it is.

Still, despite opposition from many in his party, McCain tried, and I admired him for his effort. Ted Kennedy and John McCain and I would go over our bill line by line. We would come to a progressive section that Kennedy and I felt strongly about—say, details about how a path to citizenship would work—and McCain would study it, look concerned, and ultimately say there was no way he could live with it.

"This can't be in here. I can't get Republicans to agree to it," he would say.

Kennedy would shake his head like he was sharing McCain's frustration, and then say in his Hahvad Yahd accent, "You know, John, I agree with you. But that's something that's very important to Luis. He really wanted that in there. Luis, do you think we can give that one to Senator McCain?"

I would look disappointed and reluctantly agree, figuring Kennedy knew what he was doing.

After the meeting, walking back, I would try to figure out exactly what he was up to.

"Senator, what was that all about? That was your provision—not mine."

He would smile and laugh.

"Luis, he already thinks you're just another crazy liberal from the House. I have to work with him every day. Every now and then you just have to take the blame for me," he said. And I would, happily. How many people get to be co-conspirators with Harold Washington and Ted Kennedy in one lifetime?

As we worked through our bill, both of us spent time traveling the country, pushing immigration reform and fighting for our issue. I started doing lots of national TV, and was pleased to be seen as something more than just the congressional reform guy.

One morning, on one of my first appearances on *Meet the Press*, I went head to head with Pat Buchanan. The Chicago City Council was good training for *Meet the Press*. Pat Buchanan isn't nearly as nasty as Ed Vrdolyak. I pushed the same issues I always push: Immigrants work. They perform jobs that employers have tremendous difficulty filling, from agriculture to child care to day labor. That's why immigrants come to America—they need the work and they fill specific, demonstrated needs.

As soon as I left the studio early on that Sunday morning, my cell phone rang. I thought it might be Soraida telling me I had done a good job. Instead I heard the familiar Boston accent. Ted Kennedy was laughing.

"Luis, it's your senator. Vickie and I just watched you take on Buchanan on *Meet the Press*. You were terrific. I've never been so happy to see an Irishman lose a debate. Keep it up, my friend," he said.

Ted Kennedy was like that. He would call an unpredictable Puerto Rican congressman early on a Sunday morning just to tell him he did a good job. Who was I to him? A junior member of Congress. At the time, I wasn't even on the Judiciary Committee. I was just a guy who was passionate about immigrants and wanted to get something done. That was enough for him. He thought I was on the right side of the issue, and he was happy to be in the bunker with me, no matter the gulf in our life experience.

We never passed a bill, mostly because of Republican intransigence. If our success or failure had depended only on Ted Kennedy's passion and commitment, then about twelve million undocumented immigrants would already be on their way to staying with their families, paying more taxes, and filling essential jobs in America. Many Americans were denied a champion when we lost Ted Kennedy, but America's immigrants were at the top of the list. When we finally pass comprehensive immigration reform, Ted Kennedy will be the honorary cosponsor.

* * *

WHILE I WAS working on comprehensive immigration reform in Washington, in Chicago we were still making lots of immigrants—mostly Mexicans—citizens. Our work was changing the composition of the electorate in my district, and people were noticing.

The first people to say anything to me weren't immigrants at all. They were Puerto Ricans. After a couple of years of nonstop workshops, when I was out in Humboldt Park, Puerto Ricans began to ask me some unusual questions.

"Gutiérrez—what is it with you and immigrants? It's all I see on TV—immigrant this and immigrant that. What about us? Aren't you taking care of your Puerto Ricans?"

Most of them were just giving me a hard time, finding something to have fun with. But some were serious. Puerto Ricans aren't immigrants, so what's up with all of this citizenship workshop stuff? It made some of my Boricua friends wonder what my priorities were.

After a while, if they saw me a few times on the evening news or *Meet the Press*, it became a source of pride to most of them. I would be talking to a group of Puerto Rican and Mexican constituents or friends and the Puerto Ricans would say to the Mexicans, "Hey, how come our Puerto Rican guy has to do all this stuff? Pretty good, huh—a Boricua fighting for immigrants." It was like an inside joke, a source of friendly rivalry.

Soon enough, we had a chance to test whether making so many people citizens had also been good politics.

A young Mexican American attorney decided to run for Congress. The district had just been remapped, and between the new map and all of our citizenship work, the district was more Mexican than ever. I think his political calculus was simple. As a Mexican, if he could simply solidify the support of Mexican voters, he could be on his way to being a congressman.

I hadn't run a campaign in a while, but every Saturday those workshops in field houses had a campaign atmosphere. We never said a word about politics, but I talked to tens of thousands of residents of my district. I kissed babies. People wanted to get their picture taken with me. But it was better than politics, because we were providing a very real and essential service.

Of course, many of the people in those rooms weren't yet voters. But here's the secret that it would take the Republican Party nearly twenty years to learn, a secret they didn't even try to understand until Latinos helped Barack Obama crush Mitt Romney: undocumented immigrants have friends and family who are voters. Every undocumented immigrant is surrounded by a support network of legal permanent residents and citizens who judge politicians in no small measure by how they treat immigrants. Every time I talked to 1,000 immigrants at a workshop, they went home and told four or five or six neighbors and friends and cousins that Luis Gutiérrez and his staff of volunteers had just spent eight or ten hours helping people become citizens, and they didn't charge a dollar. By the time the attorney ran against me, we were closing in on 25,000 completed citizenship applications. That's a lot of cousins and friends and neighbors, not to mention that many of those 25,000 had already become citizens—and voters.

Still, ethnic politics is powerful. Puerto Ricans are inclined to believe that other Puerto Ricans understand their needs and experiences better than anyone else. That belief helped make me alderman. Most ethnicities are no different.

Pretty soon, we found out. My opponent couldn't keep any of his campaign signs up in Mexican neighborhoods. He would blanket the street with as many as he could and they would come down within days. And then, I started hearing directly from Mexican voters.

Walking down Eighteenth Street in Pilsen, one of the main streets of Mexican Chicago, a woman came up to me in a hurry, eager to talk with me.

"Gutiérrez," she said in Spanish, "I don't want you to think that guy speaks for Mexicans. That's just one Mexican's opinion. He doesn't speak for me."

I heard similar things from a lot of people, almost as if they thought I might hold it against them that a Mexican was running against me. I heard "He doesn't speak for me" over and over.

By Election Day, we knew we were in pretty good shape. Old rivals like Ed Burke and Dick Mell were now strongly supporting me, and voters liked the reforms I had been working on. But I wanted to do well in Pilsen and Little Village, the largely Mexican neighborhoods of Chicago. I wanted to know that Latinos were united, that we could stand together against the discrimination that came with Proposition 187 and Gingrich's anti-immigrant agenda. I wanted to show unity. Eight years earlier, Juan Soliz had beat me 4 to 1—and 5 to 1 in Mexican neighborhoods. I watched carefully when the precincts started to come in.

One of the first precincts was not too far from Piotrowski Park, the site of our first citizenship workshop. I won 171 to 19. In another largely Mexican precinct, I won 106 to 9. Overall in the Mexican wards, I beat him 3 or 4 to 1. I was thrilled; happy, of course, because it's great to win an election, but that Election Day was more than that. Latinos of every background had stood with me. We were building a coalition of Latinos who were ready to band together against discrimination and fight for the rights of immigrants.

AFTER THAT ELECTION, we just kept going with our workshops. Time after time we would see the same thing—people lined up around the building, waiting in lines with seven hundred or eight hundred other people to get help from our volunteers. It was a heyday for neighborhood entrepreneurs. Mexican men would drive up with a food truck and serve tamales to people outside. When the weather got nice, the *piragueros* would compete with one another to sell Mexican ice creams. It felt like a nonstop family block party, and because I was afraid that the volume was so huge that we might mess something up, I was always there, giving office appointments, directing people toward the fingerprint line, giving high-fives to little kids who thought the whole spectacle was exciting. I directed particularly talkative applicants to the cameras from the Spanish-language TV stations that were frequently there, covering the hundreds of Latinos taking their steps toward citizenship.

The families were great. Every workshop would be filled with moms and dads who brought along their two or three kids. Children born in the United States to immigrant parents are born citizens. Families are living all across my district and America where the mom and dad have to worry about being deported and potentially separated from their ten-year-old son or daughter who was born in Chicago. Hard-line immigration opponents coined a phrase for these children—"anchor babies," because, of course, in their opinion having your children in the United States is simply a plot by immigrants to stay in the country. The fact is that having a US-citizen child doesn't help much with your own immigration status. We have to work every day to try to keep small kids from being separated from their parents.

Let's face it, if Puerto Ricans weren't US citizens, I would have been an "anchor baby." My mom and dad came to America for exactly the same reason that virtually all immigrants do—for work. While they were here, because they were in love and wanted to start a family, they also happened to have Ada and me, born right in Chicago. Just like everyone else, their strategy wasn't much more nefarious than a desire to find a job that pays the bills and to have a family. I don't feel like an anchor, I just feel like another American.

At the workshops, I would always talk to the kids, and the older they were, the more excited they were about their parents becoming citizens. It represented peace of mind for them. Any child who knows their parent could be gone at any time lives with a huge burden of worry and doubt.

"So your mom is becoming a citizen?" I would say to the kids, who acted like the workshops were a great adventure. Many of them had done their immigration homework and helped their parents navigate the process.

"And what about you?" I would ask.

They would smile. "I was born here. I'm already a citizen," they would say, proud of being a full-fledged American.

"And so pretty soon all of you are going to be one big citizen family."

I would laugh, and people would smile and laugh along with me, like they were getting an early Christmas present by waiting hours in our long lines to become Americans.

* * *

IN 2010, we were coming up on citizenship application number 50,000. We wanted to celebrate, and mark the occasion. As we were planning our next workshop, the one that would put us over the 50,000 mark, a man came into the office with questions about applying for citizenship. He was an older man, and my staff asked him why he hadn't applied before. He laughed.

"No—I'm seventy years old. I've been a citizen for years. It's not for me," he said.

We see that all the time. Parents coming in for kids, or maybe a sibling who has recently come to the country. My staff didn't think too much of it.

"So it's for your son or daughter?" my staff asked.

He smiled again. "It's for my mother," he said.

His mother, Ignacia Moya, was 106 years old. She had lived in Chicago since the 1960s. She had tried to become a citizen before, but had trouble passing the English test. Her eyesight had always been bad, which her son said gave her trouble learning English.

She was now the matriarch of generations of US citizens; four children, thirteen grandchildren, and even more great-grandchildren. Ignacia was in a wheelchair, and she could barely hear or see. She was from near Guadalajara in Mexico, but America was her home, and her family's home, and she wanted to become a citizen. What she really wanted, more than anything, was to be able to vote, even if it was just once.

"My children all vote, I want to be able to vote too," she told us.

Ignacia wasn't going to pass her English test, but I worked with the government to waive her requirement. They thought it was reasonable to relax the requirements for a 106-year-old who had lived in America for almost fifty years and dreamed of voting in the United States before she died.

It was a big summer for us. In June, we had a workshop where, after nearly twenty years of workshops, we made our 50,000th person a citizen.

In July 2010, just after Independence Day, in a community center in Pilsen, surrounded by family members and facing cameras from most of Chicago's television stations, Ignacia Moya raised her hand, took the oath, and became a citizen. In November, at age 106, she voted for the first time in America. She was the fourth oldest person ever to become a citizen of the United States, and until she passed away in 2012, was the oldest naturalized citizen in our country. When I asked Ignacia why she wanted to become a citizen, she told me, "I want to be just like my children, American citizens."

But for us, Ignacia was just one of 50,000 people who came through our door. While Lou Dobbs and Pat Buchanan were showing clips of dangerous-looking invaders climbing over fences and gleefully landing on American soil, immediately looking for something to steal or a job to take, we were sitting quietly in church basements and school cafeterias, signing up long lines of patient nannies and janitors, gardeners and construction workers, moms and dads, making them all citizens of the United States of America.

CHAPTER EIGHTEEN

Senator Obama's Fence

S ENATOR BARACK OBAMA needed my help.

He didn't need it in the way that a politician says "I need your help" while he shakes a voter's hand and asks for their support.

In late 2006, Barack Obama needed real help, and he needed it fast. He had a problem that was getting bigger every day. And Barack Obama, spellbinding orator of the 2004 Democratic National Convention and bestselling author, was not accustomed to having problems. He certainly didn't need a local political brushfire intruding on his deliberations about whether to run for president of the United States.

In September 2006, Senator Obama had voted in favor of the Secure Fence Act of 2006. Though the bill was filled with lots of rhetoric about border enforcement, what it actually did was fairly simple. It mandated that the US secretary of Homeland Security build more than seven hundred miles of double fencing along specific segments of the US–Mexico border, mostly in Texas and Arizona.

As conservatives and cable-TV talking heads turned up their anti-immigrant rhetoric, I was becoming used to bills like the Secure Fence Act of 2006. It was just one more in a long line of all-stick, no-carrot responses to America's immigration challenges. In the early run-up to the 2008 presidential election, anti-immigration chatter was becoming deafening. Immigration opponents were calling John McCain "amnesty John," and the senator went from working with me on reasonable immigration efforts to apologizing for even trying. Suddenly he was saying he would vote against his own bill, the one he had crafted with Ted Kennedy and me. My days of visiting with him were over. If I had tried to stop by, he might have held a press conference to tell everyone he kicked me out. As immigration took up more of the national political discussion, I was one of the scary poster children for the anti-immigrant movement. In McCain's presidential campaign, he was attacked from the right by people who said as president, McCain would give Luis Gutiérrez an "open invitation" to the White House and plot with me to give amnesty to millions of immigrants.

In this atmosphere, the fence was a predictable legislative response. It was also a perfect example of the one-two punch that the anti-immigrant crowd loved. Punch one: ignore the real problem. Punch two: exploit people's fears.

A fence feels and sounds like border control. On paper, it has an easy, showstopping quality. People look and say, "Boy, that's a big fence," then they pat themselves on the back and feel like they've done something.

Unfortunately, it doesn't work. The Secure Fence Act ignores a simple fact: a seven-hundred-mile fence along a two-thousand-mile border doesn't make much sense. A fence doesn't help our relationship with Mexico, which needs to cooperate with us to make border control effective. If I'm trying to work with my next-door neighbor, building a fence doesn't accomplish much. Janet Napolitano, governor of Arizona and future secretary of Homeland Security said it well: "If you build a fifty-foot wall, people get a fifty-one-foot ladder."

And here's the most interesting fact about border control: in the past few years, we've learned what actually works. What works very effectively is reduced demand for workers in America. Recent statistics demonstrate a fact that would make famed political economists Adam Smith and Milton Friedman proud—immigrants come to America to work and to fill jobs in industries that need them. They come when they can find work. Starting around 2010, immigration from Mexico has slowed dramatically. Today, there is virtually no net immigration from Mexico. We didn't blanket the border with a fence, so how can that be? Is it because immigrants are afraid Rush Limbaugh might yell at them? No, it's because our economy is slow and there is less work for immigrants. The studies are clear. When job openings slow, immigration slows. Conservatives should rejoice—the free market works much better than any fence.

The exploiting-fears part of the one-two punch was easy: Barack Obama voted for the fence less than two months before the 2006 midterm elections, and very few senators want to look soft on anything in October of an election year. Especially when fence proponents were talking of nothing but criminals and welfare cheats crossing the border, all from Mexico.

Nobody was surprised that the fence was popular with the anti-immigrant crowd. But lots of people in Illinois were surprised that it was supported by their progressive senator, a candidate who'd won an overwhelming share of Latino votes in his 2004 US Senate election.

Our senator was already thinking about a campaign for a much bigger office than the US Senate. He wasn't used to disappointed constituents, angry mail, and negative editorials. He tracked me down at home, late at night. I usually go to bed early and was just about asleep. But the ID on my ringing cell phone on the nightstand said SENATOR OBAMA, so I took it.

As I remember, he got straight to the point. "Luis, everybody's trashing me. I don't understand. I'm trying to work with Republicans. I'm establishing some credibility so I can work with them down the road. This fence just shows I have a commitment to enforcement."

The senator was perplexed by our community's reaction to his pro-fence vote. He seemed bewildered that the Spanish-language press and the immigration community were outraged. I knew everyone was trashing him. They had trashed him to me.

Juan Andrade, president of the US Hispanic Leadership Institute, bashed Obama in his *Chicago Sun-Times* column. He wrote, "Senator Barack Obama joined ranks with desperate Republicans in passing a bill that would build a 700-mile wall along the U.S.–Mexico border. Republicans were genuinely desperate. Obama was just pandering and in so doing angered many Mexican-Americans and Mexicans, a very ill-advised vote that could cause him serious political problems."

Angry people were calling my office. As more people became aware of my immigration work, my office became a kind of switchboard for complaints and compliments. Angry immigration opponents call to tell my staff they work for the devil—though they usually don't put it quite that politely. Immigrants call to ask me for my help. After the fence vote, people were calling to complain about Barack Obama. My friends and colleagues were wondering how a surefooted politician on the rise could vote for a silly policy that was not even in his political self-interest.

I liked Barack Obama. Once he was elected—even though we hadn't been close previously—he would regularly call on me to ask for advice and suggestions regarding Latino and immigrant issues. Most senators aren't great at reaching out to their humble cousins in the US House. I was happy to help. I believed in him. After all, if we couldn't count on a liberal, African American from Hyde Park to vote right on immigration, who could we count on?

I was surprised by his vote, but I was even more surprised that he hadn't anticipated the reaction. In Congress, part of the job is taking votes that make about half of America mad at you most of the time. When I vote for gun control, the NRA and its backers send me nasty e-mails and letters. When I voted against NAFTA, I didn't get any love letters from the Chamber of Commerce and corporate America. With almost every vote that matters, you make somebody mad. Any senator should know there is no gray area in my community about a huge fence. I assumed that Barack knew he would be letting the immigrant community down and had made a political decision to give a vote to the anti-immigrant tough guys.

On the phone, he told me he thought the reaction to his vote was over the top. Could I help him to understand why everyone was so upset?

The answer was simple.

"Mexico is like home to hundreds of thousands of your constituents.

It's where they come from. They have families there. We build walls to keep enemies out, to keep threats out. You are telling your constituents that their friends and families are enemies of the United States."

A fence is not only an ineffective way to slow immigration from Mexico, it also ignores most of the problem. I reminded him that nearly half of the undocumented immigrants in the United States never cross that border. Guest workers and students and tourists from around the world who don't leave are a huge part of the population. But the Fox News chatterers never work themselves into a red-faced frenzy about Polish au pairs or Iranian doctors or Irish students who overstay their visas. Rush Limbaugh never talks about Canadian welfare cheats. The zealots always aim 100 percent of their anger at a region responsible for about 50 percent of the challenge.

The senator kept emphasizing that he was trying to build bridges to Republicans, showing them he could work with them.

"But the Republicans are not trying to work with us," I said. "There is nothing good in this bill. No reforms. Only punishment. It's all for show, and our people know it. This is very personal and very emotional for our community."

The senator listened. He was interested in my opinion. He felt like he was dealing with a wildfire. He called me because he needed a fireman: he was organizing a meeting and wanted my help. He wanted to get key leaders together to talk about his vote. He had one more request. Would I please attend, and sit next to him? Could I make clear to everyone that we were still allies?

Today, President Barack Obama often sits as far away from me as he can. Back in 2006, my continued support was evidence that I believed in him. He was still a rookie senator, and I thought he had simply made a rookie mistake.

It was important to Obama that the meeting did not turn into a public spectacle. He didn't want press and he didn't want protesters. Having a US senator meet quietly with community leaders in Chicago is not an easy trick. Most of the time in Chicago politics, there is only one way to keep a meeting a secret: don't have it. Keeping a secret when most of the people in the room are angry is even harder.

To the credit of the Latino and immigrant communities in Chi-

cago, nearly fifty people who cared about immigration showed up at
the Instituto Del Progreso Latino on a cold late-fall morning without
one reporter lurking around the door to say, "Congressman, can you
tell me what the meeting is all about? Are people angry at Barack
Obama?" I think our discretion was a credit to the growing sophisti-
cation of the immigrant community. Constantly being battered and
under attack has taught people how to organize and fight back.

I greeted Senator Obama at the door and walked with him into the
modest meeting room. We did our circle of the room, campaign-style,
meeting and greeting. It looked like this was the first time in a while
that Obama was not surrounded by fans and admirers, by people who
wanted to be close to him, touch him, have him sign his book. The
senator arrived in campaign mode, ready to smile and shake hands.
Despite his vote, he considered this a roomful of friends. But he didn't
get the reception he expected. For the moment, Barack Obama was a
suspect, someone who had let them down. As he walked through the
crowd, his body language changed. He slowed, and stiffened a bit.
He withdrew a little, as if he wasn't receiving the admiration he was
used to feeling. His staff looked nervous. They were not accustomed
to tense meetings.

Many close friends of mine were at the meeting. We couldn't have
had the meeting without Carmen Velásquez. Our neighborhood
doesn't have too many people who are more outspoken and shorter
than me. Carmen is both. She's tough, she's fiery, and she stands up
for the people she cares about as the CEO of one of our community's
most important health clinics. Her clinic helps to keep thousands of
people healthy, and Carmen never worries about anyone's immigration status.

For years, Carmen has thrived by telling everyone exactly what
she thinks and exactly how she expects the immigrants who come to
Alivio Medical Center to be treated. Carmen was a strong supporter
of Barack Obama. She campaigned for him. That day, Obama saw her
and responded like any politician would to someone who had been a
strong supporter. He saw a safe harbor in the choppy waters created by
his fence vote, a friend who would welcome him.

He had chosen the wrong harbor.

"I did not come here to shake your hand. I came here to listen," Carmen said. She turned to walk to her seat to hear her senator explain himself.

By the time Obama took his seat at the head of four conference tables arranged in a square, he knew his problems were larger than he realized. We sat down and I started the meeting and introduced the senator. I said he was our friend and he was our ally. If he weren't, he wouldn't have asked us to join him in this room. I said he deserved a chance to be heard. I said he was on our side and came to our community to hear us out. He wanted to start by listening, so we opened up the floor for comments.

People were ready to talk.

One after another, people shared their personal stories of coming to the United States, of the hardship of trying to find work or go to college without papers. People told stories of families left behind in Mexico, of what it feels like to constantly be portrayed as criminals in political ads and on talk radio.

Toward the end of the comments, a young woman stood and told a simple short story that seemed to affect the senator the most. She was young and thin, and when she stood to speak her voice had a power larger than her stature.

"I came here when I was just a little kid. My family didn't have anything. My dad couldn't find work. We came across the border. My dad carried me across the border in his arms. We could have died. We didn't know if we would make it. We risked everything for a better life. And now you want to build a fence?"

Her words spoke for everyone. We're good people who risked everything to come here. Please help us. Stand with us and be our ally.

At every meeting I attend across the country, I'm asked some version of the same question. "Why is it always about us?" The immense majority of immigrants work, many of them very long hours for very low pay. Most would take any steps—fees, wait lists, criminal background checks—to legalize their status. They just want to support their families.

The constant cable news attacks that portray them as a well-organized mob of lawbreakers trying to game the US system are both threatening and mystifying to tens of millions of people living and working hard across America right now, who feel like they live with targets on their backs. How can people who work long hours for low pay in jobs like picking fruit and caring for children and bussing tables get so many rich white men in blue suits and power ties on cable TV and in Congress so excited? We've had few times in American history when a group so powerless seemed to provoke so much fear and anger in the powerful.

They depend on somebody standing up to protect them. I try. But they need Barack Obama too. At that meeting, I listened to people repeat the same basic message: We thought we could count on you. Don't you understand how offensive a wall is?

He listened. He had a response to the woman who almost died crossing the border, and others from our community.

"I want to have better communication with you. I want to hear from you." He said he would be back to meet again. He didn't spend any time talking about trying to work with Republicans, or building up some credibility with the enforcement community. He emphasized that he wanted more input, to build better relationships.

But here is what he didn't say: he didn't say he had made a mistake, or that he was sorry. He talked "communication," not that the fence was a terrible idea.

Still, as he worked his way out of the meeting, he was surrounded by a warmer crowd. We wanted to believe him. As he left, people started taking pictures and smiling. I knew that I was his cover that day. He needed Mr. 100 Percent Pro-Immigrant Congressman to look our community in the eye and say that everything would be OK.

Before he left, Obama thanked me for being there and for what I said. For standing with him and helping him during a tough time. He gave me a warm handshake and he was on his way, a possible presidential candidate who had just extinguished a brushfire. I didn't even have to wear a fireman's hat.

The truth is I don't think I listened closely enough. We deserved "I'm sorry," not "we'll communicate better." I wanted a sense of accomplishment, of progress being made. So I had helped our new senator.

Our community had stood up for itself and made their views known to him. He had made promises to me, to Carmen Velásquez, to the young woman whose father had picked her up, put her in his arms, and risked everything to carry her across the border to America.

People had walked through the door angry, and walked out feeling better. But I'm not sure I learned much that day about Barack Obama's true feelings about immigration. What I learned was that Barack Obama is a very good politician.

SENATOR OBAMA was about to leave on a vacation to Hawaii when he called and asked me to come see him in his Senate office in Chicago. On the way over, I thought about recent Senate votes. I wondered if he might have made another fence-like misstep. Had he done something to get himself in trouble again?

We met in the Dirksen Federal Building in downtown Chicago, a place that serves mainly as a courthouse, where you are more likely to see camera crews chasing the most recently indicted politician than run into your US senator. Senators don't use the offices in their home state very much. No matter how many times your senator says that he will never forget the people of his home state, you are most likely to find him in Washington. It's good to be a senator in Washington, DC, kind of like it was good to be Henry VIII in London. You're recognized and coddled, feted and pursued most every moment you're in town. You hear, "Right this way, Senator, we're so thrilled you're here" at very nice restaurants. Members of the House of Representatives who aren't named Pelosi or Boehner aren't exactly treated like serfs, but we are much more likely to hear, "Could you spell your name again?"

But even by the standards of their underutilized state offices, Obama's Illinois Senate office suite looked like a lonely afterthought. It seemed barely unpacked, sterile, a reminder that he hadn't been there very long. We met in a conference room with blank walls. The desktop was practically clean. It looked like a place where the FBI might perform an interrogation. It was filled with furniture that looked like it had started its life with Senator Paul Simon or Everett Dirksen. I thought it looked temporary. Maybe he believed from the very beginning that he wouldn't need his Senate office for very long.

Barack Obama came right to the point. "Listen, Luis. I'm leaving on vacation to Hawaii with Michelle and the girls. While I'm there, I'm going to decide whether I run for president of the United States. When I come back, I would really like your support. I hope you'll stand with me."

I had to stop myself from looking surprised. I wanted to raise my eyebrows and say, *President? Of the United States? Get outta here.* But I didn't. I nodded thoughtfully.

Presidential chatter was surrounding Obama—he had a bestselling book and had fired up Democrats with his speech at the 2004 convention. In the last few months, the idea of an Obama presidential candidacy had moved from ludicrous to enticing. Political reporters were in a frenzy over what he might do. Obama wasn't saying no—which in high-level politics usually means yes. While I wasn't sure anyone could make a serious run for president just a few years after leaving the Illinois State Senate, I knew it was a mistake to underestimate Barack Obama. And if he was asking me to stand with him, that meant it was unlikely he was going to come back from Hawaii and say, "Michelle and I kicked it around for a while and I decided I'm the only man in the history of the US Senate who doesn't want to be president, so never mind."

After recovering from the initial surprise, my quick mental calculation was simple. I thought, What you've actually told me is that you've made up your mind already. So I told Obama what I tell most everyone who asks me for their support, whether it's for a bill in Congress or an endorsement for their campaign.

"Barack—you know what's most important to me—"

He stopped me before I had the chance to finish my sentence. "Immigration."

He passed my one-question test before I even handed it out. Everyone in Washington knows that fighting for immigrants is as important to me as hating the government is to Tea Partiers. Obama knew it too. He had called me for backup on the fence vote. I'm sure he was ready for my question the minute he called to invite me over. We talked briefly about what a president could do to change our nation's immigration policies.

I told him it was all about a Comprehensive Immigration Reform bill passing Congress. I told him you could never solve this problem bit by bit. The only answer for America is to look at the entire immigration challenge and solve every angle of it. I had introduced several versions of the bill over the past ten years. My bill's always included a pathway to citizenship for America's undocumented population, which is why immigration opponents scream "amnesty" whenever I say "comprehensive immigration reform." But my legislation also includes enforcement provisions: penalties for employers and more enforcement at the border. I also emphasize learning English and giving immigrants assistance in mastering their new language. I'll work with anyone to get something done.

So when Barack Obama asked me to support him for president, I didn't ask for a cabinet position, to be co-chairman of his campaign, or to be a major speaker at a convention—all things he certainly would have given me. I didn't ask to be an ambassador. I talked to him about comprehensive immigration reform. That's my passion. That's all that mattered to me.

And Barack Obama was clear. He told me he would fight for comprehensive immigration reform.

That was enough. The most critical component for a bill's passage is a president who is willing to spend his political capital, put his muscle behind it, and sell it as an economic and moral issue. A president who is willing to take a beating from the anti-immigrant zealots because he believes fairness for immigrants is a civil rights issue. Our conversation was brief because I believed in Obama.

I thought Barack Obama could be the missing piece that immigration advocates needed. He could be a president unafraid of political advisers who told him immigration was too controversial or difficult. The day he asked me for my support, he didn't have to give me a ten-page position paper on how he would pass immigration reform. He just needed to say he would do it. Barack Obama's promise was good enough for me, and before he left for she sunny beaches of Hawaii, I got it. I was in.

IN HIS 2008 bid for president, I campaigned across the country for Barack Obama. In Chicago, I was surrounded by people who loved Barack Obama. Outside of our hometown, he wasn't an easy sell to Latinos. Hillary Clinton was Coca-Cola, reliable and beloved. Barack Obama was some supposedly tasty new soda that was completely unknown. Most of my Congressional Hispanic Caucus colleagues were backing Hillary Clinton. My Latina colleagues were particularly committed to her and thought my support for Obama over Hillary was little more than favorite-son politics and almost a betrayal. They were dismissive of his chances.

When I campaigned for Obama in Latino neighborhoods, people told me how much they liked the Clintons. When I was campaigning for Obama in Nevada, a Mexican man in Las Vegas listened carefully to my Obama pitch, then pulled a dollar bill out of his pocket.

"See this dollar bill? When Bill Clinton was president, a dollar was worth a dollar. I want that dollar to be worth something again. I'm voting for Hillary," he told me.

But Obama fought back. When he spoke at the National Council of La Raza during the campaign, he couldn't have been more direct in talking about the human toll of deportations. "When communities are terrorized by ICE immigration raids—when nursing mothers are torn from their babies, when children come home from school to find their parents missing, when people are detained without legal counsel, the system isn't working," he said. I was proud. I felt I was backing the right candidate.

When Univision hosted the first presidential debate televised nationally in Spanish, Hillary Clinton promoted the fact that she hired the first-ever Latina campaign manager for a major presidential campaign. Barack Obama was ready with a response. He told people twice about working with his "dear friend" Luis Gutiérrez to protect immigrants, and about his experience attending one of our citizenship workshops. Of far more importance, he said that night that he would fight to pass comprehensive immigration reform during his first year, a pledge he repeated in the campaign.

I appreciated his pledge, and his good words about me. But soon, things started to change. Regularly in the campaign I would get questions from people who hoped Obama would say more, give more details about how he would help immigrants. As it became clear that he was going to sneak by Hillary Clinton and win the Democratic nomination, he had even less need for specific plans and policies for our community. Latinos and immigrants weren't going to support the new, anti-immigrant version of John McCain. In politics, success means less negotiating and promising for the candidate. Every day that it became more obvious Barack Obama was going to be president, the less he had to say about immigration.

Eventually, I took my concerns to David Axelrod, Obama's media strategist and closest adviser. I had known David for years. Throughout our years in Chicago politics, we always stayed in touch, frequently having breakfast or lunch to compare notes. He helped candidate Rich Daley package my endorsement and help convince Chicagoans that he could be a bridge builder and a peacemaker. He had shot TV and radio ads of me endorsing Daley for mayor and Daley endorsing me for Congress. I was happy for David that Barack Obama looked like he was on his way to the White House. David was another Chicago success story.

When I met David in his office in the River North neighborhood of Chicago, he looked busy and distracted. Of course, David always looked a little distracted. He still looked more like a harried, rumpled newspaper guy than the brilliant media strategist who was about to make a guy who was an Illinois state senator a few years ago the first African American president of the United States. I understood. Electing a president creates a little stress. I got right to the point.

"David, I'm concerned that for a long time now Barack hasn't really said more about Latinos or immigration policy. People notice that he's not saying much in speeches, that there's nothing on immigration on his website. Other candidates have lots of detail on their websites. I want to make sure it's a priority," I said.

David looked at me over the top of his glasses.

"The website?" he asked. A guy who was about to have an office in the West Wing was making his point clear. Was I really bothering him about a website?

"Not just the website—the whole focus of the campaign. I just don't want to lose sight of this issue."

He tried to be polite. "Let's just win. There will be plenty of time for deciding priorities after the election. Let's make sure we get there."

"Let's just win." You hear that a lot. Campaigns are tough and long and complicated. And campaigns have only one goal—getting more votes than the other candidate. The goal of campaigns, particularly in the consultant-fueled era we live in now, isn't to win a college debate on fiscal policy. It's to *win*. I've heard "We can't do anything if we don't win" a hundred times from pollsters and TV gurus and direct-mail consultants. It's true, but it's also why so many winning candidates wake up the day after an election and wonder what in the world they are going to do next.

I like David Axelrod. But I can also tell when I'm wasting his time. He didn't want to talk immigration policy that day. I thanked him and left him alone. I wanted to focus on the positive. Our long-shot candidate was on his way to being the leader of the free world. After eight years of living under the leadership of George W. Bush, I was about to be friends with the man sitting in the Oval Office. That would have to be enough for the time being. We would sort out my immigration concerns later.

AFTER THE ELECTION, Chicago was pumped with the kind of excitement usually reserved for a Bulls championship. We had just elected a hometown, liberal president who promised to be completely different from anyone before him. As a minority, as a Chicagoan, as a progressive, no matter what worries I might have had, I felt the election of Barack Obama was a historic cause for celebration.

The excitement filled every room of every event in Chicago in November and December of 2008. In Chicago, we felt like we had taken over the world. That it was so unlikely made it even more exciting. We knew that the man promising a new direction for America was just another ambitious young lawyer and community organizer on the South Side a decade ago. A few years before, he was one of fifty-nine Illinois state senators, debating funding for new bridges and the salaries of prison guards. People in Illinois still couldn't quite believe it. Barack Obama was president of the United States.

In December, I was at a Christmas party at a restaurant across from City Hall. The topic of the night was our Chicago president. Celebrating and talking with my friends, including other elected officials and an up-and-coming young Latino attorney, we all exchanged "I knew Barack when" stories.

My young attorney friend looked serious. "Luis, are you in touch with Barack now?"

Well, I was more in touch with him than three hundred million other people in America, but we weren't exactly hanging out at the corner bar. I had called a couple of times to schedule a meeting to talk about immigration, but we hadn't connected yet.

The attorney had a request. "I would love to do something in the administration."

Get in line, I thought. People kept asking about jobs, and I would send them over to the transition office. I was glad it wasn't up to me to sort through the applications of everyone who wanted to join the Obama administration. But this lawyer was my friend, and we were at a party in a jovial, joking mood.

"Work for the president? No problem. I've got his personal cell-phone number right here."

I did have his personal cell-phone number. He gave it to me early in the campaign. I almost never bothered him on it. I had called him once since he was elected, to congratulate him and start the process of moving forward for immigrants. I had gotten his voice mail. I imagined by now the Secret Service had probably shut down the number. I thought the president-elect of the United States was probably not answering any old cell phone, chatting with callers who might have a tip about the Middle East peace process.

But we were celebrating, all having fun.

"Let's call him right now, and I'll put in a good word for you," I said.

My friends didn't know whether to believe me or not.

I showed them my phone. The contact said SENATOR OBAMA.

I was ready to hit the Call button, thinking if anyone answered, it would be a stern Secret Service agent, or maybe the call would go into the old voice mail and we could all enjoy hearing the voice of our old friend, the man who was soon to be in possession of our country's nuclear launch codes.

"Before I call—what job do you want? Attorney general? Just hang on; I'll set you up in one minute."

The phone began to ring. We were laughing. There was music in the background, loud conversation, glasses clinking. I put it on speakerphone in case we might hear the president-elect's old voice message.

I laughed and told my friend, "Start planning, because in just a couple of minutes, you are America's highest-ranking law-enforcement official."

The phone rang again, and then, "This is Barack."

Not a message, but the familiar voice of our new president.

My friends stopped laughing. I quickly clicked the phone off speaker. "Mr. President, it's Luis Gutiérrez."

No doubt the newly most powerful man in the free world wondered why I was calling him at night on his personal cell phone. From a party.

"Hi, Luis. How are you?"

I give Barack Obama credit; he's a good sport. I congratulated him again on his victory. I mentioned who I was with at the party, told him they were excited too. I figured if I wasn't going to make my guy attorney general, I could at least mention his name to our next president.

"Mr. President, I'm hoping we can get together. Follow up on immigration. Talk about next steps."

He said he would be happy to do it, somebody from the transition would call me and set it up. I wished him a good night, closed my phone, turned to my friends, and smiled.

"You want to talk to the president of the United States? I'm your guy. Tell your wife to get ready to move to Washington, DC." They looked at me like I had gotten the ghost of FDR on the phone. And maybe a little worried that prank calling the president might be a felony.

But I was pleased that my call had practical value. His staff called and I had a meeting with our new president. His Senate offices in the Dirksen Federal Building were being used as part of his transition office, the same place I had seen him before he went to Hawaii. Now he was receiving daily national security briefings and choosing cabinet members.

Our new president looked a little weary, like he was still getting used to the idea of running the United States of America. I expected platoons of young staffers sorting through papers, preparing position books, thumbing thoughtfully through folders with labels like CHALLENGES THE KYRGYZSTAN SITUATION PRESENTS TO THE PRESIDENT. Instead, I found a suite of offices with a similar feeling to when I met him there last time. There were a couple of young staffers closing up shop, and a new president-elect who looked like he was ready to call it a day.

I congratulated him, and looked around the office.

"Here we are. Back in the same building where you told me you were running. You did it."

He thanked me for my help.

I wanted him to know I was excited, enthusiastic. "You're going to do great things. I just have one question. How are we going to do comprehensive immigration reform? I know you have a lot on your plate. I want to help."

The president-elect said to me: "That's why you're here. See anybody else here? Do you think I meet with everybody? You're important."

OK. That's fair enough. He doesn't meet with everyone. But I've come this far in my political career because when I need something I ask for it. When I want something, I try to go get it. What I needed that cold December night was more commitment to immigration reform. I felt like there wasn't anyone else in America who was going to ask him, and it was my responsibility to push.

I asked him again. "What's the plan for immigrants, and how can I help you get started?"

His answer was simple too. "You need to give me some time. We have an economic crisis. We have to work on some other economic issues. Let's talk again in March or April."

I understood that America was teetering on the brink of financial collapse. I didn't expect him to tell me that immigration reform would be his top priority. But the president of the United States has the ability to do more than one thing at once. Now he was saying March or April. The spring. That's a lifetime in Washington, DC.

The president answers to all Americans, but I answer to a district filled with immigrants, and to twelve million or so undocumented immigrants from coast to coast who don't have nearly enough leaders who fight for them. I was not giving up hope in Barack Obama. He had an economic crisis to address. But I had an immigration crisis to address, and I knew it couldn't wait.

"You promised you would do it in the first year," I reminded him.

When Barack Obama asked me for my support for president, I didn't ask for a thing outside of his leadership on immigration. I didn't want a job for me or any of my friends—just progress for immigrants. My congressional colleagues, meanwhile, most of whom had been for Hillary Clinton, were busy fighting over possible cabinet appointments. In the primary, Congresswoman Hilda Solis attacked Barack Obama every chance she had. She campaigned hard for Hillary and acted like I had betrayed every woman in America by not supporting her. Now Solis was in line to become our new president's Secretary of Labor. None of the job-seekers would be waiting months to talk to the president.

"We need to start planning now," I said to him.

The president-elect said, "We'll get to it. We've got some other priorities."

And that was it. He seemed perfectly willing to wait. He felt no sense of urgency. It was the end of the day and he was tired. He was eager to go see Michelle and the girls. He would soon be responsible for the future of three hundred million Americans. We shook hands and he headed home.

I gathered my staff, and we made a simple decision. After traveling the country for Barack Obama, I would get back out and spend time with immigrants from coast to coast on a "Family Unity Tour," talking about their needs and challenges and what they hoped our new president would accomplish for them.

HERE'S A HELPFUL tip for the next time you visit the White House— don't bring along enough petitions to fill up the trunk of your car. Even if you are a member of Congress, and even if you think the man newly elected to sit in the Oval Office is your pal.

I took three boxes filled with stacks of petitions along to my first meeting with Barack Obama after he was elected president. We called ahead to the White House to let them know we would be bringing them. An aide came along with me to help me deliver them. The security guys at the guardhouse on the front lawn of the White House still looked at me like I was crazy.

"You can't bring those in here," they said.

"I'm Congressman Gutiérrez, and I've been collecting petitions all over the country to give to the president," I said. "I told the people who signed them that I would deliver them. Other Latino members of Congress and I have a meeting with Barack Obama. One way or another, they have to be delivered."

They kept me at the guardhouse for a few minutes. They picked them up, looked through them, ran metal detectors around the boxes. I started to worry I would miss the meeting. While the guards puzzled over my suspicious boxes of petitions, some of my colleagues in the Congressional Hispanic Caucus showed up and gave me the "What exactly is Luis up to now?" look that I've become accustomed to seeing. It's a raised-eyebrow, slightly bewildered look that suggests they think I'm the only person who would do something like bring boxes of petitions to my first meeting with the new president.

Eventually, my boxes were approved. I had the boxes on a handcart. Nobody was volunteering to carry them in for me, so I pulled them up the White House front walk, a Congressman and his legislative director tugging a cartful of signatures for the president. To tourists, I probably looked like a dressed-up UPS man. I zigzagged the cart through the White House door and into the towering State Dining Room, where I got even more unusual looks from people. An aide told me to leave them in the front of the room, behind the chair at the head of the table. My colleagues and I, and my boxes full of petitions, waited patiently for the president.

The Hispanic Caucus members had met privately before the larger meeting. We agreed that we were going to emphasize, in March of 2009, just one issue—immigration. After eight years of George Bush, we were very pleased to have an ally in the White House, and we were ready for progress.

The State Dining Room of the White House is a huge room. Unless you wait in line for the White House tour, not many Americans get to see it. The room is an impressive place for a meeting. It's usually reserved for dinners and formal events. The ceiling is so high it looks like you could park a helicopter in the room. It doesn't exactly feel like the company cafeteria. We were meeting in a room where a French king would have felt at home.

I was looking forward to telling our new president what I had been hearing from immigrants around the country. My goal for my Family Unity Tour was simple. I wanted to put a human face on the immigrant community in the United States. A casual consumer of news, particularly any news that included Fox, thought of immigrants as dangerous hordes marauding through the United States looking for jobs. I wanted to show that they were mostly hardworking people with families. Just as I heard in our Chicago citizenship workshops, people across the country said to me, "Please help me keep my family together."

Many of the people asking for help were citizens. America is home to more than five million US-citizen children of undocumented parents. Every day, the United States was deporting some of these people, either sending the children to countries they had never known, or separating them from their parents. Wives were being separated from husbands, children from parents and grandparents. Very few of the people facing separation had committed a crime other than coming to the States to look for work.

I started my tour in Chicago at a church in the Pilsen community. When the event was scheduled to start, there were a lot more empty seats than filled ones. I told Father Brendan that I was going to deliver my speech as if the pews were filled. In the next few minutes a suburban pastor pulled into the parking lot with the first of two school buses filled with people. More folks from the neighborhood just kept coming. By the time we were done, the church was packed.

It was like that all over the country. I looked out at packed auditoriums and thought, Tell immigrants you care, give them an opportunity to tell their story, tell them you will listen, and they will fill one church after another.

In Atlanta, we packed an evangelical church with over a thousand people. In that overflowing sanctuary, we heard from two American-citizen children, a brother and sister who were about eleven and twelve years old. Their parents were undocumented and had been deported the year before. So much for anchor babies—their parents were set adrift in Mexico. The mom and dad did not want their children to come to Mexico, a country the parents had risked everything to flee. They could not find families who could take both siblings in Atlanta, so the brother and sister were living apart. Crying, they said all they wanted was for their parents to come home.

John Lewis, my friend and colleague and champion of the American civil rights movement, attended that day. He listened to the stories and said, "I went to jail for civil rights for black people in the 1960s, and I will go to jail for civil rights for your people today."

We heard similar stories everywhere we went. Nancy Pelosi attended our event at a large Catholic church in San Francisco. Two older American-citizen children were there, and implored us to do something to keep their family together. Their mother was in deportation proceedings and attended the meeting with them. She was allowed to attend because she was wearing an ankle bracelet monitored by Homeland Security. As I recall, she worked cleaning houses, but Homeland Security was tracking her movements as if she might lead an effort to overthrow the government.

"I've been accepted to college, and I want to go," one of the daughters said. "But if my mom is sent away, I will go with her." She was ready to give up college and go to a foreign country to stay with her mother.

Before we finished, Nancy Pelosi stood up and said, "Taking parents from their children—that's un-American."

And everywhere we went, we gathered signatures on petitions for the president of the United States. The request was simple: please take action to keep immigrant families together.

Now, nearly 10,000 signatures, cleared reluctantly by security, were sitting in boxes in the White House State Dining Room. We waited a bit for the president. He came in and sat down at the head of the table—right in front of my boxes of petitions. He looked right at them and did a bit of a double-take, wondering if someone had forgotten to clean up the room before the meeting, and then sat down so we could start.

Nydia Velázquez, the Puerto Rican congresswoman from New York who has never been afraid to say what she believes, always says it with conviction and was serving as the chair of the Congressional Hispanic Caucus, set the tone. She was clear and articulate and forceful.

"Mr. President, our community needs action on immigration now—right away. This is the civil rights issue of our time. The lack of action on comprehensive reform, and the continuing deportations are simply unacceptable for our community. In the end, Mr. President, you will be judged by how you treat the most vulnerable—our immigrants."

I spoke after Nydia and reinforced her message. I pointed to the boxes of petitions right behind the president. "Everywhere I go, people need your help. Moms are separated from children. We can't wait—we need action," I said.

My colleagues in the Hispanic Caucus were ready to carry the same message. One after another, we said, "We need immediate action on immigration."

As soon as Nydia had started speaking, I saw a reaction from Barack Obama that reminded me of what I saw in that conference room when he walked into the Instituto Del Progreso Latino and was met with anger instead of cheers. I saw a defensive and frustrated Obama, a man who doesn't like his priorities challenged.

As all of us prodded him to action on comprehensive immigration reform, he stiffened. He looked away from whomever was speaking and into the distance. Everything about his body language said he was not ready to be told what to do just a couple of months into his presidency.

To the credit of my congressional Hispanic colleagues, we were unified and determined that day. Nydia's words that "you will be judged by what you do for immigrants," rang in the room throughout the meeting. Nydia courageously made our case to the president.

In response, Barack Obama was brief. He said he supported immigration reform, but he had more urgent priorities. We could follow up with him. As we concluded, I asked him what I thought was obvious, given his response.

"Who should our contact person be? Who should we follow up with?" I asked.

He looked back at me, dismayed. I might as well have been Katie Couric asking Sarah Palin what newspapers she read. He clearly had not put anyone in charge of immigration policy, or had any discussions about how to deal with the issue.

After a stone-faced pause, he said, "Rahm Emanuel will be in charge."

His Chicago chief of staff, and my former colleague, Rahm Emanuel. Rahm was busy running the government. His plate was too full for immigration. Telling us Rahm was in charge sent a clear message—nobody was in charge.

So I did what I always do. If I am hitting my head against a wall and not breaking through, I usually try to hit harder. I scheduled more stops on my Family Unity Tour. I spoke out more often on the floor of the House. I collected more petitions. If you want change, you have to force it. And I didn't care whether the man sitting in the Oval Office was my friend or not.

CHAPTER NINETEEN

Arrest Me, Not My Friends

AFTER THE FIRST leg of the Family Unity Tour, I was glad to be back in Chicago. The night before a huge hometown event at Our Lady of Mercy, a huge Catholic church on the Northwest Side, Soraida and I were relaxing together when she answered the phone. She looked surprised.

It was a call from the archbishop of Chicago, Francis Cardinal George, the leader of my church. I thought to myself, How nice of the cardinal to call me here at home. The cardinal had agreed to speak at our event. I thought it would be a very powerful moment for our movement. I assumed he was calling so that we could coordinate. The large Latino and immigrant population is a huge reason the Catholic Church is still an important part of the fabric of Chicago. I picked up the phone and heard his familiar voice.

"My son, tomorrow we're going to have an activity at the Catholic church, in a Catholic sanctuary," he said.

"I look forward to it, and thank you so much for coming," I told him.

He told me he had a very specific reason for calling.

"I must ask you not to come," he said. "Our faith is very clear on the issue of life, and you have a very clear pro-abortion position. I cannot share the altar with you, or be part of an activity together with you in a Catholic church."

It wasn't the first time I had been chastised by a Catholic for being pro-choice, but to be disinvited from my own event by the top guy in the church was a new one. I hoped I wasn't in line to be excommunicated. Usually whenever I'd visit Catholic churches in my district, the priest simply looked the other way on my pro-choice position, happy to have me talk to their mostly Latino congregations about immigration and my work in Congress. But occasionally, I will sit politely in the pew while a section of the sermon, prepared with their special guest in mind, focuses on the sanctity of life. Sometimes a quick preview of the hell that awaits those who deviate from the Church's position is thrown in. I don't mind. The conflict is part of being a Catholic who separates the beliefs of my Church from my public-policy advocacy. Still, the cardinal had never before called me to tell me to stay home.

My first thought was to let him know that I had just been touring from coast to coast in Catholic churches where priests from New York to San Francisco had blessed me and thanked me for coming. But I didn't want to argue with the leader of my church.

"Cardinal, as a Catholic, let me make it abundantly clear that I will obey. But I'm not sure you are accurately informed about the event. It is not a Catholic event, it is an ecumenical event that our church is generously hosting. The sanctuary will be filled with protestants and Jews and Muslims—people from all religions and all walks of life. I hope that might allow you to reconsider," I said, trying not to sound like I thought I could tell the leader of Chicago Catholics what to do in his church.

"That gives me pause," he said. He told me he would call right back, and he did.

"You're right. It's an ecumenical event," he said when I had him on the phone again. I was relieved, but it was too soon to stop worrying.

He continued, "Because it is ecumenical, I believe we have two choices. Given your position on abortion, I still cannot share the altar with you. One choice would be for me to send an emissary in my place. He will deliver a message on my behalf, and you can then speak from the pulpit. Second, I could attend and you could sit in the audience with all of the others who have gathered for the event, and I will sit at the altar and speak from the pulpit." He said this in a soothing, loving tone. It was like getting a personal mini-sermon from the most important Catholic in Chicago.

The choice was easy.

"Cardinal, everyone knows how I feel about immigration reform. I don't need to speak. I would be honored to be in the audience and hear your views. I believe you can bring more supporters to our cause for immigrants," I told him, and I meant it. I thought the support of the cardinal was vital to our efforts.

The next morning, the cardinal was true to his word. He was very welcoming to the immigrant families in the church. The cathedral was packed. Chicago immigrants and activists had heard and read about the coverage our tour was receiving nationally. I felt like a returning missionary. I entered the church just before the event began and walked down the center aisle with my whole family, with Soraida and Omaira and her husband and my grandson. I wanted people to know we were fighting for families just like mine. We walked to the pew in the front, and as we walked forward everyone in the church rose from their seats and applauded like we were about to hold a revival. It was a gratifying moment, and while I wasn't at the altar, many priests from our neighborhood made a point of sitting in the audience with me, setting aside my heresy on choice to show their support for my position on immigrants.

Following the cardinal's wishes had been the right decision. He delivered a powerful and courageous message that day. He fully endorsed the need for comprehensive immigration reform and for the importance of keeping families together. He called the division of families by deportation "immoral." Having one of America's most important Catholic leaders give us his support was in important moment for our movement. He may not have wanted me standing at his side, but in his words, he stood strongly with me and Chicago's immigrant community.

I was just fine with sitting and listening to Cardinal George lend his leadership to our cause. On our tour we talked to thousands of immigrants and generated news coverage everywhere we went. In an increasingly hostile anti-immigrant environment, we were striking back. More immigrants across the country were feeling like somebody was on their side, that help was on the way.

BUT WE STILL needed help from our most important ally. More than six months after taking office, halfway through his "do it in year one" promise, my friend Barack Obama had still not lifted a finger on comprehensive immigration reform. But he was doing something on immigration. In Chicago, and in the cities and towns that my colleagues in the Congressional Hispanic Caucus represented, we heard about more aggressive enforcement and deportations by Immigration and Customs Enforcement—or ICE—agents.

"ICE is being more aggressive, they are putting people into deportation proceedings after getting stopped for running a red light" was a common complaint. Across America, many immigrants were glad I was coming to town, but when it came to immigration, I wasn't exactly the sheriff. I was more like a deputy who wouldn't shut up. Immigrants needed to hear from the real sheriff, the president of the United States.

Soon enough, Barack Obama invited a bipartisan group of congressional leaders to the White House for a roundtable meeting on immigration. We talked in very general terms about immigration, but he made clear that he was still working to fix a struggling economy. In response, many of us emphasized the complaints we were hearing about deportations. After a cordial but not particularly productive meeting, I was ready to leave, but the president got my attention and he called me over to talk with him privately.

We stood by ourselves off to the side of the State Dining Room. It's an excellent place to have a meeting if you want to convey presidential authority. The wooden floor gleams, the furniture and paintings are hundreds of years old. All across America every day, people meet in generic conference rooms. Barack Obama gets to hold meetings under a famous portrait of Abraham Lincoln. I hoped he wanted to have a private word with me so he could deliver some good news.

As we talked, Obama leaned down and put his hand on my shoulder. The rest of my Congressional Hispanic Caucus colleagues thought I was getting special treatment from my friend the president. From across the room, I imagine we looked like two Chicago guys hanging out. But in our corner, he'd leaned down to me and said, "I called all of the right people to this meeting, right? I kept everyone focused on finding common ground, right? And we're from Chicago, we should be working together, right?"

I didn't really know what he was getting at.

"It was a good meeting, Mr. President," I said.

"So why don't you get off my back?"

That got my attention. I asked him what he meant.

He told me that everywhere I went, I was complaining about him, about the deportations. My tour wasn't fair. It was giving people the wrong impression. He said we were on the same side and I should give him some time.

Barack Obama telling you to get off his back makes you think twice. In just a few weeks I had managed to get myself in trouble with a cardinal and a president. But I really didn't think his complaint accurately captured what our tour was all about. Everywhere I went, I said something like: "Barack Obama is our friend. I want him to be the best president he can be. When he understands the impact of these deportations, he will act. When he reads your petitions, he will act. He will be on our side."

Did I want to put pressure on the president? Of course, but I wanted it to be the pressure you put on your friends to do better. But that day in the State Dining Room of the White House, the president of the United States wasn't seeing it that way. It was clear he didn't like a national tour that highlighted families torn apart by deportations— particularly now that he was the guy doing the deporting. He didn't care if I was trying to apply friendly pressure. He didn't want to be pressured at all.

I told him I wanted to try to work with him. He said he would keep trying. We shook hands. My colleagues saw that my special private time was over. They didn't know, yet, that we weren't two buddies talking about the Chicago Bulls.

ON THE TOUR, one of our stops was in New Jersey, the home of my friend US senator Bob Menendez. The place was packed. Bob is very popular and received a great ovation when he spoke. He gave me a generous introduction. When I said, "Deportations that tear families apart must stop," it brought people to their feet, as it did virtually everywhere we went. When I finished speaking, the guy from Chicago got an ovation too, almost like their hometown senator.

We walked down from the stage and Bob put his arm around me. "There aren't too many people I would let come to my neighborhood and get an ovation nearly as big as mine," he said, laughing.

The more the anti-immigrant crowd turned up their rhetoric, the more invitations I received to speak around the country. In President Obama's first year in office, I spent dozens of weekends listening to the stories of families. More national news programs called on me to be a guest, and the national Spanish-language news and public affairs shows had me on regularly. After years of combat in Congress with my colleagues about reforms, I was now consistently recognized for my work on immigration—an issue that had nothing to do with cutting anyone's pay.

On our Family Unity Tour, it wasn't just those who attended the events who recognized me. Sometimes my hosts would invite me to a nice restaurant for lunch or dinner. I would sit in a steakhouse or fancy Italian restaurant in Tampa or San Jose, and usually none of our fellow—mostly white—diners would recognize me. But the Mexican immigrant filling our water glasses would lean over and say, "Thank you, *congresista*, for fighting for us. How much longer before I can get my papers?"

Sometimes, one or two or even a whole group of Latino immigrants would come out of the kitchen, look around sheepishly because they were breaking the rules, and get a quick picture or autograph before going back to work scrubbing pots and pans. If they had time, I would tell them that I knew all about clearing tables and washing dishes, that I knew restaurants were hard work. The paying customers around me always looked astonished, wondering who the guy getting all the attention was, thinking maybe I secretly owned the restaurant.

The recognition was gratifying, but it was daunting too. When enough people carrying your dirty dishes from your table say, "We're counting on you," you feel an obligation to get something done. For the working people I met on our tours, what we did—or didn't do—in Congress was much more than an interesting policy debate. It would determine their future. A Tea Partier might think the world will end if his tax rate is 26 percent instead of 24 percent, or if government spends more than he likes on foreign aid. But nothing that happens in Washington, DC, affects whether he will be able to stay in America with his family. Across the country, I wasn't collecting helpful tips about what I should do—I was receiving pleas for help.

Being in the middle of America's escalating battle over immigration suited my nature. Immigrants were getting attacked and I enjoyed fighting back. Being a spokesperson and advocate felt natural to me, no different from selling independence newspapers in the plaza, being a soldier for Harold Washington, or fighting for affordable housing. Congress is very often all about process—about excelling on the issues of the committee you're assigned to as a freshman, about moving up slowly on your subcommittee, about making friends and allies within Congress who help you to move into leadership or get onto a better committee. It takes patience and the willingness to compromise and the ability to get along with people. I'm bad at those things. I'm good at bringing boxes of petitions to the White House.

As a survivor of the hand-to-hand combat of the Chicago City Council, I've always looked for a different way to thrive, a different niche in Congress. In a Congress that could be all too reasonable and patient, I sometimes felt like the reform-school guy who ended up surrounded by the polite kids with nice sweaters. I think my fondness for a fight came through to immigrants who felt like punching bags. At a forum in New York, a man came up to me afterward and said,

"You know what I like about you, Gutiérrez? People say all kinds of terrible things about immigrants, but immigrants are always nice to everybody. Not you. You always tell them what you think." I hear that a lot. I'm seldom accused of being too nice.

SOON, Barack Obama's first year in office was over, and with it our hope that he would keep his promise to do comprehensive immigration reform in year one. I had other members say to me, "Luis, give him some time. There is a lot going on. Just look at the economy." Of course the economy had been in crisis, but immigrants were in crisis too. I would complain to other members of Congress, remind them he promised us he would make it a priority. Some would shrug. "Like he's the first person to break a campaign promise," they said.

Many Latinos waited with high hopes that the New Year would begin with a commitment to immigration in Obama's 2010 State of the Union speech. But by 2010, Obama was betting his presidency on health-care reform. He devoted most of the speech to health care and jobs. Then he ran down a list of other priorities, including a detailed and passionate explanation of why America needed to get rid of "Don't Ask, Don't Tell," a welcome promise. After he had listed virtually every other priority, he mentioned, almost as an aside, America's immigrants.

He said, "And we should continue the work of fixing our broken immigration system—to secure our borders, enforce our laws, and ensure that everyone who plays by the rules can contribute to our economy and enrich our nation."

That was it, an "I'm glad this speech is almost done," over-the-shoulder bone tossed to America's immigrants. A total of thirty-seven words, most of them about enforcement. Latinos had been watching and hoping. Immigrants understood what it meant. We hadn't fallen off the president's radar; he had turned the radar off. Blogs began to buzz. A *Huffington Post* columnist asked if Obama had killed comprehensive immigration reform.

After the speech, I went to Statuary Hall in the Capitol to talk to reporters, a congressional tradition. The reporters line up in one place to make instant analysis and television time that much easier for members of Congress. They turn the Capitol into a mall for sound bites. The Telemundo reporter asked the exact question that was on my mind.

"This speech makes it sound like the president isn't very interested in immigration reform. What do you think, congressman?" she asked.

For more than a year I had been trying to walk the line between my disappointment in my friend and my hope that the president would eventually get to our issues. He might not have thought so, but I had been telling people to trust him. He'll respond to your petitions. We'll get it done. That day, I told the reporter exactly what I was thinking.

"You're right, the president doesn't seem very interested in immigration. It's time we demand that he get interested," I said.

Now into the second year of his presidency, you couldn't hide the truth anymore. Time was slipping away, and Barack Obama wasn't doing a thing about immigration.

VERY QUICKLY, the tone of our national tour changed. I received an invitation to come to visit Los Angeles. They wanted me to come for a simple reason. People were mad.

A good indicator of a crowd's enthusiasm is the number of home-made signs—actually homemade, not put together with the help of poster board and markers bought by a campaign consultant. The church was filled with angry people carrying real signs: OBAMA, KEEP YOUR PROMISE. KEEP OUR FAMILIES TOGETHER. STOP THE DEPORTA-TIONS. Obama's cavalier mention of immigration reform in his State of the Union had fired up our community. He probably would have done better to say nothing at all. "Oops, I forgot," would have been better than "I remembered to put you last." Murmurs started of a march to show him how we felt.

Barack Obama already thought I was a pain in his presidential back. But his indifference in the State of the Union had me genuinely pissed off and tired of waiting.

"It's obvious the president of the United States doesn't see us," I said, as the people in the room cheered. "So let's make sure when he opens his curtains from the White House, Barack Obama sees us. If he doesn't look out, let's make sure he hears us. It's time to march on Washington," I said, and the room went crazy, ready to get on buses and ride all the way from Los Angeles to Washington, DC. I thought if people will come from the West Coast, they'll come from anywhere.

And they did. Immigration advocacy organizations started planning the march from coast to coast. The date was set: immigrants would march on Washington on March 21. Inspiring people to come wasn't hard. By the spring of 2010, immigrants had plenty of reasons to be upset with Barack Obama. While he was telling me to be patient on immigration reform, Obama pushed local governments to increase their efforts to identify undocumented residents and gave them more federal resources to do it. In early 2010, Obama sided with hardline Republicans in the Senate and starting making plans to send National Guard troops to the Mexican border.

But it was the deportations that were making people irate. In Obama's first year in office, the United States deported almost 390,000 people. In George Bush's first year in office, the United States had deported 210,000. And Obama was just getting started. In 2012 he deported more people than in any year in US history. George Bush never presided over one year in which more people were deported than in any year under Obama. That was definitely change—just not change that Latinos could believe in. Eventually, Spanish-language talk radio started lighting up in frustration. Regularly, as I went from coast to coast, leaders were asking me, "What's wrong with your guy?" I had been the first Latino member of Congress to endorse him. I was not only mad, I felt guilty, like I had misled people.

I didn't know exactly what was wrong with "my guy," but I knew that he had squandered an entire year—a year with a Democratic president, a Democratic Senate, and a Democratic House. The only area where Obama was making his mark for immigrants was in setting deportation records.

While Latino activists across the country made travel plans and found friends and families to host them in Washington, DC, Barack Obama was busy working and lobbying as well. He was focused like a laser on health-care reform.

The health-care debate was up and down. It looked like he wouldn't have enough votes. The president worked incredibly hard on a very worthwhile issue. He lobbied members personally. He needed every vote of the Congressional Hispanic Caucus. In March, he called us back in to the White House to meet with him. We headed over to talk to him again. We had a decision to make. If we'd wanted to, the Congressional Hispanic Caucus could have stopped health-care reform.

We had reason to stop it. When he gave a speech to a joint session of Congress to sell health-care reform, Obama went out of his way to emphasize that his plan did not provide any benefit of any kind to undocumented residents. To make his point, he called immigrants "illegal immigrants," using the demeaning phrase of our enemies. This was a new Barack Obama. In his campaign, he always said "undocumented." When he was heckled by a right-wing congressman who didn't believe Obama's plan didn't cover the undocumented, Obama didn't defend immigrants or stand up for fairness. Instead he emphasized again that they wouldn't receive any coverage.

Had we withheld our votes and demanded immediate action on immigration reform in exchange for our support, the president likely would have faced an insurmountable hurdle to passing his health-care plan. We talked about blocking it, and maybe we should have. In the end, though, almost all of us believed in his health-care initiatives. Obama was the president of my party, the former senator from my state, and as frustrated as I was with him, I still wanted him to succeed.

Now, as we listened to his health-care pitch, the president was lobbying us hard. He was passionate in asking us to support health care, to be patient with him on other issues.

"Help me get this done, and I will work with you on immigration," he told us. We let him know how hard it was for people to wait. Everywhere we went, people were asking us to do more to help them, to do more to keep their families together, and to bring justice to the immigrant community. He responded with emotion.

"How do you think it feels to be the first black president of the

United States and not be able to do more for black people?" he asked. At that meeting, more than the other times we had been in the White House with our new president, I felt he was trying to listen to us, to show empathy. I had never before—and have never since—heard him refer to himself as the "first black president," or make such an emotional appeal that was clearly intended to connect with the Latino members of Congress in that room as one minority to another.

In the end, virtually every member of the Hispanic Caucus supported health-care reform. I felt it was the right thing to do. The president and Speaker Pelosi kept going back and forth about when the vote would be held. Finally, when they thought they could squeak by with enough support, they called the vote for March 21, 2010—the very same day of our national immigrant and Latino rally. One by one, Latino members of Congress cast their vote in favor of health-care reform, making sure it would pass. As we helped our president pass the historic bill, nearly 200,000 Latinos and immigrants and their allies were marching on the Mall, demanding action on immigration reform, shouting for attention while virtually every news outlet in the country covered the historic health-care vote.

Earlier that day, I spoke to a cheering crowd that filled up the National Mall, said the president must act, that we had been patient long enough, that we couldn't wait. Then I walked through the crowds back up to the Capitol to help the president I had just criticized pass his signature piece of legislation. I thought to myself that only Barack Obama could be lucky enough to hold his most important vote on the day one of his key groups of supporters poured in from across the country, many of them to protest his policies. On most of the English-language networks that night, five hundred Tea Partiers complaining about Obamacare received more coverage than tens of thousands of Latinos complaining about Obama.

I WASN'T SURPRISED when the earnest immigration promises Obama made when he needed our support on health care evaporated in the Washington mist. Health care passed, and so did the president's commitment. By May 2010, the deportations continued, and still nothing had been done on reform. The health-care plan wasn't playing so well across the country, and Democrats losing seats in Congress seemed like a real possibility. Time was running out.

Immigrants were mad. They were done being patient. The immigrant community simply didn't understand why their ally Barack Obama wasn't doing more. He had our votes for his signature piece of legislation. He had moved on.

Four young people who were undocumented but came to America as children—Dreamers, as they were becoming commonly known—walked from Miami to Washington to raise awareness about the DREAM Act and immigration reform. They planned to end the walk by getting arrested in front of the White House. Nobody thought it was a very good idea for them to get arrested, because they were likely to get deported. I joined a group of other leaders who made a simple decision—arrest us, not them.

So on the first day of May in 2010, I was at Barack Obama's office again, but this time I wasn't invited. I was sitting on the sidewalk outside the White House gates. You are not allowed to sit on that sidewalk; you have to keep moving. If you don't move, the police will move you into their custody. More than twenty other national immigration activists and leaders were there, sitting and waiting. On their bullhorns, the US Park Police kept warning us that we had five minutes to leave. Finally, they told us we had five minutes to move before they would start taking us away. They even said it in Spanish, just in case we didn't speak English. I thought it was nice of them to make sure Spanish-language TV had good sound bites. The paddy wagons were parked about fifty feet away, their back doors open and ready. Thousands of angry protesters stood around us, spilling across Pennsylvania Avenue into Lafayette Park, cheering for all of us who were sitting quietly in front of the White House fence. They waved signs, and people chanted, "Obama, keep your promise." Lots of television cameras were rolling.

The May Day event at the White House drew more people than the organizers had expected, and the crowd was large, frustrated, and angry. We started the day by giving speeches and firing up the crowd. My message was simple, and was repeated over and over that day: We can't wait any longer. The president must act. When we finished, I walked across Pennsylvania Avenue with other leaders and we took our seats at the White House fence. The clock began to tick and nobody expected a last-minute reprieve. Once you decide something is worth getting arrested for, you make your decision and live with it. But the few minutes before the police arrive are still tense. You know that the headline CONGRESSMAN GUTIÉRREZ ARRESTED TODAY, is about to show up all over the news in your district and in Washington.

When our five minutes were up, the US Park Police slowly worked their way down the line of protesters. A large, friendly African American policeman got to me and said hello. He told me he used to be a Capitol Hill Police Officer. As he took out his handcuffs, he said, "I've always liked you. You were one of my favorites."

He was a nice guy. He put my hands behind my back and carefully tied the red plastic handcuffs around my wrists. He led me to the back of the wagon, while the cheers and chants from the protesters grew louder. The Park Police had not done a very good job of separating us from all of our supporters that day. We were led to the paddy wagon directly by a huge crowd of fans, calling out their support for us. The officer gave me a hand up the back steps of the wagon.

"Sorry, Congressman, I have to do my job," the officer said.

"You've got no problem with me," I said. "I'm just doing my job too."

On that sunny, warm day in May, I didn't really know what else I could do. I felt I had run out of choices. As a candidate, Obama made me promises about immigration. As president, he broke them. So I took a stand. I rode to the police station with my friends. Everyone was polite and businesslike. Within three hours, I had paid my fine and I was out, about to be on the news again. The Dreamers who had walked halfway across the country to beg the president to stop the deportations gave all of us flowers. I never doubted for a moment it was the right thing to do.

IN FRONT OF the White House, I had been cheered by thousands of people as I was led away in handcuffs, but back in the Capitol, some of my colleagues thought getting arrested was going too far.

At a meeting of the Hispanic Caucus, one of my colleagues looked at me like I was crazy. "Do we want Barack Obama to lose? Nobody is complaining more than we are," he said. Another told me he had heard from the White House that if I would stop complaining, Obama could actually do more. "We're going to cost a Democratic president his re-election," someone told me.

Others would say, "Go criticize the Republicans. They're the ones who hate us. The president is on our side."

I didn't agree with my friends. I criticize anti-immigrant zealots, including my Republican colleagues, all the time. I had been going on Lou Dobbs's show as a guest and stopped just short of calling him a xenophobe and a racist. But the press is much more interested in a Democrat getting arrested in front of a Democratic president's White House than a bunch of the usual partisan name-calling. I criticized anyone I thought was slowing our cause—it wasn't my fault that the press was fixated on a Democrat criticizing another Democrat.

The truth is that I have agreed with almost everything Barack Obama has done as president of the United States. I supported him from the beginning. Many of the people criticizing me had always been for Hillary Clinton. I've voted for his initiatives, said good things about his policies on issues ranging from credit-card reform to gun control. Instead of stopping dramatic health-care reform, my congressional Latino colleagues and I helped him make it happen. But on one issue—the most important issue to me—he refused to take action. That calling out someone in your own party gets you so much attention isn't really a compliment to me—it's a criticism of the way things work in Washington.

CIVIL DISOBEDIENCE still works. President Obama called an immigration meeting at the White House within a month of my arrest. He even invited me.

The last time I was in his neighborhood, they'd taken me out in handcuffs, so I assumed the president wasn't exactly going to give me a gift and sing my praises at the meeting. But before we sat down, a leading immigration activist from Chicago pulled me aside to pass on something he had been told in confidence.

"I wouldn't worry about the arrest too much. Someone I trust told me that they want to get past it. I think they want to make peace." I was all for peace, if the peace led to some progress. President Obama came into the meeting, welcomed everyone, and started.

"I want to begin by saying something to Luis Gutiérrez." He looked right at me. "You're being unfair. You say I can end these deportations, but you know I can't."

Barack Obama did not say it in a friendly way. He didn't say it like he wanted to get something off his chest and then move on and work together. He was mad, and he showed it. In that room, with other Latino members of Congress, it was important that he make a point—my criticisms were unfair. My Hispanic congressional colleagues have always been excellent in fighting for our issues, but at that moment, I could feel everyone inching away.

Of course, Barack Obama was wrong when he said he couldn't end the deportations. The Department of Homeland Security and ICE leaders made decisions every day about where to focus their resources. There are twelve million undocumented immigrants in our nation. They can't target all of them. It's up to the agency—an agency that takes its direction from the president of the United States—to decide how to prioritize their enforcement. We never asked Barack Obama to stop deporting everyone. We wanted him to give relief to families and Dreamers and immigrants who were working and posed no threat to our nation, the people I'd heard from on my tour. Our requests were reasonable—help families, help working people. He had the authority to do it.

But I've learned something over time about our president. Maybe I should have learned it the day he expressed dismay that my community was upset that he had voted for a seven-hundred-mile fence between the United States and the country many of my constituents came from. For a man who has to wake up every day to a Congress where half of the members hate him and a country full of angry editorials and bloggers and columnists, Barack Obama doesn't have the thickest skin. After all, I'm just one member of Congress; how upset should he really be at me for standing up on an issue that's critical to me?

At the end of the meeting, I asked the president if we could talk privately. I thought we should try again for a relationship that didn't involve arrests and complaining about arrests. We walked to the edge of the room. This time, as we stood alone, none of my colleagues thought I was getting a friendly slap on the back.

"Mr. President, I want to be on the team. But we need your leadership. You need to lead the fight. People need to see you are fighting for them, leading the charge," I told him.

He wasn't very interested. "Luis, I'm learning Washington is a place where people have to tear others down to build themselves up."

OK, I thought. I understand. It's clear Barack Obama doesn't like people getting arrested on his front sidewalk. The president who ran on his record as a community organizer and grassroots activist now thinks getting arrested is about ego and self-promotion, not about taking a stand for something worth fighting for. But I knew my arrest wasn't about me or anyone else trying to tear the president down. I thought, I'm representing immigrants who are asking you to keep your promise. We don't want to tear you down. We want to lift you up.

"Maybe we could meet? I'll come back to the White House and we'll talk about this so it doesn't happen again," I suggested to him.

He wasn't interested in a visit.

"Maybe we could start with a phone call," the president told me. At that moment, I thought we would never make any immigration progress in his first term.

I MIGHT HAVE been frustrated with Barack Obama, but at least the president wasn't calling immigrants cattle like some others were.

Steve King, my colleague from Iowa who deserves his own *Jeopardy!* category titled "A Member of Congress Actually Said This," complained on the House floor that we not only needed a fence between the United States and Mexico, but it should be electrified at the top, "just like we do with livestock." Not much later, he compared immigrants to dogs, saying we should only take "the pick of the litter, not the lazy ones sleeping in the corner."

It would be nice if the anti-immigrant rhetoric were limited to one Republican from Iowa with a fondness for comparing immigrants to canines and cows, but our foot-dragging president was surrounded by say-anything, anti-immigrant extremists, many of them members of Congress. But long before the president took office, the rhetoric had been intense, insulting, and often downright loony.

We were hearing military terms like "invader" and "surrender" a lot. Immigration opponents frequently looked at people whose fondest hope was to make five bucks an hour landscaping lawns or washing dishes as an organized, advancing militia, apparently well armed with rakes and pot-scrubbers.

"My message to them is, not in two weeks, not in two months, not in two years, never! We must be clear that we will not surrender America and we will not turn the United States over to the invaders from south of the border," was the message from Congressman Virgil Goode of Virginia. And some of the grassroots activists out in the states made Goode and King look moderate. One of the cofounders of the Minuteman Project, a do-it-yourself border control group, said, "We need the National Guard to clean out all our cities and round them up. . . . They have no problem slitting your throat and taking your money or selling drugs to your kids or raping your daughters, and they are evil people."

The talking heads on TV and radio weren't quite so blunt, but they've kept up the chatter about immigrants, mostly focusing on the key myths that immigrants are dangerous criminals and that they take away jobs. Media Matters, a media analysis think tank studied the massive amount of immigration chatter on cable television, and found that in 2007, the year we brought comprehensive immigration reform to the floor for a vote, just three hosts—Lou Dobbs, Bill O'Reilly, and Glenn Beck—did 402 shows that mentioned illegal immigration. Dobbs alone did almost 200—in just one year. Their shows bubbled with half-truths, misinformation, and downright lies.

They excelled at taking individual incidents and making outrageous generalizations. When an undocumented immigrant who was drinking caused a car crash that killed two people—obviously a tragedy—O'Reilly talked about it on thirteen separate shows. As Media Matters pointed out, that year, nearly 17,000 people were killed in alcohol-related auto accidents. But Bill O'Reilly didn't rail about America's urgent need to do something about drunk driving—a topic worthy of hundreds of shows—his point was that we needed to do something about "illegal aliens." More often, the talk-show "experts" just got things wrong. In addition to Dobbs's phantom leprosy outbreak, he said over and over again that one-third of the US prison population were "illegal immigrants." According to the Justice Department, it's just under 6 percent.

In this kind of toxic atmosphere, it would be easy to do what some of my colleagues suggested—just be patient with the president. But it's not enough just to be better than the extremists and call it a day. Only Barack Obama, even if he felt that he couldn't champion real immigration reform, could take immediate action to stop splitting up immigrant families with deportations. Glenn Beck wasn't in charge of anything except his mouth—Barack Obama held the lever of power that would allow more families to stay together.

CHAPTER TWENTY

Immigrants Can't Wait Any Longer

Ａ**FTER CALLING ME** out at the meeting for my arrest, Barack Obama didn't want me stopping by the White House to chat—whether I was invited or not. But he did take me up on my offer to talk on the phone. In the summer of 2010, he reached out to me and told me that we just didn't have the votes to pass comprehensive immigration reform.

"It's not about the votes, Mr. President," I told him. "My community needs to see that you are fighting for them, that you are leading. They want you to be the quarterback of the team. Maybe we'll win, maybe we'll lose, but people will give you credit for the fight. They'll know you're their champion," I told him.

Barack Obama is a smart politician, and he can count votes in Congress. We both knew that passing a comprehensive immigration bill was tough—maybe impossible. But in Washington, there is only one way to be certain of how many votes you have: you have to call the vote. People will tell you they are against something just because they don't want to have to take a stand on a tough issue. When the vote is called and the list of members of the US House is lit up like a giant scoreboard above the House floor and their position is about to be recorded, they might have a very different opinion. I just wanted my president to lead.

The president and I had a good conversation. He seemed to get it. Immigrants knew Barack Obama couldn't guarantee a victory. They just wanted his guarantee that he would fight. Not long after our discussion, he invited Bob Menendez and Nydia Velázquez and me to the White House to talk about what he could do. Nobody put me in handcuffs as I entered the building. We had a productive meeting, and one of our key agreements was to push for passage of a comprehensive immigration reform bill in the lame-duck session of Congress, after the fall elections.

We didn't know just how lame the Democrats would be in that session. By the time Barack Obama flew home to Chicago for a pre–Election Day rally in Grant Park, you could see the panic in the eyes of my Democratic friends in swing districts. Many of them knew their constituents were sending them home for good, the victims of a midterm voter revolt.

With the president coming home to Chicago for the rally, I thought about going to Grant Park to have a quick word with him about our next steps, to remind him we had agreed to push immigration aggressively after the election. Then I realized that most of the elected leadership of our state would probably be at Grant Park to stand with him. I knew the governor and the mayor were going, as well as several of my congressional colleagues. I did a quick mental calculation. If I went to meet *Air Force One* and Barack Obama at the airport, I would probably be the highest-ranking elected official who wasn't waiting for him at the rally. I had been to the airport to greet Bill Clinton before. The highest-ranking elected official always welcomes the president. Let everyone else stand in their powerful group at Grant Park, waiting for the presidential motorcade. I was going to the airport.

I went to O'Hare and arrived at the gate where the president's security was lining people up to meet the plane. The protocol officer looked at the handful of elected officials who were there. No governor, no senators, no mayor.

"Congressman, it looks like you're the senior official here. Could you please head the reception committee to meet the president?" he asked, like I might be doing him a favor.

"I would be honored to," I told him.

President Obama stepped off of the plane, looked around, and gave a presidential wave and smile for the reporters. He looked happy to be home. He started down the steps at a jaunty pace that conveyed a young and athletic president. Then he looked at the bottom of the steps and saw that the chairman of his welcoming party was Luis Gutiérrez. He paused only for a moment and then kept right on coming. There was no other way off the plane.

He smiled and shook my hand.

"Welcome home, Mr. President," I said. He thanked me and stopped for a minute.

"I was hoping we could start planning our lame-duck strategy for comprehensive immigration reform," I said, still smiling, still being friendly. After all, he had said we would.

"Right after the election, I'm going to Asia. Let's talk when I get back," he said, and the president was on his way.

Asia. There is a small window for the lame-duck session. We didn't have time, and the president couldn't quarterback the team from Asia. All of us had to work together, and the effort would need to start right after Election Day. I knew that with the president overseas, we couldn't build enough support to pass a comprehensive bill. I wanted to make some progress for immigrants before Nancy Pelosi handed the Speaker's gavel to John Boehner. At that moment, I thought we needed to try to fight for the Dreamers. It wasn't everything I wanted, or everything immigrants deserved, but it felt like the best we could do at the time. And the Dreamers needed our help.

ABOUT SIX WEEKS later, the House gallery was packed with Dreamers. There were hundreds more outside, standing with their friends and families, some bringing their moms and dads along for the historic vote in the US House.

The Dreamers were young, undocumented citizens. They had no legal standing in the United States and they could be deported at any time. To Rush Limbaugh and Lou Dobbs, they were just a statistic, another million or so people who were part of a faceless horde committing crimes, taking jobs, and sapping our government resources.

The truth was much more complicated. The Dreamers were undocumented immigrants who had come to America at a very young age, many of them as infants. The young woman who told Barack Obama about being carried across the border to America in her father's arms as a baby was a Dreamer—she arrived in Chicago when she was months old, but has no more legal standing in our country than a man who crossed the border when he was forty.

This puts the Dreamers in a very strange legal position: they are unwilling outlaws in the only country they've ever known. They've grown up here, gone to school here, graduated from high school here. Their parents may remember life in Mexico or the Dominican Republic—or Poland, for that matter—but for this entire class of immigrants, there has never been any home other than the United States. They are entirely American except for the fact that they are missing a piece of paper showing they are citizens.

Yet, when they turn eighteen, they face a huge legal dilemma. Newt Gingrich's Congress passed legislation in 1996 that makes it very difficult for them to go to college, because even though a Dreamer may have lived in Pilsen in my congressional district since she was six months old, she can't receive in-state tuition most places in America. It's harder to get a job, because she doesn't have a Social Security number or a green card to show a potential employer. Kids who've gone to kindergarten in America, played Little League baseball, served on the student council, played on the high school soccer team, or starred in school plays turn eighteen and are treated like fugitives from the law. Government estimates vary, but nearly two million immigrants fit into this category—they came here before they were sixteen years old and had virtually no way to become legal.

For years, many of us had championed the cause of Dreamers. My home state colleague Dick Durbin led the fight for legal relief in the US Senate. We held press conferences that focused on the many great kids who were caught in this immigration trap, high school valedictorians and student council presidents. But even modest proposals to ease the cost of college had never moved forward.

Finally, these young people were about to get a vote in Congress.

Our bill didn't make the Dreamers citizens immediately, but it gave them the ability to stay in the country, attend school, and get temporary work permits to hold jobs. If they stayed out of trouble, they would eventually be on the path to citizenship. It was obvious, commonsense legislation. We would simply allow decent young people who had always lived like all other Americans to continue to live like all other Americans.

Before the vote, when the president returned from Asia, Bob Menendez, Nydia Velázquez, and I met with him again. He agreed we didn't have time to pass comprehensive reform. But we were ready to go to work, and we started a full-court press for the Dreamers.

Still, the road to the vote was not easy. Virtually no Republicans were for it. The House Democratic leadership, though very supportive of the issue, didn't think we had enough support to pass the bill.

"Luis, I'm not sure we're going to make it. I don't want to risk losing a vote that's so important," Speaker—soon to be minority leader—Pelosi told me more than once. She didn't want one of her last acts in the majority to be a high-profile legislative defeat.

To help, we set up our own whip network—members of Congress who would round up votes—of pro-immigrant advocates to enhance the House leadership network. Our whip count showed the vote as being very close, but we felt that momentum was moving in our favor. And most important, the president was helping.

I talked to Congressman G. K. Butterfield of North Carolina, an ally of the president.

"G. K., are you with us on the DREAM Act? We need you," I said. His response was immediate.

"Are you kidding? The president called me. He was clear. Let me tell you Luis, I'm voting for the DREAM Act."

"I'll tell the president you're with us," I said to G. K. He was happy.

"You let the president know, G. K.'s his man," he said, laughing. As we worked to round up votes, it was clear that the president was making calls, and working for the bill. It was making a difference.

Still, even though our count was encouraging, Pelosi and Steny Hoyer kept telling us they didn't think we were going to make it.

"But our count looks good," I would say.

"Luis, nobody wants to hurt your feelings. People are telling you they're for it and telling us they're against it. It's hard to tell a Hispanic they are voting against an immigration bill," Steny said.

We kept working. Nydia Velázquez cornered every undecided member she could find. My Illinois colleague Jan Schakowsky worked nonstop. Barbara Lee kept checking with African-American members. It was hard, but I believed we were on the right side of an important issue. In my nearly twenty years in Congress, Democrats had hardly won an immigration vote, and hadn't passed one piece of legislation expanding rights to anyone. Democrats had a pent-up desire to do the right thing by immigrants. I was optimistic.

Heeding Steny and Nancy's advice, our team made a second request of anyone who'd told us they were voting yes.

"Can you go tell Nancy that you're with us? They think you're just being nice to me because I'm Latino," I said to people.

My colleagues would chuckle and trudge off to one of the leaders to say they were voting yes.

Eventually, Nancy came up to me. "OK. Enough is enough. We get your point." She laughed.

It was still hard. Two of my moderate colleagues from Illinois had lost their elections back home and this would be one of their last votes.

I asked Melissa Bean for her vote, and she answered with a frustrated response that had become the unthinking party line of many Democrats: "Why are we doing this? This is bad politics. It's bad for our party. It's going to lead to more losses in the future," she said, even though her district was increasingly filled with immigrants and Latinos.

I tried another colleague, Bill Foster. He had lost to a Tea Party candidate in a district that had a growing number of immigrants. He paused and thought for a moment.

"You know what? It's the right thing to do," he said. "I'm going to run again and this vote will be part of my legacy," he said. Two years later, Bill Foster was back in Congress. Melissa Bean wasn't.

As the vote started, our party leadership still wasn't sure what would happen. Neither was I, but I felt good. I watched a few key members.

Foster, yes. Butterfield, yes. Every single African-American member supported the bill. Even Melissa Bean was a yes, proving that you never know how many votes you have until you call the bill. Within a few minutes, I knew we were going to make it. The Dreamers in the gallery started to clap, then cheer, then erupt in celebration. It was close—216 to 198, but we had a victory. Just a few Republicans voted with us. Democrats did it, almost alone.

With the Dreamers' help, we showed the world that immigrants had muscle, that we could win a vote. We showed that we were ready to fight back. Despite Dobbs and Hannity and Limbaugh, despite Republicans who compared immigrants to cattle, despite state legislatures who wanted to take every civil right from immigrants, we had won the vote in the US House of Representatives.

OUR CELEBRATION didn't last long. We won for Dreamers in the House, but we lost in the Senate. And John Boehner and the Republicans were about to take over. Not long after the vote, Omaira had to come into the bedroom after midnight to wake me up with the news that the White House was on the phone. The president needs to stay up later than members of Congress. He wanted me and a small group of Latino members to come to the White House to talk about the next steps to help immigrants.

We met just before Christmas, and Obama said that the Republican wave had killed our chances for comprehensive immigration reform. We couldn't make any gains legislatively. We agreed. He said he still wanted to play defense to protect immigrants. Then he asked us to "put on our thinking caps" to come up with ideas for what he could do. When the commander-in-chief tells me to put on my thinking cap, I do it. My staff and I devoted our holiday to finding ways the president could help and protect immigrants. The Republicans might control the house, but Barack Obama is still the most powerful man in the world, we thought. Soon, our thinking caps were brimming with suggestions. We recommended the president use the executive authority he had to direct ICE to use discretion on which immigrants to deport. He could take action to help the Dreamers. He could protect the undocumented parents of the four million or so American citizen children in our nation. He could protect the undocumented husbands and wives of American citizens who were raising families. I wasn't asking him to ignore or bend any laws. We just wanted him to direct the resources of the US government away from hardworking immigrant families and children who were not a threat to anyone.

We took our idea to the Hispanic Caucus. We vetted it with immigration experts and advocates. They all thought it was aggressive and innovative, but that it was the right thing to do. A former general counsel to the Immigration and Naturalization Service had written a memo suggesting the proposals were entirely reasonable. A group of law professors and immigration law experts wrote an op-ed saying it was appropriate and a good idea. We had won a vote to protect Dreamers, showing there was widespread support for it as a decent, commonsense policy. We just wanted the president to act on it. We put our proposals in a memo and waited for a response.

I KNEW we were in trouble when I saw Eva Longoria on television talking about immigration policy.

She was standing outside the White House, where she had just come from a meeting with the president and a group of other "influential Hispanics" to talk about immigration. Barack Obama had announced that he had invited "influential Hispanics from across the country to discuss the importance of fixing the broken immigration system" and to take part in a "constructive national conversation on this important issue." These influential Hispanics did not include any members of Congress.

Obama didn't just invite a Desperate Housewife. Among the influential Hispanics were other actors and celebrities. There were television commentators and radio hosts. It was the spring of 2011, almost five months after we won for Dreamers in the House. As I watched Eva Longoria and others talk to reporters, I knew the president's response to my "thinking cap" plan was clear.

The message Longoria and others were delivering to reporters that day was that they had just completed a very productive meeting with the president. They had talked about deportations. He had made it clear to them that he couldn't just stop deporting certain people or groups of people. It wasn't up to him. His hands were tied. He had to uphold the law. His chief White House adviser on immigration policy, Cecilia Muñoz, held a conference call with reporters to say, "The president can't simply say there are laws he will choose not to enforce." In the early summer, he traveled to El Paso to give a speech in which he said he could not use his discretion to protect Dreamers and other deserving immigrants.

When he cleared the movie stars from his schedule and met with the Hispanic Caucus and we pushed him to take action, he told us that if he tried to protect certain groups of immigrants from deportation that John Boehner and the Republicans would simply take his discretion away.

I thought, what is the point of having all of that presidential power if you won't use it? Bob Menendez, our only Democratic Latino US senator, responded immediately. He told him clearly that he would filibuster in the Senate to guarantee that the president could preserve his ability to take executive action.

"Even if it costs me my re-election, I will fight to protect you from any Republican attempt to dilute your power," Menendez said.

It was a courageous and forceful pledge from Bob. But the president wasn't budging, even though our senator had just offered him the ultimate Senate weapon to defend him. He kept telling us he couldn't do what we were asking, but I believed he was wrong. More than a few law professors and constitutional experts agreed with me. To prove my point, I'd already decided to take my show on the road again, highlighting the deportations and asking for relief for the Dreamers and families. Before we started, I arranged a press conference in Washington to announce the beginning of another tour and to continue to push for prosecutorial discretion for young people who needed help.

THE DAY BEFORE the press conference, I received a call from Valerie Jarrett, an old friend from Chicago and one of the president's top advisers. Valerie was blunt.

"I'm asking you to cancel your press conference and cancel your tour," Valerie said to me. When my staff told me Valerie was on the line, I expected a complaint, not an actual request to cancel meetings with immigrants. I told her I couldn't possibly do that.

"You and the president share a constituency," she said.

I thought about what she really meant. I decided that she was suggesting that the president was very popular in my district, that I should be worried about the political fallout of challenging the president.

"Are you threatening me?" I asked.

"I'm simply asking you to cancel your tour and press conference," she said.

She didn't ask that I delay it, or slightly change the message. Valerie Jarrett just said stop. The president had helped us with the Dreamers just last year, I thought. Why should he be bothered by a simple press conference? Our conversation was brief. My answer was no. That gave Valerie time to call the other members of Congress who were coming to my press conference and ask them to stay away.

My staff and I started getting calls from colleagues who suddenly said they couldn't come, who had a last-minute change of plans. I understood. Valerie's a powerful person, and most people don't want to take on the president.

Keith Ellison, a progressive leader from Minnesota and someone who has stood up for immigrants again and again, called me. He sounded worried.

"I just got a call from the White House," he said.

"You're not the only one," I told him. "I understand if you can't come, but this is important for our families. If we allow them to stop this, then more families will suffer. This isn't about me or the president, it's about those families. Please come." If someone as steadfast as Keith was wavering, I wasn't sure if I would have anyone standing with me the next day.

Keith came. So did eight or nine other members of Congress, including Jan Schakowsky, one of the president's closest allies. Valerie and the White House had probably kept just as many away. I profusely thanked my colleagues who showed up. I'm sure the president wasn't pleased with them for sticking with me. It was a courageous thing for them to do; my whole life I've been getting people who stand by me in trouble.

The press conference and the tour, where I went to more than a dozen cities and stood with many Hispanic Caucus colleagues to protest deportations, didn't move the president. A group of twenty senators, including his close confidant Dick Durbin, wrote to him asking him to take action to stop deportations. It didn't matter. "I can't do it," Obama kept saying over and over. Yes, you can, we said to him. In July, I sent him a letter, asking him yet again to consider providing relief for the Dreamers. You have the authority. Experts say so, I wrote to him. A former general counsel of your agency says you can do it. Three of my fellow members of Congress, wrote along with me. If you can't take action, we wrote, we think civil disobedience to protest is appropriate. I felt even more strongly about it than about my previous protest before my first arrest. What good was electing a president if he wasn't willing to protect the civil rights of American citizen children and kids who had lived virtually all of their lives in America?

The president wrote back to us right away. He couldn't do what we were asking, and the only real answer was comprehensive immigration reform.

In July, I was in front of the White House again. As the Park District Police started again with their warnings to stand up and keep moving in the secure area, I looked around for my other congressional colleagues who had signed the letter and threatened to protest. They were not going to be joining me in the back of any police cars that day. Along with twenty other protesters, I was taken away again to be booked and then released after paying the fine.

After Bob Menendez stood up to him at our caucus meeting, around the time of my arrest and Obama's new fascination with the "influential Hispanics" of Hollywood and Wisteria Lane, the president lost interest in the Hispanic Caucus. Maybe I don't blame him. We were about the only progressive, Democratic group of members consistently putting pressure on him. And we wouldn't let go. It's hard to oppose your president, and I was proud of our Hispanic Caucus for standing up and never letting President Obama off the hook. After May 2011, the Democratic president of the United States wouldn't meet with our caucus again until he was re-elected and sworn in as president.

Throughout the summer on my tour, I made my message clear—the president doesn't need action from the Republican-controlled Congress—he can act right now to stop his administration from deporting more than 1,200 people per day, many of them kids and Dreamers and parents of American citizen children. In July, the president spoke in Washington to the National Council of La Raza to address activists from across the country. The room was filled with Dreamers. I believe our president expected a friendly crowd.

He spoke in general terms about his support for issues that are important to Latinos—access to education and health care. Then he turned to immigration.

"Now, I know some people want me to bypass Congress and change the laws on my own," Obama said. He wasn't expecting a response. But he got one. The audience shouted back, "Yes, you can! Yes, you can!"

He looked surprised. He paused, then answered.

"That's not how our democracy functions. That's not how our Constitution is written," he said, but "Yes, you can" echoed through the hall.

I thought that day, with the crowd at the National Council of La Raza interrupting the president and telling him that he could do what we had been asking for months, that we had turned the tide. It wasn't just that pushy Luis Gutiérrez pestering the president. He was hearing it everywhere he went.

EVENTUALLY, he even started hearing it from Republicans. Senator Marco Rubio was planning on introducing legislation in the Senate to help Dreamers. It wasn't nearly as far-reaching as the bill we'd passed in the House, but still would provide help for Dreamers to stay in the country without constant fear of deportation. It was far from a perfect plan, but it was better than nothing. And it showed at least one Republican was interested in stopping the constant vilification of immigrants. True, he pushed for his proposal less than six months before Election Day and he likely hoped it would help Mitt Romney in Florida, but that was probably irrelevant if you were a good kid who had lived in the United States all your life and didn't want to get sent to live in a country far away from home.

The president didn't like Rubio's plan at all. He had already stopped meeting with me and the caucus. About the only contact I had with him was when Valerie Jarrett had called to bully me about my press conference. But the president thought the Rubio situation was urgent enough that he sent Cecilia Muñoz all the way over to Capitol Hill to talk to the Hispanic Caucus.

We met with Cecilia in a conference room in the basement of the Capitol. Cecilia had been one of the immigrant community's most ardent advocates before she joined the Obama administration. Now, most of the time I didn't know whether to feel sorry for her or be enraged at her. Instead of fighting for immigrants, she spent most of her time explaining why the most powerful man in the world could do little to help them. It's a great Washington, DC, puzzle, how so many good people get lost in the bureaucracy and insulation of the White House.

Her message that day was simple: we need you to stand firm against Rubio's proposal. She talked about how it didn't go far enough, but the unspoken reason was obvious: the president didn't want a Republican—and an ally of Mitt Romney—to be seen as doing more for immigrants than he was.

"We cannot waiver on our commitment to citizenship. Rubio's proposal would endorse the idea of second-class citizenship and create larger problems for us on immigration reform in the future," she said.

The caucus members looked to me to give a response. It's a blessing and a curse. I'm often up first when it's time to deliver bad news to the president.

"Cecilia—we don't have a Rubio problem. We have a deportation problem. As I see it, Rubio wants to help solve the deportation problem. It might not be perfect, but it is more than the president is doing.

And you want us to oppose it? It helps the Dreamers. So let me be clear. If Rubio's bill makes it to the House, I'm voting for it. Not only that, I will work with Rubio to help him pass it and I will encourage others to vote for it. The president can fix this with the stroke of a pen, so why would you come here and ask the Hispanic Caucus to be against something that helps immigrants?"

The members of our caucus spoke up. Some of us had already met with Rubio. One by one, people said they would support the bill. The president of the United States wasn't even talking to us. Rubio's bill was mediocre? It was political? So what? It would help immigrants. We made it clear that we were for it.

Cecilia responded—once again—by saying that the president simply couldn't do anything about deportations. My friend Lucille Roybal-Allard of Los Angeles, a calm and effective legislator who always stands up for her people, became so frustrated with hearing again that they couldn't do anything about deportations that she left the room in anger. It takes a lot to make somebody as levelheaded as Lucille leave a room. Cecilia went back to the White House with a clear message—the Congressional Hispanic Caucus was not solving Barack Obama's Rubio problem.

Cecilia didn't know it at the time, and neither did we, but we *had* actually solved it for him. After months of me being on his back, of the caucus standing firm, of hearing chants at La Raza and now with a Republican doing more than he was, Barack Obama didn't have any choice.

FINALLY, five months before Election Day, less than a month after Cecilia delivered the bad news to the White House, Barack Obama announced that he would take historic action to help Dreamers.

He signed a memo calling for deferred action for undocumented young people who'd come to the United States when they were younger than sixteen and who want to pursue an education or military service. Deferred Action for Childhood Arrivals, or DACA, protected undocumented young people from deportation and allowed them to work legally. In short, all across my district, and all across America, over one million young people who grew up here could pursue their futures in their home country, the United States of America. He didn't do everything we had been asking, but it was a hugely helpful step.

I was with my family in Puerto Rico when he made the announcement. My staff told me, and I had to have them explain it twice.

"He just did it—just like that?" I asked. They said he did. And Univision was on their way over to talk to me.

In his press release announcing the dramatic change in policy, he didn't mention that he had been telling the entire immigrant-rights community for nearly a year and a half that he couldn't do it. That he had traveled around the country making speeches saying he couldn't do it. He didn't say that because Luis Gutiérrez and the Hispanic Caucus had been on his back forever about it, he was finally doing it. He didn't mention that he singled me out during a White House meeting after I was arrested and said, "You say I can end these deportations, but you know I can't." He didn't say that in the end he was outflanked by Marco Rubio. He just did it. And it was the right thing to do. And even though it had taken much longer than necessary, I was extremely grateful for it.

In the end, all it took was for him to give the Department of Homeland Security some clear direction. He did just what I had recommended when he asked me to put on my thinking cap. As I talked to reporters all afternoon and into the evening, it felt like one of our greatest victories, the culmination of years of activism.

"You said all along he could do it," the Univision reporter said. It almost made me laugh. Now that it was done, it seemed so easy. For years, I'd alternated between outrage and hope for my president, but I always would rather have supported him than opposed him. All I had ever asked was that he use the immense power of his office to lead on behalf our people. I always treated the fight for immigrants as a civil-rights struggle, and I believe it is. I simply wanted Barack Obama to view it the same way, to take the same courageous stand for immigrants that presidents before him had taken for African Americans.

And now he had done it. It was only a first step, but it was an important first step. In the first six months after he took action, nearly a half million Dreamers applied for help and were kept safe from deportation. Was it comprehensive immigration reform? No. Was it done later than it needed to be, done for political reasons? Probably. But all sorts of great things get done for political reasons. That doesn't mean they aren't great. From the minute Barack Obama took action for the Dreamers, I said positive, supportive things about him. Just as crowds had chanted against him before, they now cheered his leadership for the Dreamers.

It helped that Mitt Romney had made the critical error of listening to the wackiest anti-immigrant zealots in his party when it came to immigration. His plan was for millions of immigrants to voluntarily leave the country, and take their American-citizen children with them. I went to the Republican National Convention in Tampa and bashed Romney. I traveled to Nevada and Florida and Colorado and bashed Romney. I went to Ohio on Election Day and bashed Romney. "Barack Obama stood up for the Dreamers. We need Barack Obama in the White House," I said over and over again. The Obama campaign called me regularly with requests for campaign stops and radio interviews, for Spanish-language TV, for any work I could do for our president.

I was glad to do it. After all, we'd started out as friends. All it took was four years of fighting, two arrests, boxes of petitions, and two national tours, and he took historic action to protect immigrants. Maybe we could get along again after all.

CHAPTER TWENTY-ONE

Too Puerto Rican for America, Too American for Puerto Rico

N EARLY 2011, while I was still busy arguing with my president, I started receiving angry phone calls that had nothing to do with Barack Obama or immigration.

"You can't believe what is happening in Puerto Rico," friends and activists would say.

Juano and Lucy, who now lived in Puerto Rico, were much more blunt with Soraida and me. "Luis, this new governor is out of control," Juano told us.

The same day America elected a progressive new president in 2008, Puerto Rico chose a very different leader. The island elected my former colleague in Congress and resident commissioner of Puerto Rico, Luis Fortuño, as their governor. Fortuño was an enthusiastic supporter of statehood. He was a Republican too. For me, he was two-for-two in promoting paths that led the Puerto Rican people in exactly the wrong direction.

While my opinion didn't really matter, the people of Puerto Rico soon learned that Luis Fortuño wasn't just another Republican. He governed in a way that would make Newt Gingrich or Sarah Palin stand up and cheer.

He threatened to lay off 30,000 workers and eventually put nearly

15,000 out of work. He pushed for a natural-gas pipeline that cut across the island, through forests and near homes. The plan enraged environmentalists, who thought pristine parts of the island's natural beauty were under attack. His administration attacked Puerto Rico's Colegio de Abogados, the activist bar association in Puerto Rico, a group that had always been committed to issues of social justice and civil rights. The leader was harassed and eventually thrown in jail.

But it was his conflict with students at the University of Puerto Rico that had everyone talking. Early on, Fortuño and his government announced an austerity plan that dramatically raised tuition and fees at the University of Puerto Rico. Students at the University of Puerto Rico haven't changed a whole lot since I was there, and they were angry and showed it. My friends and I once agitated for Puerto Rican independence. To me, protesting was part of the college curriculum. It's a way to learn what's important to you. Protest is practically in the DNA of college kids.

But to Luis Fortuño and the enforcers of law and order who populated Puerto Rico's statehood government, the student protests apparently looked like a civil insurrection. He decided a swift response was needed. The front gates to the University of Puerto Rico—gates I'd walked through hundreds of times as a student—were removed by the government, taken away because they had become a gathering place for protesters and a symbol of opposition to the governor and his tuition increases. The government hired a private security force that disrupted protests. Video of the security forces restraining and arresting students, particularly female students, filled the evening news and enraged Puerto Ricans. When students marched to the state capitol to confront Fortuño, the Puerto Rican Senate simply closed its doors and held its session in private—no students, no protesters, no cameras allowed. They put their riot squad in front of the capitol and attacked students who tried to get in. The government made its position clear: it didn't want to win a debate with the students, it didn't want any debate at all.

What I watched on the news of the events unfolding in Puerto Rico seemed surreal. I wondered if Luis Fortuño had met any of the people he was elected to govern. Telling Puerto Ricans they can't protest is like telling a starving man he can't eat. Debate and argue and talk is what we do. I was surprised Luis Fortuño thought he could simply decide the discussion was over.

The more I saw, the more I wanted to help. I had spoken out on Puerto Rico many times in Congress. I took on the US Navy about their training exercises on Vieques, a small island just east of the Puerto Rican mainland. Since 1941, the Navy had been using Vieques for target practice, dropping bombs and storming the beaches and using beautiful Puerto Rican land for whatever military exercise suited them. In 1999, a stray bomb from a Navy jet killed David Sanes, a Puerto Rican security guard at Vieques, crystallizing long-standing anger and opposition toward military use of the island.

The Puerto Rican people had protested and marched, and I joined them. I met with Defense Department and Navy officials, letting them know I opposed the military exercises. I delivered letters and petitions of protest from Puerto Rican leaders and activists. Navy leaders listened politely and made their position clear: they weren't going anywhere. Eventually, just as hundreds of other Puerto Ricans were doing, I traveled to Vieques, entered the restricted bombing area, and waited to be arrested for standing up to the US military. I spent a night in jail with Robert Kennedy Jr., another Kennedy willing to do more than talk about fairness and justice.

When I traveled to Vieques for the protests and sit-ins, I met with the man whose speeches in our small town square had inspired me to follow him around the island. Despite being diagnosed with prostate cancer, Rubén Berríos camped out in the restricted area for nearly a year to show his opposition to the bombing. He eventually also was sent to jail. We talked about our common commitment to returning Vieques to the Puerto Rican people. I thanked him for his leadership and the example he was setting. And I told him that if he hadn't come to San Sebastián, and I hadn't stood in the plaza and listened to him speak with pride and passion for an independent Puerto Rico, I would likely never have been in a position to talk to US military leaders about Vieques.

Finally, the Navy understood that they couldn't continue bombing the island. Fishermen surrounded Vieques with small boats. Protesters kept sneaking into the restricted area. The Puerto Rican people wanted their island back. After more than three years of protests, the Navy announced that they would leave Vieques. Today, Vieques is coming back. The people are still overcoming years of bombing and contamination, but some areas are now beautiful nature preserves and the island is a tourist destination and a place for the Puerto Rican people to live and work.

But in 2011, the challenge confronting Puerto Rico had nothing to do with the US military. Puerto Ricans were mad at their own governor, and asking: How do I make a difference? In the nearly thirty years since Dan Rostenkowski's precinct captains knocked on my door, I've learned that sometimes the best you can do is speak out. A great thing about the US Congress is that you can work to cut everyone's pay and you can annoy the president of your own party, but nobody can keep you from speaking. When my constituents re-elect me, they give me the rare privilege to raise my voice on the floor of the US House.

So that's what I did. In February of 2011, I gave a five-minute speech in the House about the civil-rights abuses in Puerto Rico. I defended the rights of students who wanted to protest tuition hikes. As I spoke, Arab Spring was happening halfway around the world, and I noted the irony that we were rightly cheering Egyptians standing up for their freedom but ignoring what was happening in our American backyard.

When you speak out, you usually learn something. That day, I learned that quite a few people were grateful for the effort, but I learned even more from the reaction of the ruling party of Puerto Rico.

The resident commissioner of Puerto Rico, an ally of the governor, was asked by reporters about my remarks. He told people that only he could speak for the people of Puerto Rico, and that after my speech, he had looked for me, and I was lucky he didn't find me. He repeated the same idea a couple of times to reporters, saying I would have been sorry if he had found me. He didn't detail what he was going to do, but I got the impression that maybe I should have been prepared to defend myself.

But it was the action of the Puerto Rico House of Representatives and Senate that taught me the most. After my modest five-minute speech, they introduced a motion to censure me, to put the government of Puerto Rico officially on record as condemning my remarks as "very hurtful and offensive to the honor and dignity of all Puerto Ricans." The House, which was dominated by Statehooders, spent the better part of a day criticizing my speech.

The reaction to my simple five-minute statement helped me understand how serious the problem was in Puerto Rico. I had spoken about civil rights and free speech. The official government reaction was that I should sit down and shut up. I wanted to send them a note thanking them for the clarification. It was as if I had accused them of being thieves and they responded with indignant outrage, and then demanded I turn over all my money.

I went to the House floor the following week and talked about Puerto Rico again. When the Statehooders sent me a copy of the articles of censure, I framed them and put them up on the wall in my congressional office.

Soon, I was receiving invitations to speak on the island. I accepted the invitation of the Colegio de Abogados. Their auditorium in San Juan was jammed beyond capacity. It was filled with television and print reporters, lawyers, and environmentalists. Some of the students and laid-off workers had found their way in. They set up an overflow room for people who couldn't get into the main room. It was an enthusiastic—almost raucous—crowd. People who were frustrated and felt under attack were happy to hear from an ally, particularly one who happened to be a member of Congress. Welcoming me to the meeting was Noel Colón Martínez—my candidate for governor of Puerto Rico in 1972—a leader whose commitment to Puerto Rico and civil rights had not wavered once, and whose speeches nearly forty years earlier had inspired me.

When I speak in Puerto Rico I often tell the story of one of the first times I said anything out loud on the island, my first day at Manuel Méndez Liciaga High School. I think back to Señor Hernández's classroom, and remember how I pronounced my name then. I wipe away a lifetime of the correct Spanish pronunciation and make myself that awkward outsider again, a kid lost on a distant island. "My name is Lou-is Goo-terrez," I will say to the crowd. People always laugh. But then I tell the rest of the story, of how isolated I felt, and people understand that it wasn't so funny for a fifteen-year old kid who felt adrift.

At the Colegio that night, I told of the time Omaira and Maritza and I were singled out by the Capitol Hill security guard and told to "go back where we came from." It's a story that resonates with Latinos, whether they are Puerto Ricans born as US citizens or undocumented immigrants. Almost all Latinos have endured a moment when they've encountered a person who regarded them as nothing more than a blur of brown skin or curly hair, a suspect with a complicated last name or unusual accent. When Latinos hear about the kid who was born in the *barrio* and made it to Congress but was still told in the US Capitol to go back home, I always see people nodding and remembering the time they or someone they knew became a stereotype instead of a person.

But in my speech at the bar association that night, I ended the story by adding something different. I said it because people around the governor kept insisting I didn't have any right to speak out on Puerto Rican issues, that I simply wasn't qualified.

I said, "It's the story of my life. I'm too Puerto Rican for America, and too American for Puerto Rico."

In Washington, I was plenty Puerto Rican for the Capitol Hill security guard. In Chicago, I looked Puerto Rican enough for the white cops who'd line me and my friends up against cars on the street corner. Ed Vrdolyak and the white guys running City Hall saw a very Puerto Rican guy who wanted Harold Washington to be in charge of Chicago. But in Puerto Rico, I was too American for Señor Hernández and the girl who wanted the "gringo" to stop bothering her, or for the kids in the school hallways who mocked my Spanish. And now, the Statehooders thought I was so American I was unqualified to criticize their governor.

Before the speech, I had dinner with Archbishop Roberto González Nieves, the archbishop of San Juan, and he echoed the comforting words of the independence leaders of my youth: "From the moment you were conceived in your mother's womb, you were Puerto Rican," he said.

But the truth was, I was caught in between, just like some people I've come to know very well. Just like America's immigrants. On my tours around the country, people who've sat in church basements and listened to me speak will sometimes come up and ask, "Why did you come here all the way from Chicago?" The answer begins in the streets of Lincoln Park, and on that first plane trip from Chicago to San Juan. I want to fight for immigrants because I've been an immigrant in my own land. Twice. I know what it's like to feel isolated, left out.

I knew I had to fight back, but as is true for immigrants today, I couldn't have done it without help. When I felt most alone, Luis and Tino reached out and befriended me. Instead of treating me as an outsider, they accepted me as a friend. The Independentistas in San Sebastián pulled me aside and said, "You are Puerto Rican. Don't let anyone tell you that you aren't." I listened, and I sold my newspapers on the plaza and followed Rubén Berríos around the island. I dared anyone to be more Puerto Rican than me. Mrs. Badillo believed in me, and told me my ability to speak English had value. I studied, and when I did well on my college boards, a quality, affordable college education was available. I might have felt lost, but good people came forward and extended their hands to help me.

So when the busboy at a restaurant thanks me for helping him, I'm really just repaying a debt. Is it unreasonable to want immigrants to have the same help I received? I see myself in those busboys. I see my parents. My mom once lived in a hut in the hills of a small town in Puerto Rico. My dad once had nothing but a job running the projector at the movie theater. She caught his eye, and he wanted to make a life with her, so they left what little they had behind, climbed on a plane, and flew away to Chicago. They worked hard and they built a future for Ada and me.

It wasn't always easy. My parents had to fight for what they had, and so have I. That night at the Colegio de Abogados, I was reminded how good it felt to stand up and speak out without worrying about offending anyone, even the governor of Puerto Rico.

As I spoke, I felt close to the people in that packed room at the bar association in San Juan. So many of the faces were familiar to me. There were people who had been Puerto Rican independence leaders ever since I was a sixteen-year-old trying to learn all I could from them. My mentor, Noel Colón Martínez, introduced me and sat next to me as I spoke. There were students who had protested and reminded me of a young Luis Gutiérrez at the University of Puerto Rico, or Albany, or Northeastern. *Claridad*, the newspaper I sold to Soraida as a student at Northeastern, my Puerto Rican newspaper of record for years, was there covering my remarks. There were young legislators who were happy to hear somebody stand up to the governor, and I hoped I motivated them just a fraction as much as Harold Washington had motivated me. I saw friends: people who'd opposed the Navy training at Vieques, people who'd supported me when the government censured me, people who wanted the same things I did for Puerto Rico.

When I finished my speech, delivered in Spanish—the language of my mother and father, and all of my Puerto Rican ancestors who came before them—the room was still for a moment, and then the quiet space filled with the cheers of my friends. And I knew I was home.

AFTER YEARS of being an outsider, I'm feeling a little more at home in Washington, DC, as well. On Election Day in 2012, America suddenly woke up to the power of the Latino and immigrant vote.

For me, the awakening to the changing face of America was heartening, but it was frustrating too. Why did it take so long? The Latino electoral storm that hit America in November 2012 had been gathering for years. It was obvious to anyone paying attention that it was coming, and just as obvious that we should have addressed my community's needs sooner. The Republican Party, and a few of my Democratic friends, had ignored a lot of thunder and lightning and were left standing in the downpour on Election Day.

Now everyone wants an umbrella. It's gratifying to be in the middle of the discussion. For years in Congress, I was like the guy at the cocktail party who corners everyone and talks only about one topic, on and on until people become uneasy and look for somebody to come along and change the subject and save them. "Don't get stuck with that Gutiérrez guy. All he'll do is chatter about immigration," people might say. But now, all of a sudden everyone's talking about it—even the most popular people at the party.

That it took so long for people to catch on to the power of the Latino vote and the need for comprehensive immigration reform is frustrating, but that we're almost there is incredibly rewarding. We are about to make history for millions of immigrants who want to be full participants in American society. That is a reason to celebrate.

The first week back after the election, in the midst of the din of astonished TV talking heads who were thrilled by their discovery that about thirteen million Latinos had voted in the election for president of the United States, many of my colleagues walked up to me and simply said, "Congratulations." People slapped me on the back, shook my hand, laughed, and said, "We're actually going to get this done," or "Luis, you tried to tell us." I knew I hadn't done anything alone. Activists across the country and organizations that fought and all of the Dreamers and the determination of the Congressional Hispanic Caucus kept the pressure on.

We wouldn't give up, and on Election Day, more Latino representatives than ever found their way to Congress, and they came ready to fight for immigrants. Whenever I discuss comprehensive immigration reform with them, I'm talking with new friends who don't know anything about my history as the upstart reformer who made Tom Foley and Dan Rostenkowski so mad they ostracized and mocked me. That's ancient history. Now I'm just a guy who keeps telling anyone who will listen that immigrants are good for America and we need new policies that help them contribute even more. Instead of threatening fistfights in the cloakroom, or arguing about what I said on *60 Minutes*, I'm working with my colleagues on an issue I've lived and breathed for almost two decades. Sometimes I almost feel like an elder statesman, which reminds me that it's probably time to start some new trouble.

Of course, if I want trouble, there's always my relationship with our president. But I'm working on that.

Latinos were crucial to Barack Obama's victory. After nearly four years of telling me that he simply couldn't do much to help immigrants, Obama took bold action for Dreamers, and it made all the difference for him with our community. Once he embraced the idea that he could take executive action to protect immigrants, he touted it in his campaign like it was as natural to him as talking about change and hope. He filmed Spanish-language television ads that focused on Dreamers, and he equated their desire to build a better future in America with the very same hopes he has for his daughters. It was powerful stuff, and it worked. Latinos always wanted to be with Barack Obama, he just needed to give them a reason.

After he was re-elected, Barack Obama finally invited the Hispanic Caucus back to the White House. He had already announced his strong support for getting comprehensive immigration reform done quickly. Of course, post-election, after Latinos and immigrants had flexed their electoral muscle, everyone was for comprehensive immigration reform, speaking up like kids at a birthday party arguing over who gets the first piece of cake. Where were all you guys last year, I thought? Or every year for the last two decades, for that matter? Even John McCain was for comprehensive immigration reform again.

At the meeting with the president, Bob Menendez, Xavier Becerra and I—the three members of Congress who were most involved in the delicate negotiations to come up with a Comprehensive Immigration Reform bill that could get some Republican support and pass—asked the president to hold off on introducing his own legislation. It seemed ironic, after four years of pushing and pleading, but now the game had changed. The president's opportunity to be the sole leader on reform had passed. To get it done, we needed to balance some delicate politics in the House and Senate. We needed to round up votes.

Barack Obama, my friend from Chicago, the man I'd endorsed before any other Latino member of Congress, looked at us like we were crazy.

"After four years of constantly complaining—and not exactly being subtle about it—now you want me to wait?" the president said.

Well, yes, we did. I have my moments of contention with Barack Obama, but I almost always support him. I frequently disagree with him on one vital issue, but there are a couple hundred Republican members of Congress who disagree with him on everything. They would vote against sunlight if it was sponsored by Barack Obama. We needed him to be patient, so we could get some Republicans to support us. To his credit, even though he complained, he listened to us, and he waited.

But it was that word he used—"subtle"—that stuck with me. He was right; on immigration, I was never subtle with him. I'm just not very good at subtle. But there's nothing subtle about deportations, either. They tear families apart. If you want to stop deportations, and help immigrants, sometimes you can't be subtle with powerful people, even a president you want to support. It's much easier to stand up to people in power if you view the ability to confront them as a privilege that shouldn't be wasted. I'm not concerned that the president of the United States might be mad at me, I'm amazed that I'm in a position where I can make the president of the United States mad.

After all, I'm the Puerto Rican son of a cabdriver and a factory worker, a kid who chopped up pig innards and swept the floor of an unsuccessful restaurant, a guy who had to drive a cab on the night shift to make ends meet. And somehow, forty years after my dad packed us up and took us on the road, I ended up sitting across the table from the president of the United States negotiating comprehensive immigration reform. And nobody ever stepped in and tapped me on the shoulder to tell me there's been a terrible mistake and I need to go back to an apartment in Lincoln Park, or San Sebastián. I'm still here.

So when people tell me I should be a little nicer, or try to get along, I think, Why? What do I have to lose? I've reached my dreams. Actually, I've done more than a kid sleeping on a cot in a Chicago apartment could ever have imagined dreaming.

NOT LONG AFTER I was first elected to Congress, I visited my parents in Puerto Rico. I had become a mini-celebrity in San Sebastián. To my mom and dad's friends and neighbors, I was no longer the kid who'd left the island and ended up involved in the world of shady Chicago politics. I was a member of the US Congress. We greeted people and accepted congratulations all day. People I hadn't seen in years stopped by the house just to say hello. My mom and dad were proud. In the evening, after my mom had gone to bed, my dad and I were sitting in his living room, relaxing, not saying much. We were both tired. Then he looked at me as if he had something to tell me and I needed to listen. He had a bemused look, one that I had seen sometimes before he made an important pronouncement.

"You know, Luis, you complained all of the time when we brought you here. On an on about your friends and Chicago and how much you missed it and how hard it was in Puerto Rico. The kids here made fun of you. Learning Spanish was hard. You wouldn't stop. And look at you now. Your Spanish is excellent—you keep winning elections because you speak Spanish better than everyone else. You got to the city council because you were such a Puerto Rican candidate. Now you're in the Congress of the United States of America. I hope you understand that coming to Puerto Rico was the best thing that ever happened to you. It made you different. It made you who you are today."

He said it all in Spanish. And then he was done, ready to play dominoes or have a beer. He wasn't really interested in my opinion. He just wanted me to know what he thought.

My dad was like that. Mostly quiet, often distracted by something seemingly trivial—maybe that my mom had spent too much on a dress. And then he would turn to you with some good advice, an insight. My dad died last year, when I was writing this book, when I was finally taking the time to reflect more about our family and our life together. When he died, what he told me that night in San Sebastián was one of the first things that came to my mind.

To him, it was simple. It was 1969, a time of riots and assassinations, and he had a choice to make. So he decided to take care of his family. He gathered our things and packed us up in the Impala, a father afraid for his son and daughter because of gangs and drugs and disorder, a father willing to do anything for them. He wanted me to know that he paid a price—all of that whining he had to hear. But just look at how it all turned out, he said.

He was right, of course. It was the best thing that ever happened to me.

ACKNOWLEDGMENTS

Soraida is more than my partner in life. She is a careful reader and smart editor. She lived it, remembered it, and helped me to tell this story in a way that honors our family, our island, and our past. Also, I couldn't make up a character as wonderful as her dad, Don Juan, no matter how hard I tried. Thank you to Juano and Lucy and my sister Ada. Family is always there for you, and they have never missed a moment.

In Puerto Rico, my friends Luis Águila and Tino Núñez deserve more thanks than I can ever repay. Thanks for seeing a person instead of a misfit at Manuel Méndez Liciaga High School, and thanks for your invaluable help in remembering our adventures together. Gary Aquino, Marciano Avilés, Reynaldo Acevedo, Lucy Rodríguez, Alicia Rodríguez, Pablo Reyes, and my high school principal, Julio Arocho, all shared memories with me. Thank you for taking the time. Ida Luz and Alicia Rodriguez are childhood friends and so much more. Puerto Ricans have sacrificed in many different ways to stand up for our rights, but few have endured more than Lucy and Alicia. Thanks for talking about the old neighborhood and for a lifetime of caring about all Puerto Ricans throughout the diaspora. I'm proud to call you friends.

I also spent a wonderful night in Puerto Rico around the table with Soraida's extended family, including her sisters Nery and Milagros, her niece Chula, and her husband Luis Negrón, remembering and laughing. And I want to thank all of my Independentista friends who have nourished and supported me now for more than forty years. Thanks to Carlos Gallisa, a larger-than-life figure who came to San Sebastián and showed me how to stand up for the little guy. Our movement is filled with heroes, but a special thanks to Noel Colón Martínez, who exemplifies honor and taught me how to fight for the Puerto Rican people. And thanks to *Claridad* newspaper. Selling your newspaper on campus not only helped me get my first date with my future wife but also kept me informed about Puerto Rico my whole life.

In Chicago, I've been lucky to be surrounded by teachers, friends, activists, staff, and so many partners in making waves ever since Dan Rostenkowski's captains knocked on my door. I can't name them all. Jose Lopez not only was my professor at Northeastern Illinois University and a guiding force in my life, but he reviewed much of the book and gave wonderful advice. Thank you Jose for all you've done for me and for all your family has sacrificed for the Puerto Rican people. I asked many of my friends in the immigration rights movement to help me remember important moments and to review parts of the book. A special thank you to Josh Hoyt, a great leader of our community. Slim Coleman has been helping me for thirty years. Without him, I might never have been alderman, and now he is a leading voice for social justice. Slim and Josh helped immensely with the book.

Immigration activists have no idea how much their courage and insight have meant to me. The people who serve immigrants every day—who run nonprofits, who provide counsel and shelter and guidance to good people in need, who analyze policy, who speak out when others are silent—make all of our successes possible. Without them, I can accomplish nothing for immigrants. They don't get nearly enough credit, and I apologize for naming just a few, but in addition to Josh and Slim, some of the heroes of our movement are Deepak Bhargava, Chung-wha Hong, Janet Murguía, Ali Noorani, Gaby Pacheco, Angélica Salas, Frank Sharry, and Gustavo Torres. I thank you so much for showing me the right thing to do. The labor movement is a key part of our coalition, and I'm grateful to leaders like Eliseo Medina and Arturo Rodriguez. And thank you to Emma Lozano, for never doubting the power of immigrants.

The determination of the Congressional Hispanic Caucus is a giant part of the reason we are on the verge of historic progress for immigrants. It's not easy for more than twenty members of Congress to stay focused on a common goal, but our caucus has been a consistent voice for fairness. Thanks to Nydia Velázquez and Jose Serrano, my Puerto Rican friends and colleagues of twenty years who have not only stood up for immigrants but have always defended the people of Puerto Rico. For their commitment, I thank all my Latino colleagues, and in particular Senator Bob Menendez. Bob remembers when just sitting next to me could get a member of Congress in trouble. He did it anyway, because Bob fights for his people and sticks by his friends. Thanks also to my Illinois colleagues for their friendship and support, particularly Senator Dick Durbin for a lifetime of working for immigrants and for mentoring me.

I've always believed immigration is a civil rights issue, and I am immensely grateful to the civil rights leaders who've come before us and shown us the way. I watched Martin Luther King Jr. speak out against injustice in my home town and across America, and to this day the example of African-American civil rights leaders has given me the courage to find my voice. Today, our movement could not succeed without the steadfast support of African-American members of Congress, and of activists like Wade Henderson and Hillary Shelton.

A member of Congress relies every day on his staff. For more than twenty years, I've been surrounded by dedicated and passionate staff members. Helping more than 50,000 people become citizens at workshops in Chicago is an accomplishment I hold very close to my heart, and my staff has logged thousands of hours to make it possible. In Washington, I've been fortunate to work with people who believe in what I do and fight every day for progressive causes. A huge thank you to every person who has answered letters, studied legislation, filled out citizenship applications, and completed the one hundred other tasks that make our work possible. Thanks to Jennice Fuentes, who was with me for twenty years, sometimes a chief of staff, sometimes my unofficial liaison to the entertainment industry, always a friend. Thanks to Enrique Fernández Toledo. Nobody has been more loyal. Douglas Rivlin does battle in the press with the anti-immigrant forces and helped make sure this book got it right. And thank you to Susan Collins, who has carried petitions into the White House with me, been arrested beside me, and carefully read many chapters.

Which category should I choose for Doug Scofield? He managed my first campaign for Congress and served as my chief of staff for ten years. He helped to make our citizenship campaign possible. I've never had to convince him to do the right thing on any issue. It comes naturally to him. And he was my partner in writing this book. Thanks for *Still Dreaming*, and for more than twenty years of friendship.

I've been fortunate to have a great publisher and a wonderful editor who saw more than a policy lecture and encouraged me to tell my story. Thank you to Alane Salierno Mason and her team at W. W. Norton for helping me find the real book within all my different ideas. A rookie author couldn't have asked for anyone better. My agent, Ayesha Pande, was eager to take on a trouble-making congressman. She's great, and the book wouldn't exist without her. And thanks to Melanie Scofield, who read every word and whose sharp pencil and good advice made the book better.

Every day that I remain in Congress, I believe it's my duty to wake up and think about immigrants. So the real thanks in this book belong to America's immigrant community. I've seen you at rallies and forums across the country; I've listened to your stories; I've shared your fears and your accomplishments. I'm amazed at your dedication to building better lives for your families. It takes courage for you to stand up for your rights when many of you know the government could deport you at any time. It takes courage to work hard at tough jobs even when you know that many people view you as the enemy. I'm honored to be able to fight for you, and I'm grateful for all you do for America.

Finally, thank you to my mother and father. They always did what was right for our family, and they made me the person I am today. Without you, there is no *Still Dreaming*.

INDEX